Ghosts of Kanungu

Fertility, Secrecy & Exchange
in the Great Lakes of East Africa

African Anthropology

Ghosts of Kanungu
Fertility, Secrecy & Exchange
in the Great Lakes of East Africa
Richard Vokes

Village Matters
Knowledge, Politics & Community
in Kabylia, Algeria
Judith Scheele

World Anthropology

Series Editors: Wendy James & N. J. Allen
Published in association with
the School for Advanced Research Press

Inside West Nile
Mark Leopold

A Greek Island Cosmos
Roger Just

The Pathan Unarmed
Mukulika Banerjee

Turkish Region
Ildikó Bellér-Hann & Chris Hann

Hinduism & Hierarchy in Bali
Leo Howe

Imagined Diasporas among
Manchester Muslims
Pnina Werbner

Modern Indian Kingship
Marzia Balzani

Melodies of Mourning
Music & Emotion
in Northern Australia
Fiona Magowan

Expressing Identities
in the Basque Arena
Jeremy MacClancy

Ghosts of Kanungu

Fertility, Secrecy & Exchange in the Great Lakes of East Africa

Richard Vokes

Senior Lecturer in Anthropology
University of Canterbury, New Zealand

Fountain Publishers

 JAMES CURREY

James Currey
is an imprint of
Boydell and Brewer Ltd
PO Box 9, Woodbridge, Suffolk
IP12 3DF (GB)
www.jamescurrey.com
and of
Boydell & Brewer Inc.
668 Mt Hope Avenue,
Rochester, NY
14620-2731 (US)
www.boydellandbrewer.com

Fountain Publishers
PO Box 488
Kampala, Uganda
www.fountainpublishers.co.ug

Copyright © Richard Vokes 2009
Reprinted in paperback 2013

British Library Cataloguing in Publication Data

Vokes, Richard.
Ghosts of Kanungu : fertility, secrecy & exchange in the
Great Lakes of East Africa. — (African anthropology
series)
1. Movement for the Restoration of the Ten Commandments of
God. 2. Fires—Casualties—Uganda—Kanungu. 3. Mass
burials—Uganda—Kanungu. 4. Fire investigation—
Uganda—Kanungu. 5. Kanungu (Uganda)—Social conditions—
20th century.
I. Title II. Series
276.7'61082-dc22

ISBN 978-1-84701-009-4 (James Currey cloth)
ISBN 978-1-84701-072-8 (James Currey paperback)
ISBN 978-9970-02-732-3 (Fountain Publishers paper)

Typeset in 10/12 pt Monotype Photina
by Long House Publishing Services, Cumbria, UK
Printed and bound Great Britain by
CPI Group (UK) Ltd, Croydon CR0 4YY

To the memory of my late mother

Mary Josephine Vokes (1946–2007)

&

to Rupert Shortt, wherever you may now be

Contents

Illustrations

Acknowledgements

No work emerges in a vacuum, and I would like to thank all those whose encouragement, assistance and suggestions have aided the completion of this book. I would like to thank Rupert Short for first alerting my attention to the subject of Social Anthropology. At the University of Kent at Canterbury, my love of the subject was nurtured by the staff of the Department of Anthropology. I would especially like to thank Alan Bicker, Glen Bowman, John Corbin, Roy Ellen, Michael Fischer, John Kesby, Axel Klein, Nadia Lovell, Peter Parkes, Bob Parkin, Bill Watson and David Zeitlyn. I am also grateful for the endless patience of Jan Horn, Nicola Kerry-Yoxall and Shelley Roffey.

At the University of Oxford, I benefitted from the encouragement, help and advice of members of the African Studies Centre and the Institute of Social and Cultural Anthropology. I would especially like to thank Nick Allen, David Anderson, Marcus Banks, Vicky Dean, Paul Dresch, Roger Goodman, Douglas Johnson, Mike Morris, David Parkin and David Turton. I reserve special thanks for my doctoral supervisor, Wendy James.

My doctoral research – upon which a large part of this book is based – was made possible by a Studentship from the Economic and Social Research Council of the UK (Award no: R00429934453). Specific parts of the doctoral project were additionally funded by the Godfrey Lienhardt Fund, the Old Enfield Charitable Trust, the Radcliffe Brown Fund of the Royal Anthropological Institute, the Tropical Agriculture Association, the Vice-Chancellors' Fund, Oxford and Wolfson College, Oxford. Following my doctorate, I have continued to work on the Kanungu material whilst holding a Postdoctoral Fellowship from the ESRC (Award no: PTA-026-27-0254) and the Ioma Evans-Pritchard Junior Research Fellowship at St Anne's College, Oxford (2004–5). I am extremely grateful to all of the agencies and institutions who have extended such generous support to me over the course of the whole project.

In 2008, I held the Evans-Pritchard Lecturership for African Anthropology at All Souls' College, Oxford. Whilst holding this position, I was able to present parts of this monograph as a series of public lectures in the college. I am extremely grateful to the Warden of All Souls, John Davis, and to all the members of the Evans-Pritchard selection committee, for having given me this opportunity, and to all of the fellows and staff of All Souls for having made my stay at the college such a pleasant and stimulating one.

Previous drafts of various chapters have been presented at the British

Institute in Eastern Africa (Nairobi, Kenya, April 2002), at the Annual Conference of the Association of Social Anthropologists (Arusha, Tanzania, April 2002), at the University of Roskilde (Bornholm, Denmark, May 2002), at the Institute of Commonwealth Studies (London, May 2002), at the Institute of Social and Cultural Anthropology, University of Oxford (November 2003), at the London School of Health and Tropical Medicine (London, November 2004), at the Annual Conference of the Australian Anthropological Society (Adelaide, September 2005), at the Annual Meeting of the Association of Social Anthropologists of Aotearoa/New Zealand (Christchurch, November 2006) and at the Annual Meeting of the American Anthropological Association (San Jose, CA, November 2006). I am grateful to the audiences at all of these venues for their useful comments and suggestions.

In addition, I would also like to thank David Anderson, Grace Carswell, the late Alison des Forges, Richard Fardon, Wenzel Geissler, Wendy James, Ron Kassimir, David Maxwell, David Mills, David Parkin, Terence Ranger, Marcia Wright, and two anonymous reviewers for James Currey for their thoughtful comments on earlier drafts of (various parts of) the current book. I would also like to thank Susan and Michael Whyte for all their advice and hospitality over the years, as well as Jocelyn Alexander, Mette Berg, Matt Cooke, Jamon Halvaksz, Mark Leopold, Steve McGee, Knut Christian Mhyre, Carolyn Morris, Graham Naughton, Helene Neveu-Kringelbach, Nafisa Shah, Benjamin Smith, Zack Whyte and Chris Wingfield for having been such good colleagues, and such good friends.

Of course, any mistakes or omissions remain mine alone.

Parts of Chapter 6 first appeared as a chapter entitled 'The Kanungu Fire: Millenarianism and the Millennium in South-western Uganda', in *The Qualities of Time: Anthropological Approaches* [ASA Monograph No. 41] (eds) Wendy James & David Mills. Oxford: Berg.

During the pre-fieldwork phase of the original doctoral research, my work was greatly assisted by Justin Willis. I would like to thank Justin for making his various materials on Ankole available to me. In Uganda, the work was assisted by too many people to name personally. However, I would especially like to thank Simon Heck and Beth Pratt for their friendship and hospitality. I would also like to thank Karen and Lawrence John for their help with my many bizarre enquiries. Throughout the period of my doctoral fieldwork in Uganda, I was a member both of Makerere University's Institute of Social Research and of the Uganda National Council of Science and Technology. I was also connected with Mbarara University of Science and Technology, and latterly lectured in that institution's Faculty of Development Studies. I would like to thank Martin Doornbos and Pamela Mbabazi for giving me this opportunity.

My research on Kanungu was greatly assisted in the early stages by Eamonn Matthews of the MBC production company. I would like to thank Eamonn for making his various materials on the Kanungu fire available to me. It was later also aided by Nicholas Hunt, in his capacity as pathologist for the UK Foreign and Commonwealth Office. In Uganda, the Kanungu research was further assisted by the journalists Mugisha Matthias and

James Mujuni. I would also like to thank Assuman Mugyenyi, Archbishop Paul Bakyenga, and all of the clergy of the Roman Catholic Archdiocese of Mbarara. Given the sensitivity of the topic, I have decided, throughout this book, to use pseudonyms for almost all of the individuals directly connected with the Kanungu group, which, of course, precludes me from naming them here. However, the names of at least some of the protagonists are already in the public domain. I am therefore able to extend my sincere thanks to Fr. Ikazire, Mrs Theresa Kibweteere and Eric Mazima for all their help.

However, my biggest debt of gratitude in Uganda is to all the people of Rushanje and Ruzinga, Bugamba Sub-county, with whom I have lived and worked, on and off, for almost a decade. At the risk of offering an incomplete list, I extend my sincerest thanks to the families of the late Mzee Busenene, Mzee Kagambwa, Mzee Kamahega, Mzee Karoori Mugyenyi, the late Mzee Koyekyenga and Mrs Topista Mbaine, as well as to Tukundane Francis and his brothers. I would also like to thank my sometime language teacher, Mwombeki Rwabahima, my sometime driver, Turyahabwe, and my long-time associate, Tweheyo David. whom I thank for granting me the honour of being the godfather of his son, Ahimbisiibwe Richard. I would also like to extend my sincerest gratitude to my three most valued research assistants, Bakyenga Marius, Innocent Atuha and Mercy Muyambi. Without the assistance of these three people, the quality of my work in Uganda would have been greatly impoverished.

Last, but by no means least, I would like to thank the family of the late Onasmus Bwire, 'my' family in Uganda, for the love and support they have shown me over the last ten years. For this, I am eternally grateful to all of the family, to Gertrude Atukunda Kobirunga, to Gladys Mushabe and her husband Herbert Muhumuza, to Grays Nomuhangi and his wife Lilian Tumuramye, and to all of their children. But a special debt of gratitude is reserved for the head of that family, Grace Bwire, and his partner Lydia Kabahenda. I thank Grace for welcoming me into his home, for being such a wise teacher, and such a loyal friend.

I would also like to thank members of the extended family, especially Mzee Ayorekire and his children, and Mbabazi Penny.

In New Zealand, the work has been further assisted by Dave Haslett, by Mark Chubb of the New Zealand Fire Service, and by two criminal pathologists who wish to remain anonymous. I would also like to thank Alex Ruhinda for his help with the final preparation of the book, Marney Brosnan for producing its maps, and my University of Canterbury colleague Terry Austrin for all his advice and support.

Finally, on a personal note, I would like to thank my family, my father Peter, and my siblings David and Joanna, for their unwavering love, loyalty and support over the years. I dedicate this book to the memory of my late mother, Jo. I would also like to thank the love of my life, and my best friend, Zheela, for sharing the whole experience with me and for putting up with it all, and for giving me the greatest gifts of all, my daughter Elisabeh Atukunda and my sons Yusuf Nshekanabo, David Tumwesigye and Michael Busingye.

A Note on Orthography

The primary language of South-western Uganda is Runyankore/Rukiga. This is a language in the West Nyanza branch of Great Lakes Bantu. Great Lakes Bantu is itself a sub-set of the Niger-Kordofanic language family.

Runyankore/Rukiga has nine principal noun classes. In this book, I have generally used only the singular form for eight of these classes. However, when referring to words in the *mu-ba* class – principally words for people – I have used both singular and plural forms. A word with a *mu-* prefix indicates a single person, a word with a *ba-* prefix indicates more than one person. Thus *mukazi* = woman, *bakazi* = women. In some cases, I have also used the initial vowel (in this class *o-* or *a-* respectively) which stands in for the English words 'a' or 'the'. Thus *omukazi* = a/the woman, *abakazi* = the women. It is worth noting that other, more complex prefixes are also available when using nouns in the *mu-ba* class. Thus, for example, the prefix *banya-* stands for the English words 'they of'. Thus *abanyakazi* = the women of. In the *mu-ba* class (as in some other noun classes) the prefix *ki-* indicates an adjectival form. Thus *kikazi* = women's.

Glossary

A glossary of the main Runyankore/Rukiga terms used in the text:

Ab'eihe rya Bikira Maria	The Legion of Mary
ahaiguru	the above, at the top, 'the beyond'; used by Christian missionaries to gloss 'heaven' (*eiguru*, *lit*: 'the place above')
buraeya	the international, or global, domain; worldwide
eizooba	the sun; the indigenous Kiga deity was known as Kazooba, which is a derivative of this word
ekibi	a misfortune, the trouble; used by Christian missionaries to gloss 'a sin'
ekidaara	the hut which was built for a new bride, to keep her in exclusion
emandwa	a spirit of the dead
endaaro	a spirit hut
engumba	barrenness
enjara	hunger
enju	a house (in which one wife, and her children, live)
nyin'eka	the male head of a household
okuhingira	to give away (a bride), the marriage ceremony in which this give-away takes place
okutamba	to sacrifice, the ritual in which a sacrifice is made
okutoija	to pay tribute (to a superior), the objects which are given in this practice
okuzinduka	to make a formal visit, the event during which this takes place
okworekwa	to receive a vision, the apparition itself
omufumu	a diviner, or 'traditional healer'
omugigwa	the role of mediumship
omugole	the new bride in a household
omukago	a reciprocal bond-partner (often glossed as 'blood brother')
omutaka	a 'villager' (*lit*: 'a person of the land')
omuzungu	a white European
orugo	*lit*: a hedge, or a fence, the word is commonly used to refer to the compound in which an extended, or polygamous, family resides (which is typically bordered by a hedge or fence)
oruhanga	*lit*: a valley, although a term of great cosmological significance; used by Christian missionaries to gloss 'God' (Ruhanga)
tonto	banana wine

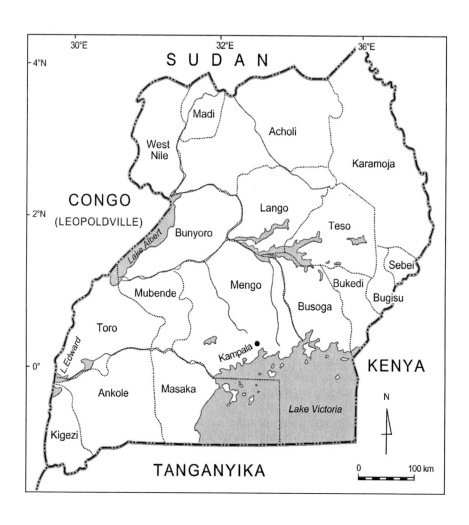

Map 0.1 Uganda district boundaries (colonial)

Map 0.2 Uganda district boundaries (2000)

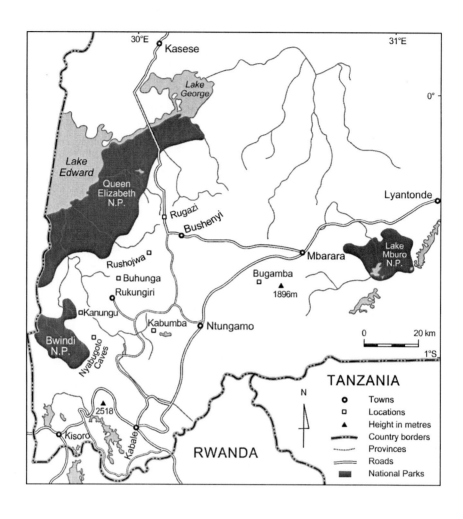

Map 0.3 South-western Uganda showing main locations mentioned in the text

Prologue
The End as a Beginning

Abafiire bagira enkuru. The dead make news[1]

Sometime around 11 o'clock on the morning of Friday 17 March 2000, Rutembo Didas was standing in his banana plantation (*orutookye*), pruning his plants, when a strange sound suddenly disturbed the morning calm. As he later described it, the noise, like a sudden uprush of air, seemed to be that of an explosion. Dropping his tools, Rutembo immediately set off in the direction from which the sound had come, and presently, emerging from his plantation, realized that a building in the compound of one of his neighbours, a religious group called the Movement for the Restoration of the Ten Commandments of God (the MRTC), was on fire. From his current vantage point below the MRTC compound, he could see tongues of fire, and a thick plume of smoke, emanating from the roof of the building. Moreover, he could also now hear the terrible screams of people who were apparently still trapped inside the building. Minutes later, Rutembo arrived at the local police station, in the nearby trading centre of Kanungu, where he found Corporal Stephen Mujuni, an officer in the Local Defence Unit (LDU) – a kind of civil guard – on duty. Together, the men dashed back to the scene of the fire, but their initial attempts to break into the building were thwarted by the smoke billowing from within. Instead, then, the pair busied themselves with searching some of the numerous other buildings in the compound. It was thus that they made a quite startling discovery, of one room, in what appeared to be the compound's main administration block, in which the remains of a lavish meal still lay on a table, and a calendar hung on the wall; in its entry boxes for the dates 16 and 17 March 2000 were written the three simple words: 'world's end' and 'bye'.

Sometime around midnight that same evening, 17 March 2000, James

---

[1] Cisternino, 1987: 253. Throughout South-western Uganda, proverbs (*orufumu*, or *enfumu*) constitute an important part of everyday speech. Whilst making a formal speech, when greeting a neighour, or while simply having an informal conversation with an acquaintance, both men and women typically illuminate their speech with these sayings, both as a way of demonstrating their own oral-literary skills and as a means of drawing on various commonly held idioms of understanding. Whilst it is beyond my scope here to examine the social and political dimensions of these proverbs in detail, I refer to a number of them throughout this book. All the proverbs reproduced here are taken from my fieldnotes, although in most cases I have also checked their details against Fr. Marius Cisternino's comprehensive *The Proverbs of Kigezi and Ankole* (1987), which reproduces 2719 of the most commonly used sayings in Runyankore/Rukiga. In some instances – such as this one – it is necessary for me to reproduce only the Runyankore/Rukiga saying itself, and its literal translation. However, in some instances, I have also included an additional explanatory note as to the proverb's meaning.

1

Mujuni, a local correspondent for the Ugandan national newspaper, *The New Vision*, was sitting with friends in a bar in Mbarara Town, when his mobile phone began to ring. The call turned out to be from a policeman in Rukungiri Town, who was calling him to report some apparently strange happenings in a place called Kanungu, which is about 20 km west of Rukungiri. Thus it was that at dawn the next morning, Mujuni set off, with one of his colleagues from the newspaper, to cover the story. Mujuni later recalled the scene which greeted the pair upon arrival at the scene of the fire:

> And there it was. So many bodies burnt beyond recognition. In fact, we got there when the fire was still on. You could see some people's scars still glowing with fire, red hot fire, somebody's scars ... for about the first five minutes, we were thunderstruck, we couldn't do anything ... [we were] supposed to take notes, we were supposed to take pictures, but we did not proceed ... because the shock was too much ... The smell of roasted meat hung all over the air ... I think it could be smelled from a very long distance.[2]

When the two did eventually come to their senses, they began trying to ascertain exactly how many people had died here – eventually breaking off their count at around 400, with many more still left to count – and to record other aspects of the scene: the presence of a large oil drum and various jerrycans close to one end of the burned-out building, the fact that many of the building's windows appeared to have been boarded up when the fire broke out (with the nails apparently driven in from the *outside*), and so on.

Sometime around 2 o'clock on the afternoon of Saturday 18 March, Assuman Mugyenyi, Chief Public Relations Officer for the Uganda Police, flew in to Kanungu by helicopter. News of the Kanungu fire had reached the national police headquarters, in Kampala, the previous evening, following which the country's most senior police officer, the Inspector General of Police, John Kisembo, had mustered a helicopter to take himself, and a small delegation of other senior officers – including Mugyenyi – directly to the scene. As Mugyenyi later described, upon arrival the group's first task was to survey the site of the fire, and then to debrief those local police officers who were already on hand, to interview potential witnesses, and so on. It was in this way that they were quickly able to ascertain that receipts had been found on the site for two twenty-litre drums of sulphuric acid, purchased six days earlier by one of the MRTC's leaders, one Father Dominic Kataribaabo, from a hardware store in nearby Kasese Town; that the MRTC membership had in recent days been selling off all the group's property, in preparation for a coming 'big event'; and that the group had published their own text which, entitled *A Timely Message from Heaven: The End of the Present Times*, signalled the group's millenarian intent (indeed, the police had found stacks and stacks of this book all over the MRTC compound).

In particular here, the group of senior officers paid special attention to the testimony of Corporal Stephen Mujuni, the LDU officer who had been the first person into the compound, along with Rutembo Didas, the previous

---

[2] This quote is taken from an interview Mujuni later gave to a film crew from the UK-based Mentorn Barraclough Carey (MBC) television production company.

morning, and who had spent the previous night in the compound. At some point during the evening, Mujuni had become aware of a foul smell emanating from one part of the same administration building in which the remains of the 'last supper' had been found. Having spent most of the morning trying to find the source of this smell, sometime around lunchtime Mujuni had come across a concealed door, which led into a pit latrine. It was here that his quest had finally come to an end, because, as he shone his torch down into the latrine pit, he realized that the smell was coming from at least 6 decomposing bodies contained therein.

Having completed their survey of the scene, and their interviewing of witnesses – all of which they recorded on a VHS camcorder – the delegation then returned to Kampala, arriving back at around 8pm local time. But for Mugyenyi, the night was still young, for no sooner had he disembarked from the return flight than he began fielding calls about the fire from the international media. In actual fact, agents of all the big international news outlets – AFP, the BBC, CNN, Reuters, and others – had already been bombarding the headquarters of national media outlets (including that of James Mujuni's employer, *The New Vision*) since about lunchtime of that day. However, with Mugyenyi's return from the scene, all these enquiries were now directed towards him, and thus it was that he was forced to stay in his office until late into the night, fielding calls not only from the Uganda-based international media corps, but also from reporters as far afield as Kenya, South Africa, the US, Australia and Japan. As a direct result of these conversations, by about midnight that night, local time, the Kanungu fire was headline news throughout the world.

Sometime around 5 o'clock on the afternoon of Sunday 19 March, I was walking through the crowded lanes of Wandegeya market, just below Makerere Hill in Northern Kampala, looking for a bar with the English football on. Having arrived in Uganda some 10 days previously, to conduct a 'preliminary' fieldwork trip ahead of my main period of doctoral fieldwork (which was due to begin 3 months hence), I had spent much of the past week in and out of government offices in the capital, arranging research permissions, visas and the like. This process complete, I was now planning a trip to the Southwest in the next day or two, to begin the search for a long-term fieldsite. However, this being a Sunday, not much was going on, and so it was that I happened to be in Wandegeya, trying to kill time. Eventually successful in my quest for a screen, I settled down in a local hotel to watch the game. All of this is significant to my story here because it was at half-time in the match, as patrons refreshed their drinks in preparation for the second half, that the barman flicked over to CNN to catch the latest headlines. As he did so, a caption popped up behind the on-screen newsreader, screaming the headline 'Cult Suicide in Uganda!'. So it was, then, that I myself first learned of the Kanungu fire.

Sometime on the evening of 19 March, Dr Thaddeus Birungi, Chief Pathologist for the Uganda Police, received a phone call from headquarters, asking him to fly to Kanungu early the next morning, with a delegation led by Inspector General Kisembo, and to include the Minister of Internal Affairs, Edward Rugumayo. Birungi's deputy, Dr Martin

Kalyemanya, had already visited the scene earlier that day (19 March), to relieve the local pathologists working there. (Kalyemanya had also travelled there on the police helicopter, which was to keep up its daily shuttle between Kampala and the Southwest until at least two weeks after the fire.) However, with the discovery of the additional bodies in the latrine, and with the growing international media interest in the event – Kalyemanya had reported seeing 'multitudes' of foreign journalists in Kanungu upon his arrival there[3] – it was now thought necessary for the Chief Pathologist to visit the site as well. Upon arrival at the scene, how-ever, Birungi concluded that there was little more he could usefully do there, and so, leaving his deputy, Dr Kalyemanya, to continue the work, he returned to Kampala. Four days later, on Friday 24 March, Dr Birungi was asked to go again to the Southwest, on a second trip that turned out to be much more eventful than his first. On this occasion, the request for him to go had followed the discovery of two additional pit graves, containing a total of 153 bodies, by a local police team working at another of the MRTC's compounds, in the village of Buhunga (also in Rukungiri District). Following this discovery, it had been decided to carry out detailed searches of all of the MRTC's (numerous) compounds, to be overseen by the Chief Pathologist himself.

Arriving on the morning of Saturday 25 March, Birungi went first to the Buhunga site, although he again discovered that there was little for him to do there, all of the bodies having already been reburied. Labour for this had been provided by prisoners from nearby Rukungiri Prison, who were used throughout the Kanungu inquiry, including for the burial of all those killed in the fire itself. However, Birungi stayed on in the Southwest, and the following day (26 March) travelled to another of the MRTC's compounds, the former home of Fr. Dominic Kataribaabo, in Rugazi, Bushenyi District. There, over the next three days, and under the gaze of the international media – many foreign journalists being present on-site as his investigations were carried out – Birungi discovered, and excavated, three more mass graves (two in the garden, and one in a former wine cellar inside the house), which together contained a total of 155 bodies.

Incidentally, by this time I myself had reached the Southwest by bus, and on Tuesday 28 March, the second day of the police excavations at the site, had been travelling around the countryside near Rugazi with my friend Frank Arinda. Frank was at the time working for a DfID-funded fish farming project, and had suggested that my travelling with him in his project vehicle, as he visited the project's trial farms, would be a good way for me to explore the local surroundings. Thus it was that, at around lunchtime of that day, we happened to be passing the Rugazi compound, and, spotting an opportunity, I suggested to Frank that we pull over to see what was going on there. However, at the entrance to the main driveway to the house, our path was blocked by a local policeman, who refused us entry on

---

[3] 'Post-mortem report on Kanungu', by 'the team dispatched from CID H/Q to Rukungiri' – including Dr M. Kalyemanya (Pathologist), Mr Z. Tumutegyereize (Senior Mortuary Attendant), Ms O. Wawire (ASP H/Q Fire Brigade) and Mr Mudungu (IP Mbarara Fire Brigade) – 19 March 2000.

the sole grounds that I did not have any proper press accreditation. So, unlike the many foreign press people who were on-site at Rugazi throughout Birungi's investigations, I spent the rest of that day counting and weighing fish!

But, to finish the story here, following their excavation of the Rugazi site, Dr Birungi's team moved on to another of the MRTC's compounds, in the village of Rushojwa (also in Bushenyi), where they discovered further pit graves, containing 81 bodies. After this, the police decided to break off the search for additional bodies, on the grounds – officially, at least – that they already had ample evidence for any future prosecutions over the case. However, their decision to do so was almost certainly also influenced by the extreme glare of the international media which, it was doubtless felt (given the nature of the incident at hand), was extremely poor publicity for Uganda (and I should point out that, by the time of the Rushojwa excavations, foreign correspondents equipped with outside broadcast vehicles and satellite dishes were broadcasting live reports directly from the site). In addition, the police were by now also being heavily criticized in the Uganda national press for their ongoing employment of prisoners as labour for their excavations, many of them – the images printed daily in *The New Vision*, and other publications, seemed to suggest – provided with neither shoes nor gloves, nor any other form of protective clothing, for the work. In a country where the handling of any dead body invokes all sorts of cultural taboos, this practice had received universal, and vociferous, condemnation. After 31 March, the police did investigate one more MRTC compound – in Makindye, just outside Kampala itself – where another excavation team (this time bedecked in full bio-chemical protective gear) found another pit grave containing a further 55 bodies.

So what, then, could possibly have happened here? The primary interpreters of events, in the days immediately following the fire, were, of course, the Uganda police. Thus, upon arrival at the scene on Saturday 18 March, Inspector General Kisembo's team had quickly ascertained that the MRTC had for long been millenarian in outlook, had recently been preparing for some sort of 'big event', had a few days earlier purchased two drums of sulphuric acid, and so on. In addition, the senior delegation had also been handed an analysis report of the scene, prepared earlier that morning by the Rukungiri police, describing the situation inside the burnt-out building, as the latter had first encountered it. This document is particularly significant, because it contained certain key details which were to become important in subsequent accounts of the fire. Specifically, the report observed – as did James Mujuni – that some of the building's windows had been nailed shut at the time of the fire. Moreover, that the bodies inside the building were piled in one spot (a later report by Dr Kalyemanya described them as having formed a 'heap'), which appeared to suggest that they had all died quite quickly. Finally, that the 'surging in of the roof and walls of the building indicat[ed] a big blast ... probably [caused by] an inflammable accelerant' (an interpretation which the report apparently goes on to confirm, in its results of tests of chemical residue at the site, all of which indicated the presence of petrol amongst the human remains).[4]

Taken together, all of these facts seemed to provide Assuman Mugyenyi with a relatively straightforward narrative with which to go to the world's media that evening: of a sect which, having decided that the end was nigh, had locked themselves in their main church building and (presumably in a state of high ritual excitement) had ignited an explosion in which all present had perished. In short, a 'simple' case of mass suicide.[5] This, then, was the story which first became amplified over the global media networks during that evening of 18 March. Indeed, in this instance, the nature of the narrative itself may be seen to have further increased this amplification effect. After all, this being March 2000, when all sorts of apocalyptic narratives related to the recent turn of the millennium were still being rehearsed by media outlets all over the world, practically *any* such story involving a millenarian suicide (from anywhere in the world) would have been guaranteed excellent coverage from the start. The BBC's very first web report on Kanungu – posted at 20.06 GMT on Saturday 18 March – was indicative of much of the coverage which was to follow during those first few days, including as it does a sidebar in which Kanungu is already compared to other millenarian cult suicides around the world, including those of 'Jonestown' (Guyana, 1978), 'Solar Temple' (Switzerland, 1994), 'Heaven's Gate' (San Diego, 1977), and so on.[6]

Over the course of the following few days at least, some additional evidence was to come to light in support of the suicide hypothesis. For example, on Tuesday 21 March, James Mujuni reported a letter, written in Runyankore/Rukiga, which had earlier been received by *The New Vision's* sister paper, the vernacular *Orumuri*, from another of the MRTC leadership, one Joseph Kibweteere. The letter, written sometime in January 2000, spoke of the end of the world. It read 'I Joseph Kibweteere, my boss Jesus Christ, has appeared to me and given me a message to all of you that there are some people arguing over the message that this generation ends on 1/1/2000. On the contrary, the generation ends at the end of the year 2000 and no other year will follow'.[7] Also on 21 March, national newspapers cited a report which had earlier been received from the MRTC by Uganda's Ministry of Internal Affairs. It turned out that the MRTC had been a registered non-governmental organisation, and as such, had had to deliver an annual report to this Ministry. Rather ominously, it was now reported, the group's annual report for 2000 had claimed that 'their mission was coming to an end, and there would be no 2001. Instead, next year would be year number 1, starting with a new generation.'[8] However, by the time these reports had gone to press, on the evening of Monday 20 March, the suicide hypothesis had already begun to be replaced with another, altogether more sinister explanation of events at Kanungu.

[4] All of these quotes are taken from the same report cited in footnote 3.
[5] Although Mugyenyi did also acknowledge that some of the children who had died in the fire had presumeably *not* chosen to commit suicide.
[6] This report is available online at: http://news.bbc.co.uk/1/hi/world/africa/682136.stm
[7] See: James Mujuni, 'Cult boss wanted to kill rivals', *The New Vision*, 21 March 2000.
[8] See, for example, Simon Kaheru, 'Kibwetere warned the government', *ibid.*

The primary agents of the subsequent shift from a narrative of mass suicide to one of mass murder, were again the Ugandan police. However, in this instance it is clear that their move was made only after sustained pressure from the cohort of foreign reporters who, by Sunday 19 March, had become a large constituent of the milieu in which the investigation was proceeding. This much can be ascertained from video footage of a press conference held by Assuman Mugyenyi and the Minister of Internal Affairs, Edward Rugumayo, on the evening of Monday 20 March, shortly after their return from Kanungu that day. The footage, which was shot by the police themselves, shows the two men trying to defend the suicide line – which was still, at that time, the official narrative of events – in the face of increasingly hostile questioning from the foreign journalists there present (most of whom had by this time been to Kanungu themselves and, having seen the bodies in the pit latrine, had become somewhat sceptical of the suicide hypothesis).[9] Thus, over the course of the press conference, a discernible shift can be noted in Rugumayo's position, in particular, away from a narrative of 'simple' suicide towards one of a 'mixed' event, made up of elements of both suicide and murder. The position he ended up taking, in the latter stages of the press conference, was that, whilst the adult members of the sect *had* intentionally killed themselves, all the children present would have been incapable of forming such an intention, and must, therefore, have been murdered (presumably, by the adults).[10]

The generally sceptical position with which the foreign press corps were now approaching the incident seems also to have galvanized certain sections of the Ugandan national media. Thus, on the morning after the press conference, the traditionally 'anti-establishment' national newspaper *The Monitor* led with a series of stories describing several other mass graves which its reporters had apparently 'discovered' in Kanungu, and news of a plot which had been described to them by the Rukungiri Police, involving one of the MRTC's leaders having planned for some time to murder all of the group's members.[11] Both stories provided very little evidence for their assertions, and neither was ever repeated again (either by any other news outlet or by *The Monitor* itself). Moreover, for the Uganda Police, this combined pressure of the foreign and national press corps only increased during the coming days.

This much is evidenced by a general shift in the language used in international reports of the incident. For example, the London *Guardian*'s report of Friday 24 March describes the bodies in the latrine as having been 'slashed with machetes, burned with acid and then dumped in the pit'.[12] Not only is this description a somewhat creative use of the facts (at least

[9] I would like to thank the Uganda Police for making a copy of this video, and all their other materials related to the Kanungu fire, available to me.
[10] This idea that the children present could not have committed suicide had first been floated by Assuman Mugyenyi on 18 March. However, the notion that this aspect rendered the *whole event* a mass murder represents an innovation on Rugumayo's part, made in the context of the press conference.
[11] See: Patson Bareire et al., 'More bodies found in pit', and Karl Vick, 'Kanungu fireball: a pact of silence', *The Monitor*, 21 March 2000.
[12] See: Anna Borzello, 'Uganda enquiry into cult deaths', *The Guardian*, 24 March 2000.

as these were recorded by the police), but its reference to 'machetes' might even have been designed, one could argue, to invoke memories of those murderous events which had taken place six years previously in neighbouring Rwanda. Yet it was as a result of the pressures these sorts of stories created that, upon first discovering the additional pit graves at Buhunga (also on Friday 24 March), the senior police team that was leading the investigation immediately declared that they were now treating the entire incident – including the Kanungu fire itself – as mass murder. This, despite the fact that, at that time, the team had yet to receive an autopsy report on the Buhunga bodies (a report which was never, in fact, to be completed).

The local police team that had excavated the Buhunga graves had included one Dr Sebudde, of Rukungiri Hospital, who, on the evening of Friday 24 March, informed the senior police team back in Kampala that, of the 153 bodies he had examined at the site, 21 showed signs of strangulation, 3 had fractured skulls, and 1 had been stabbed.[13] It was on the basis of this testimony that the police decided to make their public declaration, later that evening, of mass murder. These same senior officers also realized, of course, that further post-mortems would have to be carried out to establish the final cause of death, and thus it was that arrangements were also made for the Chief Pathologist, Dr Birungi, to go to the site the next morning. However, a breakdown seems to have occurred in the lines of communication, such that upon arrival in Buhunga the next morning, Birungi found that all of the bodies had already been reburied. As a result, no detailed post-mortems on the Buhunga bodies were ever, in fact, carried out. However, the public declaration that they were indicative of mass murder meant that, by the time Dr Birungi and his team began the excavations at Rugazi, on Sunday 26 March, all those involved, from the foreign journalists to the police themselves, were already convinced that the whole episode had been one of murder. Thus, the numerous foreign journalists who milled around the crime scene while the investigations were taking place – I later learnt from the police video (given that I was not there) – spoke of little else but murder most foul, and discussed amongst themselves various (more or less plausible) conspiracy theories. The police were therefore less than surprised to discover that, in Birungi's opinion, some of the evidence at the site seemed to suggest foul play.

Specifically, over three days of investigation at the Rugazi site, Birungi concluded that, of the 74 bodies found in two pit graves in the garden of the compound, 20 had died of strangulation (as evidenced primarily by their having a broken hyoid bone in their neck, with some also showing signs of cyanosis of the tongue – which might be caused by a lack of oxygen to the tongue prior to death), 1 of stabbing, and 1 of a fractured skull. In addition, he concluded that 3 of the bodies found in the grave in the former wine cellar had also died of strangulation.[14] Furthermore, the Chief

---

[13] Notes in police file on Kanungu incident.

[14] 'Final pathology report on Kanungu', by 'the investigating team' – including Mr Bangirana (CID H/Q), A. Mugyenyi (PRO Police), Dr T. Birungi (Police Pathologist), Mr Z. Tumutegyereize (Mortuary Attendant), Mr Aisu (Serious Crime CID 'in charge'), Mr Kinyera (Regional CID Officer, SW), Mr Kyamanyura (District CID Officer, Rukungiri) – no date (although the dates included in the report suggest that it must have been written after 1 April 2000).

pathologist also reported finding numerous small green and white bottles, like medicine vials, strewn around the house, which could have contained poison, which might also have been an instrument of murder. These vials were immediately sent away for toxological analysis (although at the time I read the police file on Kanungu, in May 2004, no record of any toxological findings was contained therein). However, the main point I am trying to make here is that these investigations seemed to provide ample evidence to support the mass murder hypothesis, as indeed did the Chief Pathologist's later findings at Rushojwa as well (where he concluded that, of the 81 bodies recovered, 3 showed signs of strangulation).[15] As a result of which, those international journalists who had been present throughout the investigation now seemed to have been vindicated in their initial suspicion that Kanungu was not, after all, a simple case of suicide.

Thus, over the following days and weeks, media representations of the episode became much darker still, if not a little sensational (for example, two articles published on successive days in the London *Guardian* led with the headlines 'Worst Cult Slaughter' and 'Uganda's Killer Cult', 29 and 30 March, respectively). More importantly, given the quite extraordinary coverage the story was now receiving – for example, the *Guardian*'s 31 March edition ran with an editorial on Kanungu – most journalists now sought to develop some sort of explanation as to *why* this sect should have suddenly committed mass murder on quite the scale that it did. Some of the more informed commentaries, such as that provided by Giles Foden in the *Guardian*, spoke of factors such as the social disorder of the Amin years, the emergence of the regional AIDS epidemic, the rise of Pentecostal Christianity in Uganda, and so on.[16] However, even these accounts remained largely impressionistic, and provided little insight into the possible proximal causes of the events at hand.

Only one plausible explanation ever really emerged, based on the fact – which the foreign correspondents had established upon arrival at Kanungu – that most of the MRTC's members had been required to sell all of their property, and to hand over the proceeds to the sect's leadership, upon entry into the group. The theory ran that if such payments had been made in expectation of a coming end of the world, and if this was expected to arrive at the turn of the year 2000, but then had not, some members might have become disgruntled and have started to demand their money back. In reaction to this, the leadership had decided to quash the dissent by killing the worst complainants (such killings as could be hidden by them among the frequent transfers that were made between the sect's various compounds). Hence, then, the bodies in the pits. However, as the dissent continued to grow – so the story went – an even grander scheme was hatched, to kill off *all* of the sect's members, in a staged suicide, allowing the leaders themselves to make off with what remained of the loot (here, much was made of various reported 'sightings' of the sect's leaders in the days and weeks after the fire, from places as far apart as Eastern Congo, Rwanda, Sudan, Tanzania and elsewhere). This, then, was the story which

[15] As recorded in the same report cited in footnote 14.
[16] See: Giles Foden, 'In the name of Mary', *The Guardian*, 21 April 2000.

was repeated again and again, in media accounts of Kanungu, in the weeks after the discoveries of the pit graves. Indeed, so amplified did it become, that by the time it was used to form the basis of an international documentary on Kanungu several months later, a film that was called *The Cult That Couldn't Stop Killing*, the thesis had become something of a 'definitive' account of events.[17] Even so, the narrative, although plausible, is also a little far-fetched (in actual fact, it can be easily challenged on a number of grounds, as we shall see). Thus, international news editors were unable to locate it within any conventional media narrative. As a result, the Kanungu story was, by and large, simply dropped, and anecdotal evidence suggests that the international readership were ultimately left confused by the apparently bizarre nature of the whole affair.

[17] *The Cult That Couldn't Stop Killing*, directed by Eamonn Matthews (MBC, 2000).

1
Introduction

This book is an historical ethnography of the Movement for the Restoration of the Ten Commandments of God, and of the Kanungu fire itself. As such, it begins with an exploration of the social context from which this particular African-Initiated Church (AIC)[1] emerged in the mid-1980s, and with an attempt to define the cultural archive which informed that process of genesis. The book's central argument is that the MRTC grew out of, and was located within, a specific – historically and geographically located – set of logics and practices related to attempts to gain redress for misfortune. Moreover, that this helps us to understand why the group later grew rapidly – during the early-mid 1990s – given that this was a period during which South-western Uganda was experiencing what was perhaps the worst social misfortune in the region's entire history: the emergent AIDS epidemic. Thus, it was as people attempted to come to terms with this new disease, and to deal with its worst effects, that they increasingly turned to the MRTC for support (and the reasons why they turned to this particular AIC, rather than to the mainstream church, or to some other sort of organization altogether, will also be elaborated upon). From here, then, the book explores what these historical dimensions tell us about life inside the MRTC, about its modes of social organization and ritual practice, about its politics and theology, and so on. In these ways, one of the book's central aims is to develop a detailed ethnographic reconstruction of the Movement, one based on interviews with surviving protagonists and former members, discussions with the relatives and friends of those who died, and so on. Finally, the book will return to the detective mystery with which it opened, to examine the question of what did, then, happen at Kanungu?

However, I begin here by noting one of the apparently more curious features of the MRTC story, as this was recorded both by the police and by journalists, at the time. According to practically every eyewitness to the events of March and April 2000, and quite unusually for an African AIC of this type, many of the MRTC's former activities seemed to have been conducted in a high degree of secrecy. Thus, upon arrival at the scene on 18 March, Assuman Mugyenyi quickly ascertained that few Kanungu residents were able to tell him very much about the MRTC, given that everything the sect had done had been 'so secretive'. He established that the whole Kanungu compound had been effectively closed to outsiders, even to

[1] Throughout this book, I refer to independent African churches as 'African-Initiated Churches' following the usage set down by Anderson (2001).

near neighbours.[2] Nor did the group's neighbours have any other way of finding out what went on at the site. Not only did most of the sect's activities take place behind closed doors, or in the middle of the night, but, on the few occasions that they did venture outside, they always did so with a view to concealing their activities.

Thus, for example, one local resident recalled one occasion on which a small group of MRTC members had gathered by a stream on the edge of the group's property in order to conduct some sort of ritual. Out of curiosity, the young man had climbed a nearby tree in order to get a better view of what was going on. However, he was himself soon spotted by the group, who proceeded to hurriedly gather up some objects they had with them, and to run off in the direction of their compound's main buildings. Moreover, such behaviour did not seem to be uncommon amongst the MRTC's members. Indeed, some local residents reported that even their daily work parties – which might be involved in sowing fields or pruning banana plantations – commonly refused to have any such contact with other residents. It later also transpired that on those occasions when sect members had ventured into Kanungu trading centre on errands – to purchase food and supplies, and the like – they had always moved about entirely in silence, speaking neither to other residents nor even amongst themselves. Both the police and journalists were later able to confirm that these same general patterns had been repeated at all of the MRTC's other compounds, as well. Indeed, at several compounds, the sect had even erected high fences around their buildings, in order to stop outsiders from being able to see inside them at all. I would add that, over the course of my own research on the sect, I documented a range of additional ways in which the sect demonstrated a commitment to secrecy.

Far from being a curious aside, these examples of the sect's secretive nature are indicative of the fact that, for much of its history, the MRTC is best understood as having been a secret network, or series of networks. For this reason, the study of this one group also offers more general insight into concealed, and informal, social assemblages of this type. In particular, it speaks to such broader questions as what makes secret networks such a compelling – in some cases a primary – mode of social action? How and why do they become reworked, or in other ways transformed, over time (and what are the consequences of these transformations)? And – perhaps most importantly of all – how and why do they sometimes become violent in nature? Finally, the study of this particular secret network, or series of networks, also enables us to think about how an anthropologist – or indeed any social researcher – might engage with the study of this sort of social phenomenon and, in a reflexive move, think about how this engagement shapes his or her analysis.

Moreover, in all of these ways, this study also speaks to a wider set of social forces, such as have shaped various other key events in the recent

[2] The few visitors who did, occasionally, stay at the compound were required to live in small guest quarters in a 'gatehouse' building at the front of the site, and were barred from venturing any further into the premises (food being served to the guests through a hatch at the back of their building).

history of the Great Lakes region. After all, it was an informal secret network with some similarities to the one examined here which was largely responsible for the planning, and the implementation, of the Rwandan genocide in 1994 (the so-called *akaju*; see, for example, des Forges, 1999). In addition, it is secret networks of this sort which have continued to shape events in the war-affected parts of the Eastern Democratic Republic of Congo (see, for example, the *Final report of the group of experts on the Democratic Republic of Congo*, 12 December 2008). Thus, although this book is not a comparative study, its case study nevertheless addresses a series of questions that might equally be posed in other regional contexts. Moreover, its exegesis develops a series of insights, and offers a series of clues, that might further assist our understanding of other, more tumultous, events as well.

On secrecy and misfortune

A key insight of this book is that, for much of its history, the MRTC is best understood as a transformation of a locally meaningful set of logics and practices which were formerly attached to a fertility goddess called Nyabingi (pronounced: '*nya-bin-ji*'). In an important sense, then, the MRTC was but the latest manifestation of the long-standing Nyabingi phenomenon. However, it is not possible to grasp the nature of this connection, nor to understand exactly how and why this sort of phenomenon should have again risen to such prominence in South-western Uganda at this particular point in time (in the late 1980s, and into the 1990s) after more than half a century of apparent obscurity, without a re-examination of the historio-graphy of earlier manifestations of Nyabingi. In particular, and as I shall argue at length in the next chapter, it is necessary to challenge here what has been a continual over-emphasis, both by colonial administrators and by previous historians of the subject, of Nyabingi's former anti-colonial aspects. In all of these earlier accounts, Nyabingi was understood primarily as a political 'society', or 'organization', or 'cult' – or, in other words, as some sort of a bounded and coherent group – which emerged in Rwanda and South-western Uganda in the early twentieth century, as a challenge to the new colonial presence.

Furthermore, by this logic, it was precisely because of its anti-colonial nature that it became so secretive – which would have been a necessity, of course, for avoiding detection by the authorities – *and* why it later turned violent: such violence as would have been primarily aimed at disrupting the colonial order. Hence also why this 'society' should have then more or less disappeared by about the mid-1930s, both as the colonial authorities became more adept at disrupting its activities and – more importantly – as local populations became more engaged with, and more accommodating of, the ongoing colonial presence.

It is indisputable that, throughout the early years of the twentieth century, Nyabingi certainly *did* act as a vehicle for anti-colonial sentiment (and between 1915 and 1928, for example, Nyabingi followers certainly did undertake a series of violent attacks against administration outposts). However, it is my argument that this was by no means its *raison d'être*, but instead simply one outcome of the broader role Nyabingi played in Kiga society as a mechanism of gaining redress for misfortunes (of which the European arrival was but one). By focusing on this one factor alone, however, by emphasizing only Nyabingi's more political aspect, the earlier literature has acted to obscure, perhaps even deny, the ways in which Nyabingi addressed *other* types of misfortunes as well. As I shall discuss in the next chapter, there were at least two additional ways in which the fertility spirit was typically drawn upon during times of misfortune.

Firstly, in the event of household sickness, or infertility (occurrences which are encompassed by a single term in Rukiga, *engumba*), one member of the household, usually one of its women, would begin to receive visions from the spirit (*okworekwa*).[3] In most instances, these apparitions would be experienced while the woman involved was moving through some 'liminal' social space (such as hilltop rangeland), or else in her dreams at night. Nyabingi was always more likely to appear in such liminal contexts, given that she was an entity firmly located in a domain 'above', or 'beyond', or 'outside' ordinary social and temporal existence (a concept which is captured by the Rukiga category of *ahaiguru*). During these visitations, the spirit would both claim responsibility for the problem at hand, and instruct the afflicted woman to attend a local Nyabingi medium, or 'handmaiden' (as May Edel terms these actors) in order to seek redress. In the context of the subsequent meetings, the medium would then consult Nyabingi on the woman's behalf, and, crucially, would demand sizeable payment both for her own interventions, and for the spirit's appeasement (with further payments being made in the event of a 'successful outcome').

Now, I say *crucially* here, because these payments (*okutoija*) were in many ways central to the whole sociology of Nyabingi. Specifically, the size of these payments was often far greater than any one household could ever, by itself, afford – demands for several cows and a bundle of produce in one go were far from uncommon – and, thus, anyone trying to make *okutoija* was invariably forced to borrow additional goods, or to seek pledges for such loans, from any number of other people. Throughout both the colonial archive and the ethnographic record, accounts of Nyabingi are replete with descriptions of the sizeable amounts of goods that were exchanged in the spirit's name, as individuals entered into such loan arrangements not only with their kin, but also with their reciprocal bond-partners, their other friends, their neighbours, and so on. Given the sheer volume of the goods involved in these transactions, it is not coincidental that the very word Nyabingi means, literally: 'she who has many things'. Indeed, so widespread were these exchanges, that they commonly formed webs, or networks, of exchange relations – ones which cross-cut other sorts of social structures, such as those of household, kinship, and so on.

A second occasion on which local people commonly turned to Nyabingi

---

[3] Throughout my research on the Kanungu fire, respondents used the terms *okworekwa* (*lit:* a vision, a revelation) and *okubonekyerwa* (*lit:* an apparition) interchangeably. However, to avoid confusion, I use only *okworekwa* throughout this book.

was during times of (what might be termed) general misfortune. In this way, in the event of a large flood, or landslide, or famine (all of which have always been relatively common occurrences in these parts), or indeed during various sorts of political upheaval, local people, and especially those who regularly participated in the kinds of networks I have just described, would again take Nyabingi to be responsible. Thus, during such episodes, they would gather at a local Nyabingi shrine to seek her mollification (again, through the offices of one of her mediums), and at these meetings, a sacrifice would be made, in a ritual known as *okutamba*. Most importantly of all, at the end of these ceremonies the medium involved would effectively hand out, or in other ways redistribute, all of the animals and other goods, which she had previously received in payment for her consultations with the spirit (always, of course, in the name of Nyabingi herself). Moreover, these redistributions would start with those people who had been worst affected by the current misfortune. In these ways, then, these *okutamba* ceremonies generally *did*, in fact, at least partly negate the worst effects of the particular misfortune at hand.

The main point I want to make here, then, is that Nyabingi was never a bounded and coherent 'society', of the type imagined both by colonial officers and by others, but was instead always a diffuse set of informal, and in many ways ephemeral, exchange networks. Moreover, this reframing of Nyabingi's social form enables me to develop alternative readings of other of its aspects, and to arrive at different conclusions as to, for example, why it was so secretive, and as to what made it (apparently) so compelling as a mode of social action. In relation to the former of these characteristics, the very fact that Nyabingi was a network already goes some of the way to explaining its secrecy, given that many types of networks, by their very nature, tend towards concealment. One of the lasting contributions of the 'classic' anthropological networks studies of the 1960s was to show how in any field of multiple partial networks – a phrase which I think most anthropologists would now recognize describes practically any social context, and not just an urban one – individual actors always have multiple, and often quite contradictory, exchange obligations. In other words, because such actors are always 'drawn in several different directions at once', they are also highly likely, of necessity, to have to try to hide details of at least some of their transactions, from at least some of their multiple exchange partners (see, for example, Clyde Mitchell, 1969).

Perhaps more importantly, some theorists have suggested that this proclivity for secrecy may be particularly marked in those networks which are characterized by uneven exchanges – i.e. those in which recipients are passed goods of a higher value than they could possibly hope to reciprocate, at least in the short term (as was indeed the case with the kind of Nyabingi exchanges I have just described). As Albert Trouwborst showed, for example, in his seminal study of exchange networks in neighbouring Burundi (1973), these uneven networks are far more likely to lead to competitive forms of exchange behaviour – attempts at 'social mobility' and the like – and, as a result, are generally more given to suspicion, intrigue and concealment. Thus, in the first type of exchange network Trouwborst looked at, one related to everyday forms of beer exchange known as *okuteerera* – the practice of which is common, incidentally, in all societies of the Great Lakes region, including in those of South-western Uganda – the general equivalence of the exchanges involved tended to result in mostly cordial, friendly and open relations. However, in the second sort of network he studied, a type of patronage network based on cattle loans called, in Kirundi, *ubugabiire*, the converse unequal nature of the exchanges – in *ubugabiire*, the very act of receiving a cow is, in and of itself, an admission of subordinate status – resulted instead in 'a certain amount of competition, mutual distrust and opposed interest' (1973: 112), and, as a result, frequently engendered what Trouwborst described as '*many elements* of secrecy and intrigue' (*ibid*.: 113, emphasis mine).

However, in addition to these more instrumental types of explanations, there may be at least one other reason why Nyabingi networks should have tended towards secrecy. It is here also necessary to look more carefully at how they were conceived by the Kiga themselves, or in other words, to explore what meanings were attached to them by local actors. Specifically, I think it relevant that people's primary motivation for participating in these sorts of exchanges, as I have just described them, was to assist other households to appease the spirit, and thereby to assist with some episode of illness, infertility, loss of crops, or whatever. Yet another way of stating all this is to say that, by giving and receiving in this way, actors sought – through the agency of the cows, or the other goods being exchanged – to address a power from the beyond – remember that Nyabingi was located in the domain of *ahaiguru* – in order to transform some part of the proximal universe (to make a sick person better, an infertile woman pregnant, a damaged field replenished, and so on). Thus, all Nyabingi networks were by intention *transformative*, of the body and of the world. Moreover, this sort of belief in the exchange of substances as a means of effecting change to the body, or to the world, is something which has long been common in many societies of the Great Lakes region. Indeed, in the case of neighbouring North-western Rwanda, as described by the medical anthropologist Christopher Taylor, such concepts of exchange have for long been so central to local understandings of transformation – as these have been associated, in that case, both with Nyabingi and with other forces as well – that, in everyday speech, local metaphors of sickness are invariably couched in terms of 'blockage' (of networks), whilst metaphors of healing are cast in terms of the restoration of their 'flows' (*ubujwa*; see, for example, Taylor 1988, 1990 and 1992).

This also enables us to develop an additional set of perspectives as to why these Nyabingi networks should have had a proclivity for secrecy. On the one hand, it is quite clear here that these networks were attempting to affect the very most private aspects of people's lives, their household members' health, their women's fertility, and so on (and in a society which draws a sharp distinction between the private and the public). On the other hand, it is also noteworthy that for the actors involved, participation in these Nyabingi networks also conformed to what Hegel famously called 'the labour of the negative' (2004 [1807]). In other words, the logic of these networks, as I have just described it, was to invoke a categorically distinct 'other' (i.e. an entity which was both in, and of, *ahaiguru*), precisely so that this could be negated, in order to restore the self to its ideal state (one which was healthy, fully functioning, productive, and so on).

Yet in these ways, the Nyabingi networks almost perfectly mimicked the very logic of secrecy itself. Because as that great sociological theorist of secrecy, Georg Simmel, first described in 1900 – albeit as part of a flawed evolutionary argument – the social life of secrecy is similarly marked by exactly this sort of 'labour of the negative'. Thus, according to Simmel, *all* secrets, by their very nature, similarly invoke a categorical 'other' (that of all the people who do not know the secret). Once cast, this category is again subject to constant erosion, and to eventual negation, as more and more of its members attempt to find out, and eventually do discover, what the secret is (at which point the secret itself also becomes eroded, of course). Finally, all of this once again acts to transform the position of the original secret-bearers themselves, who are ultimately recast as no different from all of the other members of the (now) wider community of knowledge. Thus, in Simmel's formulation, all secrets similarly invoke a 'second world alongside the manifest world [in which] the latter is decisively influenced by the former' (Simmel, cited in Piot, 1993: 365, fn. 15), whereby the inherent power of secrecy lies less in the content of the secret *per se*, than in the dialectics of concealment and revelation which secrecy necessarily implies, and which conveys a strong potential for social transformation. Indeed, this notion of the dialectics of secrecy, and its potential for transformation, has informed much of the recent ethnographic writing on forms of 'everyday' secrecy in Africa[4] – for example, Bellman (1984), Ferme (2001) and Piot (1993) – as well as the more theoretical musings of Michael Taussig (1999), and others. However, returning to my own material, it can be seen that if both the Nyabingi networks, and secrecy itself, conform to a similar logic, then it follows that for participants in these networks to have shrouded their activities in secrecy would have been to amplify the potentially transformative effects of their endeavours.

Networks and 'the other'

Therefore, a reframing of Nyabingi, as not a bounded and coherent 'society' so much as a diffuse set of informal networks, provides some insight into its secretive nature. In addition, it also helps us to understand what happened to Nyabingi during the middle years of the twentieth century. There is a general consensus in the historical literature that, by roughly the mid-1930s, Nyabingi had ceased to have any real relevance for the Bakiga. The argument is that, as the colonial authorities became better at disrupting its activities, and as local populations became more engaged with, and more accommodating of, the ongoing colonial presence, Nyabingi simply ceased to hold sway.

---

[4] I.e. those forms of secrecy which do not relate to formal ritual contexts, such as initiation cults, the installation of kings and priests, and so on (for a good definition, see Piot, 1993: 353).

However, while this argument might go some of the way to explaining why Nyabingi ceased to operate as a medium of anti-colonial sentiment during this period, it does not go far enough in addressing why Nyabingi should have also stopped operating as a mechanism of redress for misfortune at this time. In other words, it does not address why the sick, the barren, and others should have suddenly stopped turning to Nyabingi for help with their problems. At least part of the answer here, I would suggest, is that this so-called 'disappearance' of Nyabingi by about the mid-1930s, seemingly so well documented in the literature, was in fact more apparent than real. In actual fact, far from disappearing during this time, or ceasing to be meaningful for local people, the Nyabingi phenomenon instead passed through a transformation during this period. And the primary agents of this transformation were the newly arrived Catholic missionaries, the White Fathers.

Briefly stated – and as will be explored in Chapter 3 – from the time of their arrival in South-western Uganda in 1923, the White Fathers, by design or otherwise, projected an image of Catholic theology in which the Virgin Mary was constructed as a divine female similar to Nyabingi. In this way, their sermons, especially those given in the rural areas, referred to the Virgin by the same range of terms as had previously been used for Nyabingi (*omugole, nyoko'kuru*, and so on). In the context of their 'Legion of Mary' (*Ab'eihe rya Bikira Maria*) meetings, they regularly told women that the Virgin, too, was sympathetic to the issues of household illness, women's infertility, and so on (and thus, as Ron Kassimir describes of neighbouring Toro, the Legion soon became 'the exemplary Catholic lay association...and the most pervasive mode of organized lay life outside the daily purview of the church, especially in rural communities' 1999: 258). In addition, in their sacrament of confession, the missionaries invited people to enter into small huts called, significantly, *endaaro* (a term which had previously referred only to Nyabingi shrines), and to there confess their sins or *ebibi* (a word which also means 'misfortunes'). Finally, at the conclusion of these confessions, the priests would ask penitents to make an offering to the church, by way of penance. Crucially, the White Fathers defined these offerings as *okutoija*. Moreover, in keeping with all general Catholic practice for confession, this whole process was conducted entirely *in secret*.

Thus, within a relative short period of time, women experiencing sickness in their households, or those unable to conceive, or those suffering some other misfortune, again began to receive night-time visions from not Nyabingi, but instead from the Virgin Mary. Moreover, these visions now instructed the women to undertake not consultations with Nyabingi mediums, but instead confessions in their local churches. At these confessions, they were requested to make often sizeable *okutoija* payments to not Nyabingi mediums, of course, but to the church. Following all this, they would again have to approach others – usually still in secret – to raise the requisite amounts. Thus it was that, far from disappearing during the mid-1930s, the former exchange networks of Nyabingi simply became reoriented during this time towards the Catholic church. Moreover, there is no evidence here that the amount of goods passing through the networks dropped during this period. Indeed, such data as can be gleaned – based on anecdotal evidence and surviving parish records (which are, admittedly, hopelessly incomplete) – instead seem to suggest that the volume of goods passing through the networks may even have increased in the middle decades of the century. Yet it is nevertheless clear that this reorientation, or 'reversioning', of the networks into a Catholic idiom served also to amplify their transformational power.

Specifically, one of the primary operations of the old Nyabingi networks, as I have described them, was to provide actual redress – through a redistribution of goods previously received by the mediums – during periods of general misfortune. Here the Catholic missionaries always had the upper hand over the former mediums, in that, during such periods, they could draw not only on the goods they had previously received as *okutoija*, but also on a much larger amount of resources provided by their own 'outside' – national and international – networks (or in other words, those of the wider White Fathers' organization, the wider Catholic church, and so on). In this sense, then, one of the key factors here was that of scale. Thus, if Nyabingi networks had previously connected people living in one village, or a group of villages, perhaps even a whole region, through the agency of the White Fathers, they now linked into an entirely 'global' set of relations. Moreover, it was primarily through these wider connections that the missionaries were always able to offer far greater emergency relief than could possibly be procured by any local actor. To cite just one example, during one particularly bad famine in the late 1950s, the White Fathers of one parish, Rushanje (the parish in which I have conducted fieldwork since 2000), kept all of the local households in that parish in milk for an entire year. Moreover, their abilities to address misfortune in this way became particularly marked during those years of state collapse in Uganda (from roughly the early 1970s to the late 1980s). Indeed, as many of my respondents have described to me at length, the local parish was in some respects the only body capable of providing genuine assistance throughout much of this period.

Furthermore, there is at least one other way in which this translation, or reversioning, of the Nyabingi networks into a Catholic idiom served to amplify their transformative power. In order to grasp this, I return again to my discussion of their pre-existing logics, and to their inherent 'labour of the negative'. Thus, as I have already outlined, for local participants the inherent power of Nyabingi mediums, and of the networks they operationalized, stemmed from their ability to invoke a categorically distinct 'other', located beyond the realm of everyday, quotidian experience (i.e. a spirit within *ahaiguru*), and to use this, through negation, to transform some aspect of the proximal universe. And as one further piece of evidence here, I would also note that all of the verbs related to Nyabingi ended in the suffix *–mu*, which has an implication of bringing something in from without, of incorporation.

An analogy might be drawn here with the power of the mantic, as this figure has for long existed (in various different guises) in many of the societies of East Africa and beyond. As described by Anderson & Johnson, following Chadwick, perhaps *the* defining feature of the mantic is a similar ability to harness something – in this case, knowledge – which is beyond, or 'outside', the quotidian, or the normally 'taken for granted' (as they put it, 'knowledge ... of the future, or of the commonly unknown present or past', 1995: 14), in order to then use that knowledge to transform either individual bodies, or else some part of the social or physical world. Moreover, as some of the contributors to Anderson and Johnson further explore, this knowledge is marked as particularly powerful, the 'further away', or the more 'remote', it is from the people's everyday experience. Thus, for example, Waller shows how certain Masaai mantics (*loibonok*) are marked as particularly powerful precisely because they are themselves outsiders, and are thus able to introduce knowledge which is *entirely* alien to the communities in which they operate (1995: 28–64).

By this same logic, then, we can understand why the translation of Nyabingi networks into a Catholic idiom should have served to amplify their power, given that, in the process, the key symbol of the local fertility goddess was transformed into something altogether more remote – and therefore potentially more powerful – that of the Catholic Virgin Mary. After all, not only was Holy Mary also a being within *ahaiguru* – a term that the White Fathers used to translate the word 'Heaven' – she was also, local women were now told, the primary icon of fertility in *buraeya* (a term which is sometimes glossed as 'England', but which more accurately refers to a different sort of categorical other, that of an inchoate international, or 'global', domain). Thus, not only did the arrival of the White Fathers extend the scale of the networks, it also served to greatly amplify the cosmological categories which animated them.

Transforming the networks

Let me return to the key question of why all of this should have once again risen to such prominence in South-western Uganda in the 1990s, after more than half a century of apparent obscurity. Or to put it another way, why should these same sorts of networks[5] – which had been cast in a Catholic idiom and embedded in Catholic practice for almost fifty years – have suddenly become reanimated as an independent entity in their own right? (Moreover, as one which was *so* compelling that it was eventually to lead to the deaths of more than 650 people.)

I should perhaps begin by noting here that recent work in the social sciences on networks, and in particular that which has been influenced by the 'anti-foundationalist' philosophy of Deleuze & Guattari (1972 and 1980) and others, has pointed to just what a difficult task trying to answer this sort of question really is. Specifically, much of this new research has highlighted the 'rhizomatic', and partial, nature of all social networks or, in other words, their propensity, once existent, to suddenly mutate, and to re-emerge in highly complex, and often quite unpredictable, ways. Thus, they

---

[5] For a full discussion of the direct, and the indirect, connections between the historic Nyabingi networks, and the 'new' networks of the MRTC, see Chapters 4 and 5.

frequently do not play out in a linear historical fashion, but are instead characterized by long periods of inertia, punctuated by sudden bursts of activity, and transformation. One outcome of this is that all attempts to explain these networks' operation become themselves cast as, to some extent, both contingent and partial in nature. These caveats notwith-standing, the past history of Nyabingi networks, as I have just described it, does offer at least some clues to help guide our study here.

First of all, it is worth restating that one of the primary operations of these networks, throughout the history of their existence, was as a means of gaining redress for misfortune. Hence, then, the principal reason why they should have once again risen to such prominence in the 1990s, given that this was the period during which South-western Uganda was experiencing perhaps the greatest crisis of health and fertility (*engumba*) in the history of the area: the HIV/AIDS epidemic. As I shall explore at length in Chapters 5 and 6 – which will look at why so many people joined the MRTC, and how it came to have such a profound impact on their lives over the decade or so of its lifespan – the AIDS epidemic emerges again, and again, and again, in respondents' accounts of why either they themselves, or their relatives or friends, joined the sect. Specifically here, respondents speak of an increased frequency of Marian visions at that time, as a result not only of AIDS deaths but also of the profound impact the emergent epidemic had on property relations throughout the rural areas (relations that are themselves central, of course, to local understandings of fertility and social reproduction).

Secondly, it is again necessary to highlight that participants generally expected these networks, once created, to provide actual, material, assistance during such times of general misfortune (through their redistribution of past *okutoija* payments, or whatever). This aspect is worth restating, because it provides some guidance as to why the networks should have become again reversioned during this period, away from the mainstream Catholic church, and towards an independent religious movement such as the MRTC.

Specifically, by the early 1990s, a series of institutional changes within the local Catholic church – and in particular that related to the general withdrawal of missionary priests from dioceses throughout the Southwest, and their replacement with locally trained, indigenous clergy – had severely curtailed the former abilities of the church to provide these networks with the levels of material support they had previously offered. This was largely a result of the fact that the new African priests simply did not have access to the kinds of international networks of support upon which the missionaries had previously drawn. In other words, the general scale of the church's own networks became greatly reduced at this time. Yet in the context of an emergent AIDS epidemic, this led to great disillusionment amongst ordinary parishioners, and eventually, to many reorienting their exchange activities towards (potentially) more efficacious, independent religious groups such as the MRTC. Thus, at least part of the initial popular appeal of the MRTC stemmed from precisely the fact that this sect *could* provide those in need with substantial material assistance – in a way the local Catholic church could not – assistance which was provided for, in the

MRTC's case, by the enormous entrance fees the sect imposed on its new members.

Thirdly, and finally here, I would also return to my previous discussion of the internal logic of these networks, and to their inherent 'labour of the negative'. I have argued that the initial translation of the old Nyabingi networks into a Catholic idiom served to amplify, or to enhance, their trans-formational power, precisely because it replaced their existing categorical 'other' with a form that was even more remote. Yet, in many ways, the subsequent reversioning of these networks in the 1990s, away from the Catholic church and towards the independent MRTC, served to amplify their transformational power even further still.

Specifically, it is noteworthy that, throughout much of its existence, the MRTC projected an image of the Virgin Mary which was quite different from anything that had gone before, representing her as not the benign figure of missionary Catholicism, so much as a millenarian figure out to punish the whole of mankind. Of key importance for my argument here, the primary source of this new image was explicitly traced – by sect members them-selves – to a series of pamphlets they were receiving from a group of international Marian groups worldwide (contact with whom had just become permitted in Uganda under new rights of religious freedom, which had themselves been brought in following the 'structural-adjustment' programmes of the late 1980s and early '90s). In other words, what seems to have made the MRTC's Virgin so much more powerful than the White Fathers' projection was precisely the fact that it derived not just from the mainstream church of *buraeya*, but instead from something much more exclusive, from a limited, and partly concealed, network within that global domain. In a period before other sorts of international media had become common in rural Uganda, the power of this kind of imaginary must indeed have been really quite compelling.

Moreover, I would also note that, in this way, a study of these networks also contributes to recent discussions within Africanist anthropology on the influence of 'the invisible' in human affairs. A number of writers have recently drawn attention to the various ways in which metaphysical, or cosmological, influences and concerns appear to be a key factor shaping social and political life in many, if not most, African societies (e.g. Ellis & Ter Haar, 2004; West, 2005). However, at least some of this work has been criticized for its perceived implication of a return to an older, more essentialist, view of African affairs, in which African people are regarded as 'superstitious', and inhabiting worlds which are guided by 'supernatural', or 'occult', forces (see, for example, Becker & Geissler's critique of Ellis & Ter Haar, 2007: 3).

Yet such criticisms may themselves be 'throwing the baby out with the bathwater'. Because as Harry West's subtle and nuanced account of witchcraft and politics in Mozambique has shown (2005), and as my own work on these Nyabingi networks further demonstrates, 'the invisible realm' (as West calls it, in reference to a Mozambiquan idiom) certainly does impact on quotidian – productive and reproductive – realities in a variety of important ways. Yet to state this is not to imply any form of essentialism. On the contrary, the particular form this 'invisible' takes, and the ways in which it impacts upon the proximal world, vary greatly from place to place. Thus, the realm which West describes in the Mozambican context is quite different in character from the one I am looking at here. But more importantly, my own study also shows that this invisible 'other' is not static, *even within a single ethnographic context*. Thus, in this South-western Ugandan context, both the qualities, and more importantly the scale, of the social imaginary that is *ahaiguru* – and its more recent con-comitant, *buraeya* – have changed dramatically over time. At the very least here, I can demonstrate that the scale of these categories increased significantly following the arrival of the White Fathers, then contracted with the withdrawal of missionary priests, then grew again – and indeed, exponentially so – in the context of the new 'globalization'. The really key point to be made here – which I will elaborate much further below – is that, as they extended and diminished in this way, so too did the power of their influence over the proximal world.

Thus, my discussion of the nature of historic Nyabingi networks offers a degree of insight into not only why this sort of phenomenon should have re-emerged in the early 1990s, but also into what made it quite so powerful at that time. However, in relation to the second of these two points, it is again useful to draw on some of the more recent work in the social sciences on networks. In particular here, it is interesting to note that much recent writing has emphasized that the power of any specific network, or set of networks – defined in terms of its ability to mobilize people (and things) for social action – often varies directly with the degree to which its key actors recognize it as a network (and are thus able to represent it, to others, as such). In other words, and as Callon first showed in his now famous study of scallop fishing in St Brieuc Bay (1986), all networks are made more or less effective by the degree to which their leaders are self-aware, or self-reflexive, of their capabilities and limitations (the definition of which therefore becomes itself a site of political contestation, one located within what Meyer & Geschiere (1998) refer to as 'the dialectics of closure and flow' or what Strathern (1996) has simply called the competition over where, or at which 'level', to '*cut* the network'.

To my mind, this is important for trying to understand what made the MRTC so much more irresistible than anything that had gone before it. Because what the MRTC case shows is that, whilst the networks from which the sect emerged continued to be informal, and ephemeral, in nature, a key shift occurred when one of its members, in particular, became aware of the fact that this *was* a network, and moreover, one which could be mobilized towards certain ends. Furthermore, from that time onwards, this individual, Ceredonia Mwerinde (who came from a very humble background, in com-parison with certain other of the MRTC's members), further consolidated the position of the sect by strengthening the symbolic connection between the Virgin Mary and the old Nyabingi (she held ceremonies at former Nyabingi shrines, reinstated much of the ritual practice of the old Nyabingi, and so on). In addition, she began to conduct more and more of both her own, and eventually also the Movement's, practice in secret, and at one point she introduced a system of secret signs, and a special sign language, within the group. In addition, she demonstrated a keen awareness of the key importance of the sect's international network of contacts. Thus, not only did she include readings from the international pamphlets in her own sermons, to an ever greater degree, but she also later used the 'global' medium of radio advertising, as and when this became available, as a means for recruiting new members.

On violence and its negation

Moreover, an interrogation of the MRTC case study through a lens of recent work in the social sciences on networks offers at least one other set of insights. Specifically, it offers a useful frame of reference through which to understand what is perhaps the most vexed question in the whole MRTC story: *why the violence?* Certainly, I could perhaps argue that, over the course of this introduction, I have already gone much of the way towards answering this question. After all, looked at more closely, violence has been present in almost everything I have so far described. Take, for example, the kinds of misfortunes in which Nyabingi, or the Virgin Mary, becomes involved. Thus, all of the sicknesses which commonly affect households in these parts – sleeping sickness, malaria, more recently AIDS – have a violent impact on the body, causing their victims to shake, to sweat, to waste away, and so on. Yet so too infertility often brings with it a violence of its own. Here, I draw on my experience of having lived in the home of a Local Council Chairman for over two years, and of having heard all of the cases of domestic violence which were brought to him, morning after morning, during the whole of that time. As I look back now over all of my fieldnotes on all these cases – some of which involved women having their arms broken, their teeth knocked out, and even worse things still – I realize that, in practically every instance, the woman involved had been accused, by somebody else, of being infertile.

Thus, on the one hand, it is perhaps not surprising that the networks themselves should demonstrate a propensity for violence, given that, in effect, so much violence is already embedded in their rationale. For example, we might account for the fact that the visions which women receive at the outset of these processes – irrespective of whether they are of Nyabingi or the Virgin Mary – are invariably themselves violent affairs, and frequently involve their recipients going into a frenzy. On some occasions, including in a number of instances I have personally witnessed, the result can be the complete destruction of a living room or a bedroom, etc. Yet, on the other hand, it might also be correct to say that if sickness and infertility do entail such violence, then these networks might also be understood as a social mechanism for regulating its worst effects. In other words, by channelling, or translating, the actual physical violence which accompanies these misfortunes into another, potentially more constructive, method for achieving transformation, these also, in one sense, represent a means for 'controlling anger'. By this logic, those occasions on which the networks themselves have become violent might instead be thought of as anomalous, even as examples of network failure, or breakdown.

Thus from this perspective, my key research question could be rephrased as not what makes these networks violent, but rather, how, when and why do they cease to operate properly, thereby unfurling that which they might otherwise regulate, and control? However, to pose the question in this way is by no means to suggest that such a process of breakdown should therefore be seen as, in some sense, an inevitable outcome. On the one hand, there is little in the historical and ethnographic record of new Christian movements in Africa to suggest that this should be the case. On the contrary, in fact, much of this literature, from Adrian Hastings' pioneering studies of the Watchtower Movement onwards (for example, 1979), has shown that, whilst such movements frequently do draw on logics of affliction and misfortune – and they do, therefore, play on the violence that these things frequently entail – in most instances these aspects become regulated, and dissipated, over time. This much is at least partly evidenced, for example, by the fact that, whilst many AICs begin with an eschatological outlook, in most instances this declines over time, as the group involved gradually comes to terms with the world.

One particularly good example of this process is the Zimbabwe Assemblies of God Africa (ZAOGA), as described by David Maxwell in his recent *African Gifts of the Spirit* (2006a). As Maxwell carefully shows in that book, especially in his examination of ZAOGA's own printed literature, although during an earlier phase eschatological thinking represented a key concern for ZAOGA's membership, as time went on – and especially following the establishment of the church's international mission, the Forward in Faith Mission International – this element largely disappeared from their thinking. From this perspective, then, the fact that, over the course of its history, the MRTC displayed a growing commitment to a millenarian outlook – and to an increasingly violent one at that – is cast as quite *ab*normal.

On the other hand, it is also notable, from a wider comparative perspective, that the global ethnographic record is replete with examples of all sorts of networks, and 'cults', of affliction, in some features similar to those of Nyabingi (as I have just described them), which simply continue to operate for years – in some instances decades – without ever engendering violence on a scale comparable to that which occurred in Kanungu (for a very good overview of this vast literature, see Janzen, 2005). In other words, the fact that the MRTC emerged from a context of violence is not, in and of itself, enough to explain why it should have suddenly broken down around March 2000. Moreover, by this same logic, it is also possible to imagine that this sect, too, might well have continued to operate in the way that it did for a much longer period, were it not for the intervention, presumably, of some other – as yet unidentified – factor, or factors, which then caused the whole thing to collapse. So how, then, might we best try to capture these other factors, and the nature of the breakdown that they precipitated?

It is here that some recent work in the social sciences on networks again proves useful. In particular, one of the key moves of so-called 'Actor-

Network Theory' has been to highlight the fact that all social networks are, by definition, 'assemblages' (see Callon, 1986; Latour, 1988, 1996 and 1999; Latour & Woolgar, 1979). In other words, that they are all constituted of not only the people involved, but also of semiotic elements (at the very least the information which is communicated through them, and the meanings which are 'read into' them), and by material objects as well (the things which are exchanged, the media through which these transactions occur, and so on). Moreover, that each of these elements has social agency in its own right, or, in other words, that each has the potential to alter the overall constellation, in ways which might often seem quite unpredictable in advance (indeed, one of the key projects of these new network theorists has been to highlight the ways in which human affairs are frequently affected by the unforeseen influence of all sorts of non-human agents).

Moreover, this theoretical move turns out to be a particularly important one for understanding the final demise of the MRTC. As I shall argue in Chapter 7 – in which I will 'play the detective' in order to examine the circumstances which led to the downfall of the MRTC, to the bodies in the pits, and ultimately, to the Kanungu fire itself – in this instance, at least, events cannot be reduced to human agency alone. Instead, as I shall demonstrate in that chapter, the final breakdown of the MRTC network – defined in terms of its failure to meet its participants' needs, with a resultant outbreak of violence – can only be understood in terms of human intentions, and actions, played out within and through a set of complex, and unpredictable, material frameworks. Or, in other words, for purposes of telling this particular story, the various non-human agents involved – from animals to climate, to disease, to food, to land, to buildings, to technology (and other things besides) – had a particularly significant part to play as well.

A note on methods

In summary, then, the historical ethnography of the MRTC turns out to be a study of social networks, an account of their history, their mode of operation, and (ultimately) their demise as well. Yet so, too, the methods used to construct this account have also relied on the forging of network relations, and in other ways, too, have been informed by a certain network logic. The majority of this book is based on 26 months of anthropological fieldwork carried out in South-western Uganda in six periods between 2000 and 2005. For practically all of this time, I lived in the home of Mr Grace Bwire, LCIII Chairman in Bugamba Village, Rwampara County, Mbarara District. Although Bugamba is located some way to the East of the Kigezi Hills – it is instead located within the area of the old Ankole District – it nevertheless turns out to have been a good location from which to begin my study of the Kanungu fire. This stems from the fact that Bugamba is located very near to – a couple of miles away from – and is in many ways connected with, Mwizi Sub-county, which is one of the six sites to which Kiga migrants were moved, by the colonial authorities, during an assisted relocation scheme in the mid-1940s. As will be documented in Chapter 3, this relocation scheme is key to understanding the whole MRTC story, in that it was changes that this scheme brought about in the structure of the Kiga household that resulted in women within the resettlement areas being more reliant on Marian intercession than ever before. As a result, it was from the six resettlement zones that the MRTC was to gain the majority of its recruits, some forty years or so later (see Chapter 5).

Nevertheless, it is also the case that Mwizi was only one of the areas from which the MRTC gained new converts, and that, in addition, the group recruited heavily from the five other former resettlement areas (and indeed, from many other locations as well). Thus, as a totality, the MRTC membership was drawn from literally all over South-western Uganda and beyond. As a result, it follows that no one field site, wherever it might have been located, could ever have provided an adequate location from which to explore the whole MRTC story. It follows that, although my research was, of course, greatly informed by my fieldwork in Bugamba, from quite early on in my research, it was also necessary for me to travel extensively throughout the Southwest. This was done in order to trace as many of the surviving protagonists of the MRTC drama as possible, as well as the friends and relatives of those who died, local clergymen and women, government officials, medical practitioners, journalists and others – in short, all those who had some insight into the Movement story.

Most of this travelling was completed during a series of 'research safaris', of varying duration – some lasted a day or two, some a week or more – undertaken during 2001 and early 2002, in particular. In some instances, these trips away from Bugamba were completed using public transport, on others, they involved my hiring one of the village's six or so private cars for the duration. In addition, some involved my staying in people's homes, whilst others saw me staying in local hostels or hotels.

The main point I want to make here about these research safaris is that, in each instance, they involved my mobilizing a specific network, or networks, of people in order to bring them about. Thus, at the very least, most of the trips involved my gathering a small entourage of people to accompany me on the journey. Although I completed at least two of the safaris on my own, on most occasions I was accompanied by a range of other people as well. Thus, a majority of the tours included some combination of myself, the head of the household in which I lived in Bugamba, Mr Grace Bwire,[6] my wife, Zheela, one of several of my research assistants, one of several drivers, and so on. More specifically, a number of the earliest safaris were assisted by some of the journalists who had initially covered the Kanungu story – including James Mujuni – who were able to quickly introduce me to the key surviving protagonists, and to show me the main sites in which all of the events had played out. In addition, several of the later trips were joined by individuals from Bugamba, or elsewhere, who knew of friends or relatives in other parts who had been involved with the MRTC, and who were thus able to introduce me to potentially significant interviewees.

[6] Grace was particularly keen to take part in these safaris where they involved a visit to some dignitary, or to an area with which his own family had prior contacts.

More generally, most of the research trips proceeded by a method of 'snowball sampling', whereby I would follow links between contacts in order to build a network of potential respondents. Thus, I would typically arrive in a given area with the names of one or more potential contacts, and I would then ask these people to point me in the direction of others nearby who had also had contact with the MRTC (and who might, therefore, also be able and willing to assist my research). In these ways, then, over the course of the various tours, I developed my own network of contacts over the very same households that had previously been visited by the Movement (see especially Chapter 5). Thus, it could even be said that, through these methods, my own practice even mimicked that of the MRTC, in that it resulted in my retracing, or reconstructing, (at least part of) the very same network that the Movement had themselves built, almost a decade earlier.

Moreover, through its deployment of a networking approach, my own research enquiry ended up mimicking the networks under examination in other ways as well, in that it too resulted in much of the project being similarly rhizomatic, and partial, in nature. The method was rhizomatic in the sense that it did not produce the kind of steady stream of data, and insight, that might have flowed from a different kind of methodology. Instead, it proceeded in a much more uneven, or 'lumpy' – at times, an almost random – kind of a way. In other words, it included long periods of inertia, or 'redundancy' – times during which it generated little new, or significant, knowledge about the MRTC – which were then punctuated by (often unexpected) 'plateaux', moments of great insight, even revelation.

Thus, a significant number of the households I visited on these safaris yielded little by way of useful information about the Movement at all, either because the potential respondents were reluctant – for whatever reason – to talk about the MRTC, or because the person I had come to see was currently bedridden with malaria (two occasions), or was away attending the burial of a recently deceased relative (four occasions), or had themselves recently died (two occasions). In at least one instance, the potential respondent physically threatened me to leave his property, whilst on another, particularly memorable, occasion, the person involved invited me into his living room, before promptly climbing out of the window and running away! (It later transpired that he had erroneously taken me to be a police officer.) In these ways, then, whole days were sometimes lost. Yet by the same token, my arrival at some or other potential respondent's home did occasionally – and usually quite unexpectedly – result in some moment of great insight. For example, this was especially the case with one particular visit I made in November 2001 which, although I could not possibly have predicted it in advance, was to provide the final key for unlocking the whole MRTC mystery (I shall return to this visit in Chapter 7).

As a final point, I would also note that I have tried to retain at least some sense of this general 'lumpiness' of my work in Uganda – this shape of punctuated equilibrium – in the current text. Thus, like the networks themselves, and like the research process I undertook to capture them, the narrative here also unfolds through a sequence of sudden shifts. Specifically, it too develops through a series of break-throughs, or revelations, which are reproduced in this book in the same chronological order in which they occurred in the field.

In addition, the methodology was partial, in that its approach to respondent selection resulted in my conducting lots of interviews in certain areas, and almost none in others. Thus, for example, it just so happened that I was given consistently useful introductions – and was thus able to conduct many good interviews – in Kabale District, whilst I received very few contacts for – and thus achieved very little coverage of former MRTC activity in – for example, Kabarole, or Kasese, Districts. (I shall discuss my overall sample of former MRTC members in more detail in Chapter 5.) Moreover, from the very beginning the work was highly dependent upon respondents' testimonies as a source of evidence. This stemmed from the fact that the archival sources on the history of Nyabingi practice in the Southwest are hopelessly incomplete. Firstly, many of the district files relating to historic Nyabingi cases – as had been tried under the Witchcraft Ordinance of 1912 – were burnt in a bonfire at the Kabale Headquarters in the 1970s (anecdotally, to make space for additional documentation). What remains of this archive is today piled in an unusable heap in the loft of one of the main administration buildings. In addition, most of the national archive on Nyabingi – a series of historic government files which have been reference in past publications on the subject – appears also to have been (at some point) systematically removed from the Ugandan National Documentary Archives in Entebbe. I was able to gain only very limited access to wider church records for this region (especially for the periods of the 1970s and 1980s). Thus, from the outset, my research was always quite reliant on witnesses' testimonies (although I did, of course, do my best to locate these within some of the wider social contexts, and trends, which I documented – and observed – over the course of my long fieldwork in Bugamba Village).

However, one outcome of all this was that my work was invariably forced to focus upon only those topics which interviewees themselves wanted to discuss. As it turned out, most people were in fact quite willing to discuss the MRTC with me. Thus, a majority of the victims' relatives and friends I met in 2001 and 2002 were still both bewildered by, and angered at, the events in Kanungu. They were bewildered because, like everyone else, they still had no idea of how and why their people had met such a terrible end. In addition, most of those I spoke to expressed at least some degree of anger that the police investigation into the Movement had petered out in quite the way it did. It was in this context, then, that most were prepared to welcome, and to assist in, *any* investigation which might shed some light on the final days of the MRTC, even if – as I explained to all my respondents before interviewing them – that investigation was to be purely academic in nature.

Yet by the same token, there were subjects about which few of my respondents wanted to say anything at all. For example, scarcely any of my interviewees were prepared to discuss events of the politically and socially tumultuous period that was the Idi Amin presidency (1971–9). It may have been that people simply did not want to recall the traumatic experiences of that time, or that grudges and animosities developed then continue to be felt in the present (and are thus best left unspoken). Certainly, both these dynamics animate Bugamba residents' reluctance to ever discuss the 1970s. Yet the net effect was the same: over the course of my entire research, I was never able to ascertain much about how the networks with which I am concerned operated, or were transformed, during the Amin period. For similar reasons, other gaps exist elsewhere in the work as well.

Thus, if the social networks I was studying were both rhizomatic and partial in nature, then so too my research methods mimicked these aspects. Moreover, if, as I have argued, it proves useful to think of the MRTC's network as an 'assemblage' – of both semiotic and material elements – then so, too, my own research process, and the relations that resulted from it, can also be thought of in similar terms. Indeed, this is particularly true for the latter stages of the research, in the period during which I tried to develop a final explanation of what had happened in the Kanungu fire itself. During this phase – and as will be discussed in Chapter 7 – my work relied entirely on bringing together both different categories of people (in particular, various disciplinary experts such as epidemiologists, pathologists, fire investigators, and so on) *and* various sorts of material objects (including photographs of the Kanungu dead, tape recordings of MRTC rituals, video recordings of the scene, and so on). The fact that many of the elements were mobilized from my current base in New Zealand further problematizes the idea that there was – or could ever have been – a Euclidean basis to the 'field' for this particular research project. Yet it was only by assembling these different elements in the particular way that I did, that I was ever able to arrive at an explanation of what did, then, happen at Kanungu.

Ethnography on an 'awkward scale'

In summary, then, this book is an ethnography cast on the 'awkward scale[s]' described by Comaroff and Comaroff (2003). Thus, on the one hand, it of necessity historicizes the ethnographic subject, by interpreting, and contextualizing, a social formation of the present – or at least, one of the very recent past – through a lens of meanings developed, passed down, and transformed over the *longue durée*. On the other, it also attempts to develop a 'translocal' ethnography – albeit not a narrowly 'multi-sited' one[7] – in that it is concerned with a social group that was both geographically dispersed and deeply informed by various sorts of translocal imaginaries. I would add here that the research practice which produced the account also involved the mobilization of an extensive transnational network.

Yet if these dimensions have produced a number of gaps in the resulting analysis, so too they enable the book to make an important contribution to the recently burgeoning field of anthropological, and other, writings on new Christianities in Africa. The very fact that this study *does* attempt to

---

[7] For an excellent critique of the concept of multi-sited research, see Hage (2005).

historicize the MRTC is already significant here, given that relatively few recent studies of new African churches have attempted to place their subjects in a long time perspective. There have, of course, been notable exceptions to this (for example, MacGaffey, 1983; Maxwell, 1999a; Peel, 2003, and others). Nevertheless, so marked has the general trend been, and so synchronic has the overall field become, that at least two recent surveys have explicitly called for greater attention to be paid to the historical dimensions of new Pentecostal-charismatic Churches (PCCs), in particular (cf. Meyer, 2004 and Maxwell, 2006b).

Perhaps more importantly, it is only by casting the story of the MRTC on a series of awkward scales that we can understand certain features of the group which, when placed in comparative perspective, appear to be quite *ab*normal. I have already suggested that a focus on the history of Nyabingi networks offers some insight into why the MRTC, unusually for an AIC of this type, was so secretive in nature. In addition, that it also helps us to understand why the group should have, again atypically, become increasingly millenarian over time. Yet so, too, this historical scale offers a degree of insight into other comparatively unusual dimensions of the MRTC story. For example, this perspective enables some insight into why the MRTC, following its break with the Catholic church, became almost entirely focused on the activities of a Marian seer – Ceredonia Mwerinde – and thus moved away from priestly authority altogether. It is noteworthy that, whilst a number of Catholic priests – including one of the most senior priests in the Southwest, Fr. Dominic Kataribaabo – had been involved in the group's initial break with the mainstream church, the influence of these individuals then diminished rapidly within the independent Movement (Chapter 4). Yet if instances of Catholic Christian independency, such as the MRTC, are already rare in Africa – as indeed they are everywhere in the world – then it is even more unusual for such organizations, following their break with the Roman Church, to move away from all forms of clerical control in this way.

Instead, as Adrian Hastings' work has again shown, it is much more typical for them to continue to organize around the authority of a former clergyman, or clergymen, and around these actors' own (often idiosyncratic) interpretations of Scripture and revelation. For example, this was very much the pattern with the Legio Maria church, an AIC which emerged among the Luo in Western Kenya in the early 1960s, and which today has an estimated 3 million adherents. Interestingly, that church also grew initially out of local networks of the Legion of Mary organization, and it, too, then split with the mainstream Roman church (in that case, following a series of wrangles over priestly authority). However, unlike the MRTC – and as has been discussed by the long-term ethnographer of the Legio Maria, Nancy Schwartz (see for example, Schwartz, 2005) – the authority of Legio's founding priests (and especially that of Blasio Simeo Ondetto), remained largely undiminished over time. On the contrary, in fact, many members of the Legio today continue to regard Ondetto as the group's original 'pope', even as its 'Messiah' or its 'God'. All of which casts Father Kataribaabo's, and the other priests', relatively rapid loss of influence within the independent MRTC into rather stark relief.

In addition, by pitching its ethnography on a series of awkward scales, this book also offers a critical reflection on discussions of 'tradition' and 'modernity', as these have developed in the study of African Christianities. An older scholarship on the history and sociology of missionary Christianity often took these categories to be objective, or etic, analytical markers of signification (such that 'traditional' was cast as that which went before the arrival of Christianity, 'the modern' that which was introduced with it; for the best overview of this older literature, see Fernandez, 1978). Today, few scholars of the 'new' African Christianities would defend this sort of usage, implying, as it does, that African Christianity is best understood as part of the unfolding of a singular, historical Euro-American modernity (see James & Johnson, 1988: 9).

Nevertheless, many ethnographers of the new Pentecostal-charismatic Churches (PCCs), which have proliferated across Africa in the last 25 years or so, have still emphasized these categories, albeit now as descriptors of subjective, or emic, modes of identification.[8] In particular here, much of this new scholarship has drawn attention to the fact that the 'rituals of rupture' which are in many ways the defining feature of PCCs (Robbins, 2004: 127-8), are frequently cast – by the actors themselves – in a language of tradition and modernity (for the best introductions to this vast new literature, see Maxwell, 2006b; Meyer, 2004; Robbins, 2004). Specifically, they are often cast as a rejection of all forms of 'traditional religion', and an embrace of, or a rebirth in, a new – and explicitly 'modern' – form of Christianity (see Meyer, 2004: 455).[9] Yet in other instances, they are conversely cast in terms of a 'return to tradition', and as a rejection of modernity. In these cases, aspects of (an imagined) traditional religion may instead become incorporated into a new church's rituals as a positive element (Gifford, 2003).[10] Yet, either way, it is also noteworthy that these emic categories of tradition and modernity frequently become synonymous with notions of 'the local' and 'the global' as well (such that traditional religion is cast as primarily local in nature, and modern Christianity as global in form).[11]

By mapping a series of networks as these were shaped across time and space, this book makes a specific contribution to these wider discussions. Specifically, the move enables me to show that the moment of engagement between pre-existing religious forms and missionary Christianity cannot

---

[8] Deriving, ultimately, from the 'Great Awakening' within US Protestantism in the eighteenth century – although there were a number of other influences as well – PC is that form of Christianity which emphasizes 'gifts of the Spirit' and experiential forms of worship.

[9] As Meyer goes on, in some instances, this emic category of traditional religion may include only pagan forms (against which all types of Christianity are cast as modern). In others, the category of tradition may include both indigenous religious practices and missionary, or 'mainline', Christianity (against which, only the 'new' PCC is represented as modern). For example, this latter situation pertained among the Ewe PCCs with whom Meyer worked in Ghana (2004: 455).

[10] For this reason, some PCCs may also be usefully interpreted as types of 'revitalization movement' (see, for example, Wallace, 2003).

[11] Harri Englund emphasizes the constructed nature of these concepts. Thus, he demonstrates that it is not uncommon for PCCs to emphasize their local character through a denial, or obfuscation, of their international connections (2003).

simply be dismissed, as this certainly is important for understanding the later emergence of the MRTC.[12] Nevertheless, that the missionary, or even wider colonial, history of South-western Uganda is not the *only* etic temporal scale to have influenced the development of these networks. Indeed, one of the key insights of a focus on the rhizomatic nature of these social forms is a recognition that these forms are often located within and between several different scales at once (and often in highly complex, and also frequently unpredictable, ways). Thus, in my exposition of the MRTC's networks, it will emerge that, although missionary, and wider colonial, history certainly *is* important here, so too are other etic temporal scales, such as the life cycle, the domestic cycle, the flow of the seasons, longer-term weather patterns, and so on. Indeed, it will be shown that each of these dimensions had some or other crucial effect on the overall course of events, at some point in the story. Moreover, a similar set of arguments must be extended to the MRTC's emic uses of the categories of tradition and modernity, as well.

Specifically, I shall show that the sect's own perceptions of tradition and modernity are again not unimportant for understanding the course of events. Yet just as important here are various other of the group's emic temporal scales. Not least, this book will pay particular attention to the MRTC's own notion of 'the endtime' (which was itself shaped by various other etic and emic timescales). Furthermore, I shall show that similar logics must also be extended to any discussion of the sect's own under-standings of locality and 'the global' as well. Thus, just as the group's construction of the global, their category of *buraeya*, certainly *is* a key part of the story here, so too it is equally important for us to pay attention to their constructions of sacred space, their conception of the household, their view of the homestead, and so on. Thus, what emerges here is an argument that, whilst notions such as tradition and modernity, and local and global, do capture something of the reality of the MRTC story, the narrative cannot usefully be reduced simply to them (irrespective of whether those terms are conceived of in an etic, or emic, way). Neither can the story be reduced again to any other sorts of dualism nor explained through any other set of categories besides. Instead, what emerges here is a markedly – remarkably – *complex* account, one which describes a multifaceted, and in many ways unpredictable, history, which gave rise to similarly complex, multifaceted, and (largely) unpredictable events, and other happenings. Yet why should a book of this nature attempt to produce anything different? In other words, the final demise of the MRTC was – by any measure and to any observer – an extremely unusual and shocking event. So how, and why, then, would *any* account of what happened possibly attempt to be anything other than highly complex as well?

[12] I would stress my use of the word 'engagement' here, as opposed to that of 'confrontation'. One of the major criticisms of an older scholarship on the history and sociology of missionary, or mainline, Christianity in Africa relates to its emphasis upon the context of 'confrontation' that was the 'imperial high noon' of nineteenth- and early-twentieth-century European colonialism (James & Johnson, 1988: 9). In this way, one of that scholarship's key concerns was to understand the various, and complex, ways in which missionary churches operated as 'the cultural agents of [the] colonial and capitalist powers...[which] helped subdue Africans to

[12] (cont.) European domination'. In other words, it took as its focus the ways in which 'Christian missionaries brought, and enforced, specifically European cultural norms of religious, social, moral and economic behaviours, and sought to mould African individuals and societies to [this vision]' (Spear, 1999: 3). Thus, the image was of pre-colonial, or 'traditional', social and religious forms being, in effect, forcibly 'replaced' by the wider complex of European imperial 'modernity', of which Christianity was a key part.

However, as the contributors to James & Johnson's *Vernacular Christianity* (1988) point out, the very notion that the introduction of Christianity, or indeed any religion, can be understood as a temporally bounded 'moment of confrontation' and 'revelation', is itself a derivative of the Christian dogma of late nineteenth-century Europe. As the editors of that volume observe, the 'representation stems in part from an old Christian ideal, that Christianity is a challenge to the unredeemed individual soul. However, it is also part of the vernacular Christianity of late imperial, industrial Europe.' Thus, in their view, the repetition of this trope in the analysis of colonial Africa represents little more than an application, to that context, of one particular 'indigenous discourse' on the nature of religious change (1988: 9). Yet it is a discourse which, at the very least, precludes the possibility that religious conversion might be understood as an ongoing series of processes and experiences which extend over time and, in some cases, space as well (see, for example, Ardener, 1970 and Buckser & Glazier, 2003). In addition, as Terence Ranger has described, the image of a 'moment of confrontation' tends also to produce a static representation both of pre-existing systems of belief and of missionary Christianity. Thus, the impression given is of an existing 'essential African religion' being suddenly confronted by, and eventually replaced with, 'an essential Christianity' (Ranger & Weller, 1975: 11, see also 8-9). Yet one effect of this is to deny the agency of all the actors involved, including that of *both* the African converts themselves, *and* of the missionary priests.

Indeed, so marked was this essentialism felt to be, that one of the key concerns of the new scholarship on African-Initiated Churches (AICs) which emerged in (roughly) the 1970s, became to explicitly record, and to analyse, the 'manifold ways [in which] Africans [have] interpreted and appropriated Christian scriptures, practices and institutions for their own purposes, within the contexts of their own values and needs' (Spear, 1999: 3). In other words, this work aimed to document the degree to which African subjects *had* exercised agency over local forms of Christianity. This trend became especially marked in those studies which explored the role played by AICs in the processes of decolonisation (Wright, n.d., Linden & Linden, 1977), and in shaping the landscapes of the newly independent nations (for a good example from Uganda, see Waliggo, 1995). In addition, the attempt to correct the perceived essentialism of earlier works became a key theme in African missionary studies, as well. Thus, as Ranger again describes, the challenge also became to explore such themes as 'the inward history of the Central African church as a whole...the existential theology and ritual which was produced by the actual practice of missionaries and especially of African catechists...the dogmatic and symbolic content of the Revival movements inside missionary Protestantism' and so on (Ranger & Weller, 1975: 4). In other words, it aimed to explore the various forms of agency that were exercised by missionary actors (and the best example of this new scholarship, in the Ugandan context, is Hansen 1984). All of which is relevant in this case study, in which it will be seen that the transformation of an indigenous religious form into a Christian idiom occurred over an extended time and space, involved an interaction of dynamic forms, and was shaped by various sorts of agency (which were both indigenous and extraneous in origin).

2
On Fertility & Misfortune

The Nyabingi spirit is best known to Africanist scholars for the role it played in anti-colonial struggles in Rwanda, Eastern Congo and Uganda in the early part of the twentieth century – but in South-western Uganda in particular. Probably tracing its origin to late eighteenth-century Northern Rwanda (Edel, 1957: 154; Hansen, 1995: 146; although *cf.* Philipps, 1928: 313–14; Bessell, 1938: 73; Hopkins, 1970: 262–4). Nyabingi first came to the attention of the German administration of Rwanda[1] sometime around 1907, when Muhumuza, the mother of a previously unsuccessful claimant to the Rwandan throne, drew on the spirit's powers for the purposes of bolstering support for a reassertion of her son's claim.[2] Basing herself in the mountains of Ndorwa, a region straddling the present-day Rwanda-Uganda border, Muhumuza gained considerable support among the local population by styling herself a Nyabingi 'priestess'.[3] Convinced that her activities posed a significant threat to the rule of King Musinga, the German colonial government of Rwanda, themselves trying to bolster Musinga's authority, interpreted Muhumuza's activities as anti-European and eventually forced her to flee into British territory to the north (Louis cited in Hopkins, 1970: 268). However, once inside the Uganda Protectorate, Muhumuza continued to draw on the support of her Nyabingi adherents, and now became explicitly anti-European, eventually claiming to be 'Queen of Ndorwa, liberator of European domination' (*ibid.*: 271). On 28 September 1911, the British raided her encampment, captured her, and subsequently imprisoned her in Kampala until her death in 1945 (*ibid.*; Hansen, 1995: 148).

However, Muhumuza's arrest did not signal the end of Nyabingi activity in South-western Uganda,[4] nor of its propensity to serve as a vehicle for anti-colonial activity. On the contrary, between 1915 and 1928 a number of Nyabingi supporters, following Muhumuza, led, or attempted to lead, physical attacks on administration outposts. The most notorious of these

[1] Rwanda was then a district of the bigger colony of German East Africa. It remained so until its takeover by Belgium in 1915.
[2] Muhumuza was one of the widows of the Rwandan King Rwabugiri, who died in 1894. She was mother of his designated heir, Bulegeya but, owing to this boy being an infant at the time of his father's death, another of Rwabugiri's sons, Musinga, took over the Rwandan crown instead. Musinga later became known as Mwami (King) Yuhi IV (Bessell, 1938: 76; Hopkins, 1970: 268).
[3] The best account of Muhumuza is contained in Bessell (1938) a paper based on interviews with the woman herself. See also Hopkins (1970).
[4] Nor, indeed, in German East Africa, although the vast majority of Nyabingi-related unrest after 1911 occurred on the British side of the border (see Hopkins, 1970: 275–7 and *passim*).

incidents was the 1917 attack on the government station at Nyakishenyi, when over one thousand local villagers, apparently adherents of Nyabingi,[5] killed 63 staff of the Muganda Agent, Abdulla Mwanika – although he himself managed to escape – and burned down the courthouse, church, and several other buildings (the best account of this incident is Brazier, 1968). The last such incident occurred in 1928, when a plan to attack the Kabale station itself was foiled by the British authorities (Hansen, 1995: 149). However, after this time the influence of the cult seemed to wane dramatically, such that by the late 1930s the British authorities regarded Nyabingi as a thing of the past. Moreover, the substantial historical literature which exists on these incidents is largely in agreement with them on this point. There is also a certain convergence of opinion on the reasons why the cult ceased to hold sway around this time.

According to one contemporary administrator, Bessell, Nyabingi ceased to have any influence in local affairs during the 1930s because of 'the progress of Western Civilization', or in other words, the introduction to local peoples, by the British, of Christianity, 'native administration', the spread of education, and so on. Thirty years later the historian Denoon, albeit in a more historically sophisticated – and certainly less ethnocentric – argument, points to exactly the same factors for Nyabingi's demise. He argues that before about 1930, the few Bakiga who had already become Christians – having by that time been converted by Baganda catechists – had failed to be promoted beyond the lowest level of the native administrative hierarchy, the *baluka* chieftainships. Practically no Bakiga at all, in fact, had attained the higher offices of the *gombolola* and *saza* chieftainships, almost all of which were also filled by Baganda. Therefore, the religious-political leadership of Nyabingi – i.e. its key mediums – had continued to draw on the sympathies of the majority of the Bakiga unchallenged. However, as the 1930s progressed, more and more Christianized Bakiga succeeded in reaching the upper echelons of the native government, a process which was speeded up by the formation of a number of mission schools whose primary objective was to educate future political officers. They were effectively replaced, therefore, by a new religious-political hierarchy, one legitimized by the colonial regime, in a process Hansen terms the 'Christian revolution' (1995: 157; see also Hansen, 1984).

However, it is my surmise that this apparent 'demise' of Nyabingi activity in South-western Uganda by the mid-1930s, apparently so well documented in the literature, was in fact more apparent than real. Basing my argument on a rereading of the primary and secondary sources on Nyabingi, and on oral historical evidence gathered amongst Kiga elders living in and around Bugamba, I argue instead that, far from disappearing during this period, or ceasing to be meaningful for local people, the phenomenon simply passed through a transformation at this time. Moreover, I also argue that the almost universal failure of the literature to perceive this continuing relevance of Nyabingi after the 1930s derives from the continual overemphasis, by earlier historians of the subject, on the

---

[5] Although Brazier, for one, has some doubts on this point (1968: 21–2, 25).

cult's anti-colonial aspect. As my brief historical survey has indicated, it is indisputable that Nyabingi beliefs certainly did act as a vehicle for anti-European sentiment at a certain point in time. However, by focusing on *only* this one factor, historians have failed to perceive the much broader role Nyabingi worship played in local society. In particular here, I argue that the whole concept of an 'anti-colonial movement' involves a specific notion of secrecy, and secret organization, which obscures an understanding of wider local realities.

Secrecy and 'secret societies' in early colonial Uganda

One aspect of Nyabingi practice about which all British administrators – at least – were keenly aware, was the utter secrecy in which the whole thing was shrouded. Indeed, in a classified report of 1919,[6] Captain J. E. T. Philipps, then Assistant Commissioner of Kigezi District, was incredulous even at the precise degree of secrecy Nyabingi adherents were able to achieve. Writing of the Nyakishenyi rebellion of 1917, he was quite mystified by the fact that 'not a suspicion of the plot [had] leaked out beforehand, despite the fact that the British native political Agent [at the Nyakishenyi station] and his followers had Bakiga wives and boys' (1928: 319). In other features too, the whole thing seemed to exude secrecy. For example, Philipps noted that adherents communicated by way of a 'secret language',[7] and that all Nyabingi circles were surrounded by 'a vicious circle of spies' (*ibid.*: 315, 319, respectively). Indeed, the only way for the authorities to gain any information at all about Nyabingi had been by way of their becoming complicit in this secrecy. 'It has only been by means of endless tact and secrecy' Philipps wrote, 'that reliable information has been obtainable' (*ibid.*: 318, order of quotes in this section altered). A contemporary administrator of the region, M. J. Bessell, reached similar conclusions. Writing in the *Uganda Journal* of 1938, Bessell posed his problem thus: is Nyabingi best thought of as 'an organized secret society' or 'merely a local superstitious cult'? (1938: 73), before concluding that the former definition was by far the more useful of the two. Similar conclusions were also reached by other administrators at this time (see Hopkins, 1970: 303, 318, 321; and also Hansen, 1995: *passim*).

As Douglas Johnson (1991) demonstrates in his discussion of British reactions to closed associations in early twentieth-century Zandeland, for European administrators of this period, the very concept of a 'secret society' was itself loaded with pre-existent meanings. Since at least the beginning of the seventeenth century, when the first Masonic lodges emerged in Europe, such associations had been found throughout their home countries (the best history is Roberts, 1972). This long history had inevitably served to shape European governing circles' perceptions of all secret phenomena. In particular, a strong idea existed that all secret groupings were by their very

---

[6] Later published, almost verbatim, in *Congo* (1928). For ease of reference, all my references to Philipps will be to this published version.

[7] Which 'consists more of alterations in existing words than in the creation of new ones' (*ibid.*).

nature 'immoral'. For example, as Johnson describes, from the time the Freemasons came into existence, the rituals of that organization – and especially its 'oaths and signs' – were taken as proof of its sinister and immoral intent. For some observers, the fact that women were excluded from Masons' secret meetings even suggested a certain sexual immorality among its practitioners (*ibid.*: 172).[8] Later – at least from the time of the French Revolution onwards – a concomitant idea emerged that such associations were synonymous with politically subversive activity. Thus, 'the image of secret societies involved in subterranean and immoral conspiracies featured in political thought throughout the nineteenth century' and beyond, amongst most European governing groups (*ibid.*: 173).

From here then, it was a small logical step to the idea that secret societies were *by definition* politically subversive, that such conspiracies were in essence their *raison d'être* (an idea which is explored most fully explored in Roberts' *Mythology of the Secret Societies*, 1972). Therefore, it was with this model of secret societies in mind that the first European administrators arrived in the colonies. As a result, whenever a closed association was uncovered, it was immediately interpreted by the colonialists as being both essentially immoral and, more importantly, anti-colonial, in nature. As Johnson describes, 'the very term "secret society" ... transformed a local annoyance into an international threat aimed at the very foundations of colonial rule' (1991: 174). In the case of Nyabingi this perception was later confirmed, of course, when members of that association did indeed begin to attack administration outposts.

Quite convinced, then, that in Nyabingi they were indeed facing a primarily anti-colonial 'movement', the British administration in Kigezi tailored their response accordingly.[9] In particular, they began to focus intensively on the movement's form of organization, whilst effectively ignoring the actual content of Nyabingi practices. Following Muhumuza's entry into British territory, and especially following the Nyakishenyi rebellion of 1917, the British authorities in the Southwest were, of course, concerned with only one thing in regard to Nyabingi: its eradication as a threat to British interests. In pursuit of this goal, it was thought necessary to acquire knowledge of only the association's organization: How did it start? Who were its leaders? What was its membership? When and where did it meet? How could it be effectively broken up? and so on. Any in-depth understanding of the association's practices, or of the 'moods and motivations' which lay behind these, was apparently considered extraneous to these goals. Thus, throughout what remains of the colonial archive, one finds detailed discussion of the former type of issue, but only scant and passing references to the latter.[10]

[8] Somewhat ironically, in the Zande case, it was precisely the fact that women *were* admitted to the societies that convinced colonial officers of the organization's immoral intent (*ibid.*).
[9] This view was also then projected backwards, onto the history of the phenomenon. Thus, in Philipps' report, Nyabingi was seen to have been a politically subversive organization even before the European arrival in Central Africa. At one point he states 'the Nabingi [*sic*] then threw off [their] disguise and made a popular appeal to the Wahutu [*sic*] against Government by the Batussi [*sic*] and privilege of the Batwa' (1928: 314).
[10] Today, the Kigezi District Archive (KDA) of the colonial period is in an extremely poor state.

Descriptions of actual Nyabingi practices are brief and uninformative. For example, in one document a reference is made to the fact that Nyabingi activities involved an element of goods exchange.[11] In a sworn affidavit of 1925, one Acting District Commissioner similarly mentions that Nyabingi practices involved the giving of 'presents of cattle, sheep, goats, food, drink and money'.[12] Discussing the advent of the cult in Rwanda, Philipps' report even notes that 'the enormous flow of fees and presents to the Nabingi [sic] for services rendered was such as seriously to affect the royal tributes and the collections for the established [indigenous pagan] "church" and that this was even the root cause of one punitive raid against the association initiated by the Rwandan King Lwogera' (1928: 314).[13]

It is clear, then, that the exchange of goods was a key feature of the Nyabingi phenomenon. Yet, despite this fact, little attention seems ever to have been paid to it. Beyond mentioning the fact that goods *were* being circulated, questions such as how and why these goods were being given, when, and to whom, do not seem even to have been posed by the administration, let alone answered. Instead, colonial officers seem to have settled simply for impressionistic, even stereotypical, explanations. Thus, for example, in the above affidavit the movement of goods is explained as an 'extortion', exacted upon a 'semi-savage population' by way of an induced 'great dread and awe' (order of quotes altered).

With regard to its understanding of the organization of Nyabingi adherents, the administration's thinking seems to have displayed a certain circularity of logic. Just as the fact of its being secret had suggested to the Europeans that Nyabingi must be both immoral and subversive, so too the various Nyabingi rebellions which did occur convinced the administration that they were indeed dealing with the type of subversive secret society with which they were familiar. Thus, it was assumed that Nyabingi adherents must be organizing themselves in a way similar to subversive political groups in Europe: Sinn Fein, the Bolsheviks, 'the Jews' and so on (Johnson, 1991: 173). This much is revealed in the way in which the colonial administration responded to Nyabingi, in the years after the Nyakishenyi attack in particular. Firstly, it is clear that the British understood Nyabingi

[10] (cont.) Many of the documents were burned on a bonfire during the early 1970s. The few documents which survived form a shambolic and rotting pile in the attic of the current Kabale District Administration Headquarters. However, largely thanks to the industry of one former archivist of the 1960s (whose name I did not learn), I was able to recover at least some of the documents relating to Nyabingi. I have no idea how representative these documents are of the entire archive, or even how they may have once related to other parts of it. Still, a number of these documents (upon which part of this narrative is based) do offer important insights into the colonial response to Nyabingi, as I shall demonstrate below.

[11] ES A43/92 – DC Ankole District to PC Western Province, 1 January 1908. In actual fact, the Nyabingi phenomenon is here represented as *primarily* a mechanism of exchange: 'the great feature of these [Nyabingi practices] is the demand for presents'.

[12] KDA – J. R. Mcd. Elliott, Acting DC, 20 March 1925. Due to the shambolic state of the Kabale Archive, it is very difficult to give exact references for many of the documents I saw there. Many, if not most, of the files I saw had completely disintegrated, and many of the papers were simply loose-leaf. I have therefore opted to refer only to authors and dates, rather than to the files in which the particular despatches were originally placed.

[13] King Lwogera was the father of Rwabugiri. Rwabugiri took over the Rwandan crown at his father's death.

to be, in the manner of a European secret society, a formal type of organization. One element of this was the idea that the group had a fixed membership. At several points in his report of 1919, Philipps refers to Nyabingi followers as the '"ordained" apostles' (1928: 315–16, 319, etc.). Elsewhere, he talks about people 'entering' the 'movement'. He also notes that 'the careful and selective initiations of the *kubandwa* [the indigenous pagan religion of Rwanda] are in the Nabingi [*sic*] organization found in a shortened formality' (*ibid.*, 317).

Although they were less elaborate than in other local religions, the organization did appear to have formal initiation rites. This image of a formal organization allowed discussion of the practices assumed to be idiosyncratic of that membership, such as its secret language, etc. Concomitant with the idea of a fixed membership is the notion that Nyabingi was a unitary organization. One outcome of this perception was that instances of Nyabingi activity in Rwanda and the Belgian Congo were interpreted as being manifestations of the very same organization with which the British were dealing in South-western Uganda. Thus, the Kigezi District Report for 1928 claimed that 'enquiry has revealed the movement of 1928 [i.e. as it existed in 1928] to have been not only both synchronized and widespread, but also to have shown signs of a quite cunning, if elementary, organisation. Manifestations of differing importance, but the same tactics, varied only to take advantage of local weaknesses, occurred in the same period in Uganda, Belgian East Africa (mandate), and even Tanganyika Territory'. An extract from a confidential report of 1929 suggests that the British and Belgian administrations later attempted to deal with Nyabingi in this vein. The extract, initialled by Philipps, shows that the colonial powers were even attempting to identify the overall leader of the unitary society. It reads: 'the (acting) resident of Ruanda, (M. Borgers) strongly suspects Mporera, s/o Ruhara late head of the [*Biheko*] society, to be the present chief of the Nyabingi secret organization' (KDA – Philipps to PC Western Province, 1 January 1929). In other words, the search was on for the individual who sat at the apex of *all* Nyabingi activity, be it in Rwanda, Uganda, or elsewhere (see also Philipps, 1928: 313, fn 2).[14]

This last extract also reveals another, highly significant, aspect of the way in which the British authorities conceived of the Nyabingi organization. Used to thinking of all formal political organizations in Europe, subversive or otherwise, as hierarchical structures, the British placed a great emphasis on the role played by Nyabingi 'leaders'. For example, individual leaders were held solely responsible for each specific outbreak of Nyabingi violence. In one of his first despatches on the Nyakishenyi attack

---

[14] As an accompaniment to this idea of an 'ultimate leader', the British also searched for the 'headquarters' of the whole Nyabingi phenomenon. Thus, in his report of 1919, Philipps claimed that 'ordained apostles are sent out for specified areas from the headquarters of the society, of which two exist, one in ex-German Ruanda and one in Buitwa, Congo Belge. Tithes are sent by these apostles to the Headquarters of the organization' (1928: 315). A decade later, this notion of a central headquarters of the 'society' still pertained. In the Kigezi District Report for 1928 Philipps again wrote that 'the titular headquarters are still, as I reported in 1919, in Kyante, Southwest of Lake Bunyonyi'. Kyante is the former of the two sites referred to in the previous quote from Philipps' report of 1919.

of 1917, the District Commissioner was already convinced that 'there is every reason to believe that the affair was engineered by a "Nabingi" [*sic*] or witch doctor named Kaigirwa'. This, despite the fact that 'the cause of the massacre [at that time remained obscure]' (KDA – DC to PC Western Province, 30 September 1917, emphasis mine, order of quotes reversed). Elsewhere, the same Commissioner put this opinion more directly, omitting any such qualifier. In another despatch of the same period, he simply asserted that 'I consider that this [rebellion] was directly due to the machination of witch doctor Kaigirwa and possibly others with her. The 'Nabingi' [*sic*] cult has never yet failed to find a following in this district' (KDA – DC to PC Western Province, 21 September 1917, emphasis mine). By the time of later attacks, all such incidents were simply assumed to be similarly motivated by the intentions of individual leaders (Hopkins, 1970: 316). It might be noted that, in the above quotes, the terms 'Nyabingi' and 'Nyabingi cult' are used as synonyms for the movement's leaders. This textual trope was later used widely in official despatches (for example, KDA – Uganda Monthly Intelligence Report No. 13, June 1922; DC to PC Western Province, 3 March 1928; Kigezi Police Quarterly Report for third quarter of 1935, etc). It is clear that, in the minds of some members of the local administration at least, the leadership in effect *was* the movement.

The image of an identifiably hierarchical organization also acted to shape the British response to the Nyabingi 'threat'. As revealed in the Kigezi District Annual Report for 1928, the thinking was that if the individual leaders could be removed, if the organization could be 'decapitated', then the mass of Nyabingi 'followers' would soon simply give up the cause. On the one hand, it was felt that an organization without a leadership would quickly lose its structural coherence. On the other, the British hoped that only the leadership had any particular commitment to Nyabingi. It was these individuals who were both dedicated and zealous, the majority of Nyabingi's members being their 'prey'. According to this logic the mass of followers were simply an easily led, or else opportunistic, rabble, whose attention would soon be diverted, following the removal of their organizers. Thus, the following quote is symptomatic:

> the leaders are fanatics aided by elementary, but locally terrifying stock in trade developed from the natural phenomena of hypnotism, ventriloquism and mental suggestion. The followers are principally the terrorized (who include many chiefs), also the aggrieved element which King David also cleverly gathered round him in Adullam and finally, those who, hoping to gain and having nothing to lose, are the beasts of prey who, throughout the world, lurk hungrily behind the menace of every potential revolution.

As a direct result of this logic, the British focused their efforts to eradicate the Nyabingi movement from Kigezi upon only – those they regarded as – the movement's key leaders. Thus, a string of the most 'conspicuous' Nyabingi mediums (*bagigwa*) were killed, or arrested and deported out of Kigezi.[15] A number of these individuals, along with many 'lesser' leaders,

---

[15] On 23 June 1917 the British attacked and killed two of the most notorious 'leaders', Ntokibiri and Luhemba. The former was considered, by the administration, to have been the 'brains' behind the Nyakishenyi attack of earlier that year (Philipps, 1928: 320–21). However,

were also publicly humiliated, in a further attempt to undermine their influence (Hopkins, 1970: 322). However, this emphasis upon only the undermining of Nyabingi's leadership, to the exclusion of any other method of eradication, was later to have something of a peculiar effect on the colonial mindset.

Specifically, by late 1928, the British had, to all intents and purposes, neutralized all of the most prominent Nyabingi mediums. As a result, they concluded that Nyabingi must therefore have already become a thing of the past. The Kigezi District Annual Report for that year concluded as much, in no uncertain terms. It claimed that, deprived of its leadership, the Nyabingi movement had become doomed to failure, and was in the process of dying out. The only problem with this position was that it could not explain the stream of cases, involving Nyabingi 'extortions', which continued to pass through the local courts. According to Hansen, prosecutions of suspected Nyabingi mediums under the 1912 *Witchcraft Ordinance*, which had burgeoned massively after the 1917 Nyakishenyi rebellion, had by the late 1920s slowed to a trickle (1995: 149). Hopkins claims that the 'incidence of Nyabingi cases [decreased] from 1930 to 1933' and had ceased altogether by 1934 (1970: 322). Yet in fact, it would seem that, although few prosecutions were made directly for witchcraft, a sizeable number of cases involving some dimension of Nyabingi *did* continue to be heard in various legal forums, throughout the 1930s (at least). For example, in 1937, a big civil case involving allegations of Nyabingi practice was presided over by the entire Kigezi parliament, the *Lukiko* (KDA – Summary of Lukiko Case: Kinyoni son of Nyabuhende vs. T. Tebanyururwa 15 October 1937). Indeed, even today, it is not completely unheard of for some mention of Nyabingi activities to be made in civil cases. For example, I was present at two such cases in Bugamba's village courts during my time there.

The interesting point is that, throughout the 1930s, British officials in Kigezi had some trouble rationalizing these cases. Unable to explain these continuing instances of Nyabingi by reference to the movement's leadership – which was by then largely eradicated – colonial officials seem to have been bemused as to what to make of them. Their logical quandary may be summarized thus: the leadership is the movement, the leadership has been neutralized, therefore the movement no longer exists. How, then, could cases involving Nyabingi still be coming before their courts? In the end, the administrative officers seem to have collectively reached a quite peculiar conclusion, that the only possible answer was that all of the new cases involving Nyabingi had to represent purely fraudulent or 'fake' mediums. As a result, from this time onwards, any person claiming to be a Nyabingi medium was officially assumed to be a charlatan. In addition, anyone claiming to have had interaction with these characters was automatically assumed either to have been duped, or to be lying.

Thus, throughout the 1930s, instances of Nyabingi were simply explained

---

[15] (cont.) following the killing of Ntokibiri and Luhemba, the British adopted something of a softer line. After 1917, rather than killing Nyabingi leaders (or those identified as such), they tended instead to pursue such actors through the courts. A number of these cases resulted in the defendants being deported from Kigezi.

away. One extract from the Kigezi District Annual Report for 1930 sums up this general perception of the administration quite succinctly:

> No recrudescence of the Nyabingi cult has occurred, but that it has considerable influence is apparent from the large number of alleged 'witchcraft' (Nyabingi) cases submitted by the Native Courts. On inquiry, it is generally found that they are not genuine cases of witchcraft, but more charlatanism on the part of impostors who are well aware of the fear inspired in the credulous (and the tribes hereabouts seem particularly credulous), and who play upon their fears for their own personal gain.

It was primarily by way of these sorts of logics, then, that the administration concluded that Nyabingi had 'ceased to exist' by the late 1930s.

Later histories

It is somewhat curious that this colonial model has continued, for almost three-quarters of a century, to define the terms of much academic – ethnographic and historical – debate on the Nyabingi Spirit. It may be relevant that two of the first discussions of Nyabingi to appear in academic journals were those of Philipps (1928) and Bessell (1938). In other words, it was these same two administrators who in a sense 'began the canon'.[16] But even so, the extent to which subsequent scholars have reproduced the terms set out in these original treatments is nevertheless remarkable. For example, just as Philipps and Bessell – and their contemporaries – focused exclusively on the movement's form of organization, and largely disregarded the content of Nyabingi practices, so subsequent scholars of the phenomenon have done more or less the same. For instance, throughout the colonial literature on Nyabingi, references were constantly made to the exchange of goods as an integral part of Nyabingi practice. Yet at no stage did the administration examine these practices in any particular detail. Moreover, the same charge might be laid against subsequent ethnographers and historians of Nyabingi, as well.

In her 'classic' account of the Bakiga of 1957, May Edel describes the range of goods which might have been given to a medium:

> White sheep, a special kind of spotted cow, and honey beer were offerings particularly suitable for a [Nyabingi] medium, but other things might be brought – sprouted grain, fermented gruel, tobacco, butter, certain kinds of animal skins. The very poor might even bring green vegetables or firewood. Only goats, peas and potatoes were unsuitable. (1957: 151)

Both Edel and the later historian Freedman are also in agreement that mediums, who in their reading were all men, could also 'frequently demand[ ] young girls as wages for their services' (Freedman, 1984: 87; *cf.* Edel, 1957: 151).[17] Moreover, as in Philipps, the amount of goods being exchanged here is also significant. For example, Hopkins argues that the

---

[16] The first published accounts in French – all written by White Fathers – did not appear until the early 1950s (see for example, Pauwels, 1949; 1951; 1954).

[17] This is surely incorrect. As will be discussed below, male mediums did not ever 'own' these women.

volume of grain, livestock or beer that individual mediums could demand from their adherents varied according to the extent of their reputations, such that 'as the reputation of a *mugirwa* [*sic*] increased, his ability to exact offerings from the population also grew' (1970: 260–1).

Moreover, some of these accounts even go beyond the colonial descriptions. Specifically, in the earlier texts, goods were only ever exchanged by way of these tribute payments. In this way, the flow of goods was always, by definition, uni-directional, and 'upwards', in nature. However, in Edel, Freedman and Hopkins, a number of mechanisms are identified through which Nyabingi mediums would also pass on the goods they collected, and make exchanges 'downwards' as well. Thus, the picture that emerges from these accounts is of a system which was, in essence, *redistributive* in character. As Edel explains, 'part of the offerings was taken in to the spirits, and some were used for the priest's [*sic*] household; the rest was shared lavishly among the visitors' (1957: 151). The 'young girls' to whom Freedman refers would often be married off, and in this way cult mediums 'controlled, to some degree, the circulation of women' (1984: 87). And in Hopkins, mediums would use their Nyabingi booty, especially the cows, to create reciprocal bond-partnerships – known as *bakago* – which have always been an important form of sociality throughout South-western Uganda (*bakago* are an especially privileged category of non-kin with whom one is cast as having fictive blood-relations; cf. Edel, 1957: 109).[18] Thus 'the entry

---

[18] Historically, a relationship of *obukago* was formed – between two men, and their households – through the two parties consuming a mixture of each other's blood (the process is described in Lukyn-Williams, 1934). In addition, it required the instigator of the relationship to give the other party a gift of *okugabiisa* (lit: 'to give' – as *okuhereza* and *okuha*, but with the additional implication of an irreversible action. In normal usage, the verb is abbreviated to *okugaba*). Here, a female animal – preferably a cow – was handed over, with the understanding that its first offspring would be returned to the donor in a reciprocal exchange known as *empaano*. However, at least since the advent of AIDS, and probably for some time before that as well, the element of mixing blood has largely disappeared, such that today *obukago* is initiated only through animal exchange (which is usually carried out as part of a formal visit to one of the parties' homes, *okuzinduka*).

Obukago involves more than just general friendship, placing the two parties in a permanent and binding relationship of clearly defined reciprocal rights and obligations (from which, and following Peter Parkes, pers. comm., I have glossed the relationship as a 'reciprocal bond-partnership'). One key element is the obligation to provide physical protection for one's *mukago* in the event of his being threatened by some danger. In the event of any fighting, be it in a time of war or simply as part of a squabble in a local bar, a *mukago* is required to jump to the defence of his bond partner. In addition, a *mukago* is also required to provide unquestioning financial assistance, should this be required by his bond-partner. For example, I know of one dramatic case from the early 1980s, when a man from Bugamba risked his life to have his *mukago* released from a prison in Kampala, and then paid for him to flee the country. The bond partner, as a member of Museveni's NRA guerrilla force, had been detained and scheduled for execution by the government of Obote, prior to his partner's intervention.

Thus, in terms both of the way in which it is formed, and the obligations it creates for its participants, *obukago* is a relation of *substance*. As a result, it is often cast as fictive kinship. For example, people think of their father's *bakago* as their father's brothers. Marriage to one's father's *mukago's* children is regarded as incest, and is prohibited (for this to happen, a special ritual has to be carried out to break the father's bond-partnership. During a decade of research in South-western Uganda, I have known of only one occasion on which this ritual – *okugitwa bukago*, lit: 'to kill bukago' – has been carried out). In addition, it used to be common for men to inherit the wives of deceased bond partners, in contexts of polygamy. For example, I know of at least two cases in Bugamba village – one from the 1970s, the other from the late 1980s

of a *mugirwa* [*sic*][19] into a new territory was marked not merely by the acquisition of goods, but by the promise of the distribution of beer and cattle' (Hopkins, 1970: 261).

Yet, given the apparent variety of these various descriptions, it is somewhat surprising that, in most of these later accounts, such exchange practices continue to be discussed only in passing. Thus, just as in the colonial literature, these ethnographic and historical accounts seldom if ever address such key questions as who exactly was exchanging what with whom, when, and most importantly, *why?*[20] In other words, what was it that motivated actors to make these often sizeable offerings at the times they did? Again, little more than speculation is offered here. For example, in both Edel and Hopkins, it is claimed that tribute was paid simply out of fear that to not have done so would have brought a curse from Nyabingi, via one of its mediums (which would in turn lead to serious illness, Edel, 1957: 148; cf. Hopkins, 1970: 260–1).

Moreover, the ways in which later academic writers have conceived of the organization of Nyabingi adherents also followed the precedents set out in the colonial literature. The only exception here is Edel, who at the beginning of her discussion makes the interesting argument that 'the [Nyabingi] cult was *not* a cult in the same sense as [another cult] ... for there were no group rites, no group initiation or dances' (1957: 148, emphasis mine). However, this point is lost on many other historical commentators, who continue to discuss Nyabingi as an organization with a specified membership and idiosyncratic practices, into which individuals were initiated (see for example Brazier, 1968; Freedman, 1984; Hansen, 1995).[21]

In Iris Berger's account, this model is elaborated. For her, Nyabingi is clearly similar to – and is perhaps even a 'related-off-shoot [*sic*]' of – local *kubandwa* cults. These organizations 'most clearly resembled certain Central African "cults of affliction"'. Thus, in the event of someone suffering a misfortune,

> a diviner might recommend initiation [for the afflicted person]. During this ceremony, which varied in detail from one area to the next, women [*sic*] experienced a symbolic death and rebirth into a new society, superior to the profane and sep-

[18] (cont.) – in which a woman married her husband's bond partner after her husband's death. One final point here is that in contemporary parlance, the term itself –'*obukago*' – tends to be used mostly by an older generation of men. However, this is not to say that the relationship itself no longer pertains amongst the younger generations. For example, in Bugamba Village, some young men reject the term itself as archaic, yet nevertheless enter into relations of cattle exchange with their peers which are, to all intents and purposes, identical to the kind of bond-partnership described above.

[19] This misspelling by both Freedman and Hopkins reflects the similarity of the sounds for 'r' and 'g' in inter-lacustrine languages.

[20] The only partial exception here is Freedman, who does discuss how and why Nyabingi mediums exchanged the women they were 'given' in payment for their services. According to him, mediums used these exchanges to build political alliances (1984: 80-90). However, given that mediums did not ever 'own' these women in the way that Freedman describes (below), it is unlikely that they would have been able to exchange them in quite this way.

[21] Even Hopkins, who correctly observes that Nyabingi practices involved no initiation rites and no communal rites, continues throughout her work to refer to Nyabingi as a 'cult'. This word tends to imply an organization with some sort of ongoing membership (1970: *passim*).

arated from it in many respects. [Initiates][22] were given special regalia, taught to communicate with the supernatural world through spirit possession, and instructed in a secret vocabulary, food taboos, and other esoteric knowledge. As in other rites of passage, initiates passed through a liminal period in which they were abused, terrified, and humiliated before symbolically shedding their former personalities and being reborn into a new family. (1995: 67)

Of greatest significance, the colonial administration's former fixation with Nyabingi 'leaders' also became something of an orthodoxy in this later literature. For example, in Edel, the entire Nyabingi movement is again taken to have consisted of two distinct tiers, the 'priests' and their 'followers', with the latter represented as the 'subordinates' of the former.[23] According to Edel, the priests 'exert[ed] enormous power over their followers'. In particular, followers could only participate in Nyabingi practice through the offices of a priest. In other words, they could not make contact with the Nyabingi spirit themselves, but instead had to rely upon a priest to do so on their behalf. Thus, the followers 'had no ritual part of their own to play' (1957: 148). Freedman similarly talks of the 'power' priests exerted within the movement (for example, 1984: 104). Hopkins even speculates that

the ascendancy of Nyabingi over other…cults in the Mfumbiro area was based in large part on the distinctive hierarchical pattern of the cult structure. By restrict-ing access to the spirit to the *bagirwa* [sic], the cult provided considerable lever-age for the economic, political, and psychological manipulation of followers and for the extension of control over those who did not voluntarily seek the protec-tion of Nyabingi. (1970: 261)

Of course, the logic of this position leads again to the conclusion that, without its leadership, the Nyabingi movement could not have continued to operate as a coherent entity. By the early 1930s, the majority of the most high-profile priests had been either imprisoned or deported out of Kigezi. All of which brings us back to Denoon's argument. To recount briefly, Denoon argues that another factor which led to Nyabingi's demise in the 1930s was the development of a new religio-political leadership in the area. Before about 1930, the small number of indigenous people who had already become Christians – having been converted by Baganda catechists – had failed to be promoted beyond the lowest level of the native administrative hierarchy, the *baluka* chieftainships. Practically no local people at all, in fact, had attained the higher offices of the *gombolola* and *saza* chieftainships, almost all of which were filled by Baganda. However, as the 1930s progressed, more and more Christianized Bakiga succeeded in reaching the upper echelons of the native government, a process which was then accelerated by the formation of mission schools whose primary objective was to educate future political officers. For Denoon, this new religio-political group effectively replaced the Nyabingi leadership during these years (cited in Hansen, 1995: 150).

The fact that Nyabingi priests were being prosecuted by the British, whilst the new Christian chiefs were at the same time being patronized by

---

[22] Berger here uses the term 'medium' to refer to Nyabingi's 'ordinary membership'. For clarity, I have here substituted her term with my own 'initiates'.

[23] Edel further sub-divides the priestly tier into two groups: the most powerful priests, and the lesser ones. Yet all priests are super-ordinate to Nyabingi 'followers' (1957: 148).

them, must also have been a factor. The resultant fall in the overall number of mediums has been termed by Hansen, the 'Christian revolution' (*ibid.*). Once again, the conclusion is that, by the mid-1930s, the Nyabingi movement as a whole must, therefore, have effectively 'ceased to exist'. Although Hopkins alone manages to resist the logic of her own argument on this score (1970: 322–3), most other commentators are clear on this disappearance (for example, Edel, 1957: 158–9). As Freedman puts it, by the 1930s, lacking its former network of ritual specialists, the 'uniform set of legends and liturgical forms' that had once constituted the cult had 'fragmented into dozens of independent sects' (Freedman, 1984: 104).

Rethinking the historiography of Nyabingi

However, it is my surmise that the lack of attention previously paid – both by colonial officers and by past scholars – to Nyabingi exchanges, has resulted in the whole Nyabingi phenomenon, including its apparent 'demise', being largely misinterpreted for half a century or more. Specifically, my own rereading of the primary and secondary sources, and my oral historical data from Bugamba and its surrounds, suggest that, far from being some sort of curious aside, these exchange practices were in fact central to the entire sociology of Nyabingi. In other words, I contend that it is only through an examination of the operation of, and of the meanings attached to, these exchanges, that one is able to grasp the nature of the historical Nyabingi phenomenon. Yet, as already discussed in Chapter 1, any such study of these exchanges immediately faces a number of issues. Primary among these is the fact that because all of these exchanges – like all other forms of Nyabingi practice – were shrouded in such secrecy, any account of them is likely only ever to be partial, or incomplete, in nature. Indeed, Edel addresses this very point in mitigation of her own ethnography's lack of discussion about the detail of these Nyabingi exchanges. As she points out, by the time of her own fieldwork, in 1932–3, British punitive measures against the movement had been in operation for almost two decades. As a result, most local people were extremely reluctant to discuss such issues with her, a European woman (1957: 129). Thus, she was only ever able to glean a minimal amount of information about them.

However, the fact that any study of secrecy is likely to produce only incomplete data is not regarded as as much of a problem today as it would have been in Edel's time. During the last 20 years or so, a growing number of scholars have drawn attention to the fact that *all* knowledge in the social sciences (and beyond) is both partial and incomplete.[24] Thus, previously held expectations of ethnographic accounts, that they should be both complete and objective records, have been replaced by a desire to understand the range of ways in which they are all constructed and contingent (as I have already discussed in relation to my own work, in Chapter 1).

[24] In anthropology, this point was made most strongly in Clifford & Marcus' edited collection, *Writing Culture* (1986).

Yet by this logic, the study of secrecy has opened up in new ways. Previously, given that 'completeness' and objectivity could not, by definition, ever be achieved in the analysis of secrecy, concealed forms were usually taken to be a particularly difficult object of ethnographic study (see, for example, the discussion in Lyman, 1964). As a result, ethnographers describing secret systems, like Edel, tended to focus more on the 'knowable', organizational, aspects of these phenomena, rather than on the more 'opaque' content of their practice. However, in the context of more recent anthropological concerns with incompleteness and impartiality, the very fact that secret systems *are* ambiguous and incomplete instead recasts them as a particularly good object of study. This has been demonstrated in such important accounts of secrecy as Favret-Saada's (1980) analysis of witchcraft accusations in the French *bocage*. Here, Favret-Saada shows that a model of the analyst as partially positioned better enables one to understand the content of a system in which all of its actors are themselves, by definition, similarly positioned. The new interest in secrecy is also attested to by the recent burgeoning of anthropological writings in this area (for the best overviews of this growing field, see Piot, 1993 and Ferme, 2001).

In addition, I was able to avoid Edel's earlier problems in at least two other ways as well. Firstly, because I was studying events which, in most instances, occurred more than half a century previously, and which usually involved my respondents' parents, or grandparents, rather than my respondents themselves. As a result, people were generally quite willing to talk about these events at length. Secondly, it is noteworthy that almost all of my respondents on former Nyabingi practices – about whom I will say more later on – were members of the Kiga Diaspora, which had moved away from the Kigezi Hills during an 'assisted-relocation scheme' from the 1940s onwards (this will be discussed at length in Chapter 3). Thus, the events they were describing had not only taken place at another time, but also in a different geographical location. Once again, this seems to have made people much more comfortable in talking about them. For both these reasons, then, I did not experience any particular problems in getting the Kiga elders of Bugamba and its surrounds to discuss the secrets of Nyabingi (and, indeed, at great length). Yet I would also note here that all of this is yet another example of what I have described as the general 'lumpiness' of my research (as alluded to in Chapter 1). In other words, it was quite symptomatic of all of my work in Uganda that whilst people were often extremely reluctant to discuss events of certain times and places – not least almost anything that had gone on in Bugamba during the late 1970s and early '80s – they showed no reticence at all in talking at length about the happenings of certain other times and certain other places.

What emerges from my research on Nyabingi is that the secrets of Nyabingi are in large part the secrets of fertility. This general connection between the Nyabingi spirit and issues of fertility is itself nothing new. For one thing, Nyabingi is a feminine spirit. However, at least according to my respondents, Nyabingi was never thought of anthropomorphically, but was instead conceived of as some kind of energy or force (a point which is again missed by earlier commentators).[25] In addition, as Bessell first pointed out, the name 'Nyabingi' carries an additional implication of fertility, meaning as it does 'she who possesses many riches' (1938: 73; in fact, a more literal gloss here would be 'she who possesses many things').[26] A common nickname for the spirit was *nyoko'kuru* (Freedman, 1984: 27), paternal grandmother (second person), normally the person who had borne a lineage the most children.

In addition, and as several of my older informants described, in local cosmologies Nyabingi was also inextricably linked with the 'high god' Kazooba (Fr. Rwabahima). Indeed, they may accurately be termed two aspects of the same whole. The name Kazooba derives from the word for the sun (*eizooba*), and for all Bakiga the sun is the provider of all agricultural riches. Nyabingi was therefore thought to 'derive' from Kazooba. However, throughout the literature Nyabingi and the high god are represented as discrete entities, in a misleading interpretation. Edel does mention that some of her informants termed Nyabingi 'the Sun-moulder' (1957: 149).[27] This phrase, at least, captures something of the inter-related nature of Nyabingi and the Sun/god. Further, Philipps' secret report of 1919 also mentions that, in Rwanda, Nyabingi subsumed an earlier fertility practice (*biheko*), which 'profess[ed] to provide remedies for fertility' (1928: 316). Edel similarly argues that among the Bakiga, Nyabingi had overwhelmed an earlier fertility movement (*emandwa za'bakazi*) which had operated 'especially [to] help[ ]the women of the family to conceive' (1957: 146). However, in neither Philipps nor Edel are these interesting observations pursued.

In actual fact, in only Freedman and Berger is the fertility dimension discussed at all. However, for Freedman, Nyabingi's function as a medium of fertility, and in particular as '*the* divine protector of child bearing' and as a key spiritual aid to childbirth, represents only an older phase (1984: 87, emphasis mine). From about the 1870s onwards, he thinks, this original orientation began to change radically. From that time onwards, the office of the *mugigwa*, once a sole preserve of women, became instead an exclusively male domain. As this happened, a concomitant change in the meaning of Nyabingi also occurred. After this time, Nyabingi operated less as a symbol of fertility than as a symbol of secular, instrumental control (*ibid.*: 71–9, 80–90). Berger's argument is based largely on a reading of Freedman, but she also extends him, when she argues that Nyabingi was once a fully fledged esoteric fertility cult in its own right. This she compares to various other kinds of Central African 'cults of affliction'.

Now, as I shall describe presently, Nyabingi certainly was regarded as a divine being concerned with issues of fertility. However, this is not to say that the Nyabingi phenomenon was ever a *cult* of fertility. In fact, contrary to the understanding of colonial officers, it was never *any* sort of an 'organization' at all (or at least, not in any conventional sense of the word).

[25] I thank Wendy James for clarifying this point (pers. comm.).
[26] Moreover, the –b– particle in the compound word might well imply that the 'things' being possessed here are people.
[27] Unfortunately, Edel does not convey the local term to which she has given this gloss.

Instead, Nyabingi is best thought of as having been a set of ideas, from which certain practices derived.[28] The key to understanding this proposition lies in a more detailed analysis of Nyabingi exchanges than has ever been attempted before. In other words, if previous scholars have observed – usually in passing – that the exchange of goods was an integral part of Nyabingi practice, and these same scholars have also noted that Nyabingi was a spirit of fertility, then what I aim to do here is to demonstrate the logic by which these two features were integrally inter-connected, thus constituting a (more or less coherent) system. Thus, I now turn to the key questions in relation to these Nyabingi exchanges, of exactly who exchanged what with whom, when and – perhaps most importantly of all – *why?*

The polygamous household, and the 'house–property complex'

Nyin'eka ku aiba, ngu naarya ebye. When a household head steals, he takes what is his own[29]

What emerges from my own research on Nyabingi is that the phenomenon is best understood as having encompassed a series of ideas concerning the appropriate response to misfortune. In other words, it was to Nyabingi, as a spirit of fertility, that people turned during times of crisis, and a concomitant set of practices emerged from this. The majority of these misfortunes were of limited scope, and affected only a single household. It is therefore useful to begin here with an examination of the structure of the South-western Ugandan household, and of the ways in which misfortunes typically impacted upon it.

The classic ethnographic description of the old Kigezi District is Edel (1957), and a definition of the 'typical' South-western Ugandan homestead may usefully be derived from this account. Based on fieldwork carried out in the early 1930s, Edel described the basic social unit of Kigezi society as the patriarchal household, a fenced-off enclosure containing a number of separate buildings around a central courtyard which included all the domestic buildings, as well as animal stables, granaries, etc., and which commonly had only a single gateway (*ibid.*, 8–9).[30] As is still typical in some parts today, this, or several of these households – for example, those of several closely related agnates – formed a settlement, which was in turn surrounded by that unit's agricultural gardens. Edel termed this enclosure *eka*, but in everyday speech this word has come to refer more to the people

---

[28] I thank David Anderson for helping me to clarify this definition (pers. comm.).

[29] Cf. Cisternino, 1987: 306.

[30] Indeed, this basic domestic unit has for long been typical throughout the inter-lacustrine region (see Schoenbrun's survey, 1998: *passim*). The same structure is found among populations which practise a more agricultural mode of subsistence (such as those of Southern Kigezi), as well as among populations which emphasize pastoralism. This uniformity across different groups is not surprising, in light of the fact that agriculturalism and pastoralism have never been mutually exclusive modes of production in any part of the inter-lacustrine zone (a point emphasized in a new body of archaeologically-based research, e.g. Schoenbrun, *ibid.*; Robertshaw and Taylor, 2000).

living inside the household than to the structure itself.[31] Today it is more commonly termed *orugo*, and, to avoid confusion, I shall use this term throughout here.[32]

As Edel describes, an *orugo* was headed by the oldest male (*nyin'eka*) who may have been the father, or the eldest of a group of brothers, and was home to his wives, all of his offspring,[33] and any brothers who had not yet set up their own *orugo*. Furthermore, the *orugo* was 'in most respects a single social unit' (*ibid.*: 10) under this individual. Throughout her account, Edel repeats a prevailing ideology that *nyin'eka* exercised an almost omnipotent control over *everything* that went on within his *orugo*. As she states, he 'has full control of everyone and everything in it – wives, children, cattle, servants, and slaves if any. He parcels out the garden patches, makes offerings to the spirits, decides when an animal is to be butchered and how it is to be shared out...' and so on (*ibid.*).

Yet as she goes on, the separate domestic quarters of *nyin'eka's* various wives (*enju*, in Kinyarwanda spelled *inzu*) were also distinctly independent economic units within the wider *orugo*. (It is crucial to note here that South-western Ugandan society was in the 1930s, and remains today – in some parts – highly polygamous).[34] Thus, as Edel describes, each of *nyin'eka's* wives would have had to be given – upon her arrival in the homestead – her own living quarters (*enju*), in which only she and her own offspring would live. *Nyin'eka* himself would have no separate quarters of his own, but would instead sleep in each of his wives' *enju*, in rotation. As Edel states, a wife would only ever cook in her own *enju*, and her children would not only always sleep, but also only ever eat, in the *enju* of their mother. Significantly, each *enju* had its own separate agricultural gardens. These were allotted to each new wife – as parcels from *nyin'eka's* overall land holding – shortly after her arrival in the homestead (i.e. immediately after her marriage to *nyin'eka*). Moreover, each *enju* also typically controlled its own herd of animals, its own cows, sheep, goats, and so on. Indeed, it was quite common for a wife to perceive that the land she tended, and the

---

[31] Edel may simply be wrong in her gloss. Tracing the etymology of the word, Schoenbrun finds that the original meaning of the term was a 'unilineal, dispersed, exogamous group' (1998: 98). In other words, it probably always referred to a category of people, rather than to the physical homestead itself.

[32] This word derives from Kinyarwanda, and originally referred to the fence built around a cattle kraal. In Kinyarwanda, it was also used metaphorically, to refer to the fence around *any* homestead – i.e. even one in which no cows were owned – and this usage has been latterly adopted in Rukiga. Incidentally, in the burgeoning literature on Rwanda which followed the events of 1994, the word *rugo* has also been frequently glossed as 'hill' (for example, Prunier, 1995). Although space does not allow a broader discussion here, this extension has contributed to some confusing discussions about Rwandan social organization in parts of that literature.

[33] Until such time as a daughter married out, or a son started his own *rugo*, something he would not usually do until long after his first marriage, and even then only with *nyin'eka's* express permission (Edel, 1957: 11).

[34] However, it should be made clear that not *every* household in South-western Uganda was polygamous. In some cases lack of wealth, religious sensibility, or some other factor, would result in men taking on only one wife. Nevertheless, I believe that, as a general rule, the *idea* of polygamy, the concept of 'the more wives the better', has always been strong here (see Mushanga, 1970).

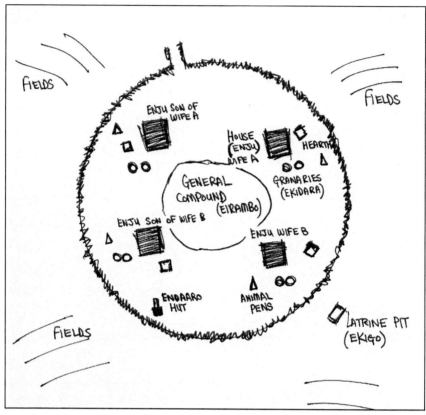

2.1 Sketch map of a 'traditional' polygamous Kiga homestead

animals she looked after, did in fact 'belong' to her own *enju*. And in these respects, at least, very little has changed in the overall organization of the polygamous household, up until the present time.[35]

Thus, according to Edel, the homestead had a kind of dual quality. On the one hand, it was unified under the authority of a single head, *nyin'eka*. On the other, each of its constituent *enju* expected to have, and in general terms did have, a high degree of independence from the others. However, following Max Gluckman's famous argument on the so-called 'House-Property Complex' (1950) – a large part of which drew, incidentally, on ethnographic material from South-western Uganda (albeit from the Bairu, rather than the Bakiga, ethnic group) – we might even go beyond Edel here, in constituting these two principles of ownership and control as a *tension* within the domestic sphere. In other words, as first described by Gluckman,

[35] Indeed, I have only ever heard of one household in which two wives have slept in a single building, which belongs to a neighbour of mine in Bugamba. Yet so queer does this arrangement seem to other villagers, that the *nyin'eka* of that particular homestead has become something of a celebrity in the surrounding neighbourhoods and is a source of continual humour. For example, in local bars, talk abounds that, to have achieved this particular arrangement, he must surely have bewitched his two poor wives! (cf. Edel, 1957: 10–11).

this sort of situation – apparently common to the polygamous arrangement – in which the male head of a homestead perceives all of the property in that homestead to be his alone, to dispose of as he wishes, yet in which each of his wives also harbours expectations as to how the husband's will should be exercised, invariably leads to conflict (for a more recent, and comparative, perspective, see Oboler, 1994). Specifically, in such contexts, the husband will be expected, by each of his wives, to 'spend' that part of his property which she controls on only herself, or on her children, or – in this case – on her *enju*. She will certainly *not* want any of the property she controls to be spent on any of her co-wives, on their children, or on their *enju*. Yet as Gluckman, and later commentators, describe, situations typically *do* arise in which husbands will exercise their ownership, and will dispose of 'their' property, in ways which are contrary to their wives' expectations. Indeed, the comparative ethnographic record suggests that it is in fact quite common for household heads to 'spend' in ways which their wives regard as 'inappropriate'.

In putting forward this argument, Gluckman and others are thinking in particular of the tensions which frequently result from property distributions which occur after a household member's death. However, it is my argument that these very same sorts of tensions played out in the polygamous Kiga household in other ways as well. Moreover, that these additional tensions are absolutely crucial for understanding Nyabingi exchanges. Indeed, as I shall demonstrate below, the entire Nyabingi complex existed as a mechanism through which people could attempt – in the context of episodes of misfortune – to engage with, and to try to overcome, these inherent tensions within the domestic sphere. In order to demonstrate the exact ways in which these two 'principles' of ownership and control constituted a wider tension within the polygamous Kiga household, I shall begin with a discussion of the types of exchange which typically occurred during Kiga marriage rites. It is not necessary to provide here an exhaustive description of Kiga marriage rites, but instead to high-light a number of its characteristic features (and my discussions here are based upon my respondents' descriptions, complemented by my own observations of the dozen or so Kiga unions I personally attended, and/or recorded details of, over the course of my fieldwork).

The main point I want to draw out here is that these rites have always involved a component of *both* brideprice and dowry. Moreover, that an ideology persisted – following the first 'principle' of the Kiga household – that the household head (*nyin'eka*) had absolute control over, and was the sole decision-maker for, *both* of these types of exchange. For example, when asked about the allocation of animals for brideprice, all of my Kiga respondents argued that the sole responsibility for making such payments has always resided with *nyin'eka* alone (and with his brothers, and his senior agnatic kin, who reside in their own homesteads). Indeed, this was said to be the case for brideprice payments made on behalf of both *nyin'eka* himself, and of any other men living in his homestead. Moreover, all respondents agreed that *nyin'eka* could make these payments out of *any* of the animals in the homestead, and could similarly distribute any of the animals received

during his daughters' marriages amongst any of his homestead's constituent *enju*, according to his own wishes. Indeed, all of this appears to tally
with Edel's descriptions. Thus, to complete the above quote from her
account, '... he [*nyin'eka*] ma[kes *all* of the] marriage arrangements for both
the sons and daughters'.

Similarly with regard to dowries. Thus, in normative terms, *nyin'eka*
alone was taken to be the sole recipient of the major part of any dowries
received at a wedding. At her *okuhingira* (giving away ceremony), a bride
was given a number of household items (*omuhingiro*, pl. *mihingiro*) by her
paternal relatives. Today, the majority of these items are made up of articles
which will be useful to her in her future married life: cooking pots, bed
mats, hoes, and so on. Yet in addition to these household items, the bride's
family used to – and in many instances still do – give *nyin'eka*, as the
groom's father, a far more valuable part of the dowry, namely the payment
of a sizeable number of animals, the exact amount of which depends on the
wealth of the bride's family.[36]

Thus, even within contemporary marriage rites, the lion's share of a
dowry still goes to *nyin'eka*. However, in the more elaborate rites of the past,
he was the recipient of an even greater range of exchanges as well. For
example, in a practice which was common until the early 1950s, every new
bride, upon arrival at the *orugo*, was placed in an exclusion hut (*ekidaara*),[37]
usually until she had become pregnant. She and her husband would then
return to her parental home – in a ceremony called *okuramukanya* – at
which point *nyin'eka* would receive yet more animals from the girl's
relatives. Following this visit, another ceremony would be performed in the
bride's marital *orugo* (*okwaruka*), after which she would go to live for a
period in her mother-in-law's *enju*.[38] Here, the mother-in-law was supposed
to teach her the ways of her new household, in such practices as cooking
and weeding the gardens. At the end of this period, which might last up to
a year, a further ceremony (*okuteekyesha*) would then be performed,
following which the new bride would finally take up full responsibility for
her own *enju*.

Given the timings, she would usually have produced her first child by
this time (and indeed, by some accounts, *okuteekyesha* could not take place
at all until she had given birth). At this stage the head of the homestead
– who was either her husband or her father-in-law – would allot a
portion of his agricultural land for her to till. Again at *okuteekyesha*, her
relatives – and also, this time, his agnatic kin as well – would give
nyin'eka livestock as gifts. These latter gifts acknowledged the completion
of the marriage rites. In practice, of course, it is unlikely that all of these
various, and elaborate, rites would have been performed for every union

[36] Within the actual ceremonies, these gifts of livestock are usually handed over to the groom.
However, because of this normative assumption that *nyin'eka* owns all of animals within the
orugo, these animals later came to be cast as *nyin'eka's* property alone.
[37] Although this word has a wide semantic range, and can refer to other sorts of structures as
well.
[38] This mother-in-law would be either *nyin'eka's* mother, or one of his paternal aunts, or else
one of his wives (depending on whether the new bride was a wife of *nyin'eka* himself, or of one
of his sons).

(or at least, in the correct order). However, the point here is to show that throughout the whole sequence – however closely this may have been followed in any given instance – gifts were frequently given to the household head, and that all of these properties were normatively taken to belong to him alone.

In these ways, then, household heads normatively controlled all of the goods which flow into, and out of, the *orugo* during marriage rites. (Although this is still the case today, it would presumably have been even more pronounced in the past, when the relative volume of the goods exchanged across the more numerous ceremonies would have been much greater than it is today.) Yet, in addition, *nyin'eka's* normative control of these goods also extended to their later re-distribution within the homestead. Thus, for example, it was generally taken for granted that, should a household head wish to make a later brideprice payment either for himself (i.e. to take on an additional wife) or for one of his sons, he could, in theory, use *any* of these animals to do so. However, to do so might well create conflict, given that – following the second 'principle' of the Kiga household – in practice expectations were placed upon him as to what are 'appropriate' uses for such animals. Specifically, even in the contemporary context, his wives would expect the property they control to be 'spent' for the benefit of only their own *enju*. For example, even today a wife regards any animal received during her daughter's marriage as belonging to her own *enju*, and thus to be spent on only the brideprice of one of *her* sons. She would regard it as totally inappropriate for any such property to be used to pay another brideprice for *nyin'eka* (in which instance she would, in her view, be 'paying' for a new co-wife), or for the brideprice of another of *nyin'eka's* sons (from another *enju* in the extended homestead). It might also be noted here that, following a marriage, these sorts of expectations were not – and still are not – limited to *nyin'eka's* use of 'his' animals.

In addition, such practical expectations extended to the household head's distribution of 'his' land, as well. Thus, when giving his new bride a plot following marriage, *nyin'eka* could again, in theory, give her any piece of land under his ownership. However, in practice, he was again expected not to give a new wife any piece of land which had been previously allocated to an earlier wife. Perhaps more significantly, it was expected that a son could only inherit – or be given at marriage – land that had formerly been under the control of his mother's *enju*, and had been allocated to her upon her arrival in the homestead. In other words, *nyin'eka* would be expected not to give the son of one wife land which had formerly been controlled by the *enju* of another wife (all of these principles still pertain in the contemporary setting).

Furthermore, these sorts of practical expectations were not only held by *nyin'eka's* co-wives. Take, for example, dowry payments. If the new wife herself had continuing expectations about the 'proper' uses for these properties, then so too did her natal kin (who are, after all, the people who have given the dowries in the first place). A bride's kin typically understood these gifts to constitute dowry in a stricter sense of the term, as goods given to help establish the bride and groom's domestic prosperity. Moreover, given that the bride's domestic sphere extended only to her own *enju*, it followed that her relatives also regarded the couple's joint domestic unit as extending to *only that enju* (and not to the wider marital homestead). Thus, later visitors from the bride's natal family would be extremely angry to discover that these animals had been used to the benefit of another wife's *enju*. In other words, although the animals were given to *nyin'eka* himself, and although he could in theory dispose of any cattle in the entire *orugo* according to his own wishes, in practice these animals were also given for the purposes of benefiting only the single *enju* of the bride. Indeed, today these animals will usually end up in the herd controlled by the new wife's *enju* (given that in most instances, her natal kin will visit her new homestead, and will in some sense 'police' the uses of the dowries they have paid).

Now, let me make the not unreasonable assumption – given the general ideology of polygamy – that any household head would at a given point in time be trying to raise enough bridewealth to secure his marriage to another wife. Yet in this circumstance, from where, then, would the requisite number of animals be raised? In other words, from the foregoing discussion, it is clear that, at any given point in time, all of his current animals would have been already allocated to his existing wives. Moreover, that each of these wives would regard the animals in her *enju's* herd as, in a sense, 'belonging' to her (and therefore not to be available to him). He might, of course, have attempted to buy the requisite stock from a local market, or to borrow the animals from his agnates, or from his reciprocal bond-partners (*bakago*), and so on. However, in practice, these options were always limited, given that to purchase animals has always been prohibitively expensive for all but the wealthiest few. In addition, an individual's ability to borrow them from his agnatic kin, or from his *bakago*, would again have been reliant upon the wealth of those actors. Instead, what seems to have often happened here – as a majority of my respondents' testimonies confirm – is that it was far more likely for *nyin'eka* to exercise instead his normative control over all of the herds in his *rugo*, by taking the requisite number of animals for the next brideprice from his existing stock. In other words, whether he would really have wanted to or not, he was often forced in this context to violate his existing wives' expectations, by 'plundering' the herds of their *enju*.

By definition, the herds of some *enju* were less vulnerable to such approaches than others. Specifically, the animals of one of *nyin'eka's* senior co-wives were less open to his plundering than those of one of his newer wives. For example, a senior wife would doubtless have already produced several sons, and she might reasonably argue with her husband that 'her' animals would be better spent on their bridewealth, rather than on another wife for *nyin'eka* himself. More dramatically, grown-up sons may even have physically defended the animals of their mother's *enju* against such advances by their father. Even today, as part of 'everyday discourse', mothers tend to denigrate their husbands in front of their children, and especially in front of their sons. Thus, any wife, as part of her everyday conversation with her children, will typically complain to them that their father 'is a drunkard', that he 'doesn't look after this *enju*', that he 'cares more about his other wives and their children than he does about us', and so on. The result is that young men often come to harbour considerable hostility towards their fathers. Indeed, it is not uncommon – in fact it is the norm – for a man's influence over a given wife's *enju* to diminish over time, in consequence.

I know of several cases in which grown-up sons have literally expelled their father from their mother's *enju*, leaving him access to only the *enju* of his other wives.[39] In one example I witnessed, two adult sons beat up their father when he tried to use some of their *enju's* herds for his own brideprice. To my knowledge, the father involved has never again entered the *enju* of those sons. However, on the other hand, a *new* wife of *nyin'eka* (*omugole*) can never, by definition, be so well protected. This is especially true if she has not yet borne her husband a child. As one of my respondents succinctly put it, 'how, oh how, can she have expected to hang on to those animals [which were allocated to her *enju* during her marriage rites] if she had not even produced a kid?' (Felicity Zahura).

Moreover, this discussion of the property exchanges which accompanied – and some of which still do accompany – Kiga marriage rites provides a suitable framework for understanding the historical logics of Nyabingi. It can be seen that, in the context of these rites, *nyin'eka* normatively controlled all of the *orugo's* exchange goods. Yet in this way he might also be said to have also controlled its very means of reproduction, or its *fertility*. Moreover, from this perspective, we might also say that if each of *nyin'eka's* wives harboured expectations as to how his control should be exercised, so too they harboured expectations as to how he should conduct himself vis-à-vis their own fertility. Furthermore, if a degree of tension existed between *nyin'eka's* control and the *enju's* expectations, we can therefore rephrase this as, in essence, a competition over the 'goods of fertility'. It is this reformulation, then, which allows us to understand the nature of the historical Kiga household's interactions with the fertility spirit of Nyabingi.

Conflict, misfortune and the spirit of Nyabingi

Omukazi tayecwa kizaire. No woman can break a childbirth taboo (i.e. overcome a problem causing barrenness) on her own.[40]

Ekibi tikiizira omwe. A misfortune affects everyone.[41]

During late 2000 and early 2001, I conducted eighteen formal interviews, and perhaps thirty or so informal interviews, with Bakiga elders living in

[39] Also as the sons of an *enju* become increasingly capable of defending its herds against his advances, so the size of these herds will also increase. It should be noted here that almost all *enju* have an ongoing supply of new animals in the form of brideprice payments received for daughters given in marriage. Again, such payments are given to *nyin'eka* himself to do with as he wishes, and again he is usually expected to give them to only the *enju* of that daughter's mother. Indeed, so seriously is this particular expectation taken, that one of my respondents suggested that a *nyin'eka* transgressing it would probably be murdered by the members of the offended *enju*. The overall effect of this general situation is that the amount of influence *nyin'eka* has over a particular *enju* tends to be inversely proportional to the size of that *enju's* herd.

[40] Cf. Cisternino, 1987: 235.

[41] Cf. Cisternino, 1987: 409.

and around Bugamba Village, in an attempt to gather some oral historical data on the history of Nyabingi practice in the Southwest. Of the formal interviewees, two were over 90 years of age, seven over 80, seven over 70, and the remainder over 60 (in all instances, it was difficult for me to be any more accurate about the interviewees' ages than these estimates). The point is that all of these respondents were selected on the basis that they had been born within the old Kigezi District, and either had had some direct experience of Nyabingi practice themselves, or else had been informed about it by their parents' and grandparents' generations. Of the informal interviewees, the majority were slightly younger, ranging in age from mid-70s to late 50s. However, most of these individuals had also been born in the area of the Kigezi Hills, and thus had some knowledge of former Nyabingi practices in that area (although, with these respondents, their knowledge tended to be based less on personal experience than upon what they had been told second-hand). Moreover, there is strong evidence that ongoing knowledge of Nyabingi practice has continued to be emphasized by people living in the Diaspora in a way that it has not been among those who never left Kigezi (for reasons that will be discussed in the next chapter). Thus, through these various interview data, I have been able to reconstruct at least something of how Nyabingi practice operated during an earlier period.[42]

Specifically, the picture which emerges here is of Nyabingi, as a spirit of fertility, being something to which people would turn during times of misfortune. Therefore, just as *nyin'eka* was normatively responsible for the fertility of his entire *orugo*,[43] so too he took responsibility during such times of trouble. Thus, in the event of any member of his *orugo* being struck by misfortune, it was his task to contact Nyabingi. For example, a wife's fields might have yielded a particularly poor harvest, a son might have caught fever rendering him unable to work, a wife's goat might have died, and so on. Yet on each occasion, it was *nyin'eka's* task to assuage Nyabingi's malevolent force. For this, each *orugo* kept a single 'spirit hut' (*endaaro*)

---

[42] It was always impossible, throughout these interviews, to be specific about dates. Thus, much of what people told me here was based on 'relational' temporal frames (such as 'when I was a young man', 'before my mother died', and so on). Whilst in a very few cases it was possible to cross-tabulate these accounts, and to thus arrive at some rough idea of when the incidents had taken place, in most instances this proved simply impossible. Thus, this section is another example of the kind of 'awkward scales' I discussed in Chapter 1.

Moreover, as one final caveat, I would also note that because most of these interviews were conducted early on in my fieldwork, when I had just started learning Runyankore/Rukiga – and my language skills were thus still rudimentary – all of them were conducted through a translator. As a result, many of their discussions lack the kind of nuance, and detail, that I was able to achieve in later interviews (by which time my language skills had vastly improved). Furthermore, because of this, I have been unable to use their transcripts to develop the kind of detailed case studies that I have developed in, for example, Chapter 5. Instead, throughout the remainder of the current chapter, I tend to discuss only the more general points and observations that these respondents made about Nyabingi.

[43] It is interesting to note that the full form of *nyin'eka* is *nyina eka*. In Runyankore/Rukiga, *nyina* is in fact the (3rd person) word for mother. It is highly curious that this term, one associated with feminine fertility, should ever be applied to a man. The very title *nyin'eka* itself therefore stresses this aspect of his role as head of household. (I thank Felicity Zahura for pointing out this interesting connotation).

through which Nyabingi could always be contacted,[44] and under normal circumstances only *nyin'eka* himself would be allowed to do this. Thus, it was within, or next to, the hut that he alone would consult the spirit on the afflicted person's behalf. Upon *nyin'eka's* death, responsibility for consultation would pass to the new *nyin'eka* – the next most senior male member of the household.

Typically, upon entering the hut, Nyabingi would somehow communicate to *nyin'eka* that either she, or one of her agents, had caused the particular misfortune at hand. The ritual part of this process varied over time and place, but seems to have only rarely involved the consultant becoming in some way possessed by Nyabingi. More typically, my respondents' accounts suggest that the consultant would instead relay a message Nyabingi had spoken to him while he was in the *endaaro* (and this also tallies with Freedman's descriptions, 1984: *passim*). In most instances, Nyabingi herself would accept responsibility for the particular misfortune, and would promise to withdraw it, in return for some sort of 'offering'. The term used for these offerings was *okutoija*.[45] On other occasions, Nyabingi would instead identify one or other agitated spirit (*emandwa*) as the origin of the trouble.[46] Yet even in this instance, she would be the one to be paid,

[44] Despite almost a century of attempts by various Christian missionaries to have all of these *endaaro* huts destroyed (because of their pagan connotations), even today many homesteads in the Southwest in fact continue to keep them. However, whereas in the past these huts were the size of a full dwelling, today they are more likely to be very small – perhaps only a few inches in height – not least so that they can be hidden from the Church's gaze.

[45] Writing of the former Ankole District – the area to the east of the Kigezi Hills – Oberg discusses *okutoija* as an animal given to an important political figure, such as a 'king' (*mugabe*). However, leaving aside possible regional variations here, Oberg's is too narrow a description of the verb. In fact, *okutoija* has always referred – in both Runyankore and Rukiga – to more or less any payment made to any agency capable of providing asssitance with one's problems (be that agency primarily political, or spiritual, in nature). Thus, it used to be applied to both kings and important 'chiefs' (*bakama*) prior to their hearing a dispute, and to the Nyabingi spirit during such periods of misfortune. However, today, the term *okutoija* is used exclusively in a church context, and it has ceased to have any meaning at all outside that context.

Okutoija was always distinguished – from various other sorts of tribute payments – by the size of the offerings it entailed. Indeed, it was precisely because of how much it involved that it was only ever given in the most serious of cases. Furthermore – and perhaps because of this – *okutoija* was always a very formal type of offering. For example, someone wishing to make *okutoija* to a chief would always inform the latter of his intention to do so some days in advance. In some instances he might even inform the chief of the size of the proposed offering ahead of time (Arnold Kashuja, Kasoro, Twesigye Leonard).

[46] The literature is confusing on the relationship between the categories of Nyabingi and *emandwa* (as indeed were many of my respondents' accounts). As a general statement, *emandwa* were the spirits of the dead, and were associated with specific lineages, or even individuals. *Emandwa* could also be consulted in the *endaaro*, but it is unclear whether the *kubandwa* complex existed independently of, or was in some way – in what way? – connected with Nyabingi devotion. Certainly Philipps sees *kubandwa* as an older metaphysical complex which Nyabingi in a sense 'replaced' (1928: *passim*). However, various sources are highly contradictory on this point. It is clear from Berger's surveys (1981, 1995) that many of these confusions may reflect regional variations. However, even among my own respondents, I found great variation. Thus, some suggested that *emandwa* were spiritual entities separate from Nyabingi (e.g. Akampurira Alex); others claimed that they were always under her guidance (e.g. Twesigye Leonard). Yet all were at least agreed that *emandwa* were somehow far less powerful, or important, than Nyabingi. However, for the purposes of the present discussion, it is not necessary for me to expand further on this subject.

In addition, I would note here that, in contemporary everyday speech, people refer to spirits

in order to 'call it off'. Following all of which, one or more animals would then be taken from the herd of the afflicted *enju*, and slaughtered. *Nyin'eka* would then place a large share of the meat inside the *endaaro*, for Nyabingi, after which the remainder was eaten by the men and children of the *rugo*.[47]

However, not all of the threats to a household's fertility would affect only that one unit. Some misfortunes, such as famines or droughts, were of a more general nature, and affected more than one home. In this situation, a more general consultation with Nyabingi would have to be organized (*okutamba*).[48] According to at least one of my respondents on the subject, this ritual was also the one aspect of Nyabingi practice that was markedly millenarian in character, which was an outcome of the circumstances in which it was carried out (Fr. Rwabahima). In addition, it is noteworthy that these rituals was usually conducted at the spirit's local shrine, which was invariably located at the top of a high hill, and in 'wild land' beyond all domesticated space. Under normal circumstances, only household heads were allowed to attend these shrines.

Yet the importance of these highly secret gatherings to the overall operation of the thing cannot be overstated.[49] For example, attenders at the ceremonies later constituted networks which subsequently assisted each other in raising the requisite amounts for offerings to the spirit. However, in the context of the ceremonies, only one or two household heads would consult the spirit at a time, although *okutoija* would later be demanded of all present.[50] Those who conducted the ceremony were those known to have had particularly 'good' interactions with Nyabingi in the past (for example, they may have benefitted from her benevolence in the past).[51] By

[46] (cont.) of the dead by two terms, *emandwa* and *emizimu*. Although these two terms carry slightly different meanings, the differences are subtle, and it is therefore not necessary for me to expand upon them here. So, for clarity, I will use only *emandwa* throughout this book.
[47] The women may have also consumed a smaller share here. However, in former times, it was generally regarded as inappropriate for women to eat any form of meat, under any circumstances.
[48] This is an archaic word, over which there is some confusion. Several of my respondents glossed it as 'sacrifice'. This is also the definition given by Taylor (1959). However, from my discussions with other respondents, I find this definition too narrow. According to these respondents (for example, Fr. Rwabahima), the word referred to an entire ritual process, rather than to only the practice of sacrifice (which constituted only one of its components). Today, the word is no longer used at all.
[49] During the course of my fieldwork in Bugamba, I had the opportunity to visit a number of historic shrines in which these ceremonies have formerly been conducted. Both at these sites and in Bugamba Village itself, I was able to gather detailed descriptions of the *okutamba* ceremony (upon which this account is based).
[50] As part of the rites, several participants were tasked with later visiting the homes of all others present, to collect these offerings. As one respondent described it to me, these individuals 'would then go carrying baskets. Empty baskets. Wherever they reached...they would fill those baskets with millet, they would put in bananas, they would put in all sorts of food. They would fill all the baskets. There would be twenty baskets, there would be whatever [sic]...they would also collect the animals, goats, sheep, whatever [sic].'
This quote is taken from an interview with Mzee Mugisha, who was in his 70s when I first interviewed him, and who had worked for over 30 years as a primary school headmaster. Given his profession, he speaks excellent English, as a result of which, all of my interviews with him were conducted in English. Therefore, this quote – and the others below – are a direct rendering of his words.
[51] On occasion, one of these individuals would even dress up as Nyabingi, and would thereby personify her for the duration of the *okutamba* rites (Mzee Mugisha).

establishing themselves in this way, these individuals might even have gone on to be regarded as particularly effective mediums. Indeed, over time, other household heads might even come to consult them in private. For example, in the event of his own consultations – in his own *endaaro* – proving ineffective, a given *nyin'eka* might turn to one of these better known mediums to contact Nyabingi on his behalf. Such an appeal for help invariably resulted in the person who asked for help having to make additional payments. These goods would be demanded by Nyabingi herself (via the medium), by the medium directly, or – most typically – both by Nyabingi and the medium. Yet it is interesting to note that such exchanges almost certainly did operate to stem at least some forms of general misfortune. Thus, particularly successful consultants of Nyabingi were able to build up substantial amounts of wealth in this way. Then, during critical times of crisis, such as during a drought, they would redistribute this wealth, thereby offsetting the worst hardships of that situation. Such a redistribution was expected, even required, of all wealthy individuals during a time of great crisis. Moreover, given that the redistribution by the mediums would have been done in the name of Nyabingi, it would indeed look, to all concerned, as if it was the spirit herself who was addressing their misfortunes. It is in this sense that Nyabingi always represented a redistributive network. Yet it must be remembered that all of this also occurred in the uttermost secrecy.

Of course, *the* greatest threat to the fertility of a household was that of a wife's barrenness (*engumba*).[52] Indeed, it would not be an overstatement to say that, for most people in this area and beyond, infertility today continues to be regarded as the worst possible misfortune imaginable. It remains every married couple's greatest fear. Obviously not a 'general misfortune' – unless all of the women in an area were suddenly to become so afflicted – barrenness was again taken to stem directly from the will of Nyabingi herself. Indeed, so serious was this eventuality that it required *nyin'eka* to bring the afflicted woman to a Nyabingi medium in person, for special consultations. Following these consultations – which took place either in the medium's own *endaaro* hut, or at a local Nyabingi shrine – the household head would then be required to make substantial *okutoija* offerings to the spirit.

However, in the event of permanent barrenness – or ongoing miscarriages – something quite different might take place. In this scenario, the afflicted woman might begin to receive her own visions of Nyabingi in her dreams (*okworekwa*). Such visions would become more frequent over time until many people, through the operation of local gossip networks, would certainly come to know of them. Therefore, these visions would be a far from private affair, and their content would be discussed openly, even enthusiastically, amongst others.[53] A woman receiving a series of these

[52] In fact, the word *engumba* has a wide semantic range in Runyankore/Rukiga, and can refer both to a woman's infertility and to any sickness which might befall her children (which is, in a sense, understood to be an outcome of her own afflicted personhood). Thus, for example, I recorded a number of instances where a child's permanent learning disability was described as an outcome of the mother's *engumba*.

[53] In recent years, such public expressions of visions – from the Virgin Mary – have been at times encouraged by the Catholic Church (see Chapter 3).

visions might even come to gain a considerable reputation as one so 'gifted' by Nyabingi. However, given that consultations with Nyabingi remained, in a normative sense, the sole preserve of household heads, still no woman could become a medium in *her own right*. Instead, the head of her household would connect her with one of the local mediums of renown. She would then work in that individual's household, and she might even be allowed – as one so 'gifted' – to enter his *endaaro* to also communicate with the spirit. Thus, as Edel describes, 'some of the most renowned of the Nyabingi mediums were women, but a woman so possessed could not practice as a priest in her own right. Some man...would build the [*endaaro*] house for her and actually speak to the spirit along with her' (1957: 154).[54] Later, other household heads, perhaps on account of her reputation, might come to seek her employer's assistance in contacting the spirit. These services were paid for, and some of the goods received would, no doubt, have eventually passed on to her. Thus, this Nyabingi 'handmaiden'[55] would ultimately bring back some riches to her marital home. Or to put it in other words, through receiving such visions, she would ultimately be able to contribute to her own *orugo's* fertility, even if she was unable to do so by giving it any children.

Therefore, in terms of seeking Nyabingi's help in addressing a misfortune *nyin'eka* was in a normative sense responsible for his entire *orugo*. However, his wives were concerned not with the reproductive fortune of the entire *orugo*, but with only that of their own *enju*. From the wives' point of view, perhaps the greatest threat to the reproductive fortunes of their particular *enju* came not from any sickness or famine, but from *nyin'eka himself*. The very biggest danger they faced was that he would dispose of that *enju's* animal wealth in ways that its members would regard as inappropriate. As one of my key respondents on the subject (Frances M.),[56] explained at length, such a misuse of animals might certainly be another cause of a wife's visions from Nyabingi. However, this time, rather than making the wife a 'handmaiden' – as with the barren wife – Nyabingi would now order the woman to take over the role of mediumship of the household's *endaaro* from *nyin'eka*, for a specific period of time. This constituted the only circumstance in which any wife could enter that homestead's *endaaro* hut.

Based on Frances M.'s testimony of how these sorts of incidents worked, let us call this wife: *Wife A*. Now, it was highly likely that some or other misfortune would afflict another *enju* within the homestead during the period of *Wife A's* stewardship of the *endaaro* hut. For example, let us say that this took the form of a sickness for someone in the *enju* of *Wife B*. In this circumstance, it would of course be not *nyin'eka*, but instead *Wife A*, who would now consult Nyabingi on *Wife B's* behalf. As Frances M. – among other respondents – described to me at length, in *this* case, Nyabingi would

---

[54] Therefore, Muhumuza could not have been a *mugigwa* herself, but, through association with several influential priests, she came to be known as 'one gifted with Nyabingi', and thereby gained considerable influence within Nyabingi circles (see Hopkins, 1970: 269, especially, for the importance of such alliances in the career of Muhumuza).

[55] In the vernacular, these actors were referred to simply as 'the Nyabingi'. I follow Edel in glossing them as 'handmaidens' (1957: 154).

[56] In recollection of a number of incidents from her own childhood.

not only claim responsibility for the affliction to the *enju* of *Wife B*, but she would likely communicate another sort of message as well. Specifically, she might typically 'describe' that she had become offended with *Wife B* as a result of the malice, jealousy, or cruelty, that either *nyin'eka* himself, or else *Wife B* – or more likely both of them – had shown towards *Wife A*. Crucially, following such a message – which was here being delivered via *Wife A* herself, of course – Nyabingi would now demand *okutoija* to be paid, not to herself but to *wife A* (by either *nyin'eka*, or *wife B*, or by both of them). Only after such a payment had been made would Nyabingi 'call off' the particular misfortune at hand.[57] Thus, throughout the period of her stewardship of the hut, *Wife A* would invariably receive numerous animals by way of *okutoija* payments. Moreover, it seems that, in many instances, these gifts could act as compensation for animals which her husband had previously 'plundered' from the animals she controlled.

Thus, it has been possible, from the testimonies of a number of my Kiga respondents, to reconstruct something of the general logic, and practices, of Nyabingi. However, I also offer a more concrete example, details of which were well remembered among the members of one particular extended family who live near Bugamba Village. One of my respondents, a Kiga woman in her 80s, called Sally Kahuru, recounted a series of events involving Nyabingi which had taken place while she was still a young women – in her teens, perhaps – living in a village in Ndorwa (just outside Kabale Town). In this instance – and unlike with a number of my respondents' other narratives – I was later able to corroborate certain details of Sally's story with two of her nieces, and with a niece's husband, who had also migrated to the Bugamba area (actors who knew the story well, even though they had learned about it second-hand; apparently, some aspects of the story had been widely discussed in the family, over a number of generations). The narrative Sally recounted involved her father and mother and events which had taken place either in the later 1930s or the early '40s (although certainly no later than the mid-'40s, given that the family had migrated to the Bugamba area as part of the 'assisted-relocation scheme' which began at that time).

The rough outline of the story, as I was told it, is as follows. One night – it was apparently some time in the long rainy season (which might well place it towards the end of the calendar year) – Sally was woken by the blood-curdling sound of her mother screaming, somewhere in another part of the house. Emerging from the room where she had been sleeping, Sally found her mother in a very distressed state, sweating, shaking and

---

[57] In one case Frances M. vividly recalled, the offending wife, *Wife B*, was openly shocked and surprised to discover that it was her behaviour towards *Wife A* which had caused such offence to Nyabingi. However, quite fearful of Nyabingi's wrath, she had been greatly disturbed by the accusation, and had been unable to sleep until the *okutoija* had been paid. I would argue that, in a number of respects here, we are not far from the logic of Azande witchcraft accusations, as described by Evans-Pritchard (1937). Moreover, following this logic, it is also noteworthy that, although malice towards *Wife A* would usually be identified as the cause of *Wife B's* misfortune, on some occasions a third wife, *Wife C*, might also be brought into the fray. Further, we might surmise that some wives – for example, *Wife A* (as the new *mugigwa*) and *Wife B* – may have occasionally formed strategic alliances against their other co-wives (e.g. *Wife C*).

moaning, while her father, and her older sister, looked on in total panic. Eventually coming to her senses, Sally's mother informed all present that she had just received a vision (*okworekwa*) of an elderly woman, with wrinkled skin, white hair, and dressed from head to toe in white. The old woman had told her that she was about to visit a terrible trouble upon this homestead, such was her anger. When this trouble arrived, it would be seen as 'a fire floating down from the hilltop, and landing in the granary of this home'.[58] Such was the reaction to the vision that a few days later, Sally's father slaughtered a cow, which Sally, her mother and her sister then cooked. However, most unusually – and Sally claims that this is why she still remembers the incident so vividly – the three women then also carried the meat to the family's *endaaro* hut, and after certain ceremonies were performed, *by her mother*, they then also ate a large part of it. This was the only time Sally was ever allowed to visit the *endaaro* hut of her natal homestead, and she had to learn a special song for the occasion (indeed, so vivid is this event in her mind, that she can still remember the words, and sang it to me during one interview I conducted with her). Moreover, this was one of the few occasions, prior to her marriage, that she ever ate meat.

Following all of this, Sally's mother apparently continued to visit the *endaaro* hut for an extended period of time (Sally thinks that it was for more than 'two harvests', although she could not be sure about this), and it was during this period that the son of one of her junior co-wives – an individual Sally describes as her 'father's young wife' – became seriously ill. Let us call this wife, *Wife B*. Sometime later, Sally's mother divined that it was the old woman of her dreams – who by now had been given the name of Nyabingi – who was the cause of the problem here. Specifically, Nyabingi was angry with *Wife B* for having 'bewitched' (*okuroga*) another of her co-wives, who I shall call *Wife C* (in total, Sally's father had 5 wives, Sally's mother being the most senior). Moreover, Nyabingi also explained the mechanism through which this witchcraft had taken place. In one dream, the spirit had spoken to Sally's mother at length, although in a somewhat incoherent manner, about dresses, and clothes, about beautiful attire, something about patterned cloth. Then, in a later dream, she had been more specific: that *Wife B* had bewitched the clothes of *Wife C* when the latter had hung them out on a tree to dry after washing. Moreover, that this witchcraft had been the cause of a death in *Wife C's* own *enju* (she had apparently lost a son some time earlier).

Nyabingi now demanded a number of animals in order to 'call off' this anger. Although Sally was never informed of exactly how many animals were requested here, she is sure that it was a sizeable number, given that her father then spent an extended period of time – perhaps several years or more – trying to raise them. Moreover, his task was made more difficult by

---

[58] This is a literal translation of what Sally said here. Although none of my respondents was able to confirm it, I think that this phrase must be an archaic metaphor for lightning. In other words, such is the spirit's wrath, that she is going to destroy the homestead's granary – i.e. its food stores, its very centre of production – with lightning. One final point here is that the word for granary (*ekitara*) is sometimes also used, even in contemporary parlance, as a metaphor for a woman's womb (i.e. her personal 'productive' capacity). In this way, the vision may be taken as a threat both to the homestead's productive, and its *re*productive, capacities.

the fact that some of the animals requested were further required to have 'special markings' (although, unfortunately, my notes do not relate the exact form these special markings were to take).[59] But the point is that this seems to have been far greater cattle wealth than Sally's father himself possessed at the time. Thus, it was perhaps no coincidence that he began to receive more frequent visits from his various reciprocal bond-partners (*bakago*), at this time. Interestingly, Sally also notes that a number of these visits were further distinguished by the fact that – quite abnormally for any visit from a *mukago* – they were conducted in utter secrecy (*omu kubonana*).[60] Indeed, Sally remembers this aspect particularly well, given that she was once beaten for trying to overhear what was being said at one of these congresses. Whatever was discussed at these meetings, over the following period the number of cattle in their homestead grew steadily. This was regarded by all concerned as particularly unusual at the time, given that no marriages had taken place in the homestead during this period (and thus, no brideprice had been received).[61] Moreover, most of the new animals were placed in the herd of Sally's mother's *enju* (which was also Sally's household, of course). Sally also remembers that at least one of these animals did indeed have 'special markings'.

From the foregoing discussion, then, it can be seen that, as a spirit of fertility, Nyabingi operated as a means through which *nyin'eka* could attempt to control the reproductive fortune of his entire *orugo*. In another aspect, it also served as a mechanism of compensation for women who had suffered specific 'attacks' upon their *enju's* own means of fertility. In other words, whilst Nyabingi was normatively a domain of men, it could also be – was more frequently? – drawn upon by women. By receiving apparitions from the spirit, women could become empowered by Nyabingi to address specific slights they had suffered.

As a final point here, it should also be restated that the most vulnerable person in this regard was invariably the *new* wife. Not only was she unable to defend her own herds. In addition, barrenness was always – and still is – a problem to which she was particularly vulnerable. In other words, given

---

[59] In this area, as across East Africa, cattle are symbolically distinguished in terms of the type, and colour, of their markings. For an overview of such distinctions as they pertain in Southwestern Uganda – albeit in the neighbouring area of Ankole, rather than Kigezi – see Infield (2003).

[60] Even today, this sounds quite peculiar, given that any visit from a *mukago* is invariably accompanied by much eating, drinking, and merriment.

[61] Furthermore, my own experiences in Bugamba suggest that any such 'unusual' growth of stock in a homestead will invariably be noted by neighbours, and other villagers, as well – and would thus lead to much gossiping and 'rumour-mongering', in an attempt to 'expose' the secret transactions which lay behind it. On one memorable occasion, the 'sudden' appearance of three new animals in the homestead of one young man led to wild stories of him having caught his wife in bed with a local vicar, who had then paid the cows in order to buy the husband's silence. In fact, the young man had bought the animals out of his salary from a carpentry job in Mbarara Town. I knew this, having seen him in town working on this job, and having subsequently accompanied him to the cattle market to purchase the animals. However, when I attempted to explain this to other villagers, my argument simply 'fell on deaf ears'. On the contrary, in fact, my own protestations as to the inaccuracy of the 'vicar story' were even met with yet further suspicion (and may even have further 'spiced up' the story still further, in subsequent retellings).

that all new wives were expected to conceive within a year or so of arriving in a marital homestead, issues of fertility were always a more pressing concern for a new wife than for one of her more established senior co-wives. Moreover, new wives, due to their lack of children, also had the greatest difficulty in 'defending' their herds. Therefore, it is not surprising that visions from Nyabingi seem to have been most frequently received by new wives. It is no coincidence, then, that the Nyabingi phenomenon was also sometimes glossed as 'the cult of the *mugole*' (Bessell, 1938: 74). The term *mugole*, a category of great social significance, refers specifically to the newest wife in a household. For example, my wife constantly toyed with the many complexities of being our household's *mugole* throughout the period of her stay in Bugamba Village (we married about halfway through my main doctoral fieldwork). I would also note that the word for Nyabingi's hut, *endaaro* (*indaaro* in Kinyarwanda), was sometimes also used to refer to the exclusion hut of the new bride. In actual fact, according to an older set of marriage rites, it was only after her *okuteekyesha* – i.e. after she had given birth – that any household building associated with a new wife could begin to be referred to as an *enju* at all.

The colonial model revisited, or the networks of Nyabingi

> *Ebisherekirwe biriibwa embeba.* Hidden food is eaten by mice. Secret problems need assistance from outsiders in order to be tackled.[62]

This reconstruction of the former logics and practices of Nyabingi high-lights a number of weaknesses in the colonial model of the movement. First of all, it challenges the common idea that anti-colonialism was the *raison d'être* of the Nyabingi phenomenon. Although Nyabingi certainly did, at one point in time, act as a vehicle for anti-colonial sentiment, it can now be seen that this was never its primary orientation. Rather, Nyabingi existed as a mechanism for addressing a range of misfortunes, of which the European arrival was but one. Certainly, the newly introduced system of administration did, at that time, place great burdens upon households' 'means of fertility', in terms of tax, labour, etc. Therefore, it might well have been construed by local people as 'a misfortune' of this type. However, it is also intriguing to note that the period of European arrival in South-western Uganda happened to coincide with a series of 'natural' disasters, including the 'great' rinderpest epidemic, and a series of other periods of heightened food insecurity as well (Freedman, 1984: 74–5). The rinderpest epidemic, in particular, affected the communities of the Kigezi Hills particularly badly in the latter years of the nineteenth century (see Hopkins, 1970: 261). Thus, we might also surmise that the increased activity of Nyabingi mediums during the early colonial period, and the parallel rise to particular prominence of certain of these actors, might also have been a response to not, the colonial presence, but to various other, more widespread, misfortunes as

[62] Cf. Cisternino, 1987: 213.

well. Or perhaps it was a response to all of these things at once? By this logic early twentieth-century manifestations of Nyabingi may well have begun as something else, but then become inflected with an anti-colonial dimension (perhaps, even, in response to the administration's attempts to deal with the natural disasters).

Yet in other ways too, my reformulation challenges the colonial model. In particular, it shows that the way in which the colonialists conceived of Nyabingi's sociology was also deeply flawed. The model of a formal organization, with a fixed membership, into which people were initiated, may or may not have once been useful for comprehending secret movements in Europe. However, exported to Central Africa, the construction certainly bore little relation to the reality. First of all, the kinds of misfortunes described above, and people's responses to them, tended to produce not a corporate structure, but instead diffuse webs, or networks, of (secret) exchange. Thus, it is noteworthy that, when trying to make an *okutoija* offering to the spirit, a household head would initially try to raise the required stock from his 'own' herds (although this may again have involved an element of 'plundering' on his part). However, as another of my key respondents on Nyabingi, Mzee Mugisha, described to me at length, in many cases the amount of stock required for these payments often far exceeded the number of animals that any one household – even an extended household – could raise, by itself.

Key to understanding this is the fact that not only were individual *okutoija* payments themselves sizeable enough, but household heads were frequently required to make more than one *okutoija* payment during a single occurrence of misfortune. This was especially the case with those misfortunes that continued over an extended period of time. For example, as Mzee Mugisha explained, in the event of an ongoing sickness in the household, or of a wife's ongoing inability to conceive, household heads often had to make multiple visits to Nyabingi mediums and shrines, for which multiple *okutoija* payments would invariably have to be raised. Indeed, in some instances, such offerings apparently continued over several years or more.

Even in Sally's story – which did not involve an 'external' medium (i.e. one outside of the extended household) – *okutoija* payments were ongoing for several years. As Mzee Mugisha summarized it,

> That one of Nyabingi, Nyabingi is Nyabingi. [His voice drops to a whisper, and slows down, to emphasize what he is about to say]: Nyabingi wanted *a lot*. [His voice becomes increasingly louder, and quicker, as he says]: It would demand that, then demand that, then she would say 'OK, so you have brought this much, ah, ah [no], that is not enough. Now, I want you to also bring that one, also that one, and that one', and so on'. As a result, '*many people were needed* to worship that [spirit].

Thus, attempts to appease the spirit typically involved household heads having to approach others for help, as well. It is perhaps not surprising that the first people to whom a *nyin'eka* would turn here were his patrilineal kin, and his *bakago*. On the one hand, his kinsmen were almost certain to assist him with animals, given that his misfortunes were also, in a sense, theirs

as well, in that something affecting the productive or reproductive fortunes
of his household also had an impact on the reproductive fortunes of the
wider lineage. Moreover, by this same logic, they might also have feared
that Nyabingi's anger here – which had caused the misfortune in the first
place – was being directed at not just *nyin'eka's* own household, but the
entire lineage (such that, were it not assuaged, it might later adversely
affect their own wives and children as well). As Mzee Mugisha put it, all of
nyin'eka's kinsmen would be likely to assist him, because 'all of those people
would be affected [by the misfortune that had occurred]. If there was a
problem, all of them had to do something to appease the spirit, because she
was annoyed. Then any of them could be hit. If there were ten [members]
of the patrilineal line, all ten would be affected.' On the other hand, a
nyin'eka's bakago were also compelled to provide whatever assistance he
required, given the nature of the *bukago* bond itself. Thus, for example, it is
no coincidence that, in the above story, Sally specifically recalled her father
being visited by his *bakago* during the family's period of crisis.

However, the amount of stock required for ongoing *okutoija* payments
sometimes exceeded even that which an entire lineage, or one man's group
of *bakago*, could muster.[63] In these instances, then, both *nyin'eka* himself,
and his agnatic kin and *bakago*, were typically forced to approach yet
further actors as well, in search of additional assistance. In this way,
nyin'eka, and/or his partners, would identify another householder whom
they knew to be active in Nyabingi affairs – for example, they might have
seen him at a past *okutamba* ceremony – and they would then visit that
person (again, always in secret), with a view to securing his help. Moreover,
as another of my key respondents on Nyabingi, Anne Arinaitwe, put it to
me, someone who was approached in this way was also under a strict
obligation to provide assistance, because such requests for help were also
thought to be in some sense 'sanctioned' by Nyabingi. Any failure to assist
with them might therefore also be an invitation to the spirit's future
displeasure (the same point was made by a number of my other informants
as well. For example, Mzee Mugisha described *any* request which was in any
way connected with Nyabingi as 'always dangerous'.) As Anne Arinaitwe
told me in her own pidgin English (and I quote here from the fieldnotes I
made during one informal interview I conducted with her. This transcript
was written during the interview itself, and is thus a reasonably accurate
transcription of exactly what was said here):

> Tomorrow you will have this person come to you to ask...he can't be tell you it
> Nyabingi who is sending there...it is done in a secret way.
> [I ask Anne] Could this request be refused?
> *No way!!!* because if this *is* Nyabingi...but if he go to ask that person for money,
> he must become like his friend, isn't it?
> [I ask Anne] What do you mean by 'friend' here? What is the vernacular for
> 'friend' here?
> The person you have cows with.

[63] This was a particular issue for poorer lineages and groups of *bakago*. However, there is also
some evidence that the size of the offerings requested by mediums would vary directly with
the wealth of the household at hand (such that the amounts required were equally exorbitant,
irrespective of the household's economic status).

In other words, what Anne is saying here is that if a person were to come to ask you for an animal 'out of the blue' – i.e. with no otherwise obvious, or good, reason for doing so – then you would probably infer that this was a request related to a Nyabingi payment (even though the word 'Nyabingi' would not be mentioned in the conversation at all). In other words, such requests would be inferred, rather than directly stated (and in this sense, would be 'secret'; cf. Favret-Saada's discussion of witchcraft discourses in the French *bocage*, 1980). Anne goes on that, given this inference, the request could not possibly be refused; that it would, in effect, place you in the position of a *mukago* or, in other words, as someone who is obliged to provide the necessary help.

Thus, the logic of these secret requests was such that they continued to 'draw people in', whether or not they ever wanted to engage with Nyabingi in this way.

All of which helps us to understand the overall description of the historical Nyabingi phenomenon that was given to me by another of my respondents, Kabwene David. Kabwene was already well into his 90s when I first interviewed him in late 2000, three years before his death. Yet he nevertheless turned out to be one of my best respondents on the whole Nyabingi phenomenon, and over the course of several months I recorded more than 6 hours of interviews with him on the subject. Kabwene had had extensive experience of Nyabingi as a younger man, in his capacity as a junior clerk in the Kabale courthouse, with some input into Nyabingi cases (and indeed, it was for precisely this reason that several people had suggested that I speak to him in the first place).[64] Reflecting on all of this experience, Kabwene wanted to stress what he saw as the key feature of the Nyabingi phenomenon: its diffuse character. Specifically, Kabwene's overall interpretation was that, given the size, and ongoing nature, of *okutoija* payments, Nyabingi practices tended to produce dispersed networks of exchange.

Kabwene's testimony may be summarized thus.

In the event of a given household head (let us call him Man A) being required to make *okutoija* to Nyabingi, yet being unable to raise the requisite number of animals from his own herd, or from those of his kinsmen, or *bakago*, he would be forced to approach another head (let us call him Man B) in secret, to request assistance. Man B would likely interpret this request as having come from Nyabingi, and would thus be unable to refuse it. However, in this circumstance, it was quite possible that Man B, too, did not have enough cattle to cover the payment either. Thus, Man B would then be required to secretly approach another household head (Man C), to further request *his* help. And so it went on. Thus, although actors themselves were not always aware of it (given the secrecy in which each of the individual transactions was shrouded), Kabwene was quite clear that Nyabingi's ongoing demands for *okutoija* – which were articulated through

---

[64] This was during the period when many cases involving Nyabingi were still coming before the courts, yet when the authorities had come to regard any mention of the spirit as an instance of 'distortion' or fraud. Indeed, Kabwene David used the English word 'distortion' a number of times in our interviews, which were otherwise conducted in Runyankore/Rukiga.

her various mediums – frequently resulted in the formation of entire networks of secret exchange (the exact word Kabwene used here was *abakuufu*, which means literally: 'a chain of people', in Runyankore/Rukiga).

Yet as Kabwene further stressed, if each request for *okutoija* did indeed draw in multiple actors, then so too the Nyabingi phenomenon was diffuse in the other sense of that term as well, such that 'chains' of Nyabingi relations often extended over considerable geographical distances. Given that all of the actors involved *did* always want to keep their actions as secret as possible, when they sought help from those outside their lineage or their group of *bakago*, they often went to great lengths to avoid these exchanges being detected by others of their village neighbours. Indeed, this would have been an especially important consideration, given that, even today, the addition or subtraction of just a single animal in a household's herd can generate a quite extraordinary amount of gossip in a given locality (as my discussion of the 'vicar story' in the above anecdote demonstrates). As a result, it seems that when people approached outsiders for assistance with *okutoija* – in the manner described by Anne Arinaitwe – they tended usually to engage people who lived some distance away from their own villages. It is, of course, impossible to say exactly what distances people might have travelled on these safaris. However, I would note that oral historical evidence suggests that at least some of the shrines used for the larger *okutamba* ceremonies could draw people in from dozens, if not hundreds, of miles away (see Chapter 4). Thus, household heads, or their partners, who were trying to raise *okutoija* payments, may well have had (potential) Nyabingi 'contacts' over a comparable distance.

Yet if Nyabingi practice did indeed produce diffuse networks of exchange, it must be emphasized that these were also, in one sense, only ever *ephemeral* in nature. In other words, although these practices doubtless did create some ongoing obligations – after all, there can be little doubt that someone approached in the manner Anne Arinaitwe describes would later expect reciprocal help with his own problems – by and large, Nyabingi was not something people ever wanted to engage with. In fact, as all of my respondents stressed to me, again and again and again, Nyabingi was instead always regarded as a highly dangerous thing, to which one would turn only as an absolutely last resort. Thus, it follows that the types of Nyabingi exchanges I have just described were specifically associated with some or other period of extreme crisis or misfortune (either in a single household, or in a wider locality). As Mzee Mugisha described it, as soon as that particular misfortune had been 'solved' – whether this took a few days, or a few years, to achieve – most people would then generally attempt to have 'nothing more to do with the thing'.

Finally here, if all of this calls into question the colonial view of a formal organization with a fixed membership, so too it challenges previous models of Nyabingi's 'leadership'. I offer here one more original insight. Throughout the literature, the term *mugigwa* is invariably glossed as a pseudonym for 'leader'. Thus, in both colonial and later accounts, 'the *bagigwa*' are discussed as the leadership of the hierarchical 'organization'. In other words, they are taken as a set of individuals who lead the majority membership of the organization. Yet, from the foregoing discussion, it can be seen that this is a somewhat misleading interpretation. In actual fact, the term *mugigwa* refers not to any individual at all, but instead to the *role* of attending a homestead's *endaaro* hut. Moreover, given that all household heads did, at one time or another, perform this task, it follows that *all* household heads were also *bagigwa*, at least for the duration of their interaction with the spirit. Further, in the event of a woman taking over control of the hut for a given period, she too would assume the title of *mugigwa* for the period of her tenure. The implications of this insight are far-reaching, for it implies that *everyone* involved in Nyabingi was, by definition, a *mugigwa*, at least for the duration of their interaction with the spirit. Some mediums certainly did build up sizeable reputations as particularly successful communicants with the spirit. Yet, given the features of the Nyabingi networks, it is extremely unlikely that such actors ever constituted a 'leadership'.

We may surmise that Nyabingi's order to attack the colonial outpost of Nyakishenyi probably did pass through one such individual. However, to read from this that such individuals had some kind of ongoing 'authority' within the Nyabingi universe seems a logical step too far. In the first place, the decision to make such a consultation rested solely with the person who was suffering the misfortune. Given this fact, it is also true that, should that person not be completely satisfied with the outcome of the consultation, he would simply move on to consult an alternative medium (Kabwene David). Thus, a respected *mugigwa's* authority was only ever consensual. Yet in various ways, *every mugigwa's* influence was always limited in scope. This much can be concluded from a number of features of Nyabingi practice. On the one hand, the fact that practically all Nyabingi activity was ephemeral meant that the influence of mediums must also have waxed and waned. Thus, although their role may have been crucial during times of severe crisis, they could never have had any kind of ongoing social importance. On the other hand, the fact that Nyabingi networks were never self-aware would have further limited the possible influence of the respected mediums. In short, it would have meant that their reputation could not be passed along, and shared by, all of the members of that network. Moreover, all of this also helps us to understand what then became of these Nyabingi networks, from the mid-twentieth century onwards.

3

The Many Lives
of the Nyabingi Spirit

The 'revelation in a swamp'

The village of Bugamba is located in the heart of the Rwampara Hills, in a steep-sided valley which runs roughly West-East from the River Rwizi, all the way up to the peak of Karamurani[1] in the village of Mwizi beyond. Like all of the valleys in Rwampara, this valley's most striking feature is the papyrus swamp which runs in a thick, unbroken band all the way along its floor. Although in some places only a few hundred metres wide, due to the encroachments of farmland, at certain points the swamp extends to a width of several miles. This is not untypical for a Rwamparan valley swamp. In the next valley south of here, the papyrus bog known as Munyere spans over six miles in some places. Many of the villages along the southern wall of that valley can only be reached by boat. It is probable that swamps such as Munyere account for the majority of Rwampara's total land mass.

Given this fact, it is perhaps rather surprising that one hardly ever finds people living in the swamps. Human settlements along the valley sides and (less commonly) the hill tops do often encroach on the swamps along their edges. Still, people never really settle within them. This is an area with some of the highest rural population densities in the entire continent. The situation is partly explicable, of course, in terms of the fact that the reclamation of swamp land for development requires a large labour input. There is also the fact that any form of reclamation is, at least in theory – although often not in practice – illegal. However, there is also more to it than that. In one very compelling argument, Heck, following Langdale-Brown *et al.*, argues that the swamp may also be a kind of 'non-social' space within the socio-ecology of 'the valley' (*oruhanga*). This stems from the fact that, in terms of agricultural production, the valley is divided into four zones of elevation. In order of descending elevation, these are: hilltop savannah, moist acacia savannah, post-cultivation community and valley bottom swamp (Heck, 1998: 58). Significantly, most agriculture is conducted within the middle two zones. As a result, most social activity is also concentrated in these places. In consequence, the hilltops and valley bottoms become non-social domains. However, I would also extend Heck here, by suggesting – in classic structuralist logic – that, within local cosmologies, the hilltops are sacred space, whilst the swamps are a polluting

[1] At 1895 metres, Karamurani is the third highest peak in the Rwampara Hills.

domain. Thus, all ritual activity takes place on hilltops,[2] and anti-social behaviour (such as pre-nuptial sex, or the smoking of marijuana) is usually conducted in the swamp (see Vokes, 2007: 810–12).

Thus, nowhere in Rwampara have I ever seen a human settlement in a swamp. Except in one location. Some three miles down the valley from Bugamba village lies the small trading centre of Kangerirwe. The primary economic centre of the middle valley, Kangerirwe hosts a number of small businesses, including a haberdashery, a carpenter's shop, and a small mechanics yard. However, the most striking feature of the place is the views it affords over the valley below. Positioned halfway up one of the steepest hillsides in the entire valley, on a wide rocky outcrop, Kangerirwe offers commanding views over the broadest unbroken stretch of swamp in the valley. The swamp here forms a Y-shape as it also continues, unbroken, up a side valley to the North. The whole view is of an undisturbed section of swamp some three miles wide, and perhaps seven miles long. On a clear morning, as the morning mists rise from the papyrus beds, the view from Kangerirwe is simply breathtaking.

However, on gazing out over this vista, the eye of the beholder is drawn not to the overall scene, but instead to the perfectly round settlement which lies in the very heart of the swamp. Surrounded by several miles of papyrus in all directions, and with no sign of even an approach route, the settlement, from Kangerirwe, reminds one of a 'crop circle' in a field of wheat. Consisting of some one hundred or so buildings, the settlement has no proper title, but is instead known to all by the nickname 'Kigali', derived from the fact that *all* of Kigali's inhabitants, without a single exception, are Rwandan. The settlement of Kigali came into existence following the infamous 'Banyarwanda expulsion' of 1982. From antiquity, small populations identifying themselves as Rwandan had lived in the area which is now South-western Uganda. However, from about 1920 onwards, the size and number of these populations swelled quite dramatically, as large numbers of people migrated from Rwanda into the region. Between about 1920 and the early 1950s, some 200,000 people crossed the international border. Then, in the years following the so-called 'Hutu Revolution'[3] of 1959, a further 160,000 came across.[4] These two waves of immigrants were received by, and interacted with, the Ugandan state in very different ways.

Specifically, the first group of refugees were generally well received by the colonial administration, which regarded the Rwandans as a cheap and mobile workforce for Uganda's growing industrial-agricultural economy (Richards, 1952). Indeed, most of the early immigrants easily found paid work in such diverse occupations as brick working, construction, fishing, forestry, industry, etc. (Otunnu, 1999:5). In particular, very many of them

[2] For example, this is where the Nyabingi shrines of old were located, where the *okutamba* ceremonies used to take place, and so on. In addition, it might also be noted here that throughout South-western Uganda, practically all Christian churches are located on hilltops.

[3] When political reforms instigated by the Belgian colonial government led to the effective replacing of the former Tutsi oligarchy in Rwanda with a predominantly Hutu native administration.

[4] Of course, all calculations of refugee numbers are highly politicized. As a result, these figures may not be accurate.

went to work as agricultural labourers in the coffee plantations of Buganda, where they constituted the largest minority of the workforce (Richards, 1952 and Mamdani, 1977: 149–56). With the wealth accumulated through such activities, many, if not most, of the first-wave immigrants were later able to buy land and settle in Uganda.

However, relations between the second wave of Rwandan immigrants (the so-called '59-ers') and the Ugandan state were always far more complex than this. Wary of the fact that many of these immigrants already appeared to be highly politicized,[5] immediately upon their arrival in Uganda the colonial government declared them to be illegal immigrants (Otunnu, 1999: 6). Throughout the period of their stay in Uganda,[6] successive regimes in Kampala continued to cast the 59-ers in a similar way, as a problematic population. In 1961 and 1962, elements within the 'refugee' group began to use Uganda as a staging post for attacks against Rwanda, actions which led to a straining of relations between the (newly self-governing) administrations in Kampala and Kigali. Obote was forced to warn the refugees against such actions, and eventually to expel some of their number. During the Amin regime, relations between this group of Rwandans and the state became more ambiguous, as some of them worked for the regime, whilst others opposed it (Mamdani, 2001: 167–8). However, during Obote II, the 59-ers once again came to be regarded as a clear problem by Kampala. This perception stemmed from the fact that a number of the refugees were involved in Museveni's insurgent Popular Resistance Army (PRA, later the National Resistance Army, NRA).[7] And in something of a self-fulfilling prophecy, the NRA even came to be regarded by Kampala as a *primarily* Rwandan organization. In response, the policy of expelling all Rwandans from the country was hatched among a group of highly placed Banyankole ministers. Thus it came to pass that, in late 1982, many thousands of Rwandans living in South-western Uganda were violently expelled from the country, mostly from the Districts of Mbarara, Masaka and Rakai. However, the implementation of the policy was always highly arbitrary and uneven.[8] In particular, although the expulsions were aimed at removing the troublesome 'second-wave' migrants from the country, in practice local government functionaries did not discriminate between different Rwandan populations. Thus, many of the 'first-wave' migrants were also forcibly evicted from their homes.

[5] Many of the refugees who crossed in 1959 were associated with the conservative Tutsi political party, the Union Nationale Rwandaise (UNAR), which had campaigned against the 'revolution'. As Otunnu points out, UNAR was also regarded with suspicion because it had been supported by a number of Communist countries in the UN's Trusteeship Council (Otunnu, 1999: 25, fn. 6).
[6] Many of them later returned to Rwanda as soldiers in the Rwanda Patriotic Front (RPF) in October 1990. Others moved back to Rwanda following the RPF's takeover of power in Kigali in 1994.
[7] A number of the NRA's leaders were Rwandan '59-ers', including Dr Peter Bayingana, Chris Bunyenyezi, Paul Kagame, Sam Kaka and Fred Rwigyema.
[8] On the one hand, some Rwandans connected with highly placed Ugandan families (either through marriage or *obukago*) were spared expulsion. I know of at least two such cases from around the Bugamba area. On the other hand, presumably due to personal vendettas, some Ugandans were declared 'Rwandan' and sent from their homes (Otunnu, 1999: 20 & 28, fn. 37).

By the late 1970s, several hundred Rwandan families were living around Kangerirwe, in the middle Bugamba valley. All were related to those who had migrated to Southern Uganda as part of the first wave of Rwandan immigration, from 1920 to the early 1950s. Nevertheless, all were forced from their homes during the expulsions. The personal narratives of the event are truly harrowing. Many people were badly beaten before and during the eviction. Several people lost their lives.[9] All lost property, animals, crops, and iron-sheet roofing. Moreover, their ordeal did not stop there. Upon arrival at the Uganda/Rwanda border, those being expelled from Uganda were effectively barred from entering Rwanda. Thus, they were essentially trapped in a 'no man's land' on the border, around Marema Hill. The plight of the 40,000 or so people camped at Marema soon came to the attention of the international refugee agencies, which quickly condemned the Ugandan government's policy of expulsion (Otunnu, 1999: 20). However, it was to be another three complicated years before the United Nations High Commissioner for Refugees (UNHCR) was finally able to return the Rwandans of Kangerirwe and elsewhere to their homes.[10]

As might be expected, the period of reintegration after 1985 was a difficult time for all those returning home. In particular, a great deal of animosity existed between the returnees and their Ugandan neighbours, some of whom had played an active part in their expulsion and many of whom had plundered the property they left behind. Throughout the late 1980s and early 1990s, a barrage of civil cases were brought before the local courts by the Rwandans, before Museveni finally declared a general amnesty on offences committed during the expulsions.[11] But even today, most people remain extremely reluctant to discuss such issues, which are frequently taken to be still far from resolved.[12] Indeed, so difficult were relations in the first few months after their return, that the Rwandans took a collective decision to move the households some way away from those of their former neighbours. As a result, the returnees founded the settlement of 'Kigali', in the very middle of the papyrus swamp. Today, although such relations have, in general terms, greatly improved, all of the Rwandans of Kangerirwe continue to live in the heart of that most cosmologically unsocial of places, the swamp.

All of which is relevant to our story here, because all of my early respondents on the subject had informed me that my inquiries about Nyabingi would inevitably lead me to Kigali. Nyabingi beliefs are well known to have derived, ultimately, from Rwanda, and as a result, the Banyarwanda are generally thought to be particularly knowledgeable about such matters. However, it quickly became clear that any approach to Kigali would have to be handled with some finesse. Early on, I was warned that

[9] Although some of these killings may not have been politically motivated, but instead 'the settling of old scores'.

[10] This was only achieved in November 1985, after the fall of the Obote II regime.

[11] This was done in the name of 'national unity', but also reflected the fact that many courts were becoming overloaded with these cases.

[12] For example, at least one of the murders which occurred during my time in Bugamba was widely rumoured to have been connected with the expulsions of 1982. Similar examples could additionally be cited.

the Rwandans of Kangerirwe were, for obvious reasons, somewhat suspicious of outsiders. Thus, it was decided – in a bar-room conference one night, with several of my research assistants – that my best chance of success here lay in approaching the people of Kigali through one of their senior elders, one Mzee Kinyaga. As one of my assistants pointed out, unless I befriended Kinyaga, no-one in Kigali would ever agree to talk to me about anything. However, my initial advances to this gentleman were met with what can only be described as a somewhat cool response. Back to the drawing board, and another suggestion was made that I hold a full-scale drinking ceremony for all of the people of Kigali. Such ceremonies are frequently used by politicians, for example, to announce themselves as the allies of the village-folk (*abataka*) of a particular area.

So it was, then, that a week or so later, I found myself hosting a public drinking ceremony in the middle of Kigali, accompanied by twenty or so friends and relatives from Bugamba Village, and carrying over 40 gallons of locally produced *tonto* (banana wine). The evening passed agreeably, and culminated in a series of warm speeches (to which I was able to contribute, in my now improving Runyankore). The final speech was given by Mzee Kinyaga, who declared me to be a new 'friend of all in Kigali'. Thus it was that two days later, I once again travelled to Kigali, this time confident that I would now be able to conduct some research interviews in the area. However, to my surprise, even after the revelry of the previous evening, people still wanted nothing to do with my work. Approaching Mzee Kinyaga, I was politely told that, even though I certainly was now a 'friend of Kigali', he had no intention of talking to me about anything at all, given that 'issues remain unclear'.[13] Frustrated, I finally gave up, and after a series of similarly unsuccessful visits to the settlement, I eventually stopped going to Kigali altogether.

It was over nine months later that I was sitting in a bar in Bugamba village drinking with some of our neighbours. A big meeting had been going on all day at the Sub-county headquarters further up the valley, and a number of delegates were beginning to drift back down through the village. A small group of men from Kigali, including Kinyaga, stopped by in our bar, obviously hoping to break their journey home with a drink or two. Several hours later, as they got up to go, Mzee Kinyaga – who had previously not spoken to me at all on this occasion – tapped me on the shoulder, and asked me to meet him outside. As I did so, he said words to the effect of 'OK, I have decided that we will now help your work'.

The following morning I met Kinyaga in Kigali, and he immediately led me off to the home of the oldest man in the neighbourhood, one Cyesha Cain. The interview which followed – and which was conducted entirely in Kinyarwanda – lasted for over three hours.[14] At great length, Cyesha discussed the nature of Nyabingi beliefs, the content of their practices, and even showed me a number of articles associated with Nyabingi séances.

[13] These were his exact words, in English.
[14] Many of the old Rwandan men who migrated to Uganda during the 1940s have never learned Runyankore/Rukiga, and continue to speak only Kinyarwanda. Thus, in all my dealings with these people, I was forced to use a translator.

However, his real 'bombshell' came at the very end of the interview, as I was packing up my things to leave. 'Of course, you've seen the Nyabingi shrine at Rushanje parish, haven't you?' he said to me (via a translator). 'They have a very big Nyabingi there.' His remarks left me completely dumbfounded. I had, of course, been to the local Catholic church many times before, but had no idea what he could possibly be talking about here. I therefore insisted that he accompany me to the parish, to show me what he meant. It was only as we walked up the driveway to the main parish grounds that I suddenly realized what the old man had been getting at. As we approached the collection of buildings, it quickly became obvious that the Mzee was now heading for the large open-sided 'Mary house' that had been built the previous year by the local Catholic Legion of Mary group (*Ab'eihe rya Bikira Maria*). At the porch of the building Cyesha stopped and, turning towards me, pointed at the seven-feet-high status of the Virgin Mary that was housed within. 'There', he said triumphantly, '*that* is your Nyabingi! Nyabingi has been a Catholic for a long time now!'

The arrival of the 'White Fathers'

> The last laugh, perhaps, was with the Great Lady Nyabingi; for when a mission-ary, on safari in 1928, asked why an unusually large crowd was following him, he was told that the local Nyabingi priestess had advised them to go and listen to what the missionaries had to say. And they were following her instructions! (Brazier, 1968: 25)

The first Roman Catholic missionaries to enter what was to become the District of Kigezi did so in late 1903. On their way to found the mission at Rwaza, in present-day Northern Rwanda,[15] three European White Fathers, including one Fr. Dufays, passed through the hills to the south of Kabale (Bessell, 1938: 78). However, it was not until eight years later that the White Fathers managed to establish a permanent presence in the area, with the despatch of several Baganda catechists to the area (Ngologoza, 1998 [1968]: 70).[16] And it was not until a full two decades after that first visit, in 1923, that the first European priests arrived in the area. In that year three White Fathers, under the leadership of a Dutch priest, Fr. Laane, took up residence at the Rushoroza mission station, on the hills above Kabale (Job, n.d., 8 & 13).[17]

From the very outset of their stay, these three priests were remarkably

---

[15] The White Fathers had established a permanent presence in Rwanda as early as 1900 (Taylor, 1992: 53).
[16] The first Muganda catechist to be sent to Kigezi was Yowana Kitagana, who arrived in 1911. He set up the first Catholic mission station at Ssebalijja, in Nyarushanje (Ngologoza, 1998 [1968]: 70). In 1914, both the White Fathers and CMS missions were invited to Kabale, by the British administration in Kigezi, to select a number of plots of land around that settlement, on which to build their headquarters in the district (Rutanga, 1991: 114).
[17] Fr. Laane was accompanied at Rushoroza by Fr. Nicolet and Br. Theofile. The station at Rushoroza had been established several years before the Europeans' arrival by a Muganda catechist, Johanna Kitagana (Job, n.d., 8). It was built on the land that had been selected by the White Fathers delegation of 1914.

successful in their efforts to convert local people to the new religion. Prior to their arrival, the total number of Catholic converts in Kigezi, who had been converted earlier by the Baganda catechists, stood at just 720 (*ibid.*). However, within just seven years of their arrival, this number had swelled to over 9,000 people (Rutanga, 1991: 116). This figure represents perhaps 10 per cent of the total population of the area at that time. The White Fathers' success in converting local people was therefore very great in absolute terms. Yet it was also noteworthy relative to the progress of the Protestant CMS missionaries who had arrived in Kigezi at around the same time. In actual fact, the first two European CMS missionaries, Doctors Sharp and Smith, had taken up residence in Kigezi (at Kabira, in Rugarama) at least two years *before* the arrival of Fr. Laane's party (Ngologoza, 1998 [1968]: 72).[18] However, despite this, and the fact that the CMS received something like preferential treatment from the colonial administration in Kigezi,[19] by 1931 their congregation stood at only 5,000 people, substantially smaller than that of the Catholics. Also by the early '30s, the White Fathers had the clear lead in numbers enrolled in education. By 1933, the White Fathers had almost 600 students enrolled in their mission schools, whilst the CMS had only 164 in attendance at theirs (Rutanga, 1991: 116). The question which immediately poses itself, therefore, is how and why were the White Fathers' attempts at proselytization so much more successful than those of their CMS counterparts during these early years?

At least part of the answer to this question lies in the fact that, within their representation of Christianity, the White Fathers, unlike the CMS missionaries, adopted not only the language and concepts, but at times also the ritual functions, of Nyabingi. Thus, their brand of Catholicism simply 'made more sense' to local people than did CMS Protestantism. In some respects, it is unsurprising that it was the White Fathers who made most 'use' of local belief systems in their attempts at proselytization. As Marcia Wright has observed, mainstream Catholic dogma in general 'contains beliefs in intercessory spirits that potentially resonate with African ideas of the supernatural ... and which provide religious assets not shared by austere, biblical teachings of Protestantism' (n.d., 4).

Moreover, the White Fathers order, in particular, has always attempted to develop these resonances further than any other missionary society. It was, after all, their founder, Cardinal Lavigerie, who first championed the idea of 'indigenous Christianities'. His original concept was one of missionaries who drew extensively on local understandings of the metaphysical as an aid to proselytization, and who always taught, as far as possible, in the

---

[18] Again, the first European CMS missionaries had been preceded by Baganda catechists. The first CMS catechist to reach Kigezi was Zakaris Balaba, who in 1912 built the first Protestant Church in Kigezi, at Kikungyere (Ngologoza, 1998 [1968]: 72).

[19] The British authorities extended preferential treatment to the CMS missions over those of the White Fathers because 'in the eyes of most officials, the educational system established by the CMS mission was better suited to training people for public office than the Catholic one' (Hansen, 1984: 336). Thus, despite complaints from the Catholic hierarchy, district administrations throughout Uganda continued to favour the CMS missions by, for example, giving many more plots of land to them than to their Catholic counterparts (Rutanga, 1991: 116).

vernacular language. As a result, and as Wright points out, the White Fathers were openly grappling with concepts of 'inculturation' long before the term became adopted by the mainstream church (*ibid.*, 3).[20] Nevertheless, some explanation is required of this particular group of White Fathers' incorporation of Nyabingi into their representation of Catholicism. For one thing, it is not at all clear to what extent this particular incorporation was ever really intended. Clearly missionaries such as Fr. Dufays and Fr. Nicolet hated Nyabingi, regarding the spirit as a '*shitaani*' (*lit:* Satan, cited in Freedman, 1984), and as competition to them in their quest to save souls (Dufays, cited in Bessell, 1938: 73 and Nicolet, cited in Freedman, 1984).

Thus, it would seem that, as with the colonial administrators of the period, the overall aim of the White Fathers was, in fact, to bring about the total demise of all Nyabingi practices. However, unlike with the governing authorities, the Catholics' strategy for achieving this end was not entirely destructive. Rather, they reasoned that a more effective approach would be to present local people with some sort of metaphysical alternative to Nyabingi. It was to this end, then, that they greatly encouraged the adoration of another sacred female, the Virgin Mary. Apparently much more aware than their contemporaries within the administration of the role Nyabingi played as a medium of fertility in Kiga society (*ibid.*), the White Fathers now sought to represent Holy Mary as an entity specifically concerned with the issues of women. Indeed, they even cast her as *the* champion of female concerns. The missionaries' efforts here were to culminate in their promotion of membership of the 'Legion of Mary' (*Ab'eihe rya Bikira Maria*), a predominantly female Catholic lay organization. Indeed, so popular did membership of this organization become that, throughout the colonial period at least, it remained 'the exemplary Catholic lay association...and the most pervasive mode of organized lay life outside the daily purview of the church, especially in rural communities' (Kassimir, 1999: 258).[21]

In many ways, this promotion of Marian adoration was a thoroughly predictable response of the White Fathers missionaries to something like Nyabingi. After all, Marian devotion has always been a key part of that particular order's spiritual repertoire. Indeed, the official name of the 'White Fathers' order is, in fact, The Missionaries of Our Lady of Africa.[22] Even today, the continual wearing of rosary beads as part of their everyday clerical garb remains the distinguishing physical feature of a White Father. Moreover, this emphasis on Marian devotion may represent more than just a simple idiosyncrasy. A vast majority of White Fathers missionaries were

[20] The concept of inculturation was not adopted within the mainstream Church until the Second Vatican Council. Inculturation was a main topic of debate throughout the meetings of that Council.

[21] In an echo of Wright, Kassimir goes on, 'the Catholic tradition of the veneration and intercession of Mary and the saints corresponded with pre-Christian appeals and sacrifices to ancestor spirits and local spirit cults' (1999: 258).

[22] The name 'White Fathers' is a preferred nickname of the order. The full official title 'Missionaries of Our Lady of Africa' is today usually shortened to 'Missionaries of Africa'. Nevertheless, the peculiar association of this order with Marian worship remains.

(and still are) recruited from the Central Pyrenees region of Southern France and Northern Spain, in the area around the town of Lourdes. Throughout that region, devotion to a feminine fertility spirit, the so-called 'Black Lady of the Mountains', has been practised since antiquity. It could be argued that the White Fathers' own peculiar connection with Marian devotion may itself represent a transformation of that older belief system.[23]

Even so, it must be stressed that the White Fathers working in Kigezi only ever promoted Holy Mary as a suitable alternative to Nyabingi. Thus, local people's eventual understanding of the Virgin as a direct transformation of the old fertility goddess – as in the above anecdote – would seem to have been an unintended outcome on the missionaries' part. It is here necessary to know something of how the Catholics' beliefs and practices were interpreted and understood by the local actors themselves. For example, at a number of points during my fieldwork, I got some of my Catholic respondents to reflect upon Christian theology, and in particular, upon the relationship between God the Father, God the Son, God the Holy Spirit, and Holy Mary. Each time I did so, I received more or less the same response, that God the Father and Holy Mary are essentially two parts of the same whole, although the latter is somehow 'derived from', or perhaps 'came from', the former (*okwaruka*, lit: 'to come out from'). Whilst God the Father is concerned with all things, Holy Mary is concerned only with issues of fertility.[24]

This model of Christian theology does no doubt stem, at least in part, from the teachings of White Fathers and later Catholic missionaries. To my mind, it also, and perhaps more significantly, represents a direct transformation of indigenous Kiga cosmology. In that system of thought, the high god Kazooba and Nyabingi also exist as two parts of one whole, although the latter derives from the former. Whilst Kazooba is concerned with, and is responsible for, all things, Nyabingi is concerned only with fertility and the misfortunes which affect it. The logic may be understood in very simple terms. Kazooba is the sun,[25] the giver of all energy and therefore life. Nyabingi is concerned with aspects of fertility, or the things which that energy 'gives life to'. Thus, Kazooba and Nyabingi are inseparably inter-connected, yet the latter derives from the former.[26]

Local people therefore interpreted the new doctrine of Christianity through the lens of their existing cosmology. More significantly, they also understood the ordinary practices of Catholicism as transformations of Nyabingi practice. As I argued in Chapter 2, the whole Nyabingi phenomenon is best understood as having been a mechanism of redress for

[23] I would like to thank Herve Maupeu for pointing out this connection to me (pers. comm.).
[24] Similarly, God the Son and God the Holy Spirit were always represented as much lesser, even irrelevant, entities in the overall scheme.
[25] The word 'Kazooba' is a derivative of that for sun, *eizooba*.
[26] The missionaries were always careful not to use the word *Kazooba*, and they therefore employed an alternative, *Ruhanga* (lit: valley). Today, the latter has entered common parlance as the word for the Christian (see for example the United Bible Society's *Runyankore/Rukiga Bible*, 1989 and MRTC, 1996). However, an earlier generation of Catholic Bakiga certainly understood the 'new' Christian God in terms of *Kazooba*. It is today still very common to hear people speak of *Ruhanga* as 'the new God' (*Kazooba* being 'the old God'). In other words, people understand the word *Ruhanga* to be a direct transformation of the (now archaic) *Kazooba*.

misfortune, which created a system of secret exchange networks. Thus, the transformation of Nyabingi into a Catholic symbol really took place when these same mechanisms and exchange practices also became incorporated into normative church practice. Again, the extent to which the European missionaries intentionally cultivated these transformations is somewhat unclear. However, their overall outcome, of convincing local people that Holy Mary was not just an alternative to, but instead a direct equivalent of, Nyabingi, was certainly *not* intended by the White Fathers. For the purposes of illustrating my argument here, I shall focus on just two commonplace church practices. The first is the ritual component of the sacrament of confession, the second a type of meeting which was regularly held, by the missionaries, for the purposes of training new catechists.[27]

In many ways, it was the new Catholic sacrament of confession which most resembled Nyabingi practice for local people. As a result, it was to this ritual that the language of the old Nyabingi became most attached. Consider, for example, a number of aspects of the ritual process here. To begin with, each convert would be led away, individually, to a small hut. This hut would be located within the main compound of the parish, but usually some way apart from its main buildings. In these ways, the process resembled the consultations with Nyabingi which took place in an *orugo's endaaro* hut. As one of my respondents explained to me at length, the confessional hut was indeed often referred to in the vernacular as *endaaro* (Arnold P.).[28] I have so far been unable to corroborate this respondent's account. However, other connections between the Catholic rites of confession and the practices of Nyabingi confirm its general plausibility, given that, once inside the hut, the convert was asked by the unseen priest to describe his or her sins.

Significantly, the word used to gloss sin here was *ekibi*. A more literal meaning of the term *ekibi* is something like 'misfortune'. In addition, it also carries a connotation of something with only a limited effect, such as might affect perhaps just one household.[29] Thus, in effect, inside the confessional the convert was being asked to describe her/his household's misfortunes to an unseen being. This was of course exactly as s/he would have done in Nyabingi's *endaaro* hut. Moreover, at the end of this description, the priest would explain to the confessant that God would forgive these 'sins' in return for some prayer, but also in return for a donation of some crops, or perhaps a chicken or goat, to the church. Most significantly, these donations quickly became known as *okutoija*, the very same term as had previously referred to the prestations made to Nyabingi. Indeed, today, the

---

[27] This being the period before the Second Vatican Council, the mass continued to be given only in Latin. As a result, there was practically no scope for this ritual to be re-interpreted by local people in their own terms.

[28] It is today impossible to ascertain exactly who – the missionaries or the local people – first used local terms in a Christian context in this way. However, it is certainly clear that linguistic borrowing was a two-way thing, given the levels of linguistic competence achieved by the White Fathers. Following a doctrine laid down by their founder, within just a few years of arrival in the field, practically every White Fathers missionary was fluent in the vernacular language (in this case Runyankore/Rukiga).

[29] As would be caused by that household's own *emandwa*. These were the very types for which people had formerly turned to Nyabingi for help.

word *okutoija* is, for most people, known only in reference to donations to the Catholic church, and has ceased to have any meaning at all outside of that context (Angela, Maria Nakacwa, Steven Ariko). *Okutoija* payments to Nyabingi, made through one of her mediums, were always shrouded in the utmost secrecy. Thus, those converts who were required after confession to make *okutoija* to the church, tended also to do so in secret.

Even today, secrecy continues to pervade these sorts of *okutoija* payments.[30] I keenly remember one old churchman telling me some amusing anecdotes about villagers who continued to bring such *okutoija* payments to him in the middle of the night (Fr. Rwabahima). On more than one occasion, he claimed to have woken up to find a goat or some chickens tethered to his front door! I also recall one insight afforded to me by another of my respondents. In this respondent's particular parish – which is located some distance from Mbarara Town – as in many Catholic parishes, it is a common practice for the confessions of an entire congregation to be heard on a specific, designated day. Therefore, this respondent, whose land backed onto that of the parish, suggested that I should count the size of the parish herd immediately before and after each of these confessional days. He predicted that the herd would almost grow in size after each of these days. This I did – in fact, on two separate occasions – and I found his prediction to be correct. Further, he suggested that, given that all of these animals had been given as *okutoija*, and given that all *okutoija* payments should be kept secret, the priest would necessarily have to do something to try to mask the existence of these new animals. Thus, he also predicted that immediately after the herd had thus grown, it would probably just as suddenly shrink again. Once again, my subsequent observations proved this prediction to be correct. I would also add that the local priests also moved their herd around a lot, often in small groups of animals, during the period when it was at its largest. It seemed to me that by keeping the herd on the move in this way, the priests somewhat reduced the chances of anyone noticing that it had suddenly grown.

In an earlier period, payments of *okutoija* to Nyabingi had led to the creation of whole networks of secret exchanges (Chapter 4). These networks emerged from people's attempts to raise the requisite numbers of animals required for making an *okutoija* payment. However, in the sacrament of confession, *okutoija*, which had previously gone to Nyabingi mediums, was now coming to the Catholic church. In a sense, then, the secret exchange networks of Nyabingi were therefore now being redirected towards the Catholic church. During this time, other Nyabingi rituals were transformed into normative church practice, and these further encouraged the redirection of Nyabingi exchange networks towards the Catholic church.

Take, for example, the meetings which were regularly held by the

---

[30] In contemporary parlance, the term *okutoija* is in fact used to refer to *any* donation made to the church. Thus, people use the word to describe everything from the small donations they make during Sunday services (which are usually made up of small amounts of agricultural produce), to the offerings they make as penance after confession, to the annual fees they pay to the church. However, for clarity, throughout this chapter I shall use the term to refer to *only* those payments that are made as penance for a sin (*ekibi*). This type of donation was historically, and remains today, the largest that parishioners make to the church.

missionaries for the purpose of training new catechists. One of my respondents (Arnold P.), a very senior member of the local Catholic laity, described these meetings to me at great length. On each of these occasions, the trainees would meet for several days, and following long prayer sessions, would slaughter animals as offerings to God. Part of the meat would be given to the deity, and the remainder would be consumed by them at huge feasts, along with large amounts of locally brewed alcohol. In these ways, the whole thing was very reminiscent of the Nyabingi *okutamba* ceremony. Indeed, further parallels may also be identified. For one thing, only household heads were entitled to attend them. Keenly aware of the authority these figures had over their households, the Catholic missionaries reasoned that the conversion of any *nyin'eka* would probably bring his entire household into the church fold.[31] As a result, they quickly became favoured converts for the European priests. This resulted in only household heads being invited to undertake the catechism. Yet most importantly, just as the *okutamba* ceremonies had alerted people to who was actively involved with Nyabingi – and therefore, to who might be approached in secret for a contribution towards an *okutoija* payment – so these catechists' meetings quickly came to serve the same purpose. Thus, any individual who had attended such a course, and who was trying to raise an *okutoija* payment demanded of him during confession, would turn first, in secret, to his fellow attenders. Thus, the networks of secret exchange which grew out of *okutoija* payments tended to revolve around these courses (Daniel T.).

The initial transformation of Nyabingi into Holy Mary was therefore more than a purely intellectual development. It also involved a transformation of many of the key practices, the very sociology, of Nyabingi. There is one other key component to be noted here. Previously, at any time of heightened insecurity such as might have resulted from, for example, a flood, or a famine, Nyabingi mediums played a key social role. By redistributing the goods they had previously received in payment to Nyabingi, they effectively negated the worst effects of that particular crisis. Almost from the time of their first arrival in the area, the Catholic missions more or less took over this role. Within just a few days of their arrival in the Southwest, Fr. Laane's party began making long safaris through the surrounding countryside. The primary purpose of these journeys was to distribute foodstuffs, medicines and safety pins for the removal of jiggers. In other words, throughout these safaris, the priests gave out goods useful for addressing various types of 'misfortune' (Job, n.d.: 10). So successful were these safaris in rallying people to the Catholic church, that they soon became a common mode of proselytization in the Southwest.

One of my key respondents on the subject (Arnold P.) also recalls this to have been the Catholics' primary mode of evangelization throughout his childhood and early adult life. As he told me, such safaris, in addition to distributing food and medicine, would also frequently hand out money to

---

[31] This was a reasonable assumption. On several occasions I witnessed household heads converting to a new religion, and each time they forced all the other members of the household also to convert. The White Fathers were quick to realize that to convert the *nyin'eka* was to convert the 15, 30 or 45 members of his household as well.

those in need. He joked that that was why his own father had first become a Catholic, because he had been paid to do so! As a result of these practices, within a short space of time it was to the Catholic church, rather than Nyabingi mediums, that people were turning during times of crisis. Moreover, the White Fathers were, of course, better placed than the Nyabingi mediums to respond to such crises. Unlike the latter, they could simply buy in goods for re-distribution, from outside markets, or even from abroad. Of course, they regularly received foreign donations to aid them in this task. Indeed, the importance of these outside sources cannot be overstated. To any local person of the period, it must have appeared as if the White Fathers had access to limitless, unseen stores of bounty. One of my oldest respondents remembered being simply amazed at a lorry-load of supplies which was delivered to the local mission one Christmas (Mukunda David).

Thus, throughout the living memory of practically all of my respondents, it was primarily to the Catholic church that people would turn in such times of trouble. For example, one of my interviewees (Mrs D.) recalled the significant role played by the White Fathers in distributing milk to the mothers of small children during one particularly bad famine of the early 1950s. Another respondent (Daniel T.) remembered how the missionaries had handed out vegetable foodstuffs to villagers during another bad period in the late 1960s. On the former occasion, the milk the White Fathers handed out had been taken solely from their own herds. During the latter crisis, the missionaries had first distributed the products of their own gardens, and when this had run out, had brought in additional foodstuffs from abroad.[32]

In summary, then, it would appear that the White Fathers had initially sought the demise of Nyabingi through an active promotion of the adoration of Holy Mary. However, primarily as a result of the structure of their sacrament of confession, the form of their catechists' meetings, and their role in distributing goods during times of crisis, Nyabingi instead became transformed 'into' the new symbol of the Virgin Mary, in the minds of many local people. All of this also helps us to answer another key research question concerning this period: why did Nyabingi become a key symbol of the Roman Catholic church, and not the Protestant one, at this time?

Certainly, Marian devotion has, of course, always been more important in the Roman Catholic, rather than the Protestant, tradition. However, this is only part of the answer here. More significant, I think, is the fact that the type of confession, the style of catechist training, and the degree of crisis management practised by the CMS missionaries were vastly different from those of the White Fathers. The CMS practices bore little or no relation to pre-existing Nyabingi practices. Take, for example, the CMS model of confession. Firstly, as members of a Protestant society, the CMS missionaries placed much greater stress upon one's personal responsibility for sin than did their Catholic counterparts.[33] In and of itself, this already limited the

---

[32] It seems that the whole of Uganda was badly hit by this famine, and that very little food was available to buy in any market in Uganda, even from the major ones in Kampala.

[33] In Catholicism, stress is laid on concepts such as 'original sin' for which individuals are not held to be personally responsible.

scope for a local interpretation of 'a sin' as *ekibi*. Household misfortunes were, by definition, externally created, and no one person could ever have anything other than a secondary responsibility for their occurrence.

Secondly, it is key to note that, from at least the late 1920s onwards, many of the new CMS missionaries being sent out to Africa had been strongly influenced by the ideas of the so-called Buchmanite, or 'Oxford', group which they directly transposed to the African setting (Stenning, n.d., 2-6). Perhaps *the* defining feature of the Buchmanite wave – known locally as the '*Balokole* Movement' – lay in its development of mutual confessions. The idea was that personal redemption could be most easily achieved when its pursuit was assisted by others. Thus, one confessed one's sins not to God directly, via one of his priests (as in the Catholic model), but instead to other lay members of one's congregation. In Kigezi, these mutual confessions were initially conducted between just two people. As one might expect, most people chose to conduct these couplings inside their existing *endaaro* huts (*ibid.*: 5, n. 1). However, as the number of converts gradually increased, it became more common for people to make these confessions to whole groups of people, even to entire congregations. For obvious reasons, such large-scale confessions could no longer be conducted inside an *endaaro* hut.

Thirdly, unlike their Catholic counterparts, the CMS missionaries rarely required any penance payment from a confessant. On the contrary, in fact, they encouraged other members of the congregation to congratulate those who had just made a public confession on their bravery, as a means of encouraging others to do the same. Some people seem to have interpreted this as a request to give gifts. Thus, at least one of my respondents recalls that, rather than having to give away any goods at the end of his/her confession, a confessant may even have expected to receive some (Natumanyisa).

Other practices of the CMS were equally incompatible with the logic of Nyabingi practices. For example, in terms of the training they provided for new catechists, the CMS missionaries took a very different approach from that of the White Fathers. It is also significant that of all of the Roman Catholic – or, indeed, all other – missionary orders, the White Fathers placed the greatest emphasis upon the catechism. For them, *all* new converts were required to have a thorough understanding of the religion they were about to enter. Thus, all were required to attend the catechism course, for an extended period of time.[34] Indeed, the catechism offered by the White Fathers was (and continues to be) by far the longest in the entire Catholic church. As a result, all such courses were offered at the local level. To have made people travel long distances to attend them would simply have been impractical. Thus, local people's interpretation of catechism meetings as essentially the same as *okutamba* ceremonies, had both the time and the space to develop. Everyone was required to attend them, and often more than once a week, for many months or even years, in their local areas.

---

[34] Or more accurately, all household heads were required to attend it. The White Fathers reasoned – quite rightly – that, given the position of a *nyin'eka* within his homestead, it was likely that any Christian education he received would certainly be passed on to other members of the household. As a result, the missionaries reasoned that it was necessary to provide instruction only to these individuals.

Compare this with the catechism offered by the CMS. Quite early on, CMS missionaries operating in this part of Uganda realized that they simply did not have the resources to offer a full catechism to every convert. As a result, an appeal for more funds was soon sent to the CMS higher authorities in Great Britain. However, the request was flatly denied. According to the higher authorities, not only were additional funds unavailable, but they were also not necessary. For them, the idea of offering a full catechism to all new converts – which may anyway have been an idea simply copied from the White Fathers – was simply ludicrous. Rather, they favoured a much more elitist approach. Rather than offering a basic training to every convert, it would be much better to offer a much fuller Christian education to an able few. This would, in the long run, create a much more effective and stable Christian society (see, for example, Hansen, 1984: 237–42 and *passim*).[35] Thus, a handful of the most promising candidates were selected for an education in one of Uganda's English-style public schools. However, such schools were very few in number at this time, and none had yet been opened in Kigezi. Thus, attending one of these establishments involved being sent away from home, for a long period of time. The CMS strategy was perhaps undertaken with an eye to getting 'their' converts into the best positions in the native administration. If this was the plan, then it was certainly highly successful. However, in that it was not undertaken by every household head, that it involved no exchanges, and was conducted far from home, the Christian training offered by the CMS bore no relationship whatsoever to an *okutamba* ceremony.[36]

Furthermore, during their 'recruitment safaris', CMS missionaries did not distribute goods in the manner of the White Fathers. On the contrary, in fact, on their tours of the local countryside, the Protestants instead *received* large offerings. This is because, during these tours, they always stayed in the households of local dignitaries (Ngologoza, 1998 [1968]: 73).[37] Then, as now, local custom dictated that, as house guests, they must be given copious amounts of presents – livestock and beer – both by their host and by their the host's associates. Moreover, the CMS missions did little to help people during times of 'general crisis'. Certainly, by 1925, Drs Sharpe and Smith had opened two hospitals in Kigezi, and were treating many local people for leprosy, in particular. Nevertheless, the CMS missions did little to help in times of general misfortune, such as resulted from a drought. On the contrary, there is, in fact, some evidence that certain missions even increased the size of contributions required of their congregations during such periods.

[35] According to Hansen, this thinking drew heavily on contemporary ideas concerning the merits of an English public school education. He quotes the minutes of a CMS Missionary Committee meeting of 11 September 1911, 'we feel that these Boarding Schools should do for these people do what our Public Schools have done for the British nation' (Hansen, 1984: 238).
[36] In adopting this policy, the hand of the local missionaries was heavily forced by the thinking of higher CMS authorities in Great Britain (see note 35). The extent to which missionaries in the field agreed with their higher authorities is not clear. Nevertheless, by that time, no such Boarding School had been opened in Kigezi. As a result, all of the catechumens had to be sent off, for substantial periods of time, to schools some distance from their homes.
[37] This contrasts with the practice of the White Fathers, who as a general rule always stayed in their own camps whilst on tour.

For example, Rutanga records one incident of 1928 during which the District Commissioner of Kigezi admonished one mission for continuing to receive donations of milk, from members of its congregation, during a drought (1991: 118–19). It would seem that the mission's own animals had died from the effects of the drought, and that, as a result, the Europeans had demanded more milk contributions, to supplement their own diet.

For various reasons, then, the practices of the White Fathers, unlike those of the CMS, came to be interpreted, by many local people, as more akin to those of the Nyabingi complex of old. It was because of this, then, that by about the mid-1930s, it was the Catholic Holy Mary which had come to represent the most complete transformation of the old spirit, in many people's minds. Further, it might also be noted here that, in the process, the old spirit had also become, for the very first time – and in a very real sense – 'incorporated'. In other words, prior to the White Fathers' arrival, Nyabingi had been a feminine-gendered entity, but not an anthropomorphic one. The new Holy Mary, on the other hand, of whom statutes and other effigies existed, was a real woman with a body, which could be located in a real space. Thus, it was to the Virgin Mary, rather than to Nyabingi, that people now turned in times of crisis. It was to the Catholic church, rather than to Nyabingi mediums, that people made *okutoija* payments. It was Mary, rather than Nyabingi, who was thought most capable of addressing one's misfortunes.[38] And as ever, the most serious type of misfortune a household could suffer was that of a wife's barrenness. Thus, it was from Holy Mary, rather than Nyabingi, that barren women received apparitions in their sleep (*okworekwa*).[39] And communicating through these visions, it was Holy Mary, rather than Nyabingi, who took responsibility for this barrenness. It was She who identified which other wife had offended Her, thereby causing Her to inflict this misfortune in the first place.

In practically all ways, in fact, by about the mid-1930s the logic and sociology of Nyabingi had become the logic and sociology of the Catholic Holy Mary. In particular, just as much Nyabingi activity had reflected a certain structural tension within the Kiga polygamous household (Chapter 2), so Marian devotion had now come to exist as a reflection of the same. It is this factor, above all else, which is crucial for understanding certain later developments, which are also central to our story here. Simply stated, from the mid-1940s onwards, the basic structure of the Kiga household began to change dramatically (among certain sections of the population, at least). As it did so, women who had previously relied upon Nyabingi/Holy Mary as a mechanism of redress for their misfortunes became more vulnerable than ever. This was especially true for those women for whom Nyabingi/Holy Mary had enabled some redress when a *nyin'eka* had used 'their' animals in an inappropriate way. Moreover, this newly engendered vulnerability quickly translated into an ever deeper devotion towards the divine female, and ever more frequent requests for her benevolent intervention.

[38] Which may have been caused by, for example, their *emandwa*.
[39] Precisely because these apparitions always occurred at night, the missionaries regarded them as 'dreams', rather than 'visions' proper, and therefore, did not regard them as being of great importance (Arnold P.).

The Kiga Diaspora

It is not my intention here to develop an exhaustive, or even a continuous, history of the Catholic church in South-western Uganda, but instead to draw out a number of episodes from that larger history which are relevant to the Kanungu story, as it later developed. The second episode from that broader history with which I am interested here concerns a series of changes to patterns of Marian devotion which occurred around (roughly) the middle of the century. From the mid-1940s onwards, the basic structure of the polygamous Kiga household, as described above, began to change dramatically for certain sections of the Kiga population.

This change was a direct result of colonial government policy. By the early 1940s, the population of Kigezi District was growing by between twelve and fifteen thousand people a year,[40] the highest in the whole Protectorate. Alarmed at the overcrowding this would eventually cause on Kigezi's southern hills in particular, the British embarked in 1946 on a programme of assisted relocation to less densely populated agricultural zones. The initial destination sites were all in Northern Kigezi, in the areas around Kambuga and Bugangari, and over the next five years more than 15,000 people were shifted to these areas.[41] Then, from the early 1950s onwards, following offers from the kings of the neighbouring kingdoms of Toro and Ankole, several sites beyond the borders of Kigezi were also selected. In Toro, to the north of Lake Edward, Bakiga settled at Nkongora and Bigodi, and in Ankole, to the north and west of the Kigezi Hills, people were relocated in Bunyaruguru and in the Eastern Rwampara Hills around Murizi/Bugamba (KDA – Dev. 4/1 II: *Kigezi Resettlement Scheme: Policy Reports and General*; Dev. 4/3 VI: *Resettlement in Toro*; Dev. 4/3 VII: *Resettlement in Toro*; Dev. 4/10 I: *Resettlement in Toro – Kibale etc.*).

Living conditions for the migrants were initially very harsh. Until their new gardens had begun to yield, the new settlers were reliant on food provided by the administration, which, despite the best efforts of local officials, rarely met demand. The archival records are replete with letters of complaint to the District Commissioner from those administering the settlements. In one, dated 23 September 1949, the local official complains that, although the Bakiga living in his area of control required more than 3 tonnes of food aid per week, the money provided him by the government for the whole month of September 1949 had purchased only 7 tonnes in total (KDA – S.C. Dwankey to DC Kigezi District, 23 September 1949, Dev. 4/1 II: *Kigezi Resettlement Scheme: Policy Reports and General*). Attacks by wild animals were another constant problem, the *saza* chiefs of the settlement areas eventually being forced to organize regular communal hunts against

[40] The total 'African' population of the District was then set at 419,588 (this figure, like all those contained in this paragraph, derives from KDA – Appendix A, *Kigezi District Annual Report* for 1949).
[41] By 1952, the number had reached almost 18,000 (KDA – C. Adm. 27: *District History and Historical Notes*)

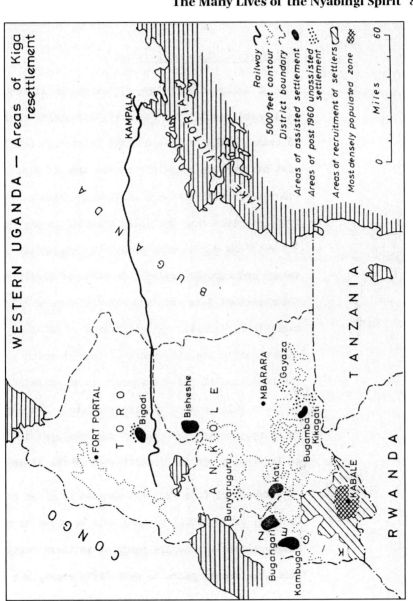

Map 3.1 Map of Kiga settlement, c. 1946–69 (Source: Yeld. n.d.. 61)

them (*ibid.*). However, perhaps the greatest risk to the settlers was that of disease. For example, several died from the poor sanitary conditions of the resettlement zones, until the administration invested in proper boreholes at the sites (KDA – DC Toro District to ADC (Land Settlement) Kigezi District, 16th September 1957. Dev. 4/3 VII: *Resettlement in Toro*). An even greater number were claimed by malaria, a disease the émigrés first encountered following the relocation. Malaria was then non-existent in their former home area of Southern Kigezi. At one point, so badly did this disease affect the migrants, that the scheme was effectively suspended for almost 8 months, in November 1948 (KDA – Appendix A, *Kigezi District Annual Report* for 1949).

Everyday life in the settlement zones was therefore more difficult than it had been in the Southern Kigezi Hills. However, the act of emigration also affected people's lives in more profound ways. In particular, the entire structure of the *orugo* became altered. In general, settlers tended to migrate with only one wife. The government strictly controlled the amount of farmland any one individual could demarcate as his own to as little as 3 acres,[42] and, as a result, there was not enough land available for more than one wife to farm. Should *nyin'eka* then subsequently bring another wife from his former home in Southern Kigezi, or should he marry a new wife in the Diaspora, he would therefore have to buy more land at the settlement site for her to live on and farm. There was no guarantee, however, that a purchased plot would be contiguous with the original one, and, in this way, the compact nature of the Kiga *orugo* broke down. In the former home area, all of the wives of a household head (*nyin'eka*) had lived in separate houses (*enju*) within a single homestead (*orugo*). In the new circumstances, the wives' *enju* tended to be spread out over different plots, sometimes as much as several miles apart. For example, at the settlement site of Mwizi in the Eastern Rwampara Hills,[43] most of the Bakiga who migrated from Kigezi continue today to have many wives, although these are rarely, if ever, located on one site.

Other aspects of the migration also led to this 'atomization' of the *orugo*. For example, it is significant that the Bakiga emigrants were not always household heads. In some cases it was sons who took up the administration's offer of assistance to move, and some used the opportunity to effectively remove their mother's *enju* from the larger structure of the *orugo*. For example, one respondent (Mary K.) recounted the circumstances surrounding her father's resettlement in Toro, in 1954. Her father was then the oldest living son of an aged *nyin'eka*. Setting up his new homestead at the resettlement site, he refused to allow his father, the *nyin'eka*, to bring any wife other than his own mother to live at the new site, informing him that, should he wish to do so, he would have to locate them on land away

---

[42] The administration's aim was for each settler to have a 12 acre plot, but use only 3 acres of this as agricultural space. Of the remaining 9 acres, 3 were to be used for domestic buildings, and 6 were to be left for future expansion (specifically, they were to be set aside for his sons to build on later, following their own marriages). 12 acres was considerably less than the size of an average *rugo's* holding in the Southern Kigezi Hills (KDA – C Adm. 27, *District History and Historical Notes*).

[43] I conducted much of my own research on the effects of the resettlement scheme in Mwizi, which is just a few miles from Bugamba Village proper.

from his plot. Thus, through the actions of the son, the various *enju* of the old man's many wives came to be dispersed in the resettlement zone.

If Kiga *orugo* therefore became dispersed in the Diaspora, relations of exchange within them remained relatively unaffected. In other words, in a normative sense, at least, *nyin'eka* continued to control all the goods flowing into and out of the *orugo*, and his wives still held expectations of how this control should be exercised. However, tensions between these two principles now increased. One primary cause stemmed from that central component of the '*obukago*' relationship which required these reciprocal bond-partners to offer each other mutual defence. Be it in times of war, or during a quarrel in a local bar, even today a man's *mukago* is compelled to jump to his defence in the event of fighting. Yet because of this, the reputation of the Bakiga amongst neighbouring peoples – as violent and warlike – counted heavily against the settlers in their attempts to form *bakago* relations with their new Batoro and Banyankole neighbours (Daniel T.). Fearing that forming such a relationship with a Mukiga would result in one becoming compelled to intervene frequently in fights, the Batoro and Banyankole neighbours of these settlers were simply reluctant to do so. Given that exchanges with *bakago* constituted the principal way, other than plundering a wife's herd, through which a *nyin'eka* could get cows for future bride-wealth payments, it is clear that tensions within the *orugo* became greatly increased in the Diaspora. In other words, within the Diaspora, Kiga house-hold heads became even more reliant on 'inappropriate' usages of their wives' herds than ever before.

As a result of this, Bakiga women in the Diaspora became more reliant than ever before on Holy Mary/Nyabingi's benevolent intervention, for purposes of seeking redress. However, given that the *orugo's* separate *enju* were now dispersed, the 'old' pattern of intervention was no longer tenable. Previously, Holy Mary/Nyabingi would appear to the offended wife (Wife A) in a dream, and communicating through her, would order another wife (Wife B) to give her an animal. However, in the Diaspora, Wife B might live as much as five miles away, and the offended wife might never even see her. In such circumstances, it would obviously be difficult for Holy Mary/Nyabingi to offer any mechanism of redress for Wife A. Such visions there-fore became less common, and attempts by offended wives to seek redress tended to take the form of a general devotion to the Holy Mother. Drawing more on a Catholic doctrine of an 'indirect divine justice' – that wrongs done to you will be compensated in the afterlife – these women simply attended church more often, and prayed more seriously to Holy Mary, requesting that she might see their troubles, and take pity on them (Juliet, Linda).

And these developments are of particular relevance to our story here, not least given the fact that a majority of the MRTC's membership was made up of Marian devotees from the Kiga Diaspora (see Chapter 5). Moreover, it is also relevant that the *entire* population of Kanungu derives from the Kigezi resettlement scheme. Located as it is in the middle of the former Kambuga resettlement zone, the valley in which Kanungu lies was completely unpopulated prior to the inauguration of the scheme. Thus, Ceredonia and several other leaders of the MRTC were in a sense themselves the 'children of the Diaspora'. However, before going on to explore the genesis of the MRTC in more detail, it is necessary to say a little more about how the practices of Marian devotion developed over time in the parishes and diocese of South-western Uganda.

The new Catholic clergy and the Legion of Mary

I am not attempting here to develop a comprehensive history of the Catholic church in the Southwest, but instead to highlight a number of aspects of that broader history which are relevant to the Kanungu story, as this later unfolded. The third, and final, episode from that history in which I am interested here is the major change in the organization of the Catholic church in the Southwest (and beyond) which began in roughly the late 1960s, reached its zenith in the mid-late 1980s, and was largely concluded by the early 1990s. I refer here to the gradual withdrawal of Euro-American missionary priests from parishes, and dioceses, throughout the area, and their replacement with indigenous clergy.

Still by the early 1960s, the vast majority of Catholic clergy working in the Southwest – as in some other parts of Uganda as well – were Euro-American missionary priests (Isichei, 1995: 325–6). However, over the course of that decade, a combination of factors resulted in this situation gradually beginning to change. On the one hand, the country's achievement of independence (in October 1962) seems to have resulted in at least some foreign priests losing faith in the missionary enterprise *per se*. More significantly, reflecting the 'general decline in priestly and religious vocations in the western world' which occurred during this period, many of the older missionary societies – including that of the White Fathers – were by this time also finding it increasingly difficult to recruit new members (*ibid.*). On the other hand, various forces within Uganda itself, not least independence, but also the major expansion of National Catholic Seminaries such as that of Katigondo (in Masaka) as well as the broader effects of the Second Vatican Council (1962-65, with its general emphasis upon the 'Africanization' of local church structures), had by then resulted in ever greater numbers of indigenous Ugandans taking Holy Orders. Indeed, it is interesting to note here that one of the first African priests to be ordained in Ankole was none other than Fr. Dominic Kataribaabo (who took Holy Orders on 8 August 1965). And that the first Ugandan to be made Bishop in the Southwest was John Baptist Kakubi (who took over the See of Mbarara on 26 June 1969). Kakubi also went on to play a significant role in the whole MRTC drama (as will be described in Chapter 4).

However, if these, then, were the general forces which resulted in the former missionary clergy eventually being replaced by a new indigenous one, it must be stressed that this process was always highly uneven. In other words, although more and more parishes were taken over by indigenous priests from the late 1960s onwards, the exact timing of this shift varied from parish to parish, and, in each instance, depended on a range of idiosyncratic factors. Specifically, it often depended on the timing of the existing missionary priest's retirement from service (even where disillusionment had set in, most missionary priests nevertheless continued to work through to their retirement). Yet this factor is itself interesting, in illustrating why the overall process also effectively 'sped up' from the late 1970s onwards, and reached its zenith in the late 1980s. Given that a majority of these missionary priests would have entered service in the 1940s and '50s (again, see *ibid.*, 325), it follows that this was simply the period during which most of them were reaching retirement age. Thus, to take just two examples here, it was in around 1989 that the last missionary priest retired – and was replaced by an African clergyman – in Bugamba's local Catholic parish, Rushanje parish. It was in 1987 that the same thing happened in Kanungu's local parish, Makiro parish. Yet the point is that, uneven though this process was, it resulted in a number of significant developments within local Catholic practice. By far the most important of these, for our story here, is the effect this shift had in promoting various forms of 'popular' religious worship, in parishes throughout the Southwest and beyond (and for ease of definition here, I will follow Kassimir in taking 'popular' Catholicism to be any 'interpretation of the faith which goes beyond the basic sacramental system of universal Catholicism', 1999: 248).

It has long been acknowledged by historians of African Christianity that the years immediately following the Second Vatican Council witnessed a marked increase in all sorts of popular expressions of Christianity, across the African continent (as, indeed, they did elsewhere in the world as well). Moreover, that predominant among these various expressions was an 'efflorescence of Marian apparitions' (*ibid.*, 328). Thus, for example, through-out the late 1960s and early '70s, sightings of the Virgin were reported from as far apart as Egypt, Nigeria, South Africa, and elsewhere (cf. Mauder, 1991). In most commentaries, all of this is usually interpreted as an outcome of Vatican II, and in particular of the specific version of 'inculturation' that was adopted at that Council. Simply put, the version of inculturation which became officially sanctioned at that time was effectively 'top-down' in nature, and therefore often resulted in local church hierarchies demonstrating a certain 'reluctance and/or incapacity to incorporate widely held spiritual concerns into officially acceptable practices' (*ibid.*: 249; also David Maxwell, pers. comm.). The argument, then, is that this situation in fact *increased* feelings of 'trouble' and 'alienation' among certain sections of the African congregation (which is somewhat ironic, given that Rome's original move towards Africanization had been explicitly designed to assuage precisely these sorts of problems, Isichei, 1995: 327). Moreover, that it was this growing alienation which resulted in people increasingly expressing their faith in ways which were not necessarily officially sanctioned by the church (for example, in the form of Marian apparitions and the like).

However, it is also crucial to note here that, as the political scientist Ron Kassimir has described – in his seminal studies of the church in the nearby Catholic diocese of Fort Portal (n.d. & 1999)[44] – Uganda always represented

---

[44] In 1999, the Catholic Diocese of Fort Portal became part of the newly erected Archdiocese of Mbarara (see Epilogue). My discussion in this paragraph is based largely on Kassimir, 1999: 251–3.

something of an anomaly to this wider, continent-wide, pattern. Unlike in so many other African countries, in Uganda, the late 1960s and '70s – and even the early 1980s – witnessed very few such public expressions of 'popular' religiosity among any of its Catholic populations. The reasons for this are various, but largely relate to the peculiarly high degree of control which Uganda's Catholic hierarchies were by then able to exercise over their congregations (and which they could thus use to effectively curtail any such expression of public religiosity).

This exceptional degree of control was itself a (partial) outcome of colonial missionary history. Specifically, although Uganda's Catholics were in many ways systematically discriminated against by the state throughout the colonial era – in favour of the country's Protestant populations (cf. Hansen, 1984) – the Catholic missions did also benefit from at least some colonial government policies. In particular, they too gained from a decision taken by the British administration, some time in the late 1950s, not to allow into the Protectorate any missionary societies outside of the mainstream Protestant and Catholic ones. Thus, in a memorandum issued by the Permanent Secretary of the Ministry of Social Services in May 1957, warnings were made against all 'small missionary sects'. On the one hand, it was felt that 'a new mission could only...succeed by dividing the existing Churches and creating another body of converts from one or the other. This is not thought to be at all a desirable development.' On the other hand, it was also feared that smaller sects would inevitably decline, leading to their members starting their own movements: 'experience in some territories has been that in a short time the breakaway Church becomes anti-Government and subversive' (R. A. Malyn, cited in Kassimir, 1999: 252, order of quotes reversed). All of which meant, then, that, although during the colonial era there was frequently 'intense competition for members and political power between followers of the Anglican and Catholic churches', at the same time 'their mutually privileged position provided incentives to Ugandans to be affiliated with one of the two mainstream churches' (ibid.). This, in turn, meant that local Catholic hierarchies always commanded strong authority over their various congregations.

Moreover, this general pattern largely continued into the post-colonial era as well. Thus, during the Idi Amin years (1971–9) all denominations other than Protestant, Catholic and Muslim were effectively banned. During the Obote II regime (1980–85) it became even less likely that anyone would attempt to affiliate with a non-mainstream organization. After all, this was the period during which even the mainstream Catholic church was itself regarded with a high degree of suspicion by the state (because of its associations with the opposition Democratic Party, DP). More significantly, it was also the time during which government forces were waging a major counter-insurgency against at least one Catholic-derived militia, Andrew Kayiira's Uganda Freedom Movement (UFM), and in which the authorities thus regarded any non-affiliated organization as a criminal threat. Thus, it would seem that once again here, 'in the context of extreme political oppression, the Catholic Church became an important component of the survival strategies of its members'. It was for this same reason that those same members 'were thus unlikely to provoke the opprobrium of church leaders, whatever the content of their private beliefs and practices' (*ibid.*). Hence, although the years immediately following the Second Vatican Council were marked by an efflorescence of popular expressions of Catholic religiosity across Africa, in Uganda, local Catholic hierarchies always had enough influence over their congregations to stop such occurrences from happening there.

However, if this was generally the case until (roughly) the mid-1980s, from that time onwards, things began to change rapidly. Specifically, from about 1985 onwards, not only did Uganda begin to witness an ever greater number of incidents involving popular expressions of Christianity involving Catholics. In addition, it also saw a range of new independent groups beginning to spring up among Catholic populations throughout the country. Thus, for example, this was the period during which a young Catholic woman called Alice Auma living in Northern Uganda began to receive spiritual messages from a dead Italian soldier called 'Lakwena'. The woman, who is better known as 'Alice Lakwena', went on to form the Holy Spirit Movement (HSM). Between August 1986 and November 1987, the HSM – now calling themselves the Holy Spirit Mobile Forces (HSMF) – waged an insurgency against the newly installed government of President Yoweri Museveni's National Resistance Movement (NRM) which was in many ways a precursor to the current war in Northern Uganda (see Allen, 1991 and 2006; Behrend, 1999). Yet the point is that Lakwena's HSM was only one such group to emerge in Uganda at this time. In addition, this was also the period during which the Catholic 'prophet' Dosteo Bisaaka began to gather followers to himself – under the auspices of his organization the Holy Quaternity Movement (HQM) – in Toro. It was also the time during which a number of Marian visionaries in the Southwest began the MRTC (a subject to which I will return in the next chapter).

However, the point here is that, in trying to understand the context within which these various expressions of popular Catholicism began occurring all over Uganda, and the circumstances in which these various Catholic-initiated groups began emerging throughout the country, Ron Kassimir points to an erosion of the control that local Catholic hierarchies had formerly had over their congregations. He sees as the primary cause of this erosion the political agenda of the new NRM government (1999: *passim*). Specifically, as John Mary Waliggo, and others, have also discussed (for example, Waliggo, 1995: 116–19), from the very beginning, all NRM policy was oriented towards 'rigorously fighting tribalism and religious sectarianism' ('The Ten Point Programme of the NRM', by the NRM Secretariat, cited in *ibid.*: 118). One of the primary ways in which the new government hoped to achieve the second part of this proposition was through the opening up of the religious space in Uganda. In this way, not only were formerly marginalized religious groups – such as the country's Catholics – encouraged to play a much more active part in political affairs (an invitation which Bishop Kakubi, for one, took very seriously, actively encouraging his regional clergy – and South-western Catholics generally – to take up positions in the nascent 'Local Council' system, Fr. Katwire).

In addition, all religious denominations and organizations were now permitted, for the first time, to operate freely in the country (indeed, in many instances they were actively encouraged to do so). This new freedom of religious association was eventually to become enshrined, as a basic right for all Ugandan citizens, in the country's new Constitution (when it was finally adopted on 22 September 1995). However, the main point here is that, from the point of view of Uganda's Catholic hierarchies, the NRM's reforms were always something of a 'curate's egg'. Whilst, on the one hand, these reforms certainly did result in the Catholic hierarchy being much better placed within the national political arena, on the other hand, they also presented ordinary Catholics with much greater scope to explore modes of religiosity, and forms of religious organization, which were not necessarily sanctioned by the mainstream church. The argument of Kassimir, and others, is that it was these new opportunities which led to an erosion of the control that local Catholic hierarchies had formerly had over their congregations, and eventually to the outpourings of popular expressions of Christianity described above.

There can be no doubt whatsoever that the new religious freedoms of the mid-1980s were certainly a major contributing factor to the increase in instances of popular expressions of Christianity which occurred in Uganda from (roughly) this time onwards. Indeed, as will be explored in detail in the following chapters, the NRM's reforms played a decisive role in shaping not only the context from which the MRTC emerged, but also the ways in which the group's theology and practice were to develop over time. Nevertheless, it is my contention here that these reforms still only constituted *one part* of the story. As my own research data from parishes throughout the rural Southwest show, an equally, if not more, important factor in the rise of popular Christianity during this period was the coterminous shift in the composition of the local clergy, which I described at the beginning of this section. Of key significance here was the way in which the establishment of this new indigenous clergy led to an even greater elevation of the Legion of Mary than anything that had been experienced before.

The Legion of Mary had continued to operate as a coherent lay organization – in the rural parishes, at least – from the time of the White Fathers' arrival in the area onwards. On this point, Kassimir notes that, by the mid-1960s, the organization had come to be regarded as something of a failure by certain elements of the Catholic hierarchy in Toro diocese. For example, he quotes a 1966 report by the then Lay Apostolate for the diocese, which lamented that the organization had become 'a reserve for old and uneducated women', and was in urgent need of modernization – '*aggiornamento*' – if it was to reach out to more 'educated' people (Magambo, cited in Kassimir, 1999: 258). Yet this it never quite managed to do, and thus, still by the early 1980s, it had 'failed to attract the elite, young people, and especially males' (*ibid.*). All of this is quite understandable, given the evidence, and the arguments, I have developed in this chapter. Given the cultural logics within which the Legion was from the very beginning embedded, it is quite understandable that the organization would have never been able to attract the (then) newly emerging urban elites, large numbers of men, and so on.

Although this may well have been to the chagrin of church leaders – during the early years of the post-colonial period, in particular – it cannot in itself be taken as indicative of some sort of general decline in the Legion's activities during the 1960s and '70s. As the testimonies of my various respondents on the subject indicate, although the Legion's membership certainly did continue to be made up of mostly rural women – and most of them members of the Kiga Diaspora – the organization's various activities nevertheless did continue apace throughout this period.

However, these same testimonies also indicate that the Legion did also experience something of a 'reinvigoration', at the hands of the new indigenous clergy, from around the early to mid-1980s onwards (Frs. Francis and Rwabahima). Specifically, it would seem that some members of the new clergy – and especially some of those based in and around the parishes of the former relocation scheme – at this time began to 'elevate' the profile, and the activities, of their local 'Legion of Mary' groups, in a number of ways.[45] And although this 'elevation' took different forms in different parishes, certain common practices can be identified. For example, I have documented at least 8 parishes in which large, and elaborate, new Marian shrines were constructed in parish compounds during the late 1980s. In addition, a number of my respondents recall new recruitment practices being introduced for the Legion at this time. These included, in one instance, it becoming a requirement for *all* of the Catholic women in one parish to attend the local branch's weekly meetings (Katume Sarah). Most significantly of all, in a majority of instances, this general promotion of the Legion also involved the introduction of new, 'popular' forms of devotional practice within the organization's weekly meetings. Indeed, from about the mid-1980s onwards, some parish priests even allowed women, for the first time, to recount publicly details of their night-time visions of the Virgin Mary (*okworekwa*) at Legion meetings.[46] At least two of my respondents had been permitted to recount details of Marian apparitions in this way (for example, Angela). As a result, discussion of these night-time visions soon became completely 'normalized'. To such a degree, in fact, that when I asked one respondent (Katushaabe) – whom I knew to have been a Marian seer at this time – to describe her apparitions to me, she talked very enthusiastically, and entirely uninterrupted, for more than an hour.

The new clergy's motivations for elevating the Legion of Mary in this way are not entirely clear, although they may well have been motivated by a desire to generate greater revenues for the parishes in which they were now taking over. Lacking the kind of transnational networks of support upon which their White Father predecessors had previously drawn, many of these clergymen lacked other sources of funds, and would thus have come to regard parishioners' contributions as a primary source of revenues

[45] However, it should be stressed that it was only *some* members of the new indigenous clergy who sought to promote the Legion during this time. In addition, at least some of the new African priests – including, interestingly, the one who took over Kanungu's local parish (Chapter 4) – were, for one reason or another, 'Marian sceptics'.
[46] Although the White Fathers' initial promotion of the Virgin had led to a proliferation of these visionary dreams, the missionaries had never permitted the content of these apparitions to be discussed in public.

for parish projects, developmental outreach, and so on. Perhaps more aware of the inherent connection between the Virgin Mary and exchanges of substance than their missionary predecessors had been, it is also not surprising that at least some of the new clergy should have come to regard a promotion of the Legion as a primary mechanism through which to achieve these revenue increases.

Certainly, this is borne out by the fact that, just as descriptions of Marian visions were now made public, so too were the demands for *okutoija* payments which inevitably stemmed from them. In other words, whereas previously, demands for *okutoija* had only ever been made within the private confines of the confessional, now such demands began to be recounted openly, in the context of Legion meetings. Unsurprisingly, my respondents recalled that the visions usually demanded these payments to be made either by the visionary's husband, or by one of her co-wives (or sometimes, by both).[47] For example, in one case I know of, one woman publicly recounted a vision in which her co-wife was ordered, by the Virgin, to pay the church two cows. In another, a visionary publicly stated that Holy Mary had ordered her co-wife to pay one cow and several goats. Interestingly, that same vision also commanded the same co-wife to stop producing any more children for her husband (Hilary Bagasora). It should also be noted that, as these two examples also show, the amount of *okutoija* being requested here was also far greater than that which would ever have been asked for in the confessional. In other words, although some priests certainly did – and still do – ask for animals in the privacy of the confessional, it is unimaginable, to my mind, that any would ever have asked for a penance payment of quite this amount of livestock.

Yet if this *was* the new clergymen's main motivation for revitalizing the Legion of Mary at this time, then this strategy was, at best, only partially successful. After all, people's primary motivation for making such *okutoija* payments had always been to provide some sort of 'insurance' against later instances of more general misfortune. Thus it follows that, with larger payments, Legion members doubtless also expected a greater degree of protection and support during such times of drought, famine, or whatever. Yet given that a majority of the new parish priests did not have access to the kinds of transnational networks of support on which their missionary predecessors had drawn, in most instances they were still simply unable to provide this kind of assistance (even where they had collected large amounts of *okutoija*).

As confirmation of this point, it is interesting to compare the activities of the few White Fathers who still remained in South-western parishes at this time, with the practices of the new indigenous clergymen. What emerges from such a comparison is the fact that the missionary priests were always able to distribute resources on a scale which was simply vastly superior to anything that could ever be achieved by (practically) any African priest. Thus, for example, I have documented the case of a Belgian White Father

---

[47] Although such requests may not be made directly. In some instances, the visions simply stated what would happen to that husband, or co-wife, if they did *not* make such a payment.

based at a parish in Bushenyi District, who, throughout the 1980s, used funds he raised abroad to fund a complex network of agricultural extension and cash-cropping work in both his own, and several neighbouring, parishes. In another example, I have recorded details of a French White Father based at another parish in Bushenyi, who during this period used monies raised in France to keep two large orphanages – each home to several dozen abandoned children – in operation. In a third example, I was given details of a German missionary priest – also a White Father – who, throughout the 1980s and into the '90s, raised money abroad to fund a sizeable industrial-agricultural complex (with a view to raising incomes throughout the whole diocese). Yet against such examples, it is simply impossible to imagine that any of the new African clergy – who were replacing the former missionary priests in ever greater numbers by this time – would have had access to the resources necessary to live up to the kinds of expectations which such actions would have engendered among ordinary parishioners. In other words, a degree of general disgruntlement among ordinary Catholics was perhaps inevitable from the very moment when the former missionary priests began to be replaced by their new indigenous counterparts.

Indeed, this certainly seems to have been the case in Rushanje Parish, at least, where the last remaining White Father – a Canadian priest called Fr. Vincent – retired in 1989. Thus, in the years before his departure, Fr. Vincent's actions – as those of his missionary predecessors had also been – were marked by an extensive range of agricultural support services, famine relief, orphan care, and various other projects besides, throughout the local area. Yet with Fr. Vincent's retirement, these sorts of services practically disappeared, almost overnight (certainly, this is how the transition is remembered by many of my respondents). The fact that a degree of general disillusionment resulted is evidenced not only by my respondents' discussions on this point, but also by the fact that church attendance in the parish dropped off significantly in real terms, in the years immediately following Fr. Vincent's departure (as can be deduced from the numbers of baptisms and marriages recorded during this period). Most significantly of all, anecdotal evidence suggests that this general pattern – following the retirement of a missionary priest – was being reproduced in parish after parish, across the Southwest, around this time.[48] Moreover, if there *was* a degree of general disgruntlement at this time, then it seems that the actions

---

[48] I have personally heard people make general comments to this effect in at least a dozen or more of the South-western parishes in which I have worked. Moreover, it would be interesting to examine what impact this shift from a predominantly missionary, to a largely indigenous, Catholic clergy had in other parts of the country as well. In particular, further research might also explore what part it played in shaping the context from which Alice Lakwena's Holy Spirit Movement – and later Joseph Kony's Lord's Resistance Army (LRA) – emerged in Acholiland, from the late 1980s onwards. To date, the institutional history of the Catholic church in Northern Uganda has remained a largely underdeveloped area of research in respect of our understanding of the social conditions from which the LRA emerged (and this, despite otherwise excellent accounts of the LRA's belief system, and the ways in which this overlaps with, and extends, indigenous Acholi cosmology; see, for example, Behrend, 1999). Yet a greater knowledge of that institutional history would clearly add to our knowledge of those conditions, not least given the fact that Joseph Kony himself was a former Catholic seminarian.

of some of the new priests in re-elevating the Legion of Mary only exacerbated this situation. Thus, by the late 1980s, the new clergy's promotion of popular religiosity within the Legion meetings – and its consequences – seem to have resulted in regular members of the Legion being even more disillusioned with the mainstream Catholic church than most.[49] Certainly, this much emerges from a study of the early history of the MRTC, and it is to this examination that I now turn.

[49] One further factor here may have related to the fact that, in the context of the new Legion of Mary meetings, details of *okutoija* payments were now, for the first time, being made public. This shift may have inadvertently reduced their symbolic transformational power (given that, historically, much of the symbolic power of these payments derived from the very fact that they were made secretly). It is possible to speculate that this would have inadvertently further increased participants' disillusionment with the church's ability to help them with their problems.

4
Genesis
Building the Network

From about the early 1980s onwards, a promotion of Marian devotion by certain members of the new indigenous clergy resulted in a significant upsurge in the number of visions of Mary that were being recorded across the rural areas. Although these visions were taking place all over South-western Uganda (and beyond), they were particularly concentrated in those areas which had previously been settled by the Kiga Diaspora. All of which is central to our story here, because it was from within this very context that the MRTC was to first emerge, also in the second half of the 1980s. In effect, the MRTC began life as a branch of – or more accurately, as a network within – the Legion of Mary, and for the first few years of its existence, its activities were largely indistinguishable from those of the organization as a whole. Thus, it too held weekly meetings in a local parish – often under the auspices of a local branch of the Legion – to discuss the visions of some Marian seer or other. It too would organize special 'rosary meetings', other prayer groups dedicated to Marian worship, and so on. Moreover, its membership was, by and large, drawn from exactly the same sorts of people who attended other meetings of the Legion as well (i.e. a predominance of Kiga women of the Diaspora).

However, over time, and especially as its popularity grew, both the MRTC's own leadership, and the local Catholic hierarchy, came to view the new Movement, and its practices and goals, as contrary to those of the mainstream church. Eventually, sometime in late 1991, the local bishop, the Rt Reverend John Kakubi, decided to censure the nascent organization by serving all of the priests who had joined it with papal interdictions, effectively expelling them – and the Movement as a whole – from the Roman church. Thereafter, the MRTC continued to exist as an organization in its own right, although now as what might legitimately be termed an African-Initiated Church (AIC), or, more specifically, as an example of 'Catholic independency'.

The purpose of this chapter, then, is to explore this early history of the MRTC through an examination of the biographies of several of its key protagonists. The argument which will emerge is that much of the early popular appeal of the new Movement – both before and after its expulsion from the mainstream church – stemmed from an attempt by its leaders to further promote the key symbol of the Virgin Mary, both as a focus of theology and as a linchpin for practical devotion. In this way, the MRTC went beyond other branches of the Legion, and became a fully fledged

Marian church (this aspect was to become increasingly marked following the group's expulsion from the mainstream church). Moreover, as I shall also attempt to demonstrate, at least part of the popular attraction of this development stemmed from a move by the MRTC's leaders (a move which was certainly at least partly intentional) to further reinvigorate – or 'revitalize' – a prior symbolic connection between the Virgin Mary and the old Nyabingi. In this way, from the very beginning onwards, the leadership adopted not only the language but also the ritual function and devotional practices, and other features as well, of the old fertility complex.

The cast

Profile: Joseph Kibweteere

Early one morning in April 1984, Joseph Kibweteere was strolling in the hills above Kabale Town. As he paused to take in the spectacular view, he was suddenly struck down by a blinding light. Eventually coming to his senses, Kibweteere found himself staring into the face of the Virgin Mary. However, she was upset, weeping. After some time, she slowly, and deliberately, began to speak, and informed him that the whole of humanity had become unimaginably corrupted. The only way for it to be saved was through a return to the biblical ten commandments, ignorance of which lay at the heart of the present malaise. On returning home, Kibweteere announced details of his vision to his wife and a few friends, and informed them that he was going to create a new organization to pass on details of the Virgin's message, an organization to be called the Movement for the Restoration of the Ten Commandments.

The creation of the Movement was but the latest event in the complex career of Joseph Kibweteere. Born in the village of Kishariro, Ntungamo District – then part of the wider Ankole District – in 1932, Kibweteere had gone on to attend the Catholic Secondary School at Nyamitanga, Mbarara Town, making him part of the second generation of students to be educated in the Catholic system.[1] From the very beginning, he proved himself to be a highly able student, and also very good at making friends, and building social networks.[2] By the time he joined St Georges Teacher Training College at Ibanda (in 1955), he was well known to practically every member of the Catholic hierarchy in South-western Uganda and, as a result, upon completion of his teacher training, he moved quickly up the ranks. For example, within just one year of taking up his first teaching post in 1956 (at Rushooka Primary School), he was promoted to the post of headmaster (at Kishariiro Primary School), and, from there, shortly became the Assistant Supervisor for Catholic Schools in the region (a post he held from 1959 to 1962).

[1] I am grateful to James Mujuni for providing me with some of this biographical information on Joseph Kibweteere. Mujuni's data are augmented here with information from my own interviews with Mrs Kibweteere, and others.
[2] Bishop Kakubi, pers. comm., 22.4.05.

Finally, in 1963, Kibweteere, by now one of the most influential – and wealthy – men in the Catholic education system, and a senior member of the regional laity, decided to start his own school, not far from his place of birth, in the village of Kabumba (at Nyakazinga Secondary School).[3] Four years later, the school – and Kibweteere's other businesses – had done so well that he was able to purchase a large piece of land nearby, and to begin constructing a large family home there.[4] It was at this stage that Kibweteere also launched his political career, by becoming an active member of the local branch of the Democratic Party (DP).[5]

The years immediately prior to, and immediately following, national independence were a time of intense party political activity in Uganda. Throughout this period, and particularly in the Southwest, the two major political parties in the country, the Uganda People's Congress (UPC) and the DP were actively recruiting new members along religious lines. Thus, many Protestants became members of the UPC, and many Catholics members of the DP. Moreover, in many cases the upper echelons of the respective laities soon came to constitute the upper echelons of the local party branches as well. Thus, it is no surprise that Kibweteere should have soon become a senior member of the Western Branch of the DP, and that this position should have stood him in particularly good stead.

In 1971, following his coup of early that year, Idi Amin sought to promote members of the Western DP to senior national positions,[6] and thus it was that, in late 1971, Kibweteere was offered a seat on the National Land Commission (a post he held until 1973). The post conferred many opportunities, but primary among them was the chance for international travel – to conferences, on fact-finding missions, and the like – which Kibweteere embraced with great enthusiasm. Indeed, throughout the early 1970s, he spent much of his time travelling to other African countries, to Europe, and elsewhere.[7] However, this period of good fortune was soon to come to an end, with the overthrow of Amin and the subsequent return to power of the UPC (following the national elections of 1980).

After that time, senior members of the Western DP were first stripped of their former positions and privileges, and later made an object of derision and attack (as indeed were many ordinary Catholics, as well). Following this, many began actively to recruit fighters for Andrew Kayiira's Uganda Freedom Movement (UFM), a guerrilla army which from 1980 to 1986 fought a sustained 'bush war' against the governments of Milton Obote and Tito Okello. It is highly likely that Kibweteere himself would have been engaged in such activities during this period. Simply put, it is quite inconceivable that someone of his seniority within South-western DP/Catholic

---

[3] Kibweteere's other business interests at this time included a beer business in Kabale, and a maize mill (UHRC, 2002).

[4] The family finally moved into this house in Kabumba in 1973.

[5] Kibweteere quickly rose through the ranks of the regional branch of the DP, and went on to become Chairman of the Public Service Commission in the (then) Ankole District government.

[6] In a move against his main rivals, the UPC.

[7] Mrs Kibweteere showed me all of his flight receipts from this period, which she still keeps as souvenirs.

networks would *not* have been engaged in such practices at this time.[8] Either way, it is certainly the case that, sometime in the early 1980s, Kibweteere was attacked and beaten in his home by local UPC Youth Wingers, and was eventually forced to flee.[9] Following this incident, he once again drew on his extensive network of contacts within the local church hierarchy, to take up residence at a parish near to the see of Kigezi diocese (in Kabale Town) where he was to remain for the next four years.

Living so close to the administrative centre of the diocese, it is certain that Kibweteere – whom Bishop Kakubi describes as 'ever the entrepreneur' (pers. comm., 22.4.05) – would have witnessed the revival of the Legion first hand, and would have noted the often sizeable wealth it was generating amongst certain sections of the local clergy. Certainly, it was during his time in Kabale that Kibweteere received his first vision of Holy Mary. Sometime around 1985, Kibweteere left Kabale, and returned home to Kabumba with his wife, Theresa, after which time both of them received additional – indeed, regular – visitations.[10] Moreover, it was once back home in Kabumba, that the couple became active members of local networks of the Legion, not only attending branch meetings – in order to communicate details of their own visions – but also travelling all over Southern Uganda (and beyond) in order to attend meetings held by other seers. Mrs Kibweteere emerges here as the key actor, since it was through her extraordinary energy and her networking skills, that the couple came to know of the existence, and activities, of Marian visionaries as far apart as Kampala, Masaka, Kibeho (in Rwanda), and elsewhere.[11]

Indeed, over the following few years, the couple spent considerable time and money travelling far and wide – to all of the places listed above, and many more besides – in order to attend the services, and other forms of consultation, of these various seers.[12] As described to me by Mrs Kibweteere, in almost all cases, the services themselves – most of which were held under the auspices of the Legion – involved the familiar format, in which the visionary either communicated a vision she had received previously, or else retired 'mid-service' in order to receive a new message, which would then be delivered to all present. In terms of the content, such messages usually focused on issues of 'backsliding', but also on abortions, polygamy, and so on. In most cases, these activities would then be followed by various sessions of faith healing, rosary prayers, all-night vigils, and the like.

[8] Although the UFM was predominantly Buganda-nationalist in ideological orientation, it also had strong links to the DP, and thus, throughout the early 1980s, recruited most of its cadres through DP/Catholic networks (and especially through the kinds of South-western networks within which Kibetweere was, at that time, so well positioned).
[9] The UPC's Youth Wing was a kind of local militia which throughout the Obote II period carried out much of the government's 'dirty work' (in the Southwest, in particular). For example, it was the Youth Wing that carried out the infamous Banyarwanda expulsions, in 1982.
[10] Mrs Kibweteere described the content of these visions to me in great detail. However, she did so in confidence, and for this reason, I shall not discuss them further.
[11] In Masaka, for example, the couple attended prayer sessions held by a young Rwandan visionary called Specioza Mukantabona. According to Mayer, this woman also claimed to be part of the group of seers from Kibeho (cited in Behrend, 2000: 93, fn. 13).
[12] In almost all cases, the seers themselves were women. However, in at least one instance, the Kibweteeres also travelled to a service which was held in Kampala by the Australian Marian Visionary William Kamm (aka 'Little Pebble').

It was as a direct result of these activities, and out of the network of Marian visionaries with whom Theresa Kibweteere had contact, that the MRTC eventually began to emerge as a social form in its own right. Throughout this period, one of Mrs Kibweteere's key Marian contacts had been a young woman seer from Rwera (also in Ntungamo District), called Jane Kasaande. Theresa had first met Kasaande whilst praying at the Marian shrine in Nyamitanga some years before, and the two women had subsequently become firm friends (Nyamitanga is the headquarters of the Mbarara diocese – and now archdiocese as well – located on a hill just outside Mbarara Town).[13] In particular, Kasaande – not least because of her convenient location at the Diocese – had proved a particularly good source of information about new Marian visions, and she had often passed on to Mrs. Kibweteere details of some or other emergent seer. More significantly, it was whilst visiting Kasaande one day, in July 1989, that Joseph and Theresa Kibweteere first met another Marian seer, called Ceredonia Mwerinde (who was also visiting Kasaande at the time).

This encounter proved to be the key event in the genesis of the MRTC, because it was at this meeting that Ceredonia first recounted a particular vision she had received, in which she had been told that she would soon meet a man called 'Joseph', with whom she would change the world. Excited by this news, the Kibweteeres immediately invited Ceredonia – and her sister, Angela Mugisha, and her niece, Ursula Komuhangi (both of whom were also seers) – back to their home, and from that evening onwards, both Ceredonia and the other two women took up residence at Kabumba. A few days later, the group was also joined by the family of one Mrs Scholastica Kamagara – another renowned Marian seer in Theresa Kibweteere's network – who, upon hearing news of Ceredonia's vision, had immediately set out from her own home in Kitabi Parish, Bushenyi District. Thus, it was following this chance encounter with Ceredonia Mwerinde at Nyamitanga that the MRTC had, in the words of Mrs Kibweteere, 'begun to pray together'.

Profile: Ceredonia Mwerinde

> She was a holy lady, very wise... She was very good at convincing [sic] ... She was a very nice person, who would even pray for you free of charge.[14]

Early media reports of the Kanungu fire made much of the character of Ceredonia Mwerinde. In particular, a lot was made of the fact that she spent some of her early adult life working as a barmaid in Kanungu Trading Centre, an occupation associated, in some local perceptions, with prostitution. However, these early reports also overlooked a number of other salient

---

[13] Mbarara diocese had been elevated in 1953, with a jurisdiction which covered much of South-western Uganda. In 1961, part of this territory was lost to erect the diocese of Fort Portal, and in 1966, further territory was lost to erect the diocese of Kabale. In 1999, these three territories were then reintegrated, along with Kasese and Hoima Diocese, to erect the archdiocese of Mbarara. Today, Nyamitanga is the headquarters of both the diocese and archdiocese of Mbarara.

[14] Winifried Aheebwa.

aspects of her early career, some of which are far more important for our story here. In particular, for purposes of understanding the key role she came to play in the MRTC drama, it is necessary to examine the circumstances through which she initially became a Marian seer.

Ceredonia Mwerinde was born on 30 July 1952 at Bugarama Village, Ntungamo District (Ntungamo is that part of the old Ankole District which abutted the Eastern border of the old Kigezi District), the daughter of a Catholic Mukiga farmer called Paul Kashako.[15] However, within a year or so of her birth, her father and mother decided to join others in their family who were then taking part in the administration's assisted relocation programme. This being the period before the additional sites in Toro and Ankole had been opened, Kashako was settled in Kataate Village, just outside the 'trading centre' of Kanungu, which at that time was close to the centre of the Kinkizi resettlement area. The land on which Kashako settled here was the very site on which the Kanungu fire was to take place half a century later. Little reliable information can be ascertained about Kashako, but it is clear that he came from a sizeable Kiga family – at the time of his move he was accompanied by several brothers, whose offspring still farm the fields near his former home – and he had a number of children, including several sons (Ceredonia's brothers). In addition, it is clear from local people's recollections that Kashako was an important member of the local laity, having served for many years as a catechist in the local parish, and that all of his children received a strong Catholic upbringing. For example, Ceredonia received at least some education at a local Catholic school. Finally, Kashako is also remembered as a renowned 'traditional healer' (*omufumu*), and as one particularly well versed in the knowledge of local herbal remedies.

At around the age of 20, Ceredonia began a relationship with a local man, and in 1973 gave birth to a child by him, a girl called Agatha.[16] However, that same year the family was struck by tragedy, as the husband died of a 'mysterious illness' whilst away working at the Kayonza tea factory in Rukungiri Town. Following this event, Ceredonia was taken in by one of her older brothers, who later set her up with her own small business – a bar selling locally brewed millet beer (*omuramba*) and distilled gin (*waragi*) – in a property he had rented for her in Kanungu trading centre. Sometime during the next five years, Ceredonia began another relationship, with a clerk at the local county headquarters (which are located in Kanungu trading centre),[17] and she once again gave birth, to a boy called Mujuni. However, once again the relationship was to end in tragedy, as this man also soon passed away (at his home in nearby Lubanda Village). Perhaps significantly, a number of local people now recall

---

[15] I am again grateful to James Mujuni for providing some of this biographical information. Mujuni's information is again augmented here by my own interviews with various actors, including Mwerinde's former husband, Eric Mazima.

[16] Several sources suggest that she may have had a number of miscarriages around this time as well.

[17] In July 2001 – following the fire – Kanungu was made a district in its own right, since when these buildings have become the district administrative headquarters.

that the symptoms the man displayed, prior to his death, were typical of those of a contemporary AIDS patient.

In late 1979, Ceredonia then entered into another relationship, and became the new wife (*mugole*) of another local Mukiga man, Eric Mazima. A few months later, Mazima – an older man of some considerable wealth (much of which derived from his successful carpentry business) – bought out the lease on Ceredonia's bar in Kanungu, from Ceredonia's brother, a move which allowed her to stay on in the business. However, sometime in 1984, the landlord of the property decided to sell up, and unable to find another rental in Kanungu, Ceredonia was forced to move to one of Mazima's (several) pieces of land in the surrounding areas (he eventually built a house for her on a plot he owned about 5 miles from the trading centre).

However, from the time of the move, problems began to develop within the marriage. In particular, serious arguments began to occur between Ceredonia and her co-wives, especially over access to Mazima's fields and to his animals. Himself an émigré of the relocation scheme, Mazima had come to the Kanungu area from Rugarama in Kabale (which is part of the old Kigezi District) as a young man in the 1950s. Since that time, not least as a result of the wealth he had acquired, Mazima had taken on a number of wives, Ceredonia in fact being his seventh (and he subsequently married at least two more). Moreover, shortly after her move away from Kanungu, Ceredonia had begun to suffer convulsions, fits which would last from a few minutes to a few hours. On several occasions, she herself claimed to her husband that these episodes were being caused by spirits (*emandwa*) for which her co-wives were responsible. However, we may note here in passing that because none of Mazima's wives lived together – still today, they live over many of his small plots, which are in some cases several miles apart – it is unlikely that Ceredonia would have had many opportunities to express this opinion to her co-wives directly.

Yet most seriously of all, it gradually became apparent that Ceredonia was also unable to produce a child for her new husband.[18] Thus, although Ceredonia had already borne at least two children by earlier liaisons, in the context of the new union she was deemed barren (*engumba*). On at least two occasions, Mazima now recalls, the couple had visited local healers (*abafumu*) to seek help with this affliction, and on both occasions had been told that the infertility was probably being caused by the spirit (*emandwa*) of Ceredonia's deceased father, who was angry that Mazima had not paid a brideprice following the couple's marriage. However, at no stage does Mazima seem to have considered the possibility of his therefore paying any brideprice as a means of trying to remedy the situation – on the contrary, when I spoke to him at least, he found the idea laughable – and thus, as Ceredonia's barrenness continued, tensions continued to grow within the marriage.

On the night of 24 August 1988, Mazima was woken by his wife, who calmly informed him that she had just received a vision from the Virgin Mary, telling her, amongst other things, to divorce him immediately. A few days later, as news of the vision began to spread throughout the local area, 'many people' – in particular, women – began to gather at the house, to

---

[18] She did in fact become pregnant on several occasions, but each time miscarried.

hear details of the apparition, and to pray with Ceredonia. However, as Mazima recalls, most of these people were initially rather unimpressed by the authenticity of her account, and as a result, few stayed on. As Mazima himself put it to me, following Ceredonia's apparition, 'many believers began to gather at her house, but they didn't agree with her visions, nor with her methods of worship, and so they left again. They returned to whatever religions they were involved with before.' However, the visions continued, and a few days later, Ceredonia was informed that she should now go to the nearby caves of Nyabugoto – which lie about 9 miles from Kanungu, and can be reached in about 4 to 5 hours on foot – where the Virgin would reveal herself in person to her.

Thus it was that the very next morning, both Ceredonia and Mazima, and about 10 other people as well, set off for Nyabugoto, to see if this promise would come true. Arriving shortly after lunchtime, the group climbed up to the cave complex – which is located about 30 minutes' climb from the nearest tracks below – and settling underneath the large circular rock which lies in the middle of the uppermost cave, began to pray the rosary. After some time, Ceredonia fell into a trance-like state, becoming very quiet and withdrawn. Eventually coming to her senses, she informed the group that, moments beforehand, the rock above her head had been transformed into the figure of the Virgin Mary herself. Moreover, that the Virgin had spoken to her, telling her that 'I have appeared to you Ceredonia, and I am commissioning you to take my message to the believers'.[19] Later, as the group sought further details of the apparition, Ceredonia added that, during the visitation, the Virgin had not shown her her face, but had instead informed her that she was deliberately 'turning her back on the world' in order to shield herself from all the sinful practices which were taking place there. A few days later, the group returned to the caves a second time, although this time their numbers were swelled by a party led by Gauda Kamushwa (a Marian seer from nearby Rubaabo, to whom Ceredonia had written informing her of events). In all, some 40 or so people attended this second meeting. Again, during a round of rosary prayers, Ceredonia received another visitation.

Following the second trip to Nyabugoto, Mazima, who remained firmly unconvinced by the whole thing, decided to divorce Ceredonia, and a few days later, she returned to her natal home in Kataate. However, thereafter her visions seem only to have increased, and within a short space of time, she and her companions – who within a short period numbered a few dozen or so (some of whom were already staying with her in the compound, others of whom visited from surrounding areas) – were returning to the caves almost every day. On every occasion, the rock at Nyabugoto transformed itself into the Virgin Mary, and spoke to Ceredonia Mwerinde.

Following her move to the Kibweteeres' home, in July 1989, Ceredonia continued to receive her daily visions from the Virgin Mary (indeed, on many occasions, her apparitions were even more frequent). Moreover, from

[19] Several of those present remember these as the exact words Ceredonia spoke during these sessions.

the time the nascent Movement took up residence at Kabumba, the group began to structure its daily routine, and its practices of worship, around her visions. It must be stressed here that although a number of other Movement members, including Kibweteere himself, had also experienced visions from the Virgin *prior* to the formation of the sect, from the time the group took up residence at Kabumba, these apparitions became the exclusive preserve of Ceredonia alone. Certainly, a number of the sect's other founders, including both Angela Mugisha and Fr. Kasapuraari, did conduct 'healing ceremonies', aimed at exorcizing people of malevolent *emandwa* (Jason Nkunda and Mr Sebataka, Patience N.). However, from an early stage onwards, communication with the Virgin was conducted by Ceredonia, and Ceredonia alone.

Thus, from quite early on, a typical day for the MRTC involved its members waking up shortly after dawn – as is typical for all people living in this part of rural Uganda – and then spending a couple of hours doing household chores, such as sweeping the compound, preparing breakfast (*kyantsya*), and so on. At around 10 am, the whole group would gather to eat the morning meal, before heading out into the Kibweteeres' (extensive) fields to do several hours' agricultural work.[20] Sometime in the mid-afternoon, the group would then reconvene in the house to begin the first of the day's prayer sessions. These sessions involved all present saying multiple rounds of the rosary, singing hymns to the Virgin Mary, and so on.

Most significantly, during each of these sessions, Ceredonia would move in to take centre stage (with all the other members gathered in a circle around her). As described to me by Mrs Kibweteere, and by several other people who had attended these sessions, at some point during the proceedings, Ceredonia would invariably then begin to drift off into a trance-like state, during which 'her manner changed', she began to shake, she dropped to the floor, and other things besides. At this point, all present knew that Ceredonia was experiencing one of her apparitions. As Mrs Kibweteere now recalls, following this occurrence, the group would then eagerly await Ceredonia's 'return', following which she would deliver details of the Virgin's message, and be open to members' (often eager) questioning – 'What was the Virgin's mood like when she appeared? What clothes was she wearing? What may she have meant when she said x, y, or z?', and so on.

At the end of this prayer session, which usually lasted for several hours or more, Ceredonia would then retire, exhausted, to a back room, and remain out of sight for much of the rest of the day. Meanwhile, all the other members would sit down for their evening meal (*kyakiro*), before reconvening for another, longer round of worship, which usually lasted until shortly before dawn (in this way, the majority of the MRTC's membership rarely had more than a few hours' sleep each night). On most evenings – perhaps two out of three – further visitations would occur during these night prayers. In this way, Ceredonia, who was invariably absent at the

---

[20] Later on, this part of the day was used for other sorts of economic activities as well, such as making various sorts of handicrafts – woven baskets, mats and the like (which the group would then sell to local shops, and occasionally in local markets as well, Winifred Aheebwa).

start of the sessions, would burst in to announce that, while alone in her room, she had just received an additional apparition. Details of these additional visions would usually be written down on a piece of paper,[21] although on some occasions they were also recorded on tape (following which the congregation gathered there would be able to hear the actual words of the Virgin, as spoken through her visionary, Ceredonia, Winifred Aheebwa). Following this, the remainder of the night session would then be taken up with discussion of that particular apparition, and with Ceredonia answering further rounds of eager questions about it.

By the end of 1989, between 50 and 60 people had joined the MRTC on a more or less full-time basis, and had taken up permanent residence at Kabumba. In addition, several hundred more, almost all of them women, were attending on an occasional basis. These others tended to drift in and out – sometimes staying for a few days at a time, sometimes for longer – but their presence meant that, at any given time, perhaps 100 to 150 people were living at the Kibweteeres' home. Just two years later, by the turn of 1992, that number had risen to perhaps 300 souls.

Profile: Dominic Kataribaabo

From the time the nascent Movement took up residence at the Kibweteeres' home, in July 1989, news of their existence had begun to spread. Thus, evidence I have collected from across the region suggests that, already by the end of 1990, clergy located in parishes throughout South-western Uganda had heard of the group, and had at least some knowledge of their activities. This is unremarkable, given that the Movement had been started by one of the most senior members of the Catholic laity in the region, given that it had grown out of a network which was centred upon the head-quarters of the diocese, at Nyamitanga (which all members of the regional clergy, even today, visit regularly, and with which all parishes have daily contact via two-way radios), and given the nature of its ongoing activities. It is also unsurprising, in this context, that a number of the clergy – and especially those who had previously been promoting the Legion of Mary, in particular within the Kiga Diaspora – should eventually also have begun to attend the MRTC's sessions themselves. The first priest to become involved with the group was the son of Scholastica Kamagara, a young man called Fr. Joseph Kasapuraari (Kasapuraari was at the time in his late twenties, and had only recently been ordained). However, more significantly, towards the end of 1991, the Movement's leaders were also invited to preach at Rugazi Parish, in Banyuruguru, which at the time was presided over by one of the most senior clergymen in South-western Uganda, one Fr. Dominic Kataribaabo (and his deputy, his former teacher, Fr. Paul Ikazire).

Dominic Kataribaabo was born on 20 December 1936 in Kigabiro Village, Banyuruguru. A member of the 'abakunta' clan – a group which traces descent from a group of Buganda migrants who first settled the

---

[21] According to Fr. Ikazire – who spent three years in the MRTC between 1991 and 1994 (see below) – the details of Ceredonia's visions were usually written down by her niece, Ursula Komuhangi, because she herself was practically illiterate.

shores around Lake Edward in the late nineteenth century – from a young age Kataribaabo proved academically gifted, and later won a series of scholarships to attend Catholic seminaries, and later Makerere University as well.[22] On 8 August 1965, he took Holy Orders at his home in Rugazi, becoming only the fifth African priest in the area (the second was Paul Ikazire),[23] and the first to be ordained in his home parish. A few years later, he was made Rector of St Francis Xavier Kitabi Seminary, in Bushenyi District (which at that time was the only seminary in this part of the country).

At Kitabi, Kataribaabo counselled practically every trainee priest in the region, with the result that today it is rare to find any clergyman in the Southwest who did not know the man personally. It is equally rare to find any priest who does not still speak of him in the highest terms. In particular, he is today still remembered as a great intellect – for example, as a man who spoke at least nine languages with a good degree of fluency – as a quiet and thoughtful personality, as a very good organizer, and above all as a wise and helpful counsellor. As a result, the vast majority of the churchmen I spoke to as part of my research on the MRTC – perhaps two dozen or more – expressed great surprise that Kataribaabo should have become involved in the events which were to follow.

However, in 1985, Kataribaabo won yet another scholarship, this time to study for an additional Masters degree – this time in Religious Studies – at the prestigious Jesuit Loyola Marymount University in Los Angeles,[24] and upon his return to Uganda, in 1988, he was widely rumoured to be in line for a senior post in the national church hierarchy. Fr. Kataribaabo may have had designs on becoming the next Bishop of Mbarara – with the impending retirement of the incumbent, John Kakubi – or else the chaplain of St Augustine's at Makerere University (one of the highest ecclesiastical offices in the country, Likoudis, 2000). However, whether because of internal church politics, or for other reasons, none of these appointments came to pass,[25] and, as a result, in early 1988, Kataribaabo returned to parish duties, first at Rubindi, and then at his home parish, in Rugazi (where he was joined, in early 1990, by Fr. Paul Ikazire as his deputy).

It is now clear that, over the course of his long career, Kataribaabo had become increasingly interested in the Marian Movement within the Catholic Church. This may have begun during his Makerere days, when the Legion was quite active on the campus (Ariseeni Oworyanawe). Certainly, it is clear that, whilst in the US, Kataribaabo had attended meetings of a

[22] Having begun his education at Rugazi Primary School, he later joined Kitabi Minor Seminary (in 1952), and then Katigondo Major Seminary (where he studied between 1959 and 1967). Later, he studied for a Bachelor of Arts degree in History at Makerere University, followed by a Masters in Theology (1974-77, Banura *et al.*, 2000: 20).

[23] Most of the details of this biography are taken from my interview with Kataribaabo's brother, Ariseeni Oworyanawe.

[24] He was awarded a Loyola Marymount scholarship, which is funded by the Archdiocese of Los Angeles to help educate priests from the 'Developing World' (Likoudis, 2000).

[25] For example, in 1989, Paul Bakyenga was consecrated Bishop, with a view to his later becoming Bishop of Mbarara (a post he eventually took over – from Bishop Kakubi – in November 1991). In 1999, Bakyenga also became Archbishop of Mbarara, following the erection of the archdiocese of Mbarara.

number of Marian groups – including one organized by Stefano Gobbi, the founder of the Marian Movement of Priests (MMP)[26] – and had travelled to the shrines of several Marian seers (including the famous Necedah Shrine, in Juneau County, Wisconsin).[27] In addition, Bishop Kakubi recalls that, on his way back to Uganda from California, Kataribaabo had also made a short (10-day) pilgrimage to Lourdes, at which he had been deeply moved both by the sight of a young girl being healed of paralysis, and by some sort of 'spiritual experience' of his own. The main result of all this was that within just a few weeks of his return to Rugazi, Kataribaabo had revived the Legion of Mary, and from about April of that year onwards, was hosting bi-weekly meetings of the group.[28] In addition, within just a few months of arriving back at the parish, he had also raised enough money to build a large and elaborate Marian shrine close to the entrance to the church grounds (which still stands on the main approach to Rugazi today).

More significantly, he had also begun to seek out Marian seers from across the region, to invite them to Rugazi to preach. Thus it was that on 5 May 1991, Kibweteere and Ceredonia received an invitation to Rugazi to come and present details of their own visions, to a meeting of the Legion. As it turned out, over the following weeks and months, these visits were to become increasingly frequent, to the point, in fact, that, by about early November, the pair had become more or less permanent residents in the parish.

In Rugazi, Kibweteere and Ceredonia conducted the Legion's meetings in much the same way as they did their own prayer sessions in Kabumba. Thus, according to Kataribaabo's brother, Ariseeni Oworyanawe – a regular attender at the sessions – each meeting would again start with the congregation praying the rosary, and singing Marian hymns. Again, Ceredonia would take centre stage, and at some point in the proceedings would drift off into a trance, and upon returning from this, would claim to have had a vision of the Virgin Mary. Once again, all of this would then be followed by a question and answer session. In fact, the only innovation at all in these meetings at Rugazi was the introduction of 'faith healing' at the end of each session, during which Holy Mary, working through Ceredonia, would cure people's ills. For example, Ariseeni recalls one occasion on which Ceredonia stood on the stomach of a young woman, in order that the Virgin might cure her affliction. Moreover, all of this seems to have proved quite popular: by November 1991, the meetings in Rugazi were being regularly attended by as many as 300 people, most of them visitors from surrounding villages.

[26] Stefano Gobbi is an Italian priest who began experiencing an interior locution with the Virgin on 13 October 1972. Although Gobbi and his movement, the MMP, are still in communion with the Roman church, the group has been criticized in some quarters for the millenarian nature of their message. Specifically – and of most significance for the MRTC story – Gobbi's locutions with the Virgin sometimes spoke of an impending apocalypse, in which only Mary herself would be able to save mankind (Behrend, 2000: 79-80).

[27] At which a young woman, Mary Ann van Hoof, claimed to have had a number of visions of Holy Mary between 1949 and 1950 (although these were never recognized by the church, and van Hoof herself was later interdicted).

[28] Although the Legion had first been introduced to Rugazi in 1958 – by the White Fathers – its membership, and activities, had dwindled prior to Kataribaabo's return.

By late 1991, Bishop Kakubi had become increasingly watchful of events at Rugazi. In actual fact, the Bishop had been closely monitoring all Marian visions in his diocese since they had first begun, at Kikagata, in the late 1970s.[29] Following the rapid growth in the number of visions during the early 1980s, in particular, he had set up a permanent commission of enquiry to look into the validity of the seers' claims, and on several occasions had contacted his superiors in Rome to seek their advice on such matters. Moreover, it was in the course of the commission's routine activities that Kakubi had first become aware of Joseph Kibweteere's visions. Thus, in early 1986, the Bishop had dispatched one of the commission's members – a priest based at Nyamitanga – to the Kibweteeres' home to examine details of Joseph's visitations. In the event, the priest returned with a number of tape recordings of the visions themselves, of the Virgin speaking through Kibweteere. Bishop Kakubi still recalls the strange sound of the distorted speech which was caught on that tape. He remembers its eerie, high pitched, and somewhat distant tone, something quite unlike Kibweteere's normal voice. In addition, he still recalls some of its content, in particular one section in which the Virgin spoke of Kibweteere suckling at her breast. Yet such recordings were not unusual during this period. Indeed, throughout these years, Kakubi received a number of similar tapes, of various other local seers as well.[30] Finally, at some point in the middle of the decade – he does not remember in exactly which year – the Bishop decided to submit a full report on the proliferation of Marian visions in South-western Uganda to the Vatican itself, following which he was granted an audience with Pope John Paul II, to discuss the report's findings. On that occasion, the Pope reiterated to Kakubi the conditions under which any Marian group could be recognized as an ongoing member of the Roman Church; in particular, if it was charitable in intention, if it was not divisive in its effects, and if it still recognized the authority of the Pope.

Yet some of what was going on in Rugazi seemed to indicate that the MRTC might indeed be a divisive influence, and that some of its nascent 'leadership' were beginning to reject the authority of Rome. Kakubi was particularly worried about reports that Kataribaabo – whom he knew to be disgruntled at his recent failure to be made a Bishop – had begun to preach that the Vatican was populated with sinful cardinals, and had begun to suggest to other clergymen that they too should now join the Movement.

In the end, a series of summit meetings was arranged, first with Kibweteere and Kurambano (another senior member of the regional Catholic laity, and a long-time friend of Kibweteere's, who had also recently joined the MRTC), and then with Kataribaabo, Ikazire and Kasapuraari themselves. At the first meeting, Kakubi tried to convince Kibweteere that his visions were not real, by arguing that the human senses cannot ever comprehend the divine presence. At the second, he told the three priests that, unless they distanced themselves forthwith from Ceredonia's visions, and signed statements confirming their commitment to ecclesiastical

[29] Much of this section is based on my own interview with Bishop Kakubi.
[30] Neither was this the last time that tape recordings were to play a part in the MRTC drama (see Chapter 5).

4.1 Ceredonia Mwerinde. This image – one of only two known pictures of Ceredonia – was taken as part of a 'delegation' she led to a potential new recruit's house
(© MBC Productions)

4.2 Joseph Kibweteere (left) and Fr. Dominic Kataribaabo (right). This photograph was taken just a few days before the Kanungu fire, when all members of the Movement had their pictures taken to be used in 'passports' for a coming journey
(© MBC productions)

4.3 From left to right: Ursula Komuhangi (Ceredonia's niece), Eutrazia Nzelreoha (Ceredonia's mother), Fr. Joseph Mary Kasapuraari. This image was taken at the same time as the one in Figure 4.2 (© MBC Productions)

authority, they would be interdicted. When this offer was rejected, Kakubi initially discussed with senior colleagues the possibility of excommunicating the three priests. However, given the near-universal high standing in which Kataribaabo, in particular, was held, the possibility was deemed overly punitive, and, as a result, *papal interdictions* were served instead.

As it turned out, the serving of these notices was to be one of Kakubi's last acts as Bishop of Mbarara, prior to his handing over of the see to Paul Bakyenga (on 23 November, 1991). It also marked the inauguration of the MRTC as an independent organization, as an African-Initiated Church (AIC) in its own right. Thus, following their interdictions, Kataribaabo and Ikazire left the parish at Rugazi – where they were replaced by other appointees – to take up residence in the MRTC's emerging network of 'compounds' (to which they also contributed their own personal residences, both of which are located within one mile's radius of Rugazi). Thus, by early 1992, the MRTC network included at least 6 compounds (or 'study centres', as the members themselves called them): the Kibweteeres' home (Kabumba), Ceredonia's place (Kanungu), the Kamagaras' residence (Kitabi), Kurambano's home (just outside Mbarara Town), and Kataribaabo's and Ikazire's residences (Rugazi). Various others were shortly to follow.

There is little doubt that the decision by Bishop Kakubi to effectively expel the MRTC from the Roman Church must be seen, ultimately, as a move against two independently-minded members of the senior laity – Kibweteere and Kurambano – and against a group of (what had come to be regarded as) renegade priests – Kataribaabo, Ikazire and Kasapuraari. Moreover, from the perspective of the literature on Catholic AICs, none of this appears to be particularly remarkable. Thus, although movements of Catholic Christian independency are relatively rare in the ethnographic record in Africa – as, indeed, they are worldwide – where they have occurred, the independent church involved has almost always grown out of political wrangles within the local clergy, and has invariably entailed questions of priestly authority. For example, this was also the case with the Legio Maria Church, which emerged amongst the Luo of Kenya in the 1960s (a church which also began, incidentally, within local chapters of the Legion of Mary). However, what makes the MRTC particularly unusual here – and perhaps even unique? – is that, following their break with the church, the various priests who had become involved with the Movement in fact continued to exercise very little influence at all over the group. In fact, it would not be an exaggeration to say that, from quite early on, they even became relatively marginal figures within the new church. Instead, the picture which emerges from respondents' narratives is that from 1992 onwards – and probably beforehand as well – the group was increasingly dominated by one central personality: that of Ceredonia Mwerinde. Of course, the MRTC's mode of worship had, since 1989, revolved around her visions. However, as the Movement gradually emerged as an entity in its own right, Ceredonia began to take control of all other aspects of MRTC life – and ultimately of the very group itself as well. Once again, her visions acted as the primary vehicle through which this was achieved.

Throughout the first few months at Kabumba, the content of Ceredonia's visions – like those of other Marian visionaries at the time – had focused primarily on a more strictly 'religious' set of topics: people's sinful practices, observance of the ten commandments and rosary prayers, how to be a 'good' Christian, and so on. However, over the next 18 months, and certainly after the group parted company with the Catholic church, a discernible shift occurred, and the range of subjects on which the Virgin spoke – through Ceredonia – began to widen significantly. Thus, in addition to discussion of spiritual matters – about which the Virgin continued to give guidance – she began also to speak about how the community of believers should conduct themselves in everyday life, how the group should be organized, and so on. For example, at some point in 1990, the Virgin decreed that, henceforth, the entire membership should conduct all of their (non-ritual) activities in silence – and should only communicate by means of sign language – that they should fast every Monday and Friday, that they should all possess only one set of clothes, and so on.

Furthermore, over time, the detail of these instructions became ever more specific. Thus, the Virgin began to speak of not only the general structure of the group's work routine, but also to give specific details of which people were to do which specific jobs, on which specific days. For example, one of my respondents recalls one of Ceredonia's visions which commanded three named individuals to grow a field of potatoes on a specified piece of land. Later, a second vision then ordered two other members to harvest the plot, and to sell the produce at a local market (Kahuru Richard). The implications of these sorts of edicts – and of the others that were to follow – will be discussed at length below. However, what I want to highlight here are the ways in which the content of Ceredonia's visions also impacted upon power dynamics within the group. This is because they seem to have also resulted, from an early stage, in Ceredonia taking over practically all aspects of the group's organization (and in so doing, undermining the role of practically all the other senior members).

For example, shortly after her arrival at Kabumba, Ceredonia received one vision in which she was informed that the Movement should be made hierarchical in structure, with her at the apex, a group of leaders below her – to include the Kibweteeres, Kasaande, Ursula, Angela Mugisha, the Kamagaras, Fr. Kasapuraari, Kurambano, and so on[31] – a group of permanent members below them, and a further group of casual members below that. Moreover, later visions then indicated specific promotions within these grades. Thus, for example, one vision indicated that Steria Kyakunzire – a young seer from Ceredonia's home area, and a late entrant into the Movement – should be promoted to the group of 'leaders'.

More significantly perhaps, later visions similarly indicated people to be demoted. Thus, for example, one of Ceredonia's vision severely admonished Mrs Kibweteere – in whose house the Movement was, of course, staying at the time – for buying expensive clothes, as a result of which she was no longer to be classed as a leader (and her entire wardrobe was to be destroyed). Later, another vision attacked Mrs Kibweteere for having bought a set of blankets for the children who were staying in the house (an act which the Virgin again claimed to be a wasteful extravagance).

As tensions grew, Ceredonia received another vision in which the Virgin ordered that Joseph Kibweteere was to be made the Movement's first 'Bishop'. This was followed, a few days later, by an elaborate 'ordination' ceremony, in which several hundred members of the group's followers processed through Kabumba Village. The column was led by Angela Mugisha, dressed as the Virgin Mary, with Kibweteere following at the rear, complete with mitre and crosier. For Kibweteere himself, the ceremony seems to have confirmed his role as the divinely-sanctioned leader of the new church. However, for Mrs Kibweteere, and for her son Juvenal, the event could be interpreted in a quite different way, as evidence of just how corrupted Ceredonia's visions had become, a means through which she was manipulating the group, in order to remain the 'power behind the throne'. In the end, a secret summit was held by members of the family, at which it was decided to expel Joseph Kibweteere, and the entire MRTC, from the family home. Thus it was that in late 1992, Mrs Kibweteere, and the rest of the family, parted company with the Movement.

Members of the Kibweteere family were not the only people to fall foul

---

[31] Some respondents referred to this group, like others, as the *'ekigo ky'entumwa'* (lit: 'The Tower of the Apostles', for example, Jane Bakyenga).

of the Virgin's pronouncements – as received by Ceredonia – during this period. For example, shortly after the group parted company with the church – and whilst both Kataribaabo and Ikazire were also staying at the Kibweteeres' home – a further vision indicated that only the leadership would henceforth sleep in beds, whilst all other members would now sleep on mattresses on the floor. Following this, a second vision clarified that in fact only Ceredonia was to have a bed, and that all of the leaders were to join the rest of the group on mattresses. As both Mrs Kibweteere and Fr. Ikazire recall, this latter pronouncement was much to the chagrin of the two elderly priests, in particular. However, when Ikazire complained about it to Ceredonia, a further vision was received informing them that all of the group, including its leaders, would now sleep on the bare floor (i.e. without even a mattress), in communal dormitories, along with all the 'ordinary' members.[32] When Fr. Ikazire again complained, Ceredonia received yet more visions admonishing him as well, in which the Virgin claimed that he had been secretly breaking the group's vow of silence whilst Ceredonia was not around.

In another incident – Ikazire thinks it was on a Trinity Sunday – Ceredonia began to recite the Liturgy of Santo Dadao, but reordered the introduction, by praying first to the Virgin Mary, and only afterwards to God the Father and the Son. However, when Ikazire questioned Ceredonia on this ordering – by arguing that all Catholic liturgies should properly begin with prayers to God the Father – he was again attacked, and a subsequent vision questioned his very faith in the Virgin's appearances. At this point, he too arrived at the conclusion that Ceredonia was little more than a fraud, and thus it was that, in early 1994, he also withdrew. Interestingly, after this time, he decided to write to Kataribaabo, to try to convince him of his own doubts about Mwerinde. However, knowing that Ceredonia read all the mail which came into, and went out of, the group – or rather, had Ursula read them to her (given her own near-illiteracy) – he decided to write the entire letter in Latin. But he never received a reply to this letter, and, still today, does not know if Kataribaabo ever received it.

Thus, from quite early on – and certainly from the time the Movement first parted company with the Catholic Church – the MRTC focused upon, and was to a large extent controlled by, the Marian visions of the group's central charismatic figure: Ceredonia Mwerinde. In other words, from almost the very outset, all of the sect's ritual practices, others of its everyday activities, and its mode of social organization, were shaped by, and in some senses flowed directly from, the content of Ceredonia's visions. The key research question here is what, then, made these visions quite so compelling?

---

[32] From quite early on, the MRTC's sleeping arrangements reflected its system of social ranking. Thus, Ceredonia, and Ceredonia alone, always had her own room. Other leaders then shared out whatever additional bedrooms remained (which usually required them to sleep between 2 and 5 people to a room). The ordinary members then slept in one of two communal dormitories, which were divided along gender lines (reflecting the fact that sexual relations were strictly prohibited at all MRTC compounds). At Kabumba, the communal dormitories were housed in two makeshift buildings which were erected in the compound of Kibweteere's home. However, at other MRTC centres, including at Kanungu – these sleeping arrangements were repeated at all of the sect's compounds – dedicated dormitory buildings were constructed.

In other words, how might we account for the fact that, in a context where many women in rural areas were experiencing Marian visions, hers apparently came to be regarded as so much more irresistible than those of other seers? Indeed, to such an extent that a senior layman such as Joseph Kibweteere was prepared to invite her to his house upon first meeting her, that two senior, and highly learned, priests were willing to risk a split with the Church itself in order to dedicate themselves to them, and that all – or, at least, most – members of the MRTC were later willing to submit to their authority. In other words, what exactly made Ceredonia's visions – and/or her as a person – quite so convincing here? It was with these questions in mind that, in November 2001, I made my second trip to the key site of Ceredonia's early visions: the caves at Nyabugoto.

The 'revelation in a cave'

Okugyenda kutera okuboona. Travelling means finding[33]

I had in fact been to the caves at Nyabugoto once before, during my first fieldwork trip to the Kanungu area, in May 2001. On that occasion, Grace Bwire and I, and our driver for the trip, Katwiire (Grace's fictive cousin), had been taken by James Mujuni on a tour of all of the 'key sites' of the Kanungu story, and to meet many of the key surviving protagonists of the MRTC. Mujuni had, of course, already been to all of these places in the days immediately following the fire, and had already interviewed most of the actors involved, and established a rapport with them. Six months after that first trip, I was beginning a second tour of the region, this time to interview former members of the Movement, and/or their surviving relatives – through a method of 'snow-ball sampling' – all of whom were dispersed in villages throughout the area (and far beyond). On this occasion, my travelling companions were my wife, Zheela – whom I had married, in London, in the intervening period – my long-time research assistant, Mercy Muyambi, and our driver for the occasion, Turyahabwe.[34]

As we proceeded between two interviews, I suddenly recognized the turn-off to Nyabugoto and, keen to show the site to my wife and research assistant (neither of whom had previously been there), decided to make a short stop at the caves. Having parked the car on the nearest track, to begin the 30-minute or so cross-country climb to the caves, we approached the farmer whose land we were about to cross – he was pruning his banana plants at the time – to ask for his permission to do so. He agreed, and even offered to escort us up, and as we climbed, the entourage grew still further as several other local people – and at least 5 children – also decided to escort us. By the time we reached the caves themselves, there were perhaps 15 or more people in our party.

---

[33] Cisternino, 1987: 454.
[34] Turyahabwe is the operator of one of the few permanently running cars in Bugamba Village, which operates as a daily taxi service between the Village and Mbarara Town. In order to make this second research safari, I had hired this village taxi for a few days.

As we reached the top, the party paused briefly, to catch their breaths, and as we did so, a thought suddenly struck me. Turning to the farmer and a number of the other people present, I asked how far we were from the site of the Nyakishenyi attack of 1917. Without hesitation, the farmer turned down the hill, and pointing to a school lying immediately below the caves and in full view of them, (perhaps half a mile away, or less), replied: 'oh, the *gombolola* which was attacked stood there, where that school now is'. The others all concurred. In a moment, I realized that the biggest attack of the entire Nyabingi anti-colonial struggle had, in effect, taken place at Nyabugoto, and that this site must therefore have been particularly auspicious or important for the old Nyabingi movement. Moreover, that the fact that Ceredonia's own Marian visions had occurred in the very same location must surely therefore have been more than a coincidence.

Subsequent research confirmed these initial insights. In relation to the first point, it later transpired that not only was Nyabugoto *an* important site for Nyabingi worship, but that it was *the primary* Nyabingi shrine in the whole of South-western Uganda (and beyond). Upon one's first ascent to the caves it becomes apparent why this should have been so. Indeed, everything about the site, from its location to the rock formations themselves, seems to symbolize fertility (with which Nyabingi was, of course, primarily concerned). For example, the caves are located on the highest outcrop for miles around, and thus provide a panoramic view of the richly fertile farmlands below (one can see for tens of miles from the entrance to the caves). In addition, the overall shape of the main cave bears a quite striking resemblance to the female sexual organs. The outer part of the cave forms a kind of tunnel shape, constituted of a series of concentric rock formations, whilst the centre is dominated by a single large, round rock, thus giving the overall impression of a vagina and clitoris (in Ceredonia's visions at the cave, it was the central rock which was transformed into the Virgin Mary).

Moreover, such associations are not lost on any of the local people with whom I have attended the site. Several of the local oral historians whom I later interviewed about the caves suggested that it was for precisely these reasons that already, by about the mid-eighteenth century, the site was being used for a variety of fertility rituals, by at least two of the largest local 'clans' (*oruganda*): the Abasasira and the Abakicu. In particular, both of these clans held large 'harvest festival' gatherings there, during which a part of their harvest would be offered up, and animals slaughtered for a feast. In addition, both groups also took their barren women there, to make 'offerings' to assist fertility (although all of the respondents with whom I spoke about this were somewhat vague as to what the content of these 'offerings' might have been). More dramatically, both clans also took girls there who had become pregnant out of wedlock, in order to kill them ritually at the site – by casting them down from the central cave, an act which was held to preserve the fertility of the wider social group.

More importantly for our story here, as many older fertility practices in the region were gradually subsumed by the beliefs associated with Nyabingi (a process which was largely complete by about the mid-nineteenth century, Philipps, 1928: 316 and Edel, 1957: 146), the site also then became a key Nyabingi shrine.[35] After this time, it was to Nyabuguto, and to Nyabugoto alone, that all the people in the local area would travel either to make an *okutoija* payment, or to engage in an *okutamba* ceremony (and indeed, it was following one particularly large *okutamba* gathering at the caves that the infamous 'Nyakishenyi rebellion' was launched, in 1917). Indeed, one local historian recalled that the caves at Nyabugoto, and a small rocky plateau located a few hundred yards from the cave proper, were even the primary site for *okutamba* ceremonies during the early nineteenth century, in particular.

Thus, the very fact that Ceredonia's visions occurred at Nyabugoto served to forge a connection between the Holy Mary of her apparitions, and the old Nyabingi. Moreover, as the testimonies of a number of people who attended these sessions confirm, this association is something of which Ceredonia was herself aware, and something which she actively sought to manipulate within the gatherings. For example, before receiving a vision of the Virgin whilst at the caves, Ceredonia would stare directly at the sun for a period, telling all present that, by so doing, she was looking at the face of God himself. This, she claimed, was a necessary precursor to seeing the Virgin, given that the latter somehow 'derived from', or 'grew out of', the former.[36] Upon turning back from the sun to the central rock, Holy Mary would appear to her. All of which was an almost certainly conscious attempt by Ceredonia to forge a connection between the Mary of her visions and the cosmology of the old Nyabingi (the latter of which held that Nyabingi, as the essence of fertility itself, grew out of – and was therefore in some sense the same as – the sun/God, *Kazooba*). In addition, throughout these sessions, Ceredonia constantly referred to the Mary of her visions by the name *nyoko'kuru* (paternal grandmother, second person), which had formerly been a common pseudonym for Nyabingi.

Furthermore, one early vision at the caves suggested that all of the 'true believers' in Mary should cut off all their body hair, pray the rosary over it, and then burn it. This act of ritualized hair cutting has a long history in many parts of South-western Uganda, in which the removal of old hair is deeply symbolic of a severance of old social ties or bonds, and the growth of new hair, which replaces the old, representative of the new relations which replace these. Today, the act is most commonly associated with the funeral of a household head (*nyin'eka*), during which all the members of a household shave their bodies, to symbolize both the demise of the former extended family, over which that particular head held sway, and the genesis of a new social unit in its stead (I have never witnessed these rites personally, but I have recorded accounts of them from a number of households in Bugamba Village, for example.) During an earlier period, they were

---

[35] It seems that the Nyabugoto site had formerly been used particularly for ritual activities pertaining to another fertility goddess, called Nyakituru. However, by the mid-nineteenth century, worship of Nyakituru seems to have become largely subsumed by Nyabingi devotion.
[36] This section is based on interviews with a number of respondents, including Fr. Rwabahima, Simon Naheza, Tugume, Eric Mazima and Atugonza John.

4.4 Looking up the hill towards the Nyabugoto caves

4.5 The main cave at Nyabugoto. During Ceredonia's vision at the site, the rock in the centre of this cave transformed into the Virgin Mary

4.6 The view from the cave. The school building on the hilltop in the middle distance stands on the site of the Nyakishenyi rebellion of 1917.

also performed as part of the ritual cleansing of murderers (Edel, 1957: 139) and – most importantly, for our story here – as part of the rites through which a barren woman became a Nyabingi handmaiden (thereby symbolizing both the break from her existing household and the beginning of her 'new life' as a devotee of the spirit).

Interestingly, Ceredonia was not the only Marian visionary to experience apparitions at Nyabugoto during this period, and at least two other seers – Gauda Kamushwa and Blandina Burigye – had briefly achieved fame a few years before Ceredonia's arrival.[37] However, within a short period of her first visit to the caves, Ceredonia's visions came to be regarded as by far the most compelling – as is evidenced by the fact that, following those initial sessions, Ceredonia quickly became the only visionary associated with the site – and it was because of this that her reputation quickly spread. Furthermore, it is my surmise that the reason why they came to be regarded as irresistible – vis-à-vis the other women's apparitions – was precisely because they specifically referenced the beliefs and practices of the old Nyabingi. Moreover, it is also

[37] In addition, Nyabugoto was not the only former Nyabingi shrine in which Marian apparitions were being received during this period. For example, the caves at Kibeho, in Rwanda, in which other visions were also taking place at this time, was also a former Nyabingi shrine. In addition, it is interesting to note here that the Nyabugoto caves were also visited, on at least one occasion in the early 1980s, by Specioza Mukantabona, a young Rwandan woman who claimed to be one of the Kibeho seers, and who later became established as a Marian visionary at Masaka (which is where the Kibweteeres later attended her prayer sessions).

clear that Ceredonia continued to invoke this connection even after her entry into the sect. Thus, for example, she renamed her father's compound as Nyabugoto, and it was later referred to as such by all members of the MRTC (indeed, local people in Kanungu still refer to the site as Nyabugoto, even today). In addition, and as will be explored at length in the next chapter, she also oversaw the recreation, and promotion, of the very same sorts of material exchanges, and redistribution networks, which had previously been the defining feature of the Nyabingi phenomenon.

Thus, in answer to the key question with which I began here, of what exactly made Ceredonia's visions quite so important – to such an extent that they became so central to the entire ritual practice, and to the social organization, of an entire AIC – it is crucial to note both that they occurred at the formerly most important Nyabingi shrine in South-western Uganda, and that the seer herself actively cultivated the various connections this implied. Thus, to put it in other words, during this early period at least, the entire MRTC can be understood as a full-blown revival of the old Nyabingi movement, at the centre of which was placed a key visionary 'hand-maiden'.[38] All of which helps us to understand a number of things, including why two senior priests like Kataribaabo and Ikazire should have fallen under the influence of Ceredonia in quite the way that they did. From this perspective, it would seem that the two priests' entry into the Movement is better understood as an attempt by them to harness the power of Ceredonia's visions, rather than the other way around (i.e. as an attempt by her to exploit the ecclesiastical authority that they would have represented). Moreover, this also helps us to understand why the two priests, whose involvement was so central to Bishop Kakubi's decision to expel the group from the Roman Church, quickly became such marginal members of the Movement thereafter.[39] But perhaps most importantly, the insights I have developed here are also crucial for understanding key aspects of the story which was to follow, including how and why the Movement grew so quickly in the years 1993–95. It is to these developments that I now turn.

[38] Interestingly, in this context, the key relationship between Kibweteere and Ceredonia – especially after the former's promotion to 'bishop' (a move which made him the, at least nominal, head of the Movement) – can also be said to have mirrored that which formerly existed between the *mugigwa* and the handmaiden (in which the former was nominally in charge, whilst the latter possessed the real power).

[39] In fact, Ceredonia herself had been summarily dismissed by the Church some years before the MRTC's general expulsion. Eric Mazima recalls that shortly after her first vision at Nyabugoto, Ceredonia had approached the resident priest in her local parish of Makiro (just outside Kanungu Trading Centre), to convey details of her apparition. This priest was the first indigenous clergyman to be based at Makiro, having only the previous year replaced the last White Father missionary to be based there. However, it turned out that the young man (whose name I never traced) was himself somewhat conservative, and a sceptic of Marian visionaries. According to Mazima, upon hearing Ceredonia's testimony, the priest dismissed her claims out of hand, and informed her that she was henceforth excommunicated from the Church.

5
Numbers
Religion in the time of AIDS

Otamwine amwine omu'nda. A woman's womb may be barren; not so her heart[1]

If an earlier revival of the Legion of Mary had, in a sense, developed out of a prior symbolic connection between the old Nyabingi and the Catholic Virgin Mary, in the context of a nascent MRTC this association was strengthened still further. Specifically, by receiving her visions at Nyabugoto, by reinvoking the earlier cosmology of Nyabingi, and by re-establishing the language, and ritual practices, of the old spirit – now in the context of Marian devotion – everything about Ceredonia's story suggests that her intention was to create something akin to a full-blown revival of the old religion. Indeed, it was because of her general success in this area, I have argued, that her visions came to be regarded as particularly compelling – more so than those of other seers of the period, and even amongst some quite senior members of the local Catholic hierarchy. Thus it was that her visions, and hers alone, came to quickly dominate the Movement's own forms of ritual practice, and its mode of social organization. Moreover, and of greater significance for my argument in the present chapter, this insight is also of key significance for understanding how and why the movement grew so quickly in the years immediately following its expulsion from the Catholic Church, (and for understanding the subsequent implications of this rapid growth).

By the end of 1989 – the year in which Ceredonia entered the group – the MRTC had between 50 and 60 'full-time' members, who lived permanently at the group's then main residence, at Kabumba. In addition, it had another 200 or so irregular followers, who would attend the daily prayer sessions, perhaps staying for a night or two as they did so. Over the following three years, these numbers grew steadily, although not remarkably so. Thus, according to both Mrs Kibweteere and Fr. Ikazire, and to other respondents as well, by the time the Movement left Kabumba in late 1992, it had about 300 permanent members, and perhaps 500 or so other followers. However, sometime between late 1993 and early 1995 – 1994 emerges as the key year in the narratives of many former members – these numbers suddenly jumped, and quite dramatically so. Thus, by early 1995, my sources suggest,[2] the MRTC had as many as 2000 permanent members, and several thousand more visitors. In other words, during this

---

[1] Cisternino, 1987: 357.
[2] Galasiano, Mr Sebataka, John Kihama.

one crucial period of 12 to 18 months around 1994, the sect grew more than sixfold in size.

The purpose of the current chapter, then, is to look at the history of recruitment to the now independent MRTC, and to explore how and why the numbers swelled in quite the way they did. The central argument I shall develop is that, whilst the sect engaged in a range of practices through which to bring in new members, the central strategy of their recruitment can again be understood with reference to the MRTC being a revival of Nyabingi. Specifically, throughout these years, the content of Ceredonia's visions – which was duly passed on to would-be recruits both by Ceredonia herself, and by the other leaders – emphasized that the Virgin Mary was a divine being capable of helping women to gain some redress for their various misfortunes (in much the same way that Nyabingi once had been). Hence, then, the timing of the sect's growth, because during the key period of MRTC expansion, around 1994, misfortune was literally everywhere in rural South-western Uganda, as the effects of an emergent AIDS epidemic began to be felt. Moreover, throughout these years, the Movement's key discourse of divine intercession was further emphasized by other of the Virgin's appearances, in which she constantly demanded sizeable offerings – much larger than those which had ever been required by the Legion – in payment for her intervention. Such demands can again be understood with reference to past Nyabingi practices which, as I have argued at length, historically centred upon various forms of material exchange.

Building the network

From the time the MRTC first took up residence at Kabumba, in July 1989, its leadership began to engage in a series of practices aimed at recruiting additional members. In a majority of cases, these early efforts centred around the class of 'leaders' drawing upon their pre-existing networks of contacts – which were in some cases quite extensive – to bring in more followers. Thus, a typical mode of recruitment involved a leader sending out a letter to some or other priest, relative, friend, or to some other contact with whom he or she was acquainted, informing them of the Movement's existence, and requesting a visit (*okuzinduka*). If this was positively received, a date would then be set, during which the leader involved, often accompanied by a small delegation from the Movement – which frequently included either Ceredonia herself, or else her sister or niece (Ceredonia's presence on these missions depended upon the relative standing of the person to be visited) – would visit the contact's parish, home, school, office, or whatever, and would stay there for a few days or more.

Here, the leader would initially focus on preaching to, and in a sense 'converting', the contact person him or herself. In addition, they would also seek out others in the local area who might be brought into the Movement. In some instances, this meant visiting other homes as well (such as those of the initial contact's relatives, friends and neighbours). In others, it involved inviting these other people to the initial contact's place, to attend

5.1 All of the sect's study centres were sited in members' homes. This centre, at Rugazi, was Fr. Kataribaabo's house. It was here that a number of mass graves were later discovered.

5.2 The sect's study centre at Makindye, just outside Kampala. A pit grave containing 55 bodies was also uncovered in the compound of this home.
(Source: This is a still from the police video of the Kanungu sites)

prayer sessions and, if Ceredonia was in attendance, visionary sessions as well. Following these visits, all those so inclined would then be required to leave their homes for a period – initially for about a week or so – to attend one of the group's initiation 'courses', at another of the MRTC's compounds (at Kabumba, Kanungu, Kitabi, or wherever).[3] Following this course, each initiand would decide whether or not they wanted to join the Movement on a full-time basis. If they did, they would then be required to return home and begin planning for a more permanent move to one of the group's centres (although it should be pointed out that, of the people who attended one of the MRTC's courses, by no means all went on to join up full-time). In a smaller number of cases, new recruits would instead be required to return home permanently, and begin preparations for their own home to be converted into a new 'study centre' for the Movement (after which other initiands, usually in groups of 30 to 50, would begin to attend courses held in them, as well).

Throughout the early years, and especially in the period between mid-1989 and late 1991, the personal social networks of Joseph Kibweteere emerged as particularly important for the group's efforts to arrange such visits to potential new recruits (although so too were those of Scholastica, Kurumbano, and Fr. Kasapuraari, albeit to a lesser extent). As a senior, and extremely wealthy, member of the Catholic laity, Kibweteere had not only a wide, but also a diverse, set of contacts on which he could draw. First of all, he was well known, and remained on good terms with many clergymen throughout the diocese. Thus, throughout the period, he was easily able to arrange introductory visits to parishes, as he was eventually to do to Rugazi (although unusually in that case, he had not requested the visit from Fr. Kataribaabo, but the other way around). Indeed, it is testament to Kibweteere's general standing in local Catholic circles that he was still able to introduce himself at local parishes, and to speak to local Legion of Mary groups, even after the MRTC had been officially expelled from the Church (although, after that time such visits tended to be restricted to the more rural parishes only). For example, sometime in 1992 or 1993, he spent several weeks at Kibale parish, in a rural part of Rwampara County, with a delegation that included both Angela and Ursula. On that occasion, the local priest opened a meeting of the Legion on his behalf, with a caveat that Kibweteere's group did not represent the mainstream Catholic Church, before allowing them to take over the meeting, and to conduct it according to their own design.

In addition, throughout these early years, Kibweteere also drew on a number of other personal networks, not all of which could be traced directly to the Church. For example, as a former headmaster, and a former Assistant Supervisor for Catholic Schools in the region, he also had a range of connections amongst local educational circles. Thus, throughout the years 1989 to 1991, he also regularly led delegations to the homes and schools of other headmasters, to the dwellings of his former students, and even, in

---

[3] Over time, the structure of these 'courses' – which were always the prerequisite for joining the group – became more elaborate. The courses themselves, and how they changed over time, will be discussed in detail in the next chapter.

one case, to the home of a former classmate of his son, Juvenal (Dodozio Innocent). Moreover, given Kibweteere's sizeable personal wealth, his former membership of the DP, and so on, he also had a wide range of other contacts on which he could draw, including various *bakago* relations, at least a dozen godchildren and their families, and various other young people for whom he had previously paid school fees (payment of educational expenses being a common means through which local 'big men' build up their social capital in this part of the country).

Following the entry of Frs. Kataribaabo and Ikazire into the MRTC in late 1991, the extent of the Movement's network of potential supporters *should* have grown significantly. After all, Kataribaabo, as the former Rector of Kitabi Seminary, was on personal terms with practically every parish priest in South-western Uganda. However, aware of the potential threat the new Movement posed – its apparently divisive nature was, after all, one of the main reasons why the MRTC had been expelled from the Catholic Church in the first place – the local Catholic hierarchy moved quickly to close off this potential avenue for recruitment. Thus, all parish priests were told, in no uncertain terms, that for them to even receive Kataribaabo's group as visitors would be taken as evidence of complicity with the Movement, and would be considered grounds for interdiction (or worse). Moreover, when one senior member of the laity received a letter from Kataribaabo requesting a visit, and she took this to her Bishop for advice, she was even told that, should she receive Kataribaabo at her home, her son would be expelled from Kitabi (where he was then studying in preparation for Holy Orders, Kyozeire Immaculate). In these ways, then, Kataribaabo soon became *persona non grata* within Catholic circles. Yet as a priest, he also had fewer of the kinds of additional contacts – of *bakago*, sponsored children, and the like – that the wealthier Kibweteere enjoyed.[4]

Thus, from quite early on, Kataribaabo's attempts to recruit new members were always rather limited, and seem to have involved little more than his contacting former members of Kitabi who had, for one reason or another, dropped out of their training (and were thus usually beyond the influence of the Catholic Church). For example, some time in 1992 or 1993, he wrote a letter to, and was subsequently received by, one Samanya Paul, an individual who had been mentored at Kitabi by Kataribaabo, but who had subsequently given up on the priesthood, and now worked as an office administrator. (On this occasion, Kataribaabo led a delegation to Samanya's house that included Ceredonia, Ursula, and others.) All of which is not to say that Kataribaabo's – and Ikazire's – efforts at recruitment were not

[4] Although this is not to say that he did not have any patronage networks at all. For example, over the course of my research, I spoke to at least two people whose school fees had been paid by Kataribaabo. In one of these cases, Kataribaabo had started to pay the young woman's fees, and to support her in other ways besides, following the death of her own father. Nevertheless, it is quite clear that his networks were nothing like as extensive as those of Kibweteere. Moreover, it is also noteworthy that, following the MRTC's expulsion, the church also moved to cut off Kataribaabo's networks. Thus, the young woman in the above example received a letter from the Bishop of Kasese informing her that, as someone who was known to have had her school fees paid by Kataribaabo, she should be aware that he had been expelled from the church, and that she should therefore have nothing further to do with him.

important at this time. On the contrary, a number of respondents remember their presence on these delegations, and the degree of authority which they brought to them. Rather, it is to say that, whether or not either of the senior priests was involved, the people to whom these delegations were sent were more often than not Kibweteere's contacts, rather than their own.

Yet if Kibweteere's networks were particularly important for the early growth of the MRTC, from about the time the group left Kabumba, in late 1992, onwards, things began to change significantly. In particular, from that time forward, the Movement increasingly recruited from amongst the networks of its ordinary membership, rather than relying exclusively, as before, upon only the connections of its leaders. Thus, as one respondent who was a member of the MRTC between 1992 and 1994 recalls, during 1993 Ceredonia's daily messages from the Virgin began to speak increasingly about the responsibility of all believers to persuade their friends and relatives to also join the group. In addition, discussion of recruitment came to predominate at many of the group's initiation 'courses'. Thus: 'at the one I attended, the most important part of the course concerned bringing your relatives [into the Movement]. They would say, over and over again, day after day: go and tell everyone, all of your relatives and friends, to come' (Ariseeni).

Indeed, my own evidence, which is based on interviews with surviving members, and with the relatives and friends of former members, suggests that, by about late 1993, it had indeed become more typical for new members to be recruited by way of their own contacts, rather than through one of the group's leaders. Moreover, my evidence further suggests that the methods of recruitment employed in these instances followed a certain pattern. Thus, in a majority of cases, an existing female member – 72 per cent of the MRTC's membership were female[5] – would arrange a visit either to the home of one of her natal kinswomen (to a sister's place, an aunt's house, or some such), or else to the dwelling of a sister-in-law, a close friend, or someone else again. Once again – and following a pattern which had already been established by the Movement's leadership – her mission there would typically last for a few days or weeks, during which she would preach both to her host and to her host's own family, friends and neighbours, and would play them tape recordings of Ceredonia's Marian visions.[6]

[5] How I arrived at this figure will be discussed in detail below.
[6] This use of tape recordings as a mode of proselytization became increasingly common from this period onwards. Thus, for example, a neighbour of the MRTC compound at Rushojwa – the site at which 81 bodies were later unearthed – recalls tape recordings of Ceredonia's visions being central to the early attempts of Joseph Nyamarimba (the owner of that compound) to recruit new members. As this respondent described to me, Nyamarimba was himself recruited to the sect through a delegation, in early 1993, but then returned home, later that same year, in order to convert his own compound into a new study centre for the group (a status it retained until the sect's demise in 2000). From that time onwards – and certainly throughout 1994 – the daily routine at Nyamarimba's home focused upon an afternoon/ evening prayer session, at which a tape of Ceredonia's visions was invariably played. According to this respondent (Patience N.), it was precisely because of these broadcasts that the sessions became so popular. Indeed, it was in order to listen to the tapes that she herself decided to attend some of the meetings, and because of them that various of her other neighbours did likewise (although it is impossible to know how many of these individuals might have gone on to join the Movement on a more full-time basis).

After this time, those who were so inclined would again leave home to attend an initiation course, after which they would decide whether or not to join the Movement on a full-time basis.

Case 1: Kiconco (Part 1)

To cite just a few examples here (although all of these are, as I have said, quite typical of the vast majority of cases I recorded during my research), this was very much the pattern through which the sister of Margaret Angabeire first joined the group, in late 1994. Margaret's sister, Kiconco, had some months earlier received a visit at her marital home, in Toro, from an old school friend of hers, called Jusenta. At the meeting, Jusenta had informed Kiconco that she was an active member of the MRTC, and that she had recently converted her own home – which was located in the two women's natal village, in Rukungiri District – into a new study centre for the Movement. Herself an active member of the local Legion of Mary group, Kiconco agreed to call in when she was next at home visiting her natal family. Thus it was that during her next visit home – to her sister Margaret's place, in December of that year – Kiconco spent a few days visiting Jusenta's house, engaging in worship with all the other initiands who were gathered here. As Margaret recalls, so taken was Kiconco by her experiences during these few days that, within barely a fortnight, she had once again returned from Toro, this time to participate in a full initiation course, and shortly after that, she joined the Movement on a permanent basis. (Margaret thinks that, after this time, her sister took up residence at the MRTC's compound in Rushojwa.) Significantly, Kiconco's husband did not join her in the sect, and she entered with only her teenage son.

Case 2: Mrs Sebataka

A similar pattern marked Mrs Sebataka's entry into the sect, in early 1996. In this instance, Mrs Sebataka had some months previously received a letter from two of her sisters, informing her that they had recently joined a 'new religion', in which she might also be interested. Just before Christmas 1995, the two sisters arrived at her marital home (in Mbarara District) for several weeks. The two spoke at length to Mr and Mrs Sebataka about the Movement (and to various other people around, especially women). Eventually, both Mr and Mrs Sebataka – and a number of other people besides – were persuaded to attend an initiation course, which they did, at Rugazi, in July 1996. The couple were asked to join the group, and to convert their home into a new 'study centre' for the Movement. It was with this aim in mind, therefore, that they returned home, along with four other 'ordinary converts' (three women and one man), and over the coming months hosted a number of additional courses at their home. Some of these courses were attended by Fr. Kasapuraari and Ursula, although never by Ceredonia, or any of the other leaders.

However, all did not go well, as Mr Sebataka soon became disillusioned with the Movement, and eventually decided to withdraw from it and, some time in late 1996, to expel it from his home (the reasons for his actions will be discussed below). However, Mrs Sebataka did not share her husband's views about the sect, and wishing to stay on, prepared for a permanent move to another of the MRTC's compounds. When she eventually left, she went with a number of her natal kin, all but one of her own children, six grandchildren, two sisters-in-law (HZ) and their children, and one affinal niece (HBD) and her children.[7] In total, over 45 people from Mrs Sebataka's kin network perished at Kanungu.

Case 3: Jolly Habusa (Part 1)

A similar general pattern can be observed in the story of Jolly Habusa's entry into the MRTC, in 1999. In this case, Jolly's daughter, Glenda, had previously – just prior to Christmas 1998 – received a letter from an old friend, informing her of the MRTC's existence, and requesting a visit to her marital home (also in Mbarara District). Glenda had initially agreed, and early the next January received the friend, along with two of her colleagues from the MRTC. However, as another of Jolly's daughters, Linda, now recalls, from an early stage Glenda regarded the visitors' message with a degree of scepticism, and showed little interest in herself attending any of the Movement's initiation courses. However, she did allow the delegation to remain in her house, and for the next three or four weeks, they used it as a base from which to hold daily prayer sessions, and to visit various other homes in the vicinity.

One of the homes they visited during this time was that of Glenda's mother, Jolly. Jolly was a long-term member of the local Legion of Mary group, and was initially quite excited by the story of Ceredonia's visions. However, as a senior member of the local laity, she was also concerned that some of the Movement's teachings were at odds with those of the mainstream church, and, for this reason, discussed the matter with her local parish priest. The outcome of the latter meeting is in little doubt: as Linda now recalls, her mother came back from this consultation loudly exclaiming that the MRTC was 'evil', and that 'under no circumstances would she ever allow those people to ever again enter her house'. However, she did not keep to her word and when, several months later, the same three women returned to her village, she not only let them enter her house, but had them stay there for over a month. Following this, both she, and her elder sister, travelled away to an initiation course, following which they returned only once more to their village, to tie up their affairs. In late 1999, the pair left the village, along with five of their children and one other young person (a local itinerant worker, *mupakasi*), and were never seen again.

---

[7] Interestingly, Mr Sebataka told me that the timing of his wife's permanent move was set by an announcement (*ekirango*) that the MRTC put out on a local radio station, Radio West, which asked her to travel to a specified Movement compound, on a specified date. This is the first example we have of the sect using radio as part of their recruitment process (which is something that they were later to do in a more targeted way, see Chapter 7).

Towards 'a coalition of frustrations'[8]

The most pressing question which emerges here, of course, is what exactly attracted these people – most of them women – to the MRTC? In other words, what was it about the various missionaries' message, and the content of the Movement's initiation courses, which made the whole thing seem quite so compelling that people were willing, within a relatively short period of time, to leave their homes on a more or less permanent basis in order to join it? Certainly, the very fact that the Movement was an independent Marian sect, which centred around the visions of a local visionary, must already have made it attractive. In addition, the very same factors that had made Ceredonia's visions so persuasive for the Movement's leadership – the Nyabugoto connection, their re-invocation of the cosmology of Nyabingi, their references to the language of Nyabingi, and so on – must also have made them appealing for other local women as well. In other words, Ceredonia's conscious attempt to lead a renewal of the old Nyabingi would surely have resonated with other local people as well (and not just with the senior laity and members of the clergy). Moreover, the overall connection with Nyabingi was something which was developed further still in the content of the Movement's teachings, all of which stressed that 'their' Virgin Mary was a divine figure capable of helping women to gain redress for the same kinds of misfortunes – in particular, those misfortunes related to the actions of *emandwa* – for which women had previously turned to the old Nyabingi.

Over the course of my research, I spoke to a range of individuals who had received visits from existing Movement members, and who had gone on to attend initiation courses, without subsequently joining up. Indeed, although it is impossible to be precise about numbers, it seems that it was not uncommon for people to attend initiation courses and then later to drop out (a point to which I shall return). Yet the point here is that a number of my respondents had witnessed the content of MRTC preaching first-hand, both during their initial visits to people's homes and during the initiation courses. What emerges from these people's testimonies is that much of the MRTC's teaching, couched as it was in a discourse of restoring the biblical Ten Commandments, centred around discussion of the kinds of misfortunes with which people in rural Uganda are commonly concerned. Moreover, within this, particular emphasis was given to those sorts of misfortunes which specifically affected women.

For example, one respondent, Godfrey Gimisiriza, recalled the homilies which were given by a group of MRTC members who visited his home, in Kabale District, sometime in the early 1990s. In this instance, the initial talk was of a general need to observe the Ten Commandments, to pray the

---

[8] Samanya Paul (not his real name), interview with film crew from the independent production house Mentorn Barraclough Carey (MBC). I would like to thank Eamonn Matthews of MBC for making the transcript of this, and all his production team's interviews on Kanungu, available to me.

rosary, to avoid backsliding, and so on. However, as the discussion became more specific, it soon turned to questions of misfortune, and in particular to those misfortunes which specifically affect women. Thus, for example, throughout these sessions there had been much talk of one of Kasaande's early visions in which Holy Mary had spoken about barrenness (*engumba*) in terms of its being not a curse, but a blessing (one which indicated that the Virgin had selected that young woman for 'special purposes'). In addition, there was lengthy discussion about polygamy – what the group usually referred to as 'illegal marriage' – about all the problems it caused, about how it was an especially wretched sin, about how it was particularly at odds with the Ten Commandments, and so on. There was also talk of another of Ceredonia's visions in which the Virgin had spoken of *emandwa*, to assure all of her followers that she would 'cure' all such troublesome spirits.

Significantly, this general pattern of discourse seems to have been repeated across the large part of the MRTC's missionary enterprise. Thus, another respondent recalls a visit by MRTC members to her home, in Mbarara District, in which the group similarly spoke in general terms about the Ten Commandments, the rosary, and so on, before going on to focus, in detail, only upon issues of fertility (Rachel, Silver Rose). Another recalled the group which visited her home, in Ntungamo District, also in the early 1990s, speaking mostly of 'problems' associated with polygamy (Mrs Tumwebase). Another told me about one initiation course he had attended, in Mbarara District, in which the 'main focus' involved discussion of *emandwa*, and a subsequent attempt to banish them from a number of the women in attendance (through the praying of multiple rounds of the rosary, Mr Sebataka's brother). And so on.

Yet if the MRTC's attempts at proselytization therefore involved their projecting an image of Holy Mary as a divine being capable of addressing people's – and especially women's – misfortunes, from quite an early stage (from about 1991 onwards) a particular emphasis was placed on one, quite specific, misfortune with was then affecting many people in South-western Uganda: the emerging AIDS epidemic. Thus, from early on, Ceredonia's visions pronounced that, when arranging visits to the homes of potential new recruits, members should focus their efforts on those households which were known to have been affected by the disease. One respondent, Georgina, recalls that one of the first actions of the MRTC delegation which visited her house, some time in 1992 or 1993, was to draw up a detailed list of all the households in the vicinity in which known AIDS victims had lived. As far as Georgina knows, this list then formed the basis of all of the group's subsequent activities – the invitations they sent out, and the visits they made – during the remainder of their stay in her village.

Moreover, from quite early on, discussion of AIDS also became central to MRTC discourse. The common line was that AIDS was a punishment from God, which had been sent down in response to people's failure to adhere to the Ten Commandments (indeed, this trope seems to have been propagated by a majority of the Movement's delegations, and was recalled by practically all of my respondents). Moreover, that the only way to avoid the deadly effects of the disease was to devote oneself to the Virgin, by joining the Movement. Delegations frequently told their initiands that 'if you have AIDS, and you join the Movement, then you will be cured' (Vincent Bwenungi).

More specifically, another respondent recalled one conversation he had with the delegation which had visited his home, in which the members claimed that, in one of the apparitions she had had from the Virgin, Ceredonia had been told how to cure AIDS (using a secret, herbal remedy, Mabega David). Moreover, this correlates with other accounts, some of which refer to various public 'faith healing' sessions held by the Movement, in which the Virgin – acting through Ceredonia – would actively 'cure' people of AIDS, in front of a congregation gathered there. Finally, other respondents recall that some delegations also claimed that for those people who had already lost their spouses to the disease, entry into the Movement would guarantee that they themselves would not contract the disease as well (for example, Silver Rose).

Such, then, was the nature of the MRTC's attempts at proselytization, at least as this was remembered by my respondents. Significantly, people's accounts here seem to be corroborated by the content of the Movement's key piece of literature, their own book, *A Timely Message from Heaven: The End of the Present Times* (1996 [1991]), which, from the time of its first reprinting, in 1994, became increasingly important to the group's attempts to attract new members (see Figure 5.3). The book was first printed in 1991, in both Runyankore/Rukiga and English. However, the print run of that first edition seems to have been quite small, and the book does not therefore emerge in people's narratives about the MRTC until after it had entered its second edition, in 1994 (which was again published in both Runyankore/ Rukiga and English, and also now in Luganda as well. A third edition of the book was then published in 1996 – again, in all three languages).[9] Yet after 1994, the book seems to have become central to the informal prayer sessions which the visiting MRTC delegations held in villages throughout the Southwest. Moreover, it also came increasingly to dominate the initiation courses, such that, by about mid-1995, the courses in practice consisted of little more than readings from the book, and discussions of these readings. Significantly, those leading the courses stressed that study of this book should replace conventional bible study, with the result that bibles became effectively banned at all of the MRTC's compounds.

The book thus offers an important insight into the Movement's key beliefs and practices. The text is made up of sixteen chapters, the majority of which – ten of them – detail visions (*okworekwa*) of the Virgin Mary, which had been received by one of the Movement's senior leaders.[10] Specifically, each of these ten chapters details one particular vision, as had been received by one named member of the leadership, at the point of his or her entry into the

[9] Indeed, so small was the print run of the first edition, that. despite numerous attempts to track down a copy, I have to date never been able to locate one.

[10] For the chapters on Frs. Ikazire and Kataribaabo (Chapters 8 and 9, respectively), the visions are instead claimed to be from Jesus Christ.

OBUTUMWA BWARUGA OMU EIGURU:
OKUHWAHO KW'OBUSINGYE OBU

IN HOC SIGNO VINCES

OMU KAMANYISO AKA NIMWE ORASII NGURIRE

"Abantu mwena mujuumure ebiragiro ikumi bya Ruhanga"

5.3 The front cover of the MRTC's main publication, A *Timely Message from Heaven: The End of the Present Times.* The book went through three editions (in 1991, 1994 and 1996)

sect. (Thus, although the daily ritual practice of the Movement had already, by this time, revolved around the visions of Ceredonia only – who was, in effect, the only person to ever have Marian visions *within* the Movement – the fact that all of the leaders had had an 'initial vision' becomes, in the context of this book at least, a marker of their divinely sanctioned authority.) However, the key point I want to make here is that the overall content of these various visions correlates quite directly with my respondents' descriptions of the MRTC's preaching. Thus, across all of these visionary chapters, the principal theme is the return to a life based on the Ten Commandments, the observance of rosary prayers, Marian devotion in general, and so on.[11] Within this, each chapter addresses a specific theme, and elaborates the ways in which a particular set of sinful behaviours contravenes a specific Commandment, or Commandments. Thus, for example, the vision of Ursula Komuhangi (Chapter 3) outlines the ways in which pre-marital sex specifically contravenes the Sixth Commandment – 'thou shalt not commit adultery'. The vision of one Byarugaba (Chapter 6) details the

[11] Whilst correct observance of the rosary is a theme which runs through all of these chapters, one vision, that of Mrs Kibweteere (Chapter 12), is devoted entirely to it.

ways in which drunken behaviour leads to contraventions of the Sixth and Seventh Commandments – 'thou shalt not commit adultery' and 'thou shalt not steal'. The vision of John Kamagara (Chapter 7) explains the ways in which contemporary behaviours contravene the Third Commandment – 'thou shalt respect the Sabbath'. And so on. Meanwhile, a number of the visions, including those of Ceredonia, Kibweteere, and Fr Kasapuraari (Chapters 1, 2 and 10, respectively), describe the ways in which people's current actions break *all* of the Ten Commandments.

The main point I want to make here is that practically all of these visions make frequent reference to various of the key themes I have already discussed. Thus, for example, Ceredonia's vision attacks those women who, in the event of infertility, turn to traditional healers (*abafumu*) for help. At one point, the vision condemns traditional healers as being 'in company with the devil' (1996 [1991]: 8).[12] More significantly, a number of the visions attack polygamy, and urge those women who are involved in polygamous arrangements to exit them forthwith. Thus, for example, in the vision of Ursula, it is stated: 'Our Blessed Mother...says that all those who are the second, the third or more wives to your husbands should leave such husbands' (*ibid.*: 40). In the vision of Kamagara (Chapter 7) believers are similarly urged to pray particularly for 'those who are in unlawful wedlock' (*ibid.*: 73–4). Again in the vision of Fr. Kasapuraari, women who enter into polygamous marriages are attacked on the grounds that they disrupt existing 'legal' marriages, and engender hatred in their senior co-wives. Indeed, according to this vision, the arrival of a junior wife might even motivate a senior wife to kill the former's children, in order that they '[will] not share the property with her [own] children'. In addition, this vision also attacks the senior co-wives of polygamous unions, arguing that their infidelities often account for their husband's seeking out an additional wife in the first place (*ibid.*: 96–7).

Finally, almost all of the visions also make explicit reference to the actions of *emandwa*, again emphasizing that such forces are 'satanic' powers, and, as such, are not to be feared by the true believer. Thus, the vision of Ceredonia speaks at length about the effects of these 'devils', and claims that only Jesus and the Virgin Mary have the power to 'drive them out' (for which they demand that the devotee fast, *ibid.*: 12–14 & 19). They

[12] A note here on references. The discussion of the MRTC's publication in this, and the next, chapters, is based on my use of the 1996 Runyankore/Rukiga and English editions of the book. During my research on the sect, I initially worked on the 1996 Runyankore/Rukiga edition, from which I produced my own, full English translation in late 2001. However, later on – during a research trip to Uganda in 2004 – I also secured a copy of the 1996 English edition of the book. As I now compare my own translation of the 1996 Runyankore/Rukiga edition with the MRTC's own 1996 English edition, I realize that the former is more linguistically accurate. Simply stated, my own translation is rendered as grammatically accurate as possible, whilst the MRTC's English edition is written in a recognizably colloquial 'Ugandan English' (which is markedly idiomatic, and grammatically incorrect, in a number of ways).

Nevertheless, I have decided, throughout this book, to quote not my own translation, but instead the MRTC's 1996 English edition. The reason for this decision is that, linguistically inaccurate as this edition might be – as is evidenced by many of the quotes included below – it nevertheless conveys a better sense of the 'flavour' of the sect's thinking, and thus brings us closer, I think, to the nature of its discourse and ideas.

are discussed in similar terms in the visions of Sempa (Chapter 5; *ibid.*: 64–5), and of Kamagara (*ibid.*: 71), amongst others.

Moreover, it is also worth noting that some of these themes are also repeated in other chapters in the book (i.e. in chapters other than those which recount the individual visions). Significantly, they constitute some of the key themes in the final two chapters, which are entitled 'Messages of Jesus and Mary to Various Institutions' (Chapter 15) and 'Questions and their Replies' (Chapter 16). This is significant because anecdotal evidence suggests that these two sections – which arguably are written in a more pedagogical style than any of the others – were the ones most frequently referred to during initiation courses. (This certainly makes particular sense in relation to the last chapter, which is made up of specific questions asked by initiands at various courses, as well as the leadership's answers to these. In some instances, the date of the course at which the particular question was asked and the compound where it was held are recorded in the book.)

It is important to note that once again here – and mirroring the earlier descriptions of Godfrey Gimisiriza – particular virtue is ascribed to those women who do not get married, and never produce children. Indeed, this is taken as evidence of particular devotion to the higher task of preaching the Virgin's message. Thus,

> marrying and getting married should be left to those who have got the time for it. In your case you know many things about what has happened in the past and what is still to come...can we really send you to go and tell what the people of the world should do...at the same time as we tell you to go to marry and to get married? Not at all...Would you really be in child labour and as well be able to go here and there to take our messages to the people at the same time?' (*ibid.*, 137–8).

Similarly, close attention is paid, in the question and answer section, in particular, to the subject of polygamy. Thus, the second question comes from a young woman who asks 'If I got married illegally [i.e. as a junior co-wife] to a legally married person and now I want to repent but my father and brothers have already taken the brideprice from the man; if they refused to return it to him what should I do?' To this, the author replies that the young woman should first of all tell her father and brothers that they themselves have sinned – by agreeing to a polygamous marriage, and thereby disrupting an existing, legal union (between the husband and his existing wife) – and should then withdraw from the union entirely. She is told that 'you on your part, should leave the man and save your soul. If you stay with him; both of you and the children will not get to heaven, you will be thrown into hell' (*ibid.*: 141). I shall return to the content of these final two chapters in due course.

However, it is fair to say that by any reading of this book, the *primary* theme to emerge across all of its chapters – across both the chapters concerning individual visions, and the other chapters as well – is that of AIDS. Thus, most of the chapters concerning visions refer specifically to the epidemic. For example, it is mentioned in the vision of Ceredonia (*ibid.*; 3, 12 & 17), in the vision of Kibweteere (*ibid.*; 32), in that of Ursula (*ibid.*; 38), that of Sempa (*ibid.*; 62–6), that of Byarugaba (*ibid.*; 67–70), that of Fr.

Ikazire (chapter 8, *ibid.*: 78), that of Kasapuraari (*ibid.*; 93–4), and so on. Moreover, the first three of these visions – i.e. those of the three key leaders Ceredonia, Kibweteere and Ursula (which constitute the first three chapters of the book) – all conclude with discussion of AIDS. In other words, all of these chapters build up to an engagement with the epidemic, and thus cast it as the central focus of their arguments. In addition, the chapter concerning the vision of Sempa is devoted entirely to discussion of the disease (indeed, it is subtitled 'About AIDS, Medicinal Shrubs and the Shrines for Satan', *ibid.*: 62). A number of the other chapters in the book – i.e. those which are not concerned with individual visions – also refer to the disease (in some cases, at length).

Thus, across the whole book, the AIDS epidemic is discussed as the result of all types of sinful practice. For example, in the vision of Kibweteere, the epidemic is caused by general 'negligence' of the Ten Commandments (*ibid.*: 32), in the vision of Ursula, by adultery, and by a failure to recognize parental authority (*ibid.*: 38), in the vision of Sempa, by greed and theft (*ibid.*: 62), in that of Byarugaba, by alcoholism (*ibid.*: 67), in that of Fr. Ikazire, by failure to observe the sacrament of Holy Communion (*ibid.*: 78), and so on. Moreover, in a majority of these references, the epidemic is discussed as divine retribution for the said sins. One early statement in the vision of Ceredonia sets the tone for all of the references which are to follow, when it states that 'the chastisement He [God] released...the world calls it the AIDS disease or SLIM: but from the Lord, it is a punishment' (*ibid.*: 3).

Moreover, it goes on to warn ominously: 'please, be informed that the punishment of SLIM, AIDS, which today claims the lives of the people, one by one, is not going to be revoked' (*ibid.*: 12). Perhaps most significantly, this same part of the book also contains a message about how one is to avoid this great 'divine punishment'. Here, the book once again mirrors the descriptions of my repondents, in claiming that the only way to survive the disease is to repent, and to join the Movement. Thus, 'the Father said; "I will not give them any medicine, its medicine will only be to repent and restore my Ten Commandments...I will only take away that punishment from them when they all repent, when they cry out to me and restore my Commandments".' Further, 'if [one] repents after getting that punishment of the AIDS, and even if one is on his death-bed and repents, both his spiritual and physical life will be restored to him' (*ibid.*: 3).

On having 'good reasons to join'[13]

All of the people who joined the MRTC during the 1990s – most of them women, and many of whom went on to die at Kanungu – had their own individual reasons for joining the sect. Thus, from the sizeable body of evidence I have collected about the MRTC, I can confidently state that no two members' stories, or motivations for entering the Movement, were ever exactly the same. Nevertheless, across this same body of evidence, certain general patterns can certainly be identified. Moreover, it is perhaps not

[13] Winifred Aheebwa.

surprising – given the arguments I have just developed, and the evidence I have presented in support of them – that, in relation to these patterns, the issue of infertility (*engumba*), problems related to polygamy, and the matter of troublesome spirits (*emandwa*) all emerge as key factors.

Case 4: Deidre Masimbi

Thus, for example, the story of one Deidre Masimbi's entry into the Movement is quite typical of many of the cases I have recorded. In this instance, the 22-year-old Deidre had, sometime in 1991 or 1992, entered into a relationship with, and subsequently got married to, a young man in her natal village, in Rukungiri District. However, barely two years later, following the visit of an MRTC delegation to her home area, she had decided to leave her new husband, and to take up permanent residence at one of the Movement's compounds (at Rushojwa). According to one of my respondents, Winifred Aheebwa – a long-time neighbour of the Rushojwa compound, and a person for whom Deidre had briefly worked as a housegirl – the primary reason for this move was Deidre's infertility. Winifred told me that over the two years of her marriage, Deidre had in fact become pregnant twice, yet on both occasions had miscarried. Finally, she had decided to seek medical advice on the issue – at a private clinic in Rukungiri Town – but had then been told that a problem with her reproductive organs meant that she might never be able to go full-term. According to Winifred, this news resulted in tensions within Deidre's marriage, which were in turn the primary reason for her initial decision, made shortly afterwards, to pitch in with the MRTC.

Case 3: Jolly Habusa (Part 2)

Similarly, the case of Jolly Habusa – some details of which have already been discussed (in Case 3, Part 1) – is again archetypical of various others I recorded in the field. In this instance, Jolly's decision to join the MRTC had been largely motivated, her daughter Linda argues, by growing tensions within a new polygamous arrangement. Thus, she told me that, during the crucial period between the MRTC delegation's first visit to her village and their second stay – the period during which Jolly's attitude towards the Movement shifted dramatically, from her describing them as 'evil', to her allowing the delegation to stay in her home (after which she herself joined the Movement) – Jolly's husband had taken on a second wife. As Linda describes it, sometime in early 1999 the family was surprised to learn that, after more than thirty years of living in a monogamous relationship, her father had decided, apparently quite suddenly, to take on another spouse. Barely a few weeks later, this second wife had arrived at his home and, more significantly, Linda's father had divided his land – all of which had previously been cultivated by Jolly alone – into two parts (in order to provide his second wife with her own piece of land on which to build a house, and to cultivate as well).

According to Linda, this perceived 'loss' of her former gardens greatly irked her mother, as did the degree of 'neglect' which her husband now displayed towards her. In the period after the arrival of his second wife, Jolly's husband stopped working in her fields (in the ones she remained with following the sub-division), ceased eating in her house (*enju*), and even stopped spending the night there. Finally, as the tensions all this created grew, Jolly's husband decided to use part of the brideprice he had received from his daughter Linda's recent marriage – livestock which Jolly would, of course, have regarded as belonging exclusively to her *enju* – to buy a new piece of land, several miles away, on which he and his new wife could settle. From that time onwards – and, indeed, up until the time I interviewed her – Linda never saw her father again. More importantly for our story here, these tensions were the primary reason, Linda feels sure, that her mother decided, shortly afterwards, to join the MRTC.

Case 1: Kiconco (Part 2)

Once again, the case of Kiconco – various aspects of which I have already discussed (in Case 1, Part 1) – is also quite typical of a number of others I documented during my research. In this instance, Kiconco's primary motivation for taking up with the Movement seems to have related to her son's disability. Shortly after her marriage in Toro, Kiconco had given birth to a baby boy who, from an early age, had suffered from some sort of physical and mental disability. To begin with, both Kiconco and the rest of the family had suspected that the child's disease might be symptomatic of an underlying 'cancer', and they had therefore taken him, on several separate occasions, to the hospital in Kasese Town. However, as Kiconco's sister, Margaret Angabeire, recalls, the doctors could find no medical reason for the boy's condition, and thus the family began to suspect the operation of *emandwa*.

Kiconco's – and Margaret's – mother had died a couple of years before Kiconco's marriage, and attention was now turned to the possibility that it was the dead woman's ghost – presumably angry, for some reason, with her daughter – that was the cause of the child's malady. As a result, Kiconco began attending a number of diviners (*bafumu*) both around her marital home and in her natal village, but again with little apparent success. Nevertheless by the late 1980s, the boy, now in his early teens, continued to be completely paralysed down one side of his body, and to display severe learning difficulties. Thus it was that sometime in the late 1980s – in 1988 or '89, Margaret thinks – that Kiconco announced that she had recently received a visitation from the Virgin, informing her that the boy's condition was indeed the result of *emandwa*, and reassuring her that the Virgin herself would soon make him better. Moreover, Kiconco went on that, a few days after her own visitation, Holy Mary had also appeared to the young man himself, to give him the same message. It was after this time, Margaret recalls, that her sister had become a keen member of the local Legion of Mary group, and it was in this context that she had later taken such an interest in the MRTC. As Margaret told me, from the time of her initial vision onwards, Kiconco had effectively 'dedicated that boy [her son] to Mary', and had later come to feel that the MRTC represented the best setting within which that dedication could be realized.

The Virgin Mary in the time of AIDS

Orwitsire nirwo ruhumba. That which kills also sweeps away. No one knows how a misfortune is going to play out[14]

Across all of the evidence I have gathered about the Movement, it is also clear that in the vast majority of cases of MRTC membership – including a number of the cases already discussed – these various issues of infertility, polygamy and affliction were greatly exacerbated by an emergent AIDS epidemic. Thus, across my entire body of data, AIDS emerges as perhaps the primary causal factor for people's decision to join the MRTC. Moreover, this insight also helps us to understand the timing of the sect's growth and, in particular, its large expansion in the period around 1994. After all, this was the very time during which the worst effects of the AIDS epidemic were beginning to be felt throughout South-western Uganda.

It is important to note here that, from the outset of the African HIV/AIDS epidemic, the hills of the Western Rift Valley – of which the Kigezi Hills are one part[15] – had been particularly badly hit by the disease. Thus, data from sero-surveys of HIV-1 prevalence point to the conclusion that, already by the mid-1980s, the area's infection rates were abnormally high, compared even with other parts of the Great Lakes region (which was in turn the worst affected part of the continent, at that time). For example, in a nationwide sero-survey conducted in Rwanda in December 1986, returns from Ruhengeri and Gisenyi Towns recorded the highest rates of HIV prevalence of anywhere in the world at that time.[16] The former recorded total infection rates of 22 per cent,[17] the latter, an even more dramatic 31 per cent (Bugingo *et al.*, 1988).

Contemporary data are lacking for South-western Uganda. However, given the close proximity of both Ruhengeri and Gisenyi to the Ugandan border,[18] and given the particularly high degree of cross-border trade – and other social activity – which has long characterized these border zones (MacGaffey, 1991: *passim*), prevalence rates in South-western Uganda must have been roughly equivalent to those of Northern Rwanda at this time. Certainly, by the time the first reliable HIV-1 prevalence data were collected in Uganda – at a number of sentinel sites in urban ante-natal clinics, from the late 1980s onward – it is clear that the Ugandan situation was at least as bad as the Rwandan case. Indeed, early data from these sentinel sites

[14] Cf. Cisternino, 1987: 405.
[15] This topographical zone extends into Eastern DRC, Western Rwanda and Western Burundi.
[16] Although both of these towns were later overtaken by Lyantonde in Uganda.
[17] The phrase 'total infections rate' refers to the number of cases across a total population (i.e. across all men, women and children, of all ages, in a particular locale).
[18] Ruhengeri Town lies just 10 miles south of the Ugandan border, and less than 20 miles from Kabale Town. Gisenyi lies just to the South-west of Ruhengeri.

suggest that by 1990, HIV-1 prevalence was running at about 25 per cent, throughout the rural Southwest (*HIV/AIDS Surveillance Data Base*, US Census Bureau, December 2006). Moreover, all of this meant that, by the early 1990s, people were beginning to die of the disease in large numbers, across the Kigezi Hills and beyond.

Reliable data on AIDS-related deaths in Uganda are notoriously difficult to come by.[19] However, anecdotal evidence, at least, would suggest that it was in the years between 1992 and 1994 that the aforementioned high prevalence rates began to result in significant numbers of AIDS deaths. Certainly, this timing would be consistent with what we now know about the 'natural' life-cycle of HIV/AIDS (i.e. its progress in the absence of anti-retroviral drug interventions). Thus, the years 1992 and especially 1993 are remembered as particularly significant in my main field site of Bugamba Village, in Mbarara District, as the time when the ultimate effects of the epidemic began to be felt. More importantly for the story here, these same years are also remembered as significant by a majority of my respondents on the MRTC.

The AIDS epidemic emerges in individual narratives related to the MRTC in a number of ways. Firstly, it is clear that some of the people who joined the Movement – especially in the key years of the sect's growth, between 1992 and 1994 – were motivated to do so by the fact that they themselves were already suffering from the disease.

Case 5: Lawrence Kamukama

For example, this was the case with one Lawrence Kamukama, the father of my respondent Michael Twinomujuni, who joined the Movement in early 1993. Some time in the mid-1980s, Kamukama had joined the Ugandan police force, and in 1991 had been posted away from his home area in Kabale District, to Kampala. However, it soon became apparent that Kamukama was suffering from AIDS, and after a slow – and rather unpredictable – decline (the typical profile for an AIDS patient), he had, by the end of 1992, become too sick to continue working. As a result, the family arranged for him to return to his home village, where they could look after him better.

It was about two months after this, Michael thinks, that an MRTC delegation first arrived in their village, to visit the home of Kamukama's mother-in-law (Michael's maternal grandmother). At first reluctant to receive the delegation – which was led by Ursula – Kamukama eventually gave in to his mother-in-law's constant entreaties to have the group run some prayer sessions in his house. Thus it was, that over a period of several weeks, the group held a number of prayer sessions at Kamukama's home, which were attended by at least two other AIDS patients as well. As Michael recalls, throughout these prayer sessions, the congregation was constantly told that if they joined the MRTC, then the Virgin Mary would cure them of all disease. In addition, after one prayer session, Ursula gave Kamukama a set of rosary beads which she claimed had 'special powers' to

---

[19] The best introduction to the vast literature on HIV/AIDS in Uganda is Allen (2006).

ward off AIDS, whilst on other occasions, she sprinkled holy water around his home, for the same reason. Thus it was that a short time later, Kamukama decided to join the MRTC, after which he was transported to one of their study centres by car (for he was still too weak to get there under his own steam). He was accompanied into the sect by his mother-in-law, his wife, and his three daughters (Michael's maternal grandmother, mother, and three sisters, respectively). A short time later, Michael received news that his father had died at the MRTC compound in Rushojwa. However, all of his other relatives stayed in the Movement and later died, Michael presumes, in the Kanungu fire.

The story of Michael Twinomujuni's mother here highlights another way in which the AIDS epidemic shaped people's motivations for entering the MRTC. In her case, there seems to have been no evidence, at the time of her entry into the sect, that she herself had already contracted the disease (certainly, Michael claims that she was not displaying any of the distinctive symptoms of the disease). However, given her husband's demise, she would have realized that she too was at grave risk of contracting the disease. This seems a reasonable assumption, even though the causes of AIDS would not have been well understood across all parts of rural Uganda by this time. Thus, the message of entering the MRTC as a means of being 'cured' of AIDS would have been equally appealing to her as it was to her already dying husband. Moreover, this narrative of the 'AIDS widow' – or potential AIDS widow – emerges again and again in respondents' descriptions of the type of people who were joining the Movement during this period of the early to mid-1990s. For example, one respondent (Michael Twinomujuni's aunt) told me that 'most of the people who joined [at this time] were women who had lost their husbands to AIDS. People who had lost their partners to AIDS', whilst another similarly stated 'you must understand that most of the people who arrived there were desperate people, people with grave problems. Most of them were widows, wives who had lost their husbands, and were therefore desperate...most of these [women] had lost their husbands to AIDS' (Lucy Kamuli, interview with MBC). Again 'a lot of the people in the Movement were AIDS widows' (Vincent Bwenungi).

In local understandings, the death of a spouse to AIDS – or indeed, to any other disease – would in many instances be more problematic for a woman than for a man. Hence, I would suggest, the reason why it was mostly AIDS widows, rather than widowers, who were joining the Movement, despite the fact that AIDS has always killed roughly equal numbers of men and women across the Southwest and beyond. The key issue here is that in local ontologies women are normatively regarded as the primary agents of their household's entire fertility. In other words, women alone are often held responsible for the healthy reproduction of all aspects of their *enju*.

However, by extension, this also means that any failure in that reproductive capacity can also be cast as primarily *her* 'fault', or her 'misfortune' (*ekibi*).[20] Thus, the possibility exists – and on many occasions over the

[20] As discussed, the word *ekibi* has a wide semantic range, and encompasses both 'fault' and 'misfortune', and also 'sin'.

course of my fieldwork I have witnessed it being realized – for *all* deaths in a household to be, in effect, 'blamed' on her. Therefore, her own death, that of her husband who stays in her *enju*, that of one of her children, that of an animal, or even some crops, might all be put down to *her* misfortune, to a failure of *her* fertility. Moreover, this notion is in some senses captured by the concept of *engumba*, which, in addition to referring to a woman's physical inability to produce a child, is sometimes also used in reference to a woman's death, to the death of her husband or child, the demise of one of her animals, or some other occurrence along these lines. However, the main point here is that, as a result of these logics, the advent of the AIDS epidemic in the early to mid-1990s, although it probably killed as many men as women, nevertheless had a particularly detrimental effect upon only the latter, exacerbating as it generally did the problems of female *engumba*, or 'infertility'.

Case 6: Mbabazi Eunice

Consider, for example, the case of Hilary Birungi's sister-in-law, Mbabazi Eunice, elements of which mirror the story of Michael Twinomujuni's mother. Sometime in early 1993, Mbabazi's husband, Frank, had fallen sick with AIDS and, unable to continue with his existing job in Mbarara Town, had returned home to his village, some 15 or so miles away. Again, shortly afterwards, an MRTC delegation had begun to attend his home, and had promised him that devotion to the Virgin Mary would cure him of his illness. In addition, the delegation had also given him a special herbal remedy for his sickness (presumably the same 'cure' for AIDS which had previously been passed on to Ceredonia in a vision). Once again, the delegation's message seems to have been convincing, because shortly afterwards both Frank and his wife decided to join the Movement. However, in this instance Frank never made it into the group, because just as the family was arranging transport to the compulsory initiation course, his condition suddenly deteriorated, and he died. Moreover, in this instance her husband's death seems to have initially caused Mbabazi to doubt the veracity of the MRTC message, and, as a result, she had no further contact with the Movement for several months following.

However, two factors soon changed her mind on this, and eventually led to her moving into one of the MRTC's compounds, sometime in mid-1994. As Hilary recalls, the first key factor was that much of Mbabazi's affinal family – on whose land she continued to live, even after Frank's death – effectively blamed her for her husband's death. Her father-in-law, in particular, claimed that it was as a result of her *ekibi* that Frank had become sick in the first place. Later, he even tried to run her off his family's land (further claiming that, were she to stay, her *ekibi* might affect other members of the household as well). To begin with, Mbabazi resisted these threats. However, shortly afterwards, one of her six children – an 18-month-old boy – passed away, the likely cause again being AIDS. According to Hilary, this death was immediately taken by the family to be yet another instance of

Mbabazi's *engumba*. Thus it was that, a few weeks later, Mbabazi left, with her mother and five remaining children, to join the MRTC.

Moreover, the fact that women could be, in effect, 'blamed' for AIDS deaths, that such deaths could be explained with reference to their *engumba*, had particular implications for young, recently married brides (*bagole*). On the one hand, the households in which these women lived were the most likely to be affected by AIDS. As the Ugandan anthropologist Stella Neema has shown in a survey of local sexual practices, both men and women in rural South-western Uganda – as doubtless elsewhere as well – are at their most sexually active, and are most likely to have multiple sexual partners, in their late teens and early twenties (in other words, in the years immediately prior to their first marriage) (Neema, 1994: 141). However, in the context of the AIDS epidemic of the early to mid-1990s, this also meant, of course, that this group was also at greatest risk of contracting the disease, and of dying from it. Moreover if, as the case of Mbabazi Eunice highlights, any wife whose husband has died of AIDS is left in a somewhat 'vulnerable' position in her affinal household, this was particularly true for younger wives. Specifically, the example of Mbabazi demonstrates the range of risks an AIDS widow might face: of being ostracized by her affinal family, of having her productive gardens and her animals – her very means of livelihood – taken away, of perhaps even being forced out of her marital home entirely, and so on.

A number of cases of AIDS widows I have recorded in Bugamba Village – all of which were quite unconnected to the MRTC, or to Kanungu – suggest that all of these risks are very real indeed. However, from my earlier discussions it is also clear that, in all such cases, the exact degree of risk any individual wife faces is directly proportional to the means she has available to 'defend' her position. Moreover, it is clear that younger wives were almost always placed in a particularly vulnerable position here – vis-à-vis the more senior wives within an extended household (who might be their own co-wives, or other senior women in the household). This stemmed from the fact that often these younger women had still to 'establish' themselves in their affinal homes (through the raising of adult sons who might 'defend' their interests, through the bringing in of wealth through their adult daughters' marriages, and so on). Once again, all of this is supported by my wider body of ethnographic data.

For all these reasons, then, throughout the early to mid-1990s, a growing number of young AIDS widows were present in South-western Uganda, many of them living in socially precarious situations in recently entered affinal households. Moreover, for most of these young women, a return to their natal homes was not an option, even when they had been effectively 'forced out' of their affinal homes, given that such a move would necessitate their fathers, brothers and uncles returning the brideprice which had been paid to them at the woman's marriage (livestock which, as my long research experience in South-western Uganda has shown, is generally disposed of quite quickly after a marriage, and is therefore not usually available for redeployment). It should also be pointed out here that, during 1993 and 1994, in particular, brideprice payments were being especially strictly enforced within most marriages, as a result of the concurrent spike in the global coffee price (which, in the context of Uganda's newly liberalized economy, had left many households with far more cash than ever before, and therefore in a much better position to raise such payments).[21] Faced with these circumstances, then, and as the above cases demonstrate, some of these women turned directly to the MRTC.

However, it should also be noted that this was not the only strategy available to them. For example, my data also show that, in other instances, young wives 'forced out' of their marital homes could simply run away, and seek a new life in the anonymity of an urban centre. For example, this was the case with one of my respondents, Lilian Suolisia. In other cases, and perhaps more commonly, the women involved could seek out a second marriage (as was especially the case for those women who lacked the necessary contacts to become established in a town in their own right). Certainly, a small percentage of these women do appear to have found other men with whom to enter into new monogamous unions. For example, such was the case for my respondents Donna Sekibibi and Maria Nakacwa. However, more commonly, especially when the circumstances of the first marriage were widely known, and *especially* when the woman had produced children from the first marriage, this was less likely to happen. In these circumstances, the only other option available to these women was for them to try to re-marry into other polygamous households.

On senior co-wives

Obushwere bwa juba tobushendera mukazi mukuru. Don't divorce your old wife because of your new one [22]

---

[21] It had become an increasingly common practice, from about the late 1970s onwards, for young people from households which were unable to afford the full cost of a marriage – especially the costs of the brideprice and/or dowries – to enter into 'informal' marriage alliances (called *okutaasya*, or *okutaasya omukazi*, lit: 'to bring in a wife'). These arrangements – which are still relatively frequent amongst poorer households, especially in the rural areas – usually involve one or more of the 'traditional' wedding ceremonies being carried out, but crucially, almost always involve brideprice payments being deferred, sometimes indefinitely so (at the very least, until the birth of the couple's first child). However, because of their informality – and for other reasons besides – they are generally regarded as anathema by the church. Indeed, even today, it is still quite common for those who have been married only by means of *okutaasya* to be barred from their local parishes. For this reason, most people consider 'formal' marriages (i.e. those in which brideprice and dowries are paid, and which are sanctioned by the church) to be a superior form of arrangement, and they will usually opt for a formal marriage if funds allow. In this context, then, during the coffee price spike of 1993 and 1994 – when even some of the humblest households suddenly found themselves cash-rich – the number of informal arrangements amongst younger couples dropped dramatically, and the number of formal unions rose accordingly. Thus, for example, in Bugamba's case, anecdotal evidence suggests that almost no *okutaasya* ceremonies at all occurred during these years, whilst local parish records confirm that, when compared with the preceding two years, 1994 and 1995 saw more than a four-fold increase in formal church weddings. However, the point is that, for many of these young AIDS widows, the fact that brideprice *had* been paid for their unions in fact made it more difficult for them to leave their affinal homes, because of the reasons outlined.

[22] Cisternino, 1987: 351.

Otaine mutima abinga omukazi owaabandize. He who is out of his mind divorces the first wife (when taking a second one)[23]

Abakazi ku bashaaga, abamwe bahinduka abazaana. When wives are many, some of them are slaves [24]

Abakazi bashweirwe hamwe nigo mahari. Polygamy is jealousy[25]

Narira eriisho riimwe nk'orikuziika muk'iba. You only cry from one eye when burying at your husband's home. One sheds only 'crocodile tears' at a co-wife's funeral

Thus, throughout the early to mid-1990s, a growing number of young AIDS widows were becoming junior co-wives in polygamous arrangements. It is impossible to say exactly how many AIDS widows entered into such marriage arrangements at this time. However, it is clear from the various stories from Kanungu that a significant number of older, married men were willing to take them on – as second or third wives – at this time (it seems to have been much less common for these women to marry younger, as yet unmarried, men). The older men's motivations for acting in this way might be again at least partly explicable in terms of the fact that many of these women, as AIDS widows, might well have been regarded by the time of these second marriages as afflicted with an *ekibi*, as perhaps even suffering from *engumba*, or as in some other way lacking in 'complete' fertility.[26] On the one hand, this may have been less of an issue for an older married man, given that, at the time of his second union, he would almost always have already had children with an existing wife (and perhaps even grandchildren as well). On the other hand, the fact that these women did have 'problems of fertility' – or were at least perceived to have had such problems – meant that only a minimal, and in some cases no, brideprice had to be paid to secure their union. Indeed, for many less affluent older men across the rural Southwest, this meant that in the figure of the AIDS widow, a second marriage – with all of the statuses and prestige which attach to this institution – now became 'affordable' to them for the very first time.[27]

[23] Cisternino, 1987: 356.

[24] Cisternino, 1987: 356.

[25] Cisternino, 1987: 356.

[26] As already seen in Ceredonia's own case, such perceptions could persist within a new marriage even when a woman had already produced children by previous unions. Incidentally, it is interesting for us to note here what might happen, in such cases, to a woman's children from previous alliances. I know of at least two cases where the head of the household took these youngsters, and brought them up as their own. However, more commonly, these children might become a source of resentment – and possibly even abuse – by other members of the household (who might well come to regard them – as a 'stranger's offspring' – as a corrupting influence on the household's own fertility). As a result, it is not at all uncommon, in such circumstances, for a woman to have to send her children away to a natal kinswoman's home. However, how well looked after these children are following such a move is highly variable, with anecdotal evidence, for example, suggesting that at least some of them then end up as 'street children'. Certainly, it is clear that, for these reasons, the number of children who were (in one way or another) socially 'dislocated' increased significantly during these years of the emergent AIDS epidemic, in the early to mid-1990s.

[27] It must be remembered that all of this was taking place in the context of the then recent coffee price spike, an event which created substantial amounts of new wealth for many households in the rural Southwest (and beyond), and which resulted in the practice of bridewealth payment being more strictly enforced that it had been previously. In addition, it almost certainly created a degree of inflation in the amounts of brideprice being requested (a point which was made by a number of my respondents, even though I do not have accurate data

Moreover, it might also have been the case that older men were simply less concerned about catching HIV, a disease which, by taking the best part of a decade to kill, would not significantly reduce their existing life expectancies. However, this latter point is entirely speculative, and would now be impossible to investigate further. The main point here is that, whatever the actual reasons were, the evidence points to the fact that throughout the early to mid-1990s, many older men *were* taking on these younger AIDS widows, and entering into polygamous arrangements with them (and through these actions becoming themselves polygamous for the first time). Moreover, that this situation had a number of important effects. In particular, and of the utmost importance for our story, this situation resulted, in almost all instances, in the emergence of new, and particularly serious, tensions in the older men's households, between the men themselves and their existing wives and children. All of this is particularly relevant for our story here because many of these other women (i.e. the senior co-wives in these new polygamous relationships) soon enough also began to join the MRTC.

Case 7: Constance Tumuheki

Consider, for example, the circumstances whereby Constance Tumuheki joined the Movement, in early 1994. As described to me by her daughter, Juliet, in this case Constance had been married to her husband for over 30 years, and by the early 1990s, the couple had at least three adult daughters. One night in early 1991, Constance's husband (Juliet's father) returned home to inform her that he was taking on a second wife. However, being something of a 'drunkard' (Juliet's word), the man owned no animals for use as brideprice. On the other hand, his three daughters – including Juliet – did own a number of animals. Although all three of the daughters were unmarried, all had jobs in nearby Kabale Town – two as teachers, one as a hotel maid – and had invested part of their earnings back into live-stock, which they kept at their natal home. One day, Juliet received a visit from her mother in town, informing her that her father had just 'stolen' two of her (Juliet's) cows for use as brideprice for his second wife. Moreover, that this second wife had now come to live in the family home. However, this second marriage soon proved ill fated, as barely nine months later, the young woman – who was several years Juliet's junior – died of AIDS.

Apparently undeterred, some six months or so later, Constance's husband yet again began preparations to marry another wife. A young woman in his village had recently been widowed, and Constance's husband was apparently keen to take the young woman in. However, as the daughter of

[27] (cont.) on the matter). In this context, then, a new wife for whom very little brideprice was required would have been a particularly attractive proposition. (Moreover, this may have been especially so for those household heads who, for one reason or another, had *not* benefitted from the coffee price spike.) It must also be borne in mind here that a lower brideprice would have anyway been less of an attraction for a younger man, for whom the collection of brideprice, when it is available (from his father, uncles, and so on) is an important *rite de passage*, one which confirms his place in the wider agnatic lineage.

an important local dignitary, a larger brideprice was required this time, which he had little realistic chance of mustering. Once again, then, his solution here was to plunder his daughters' herd, so that the marriage could go ahead. A short time afterwards, all four of the senior female members of the (now polygamous) household – i.e. Constance and her three daughters, including Juliet – were struck down by a mysterious illness, which left all four bed-ridden in the family home, for the best part of a year. At this point, the women themselves, and many other people around, suspected that all must now also be suffering from AIDS. However, none of them seemed to be developing the kinds of infections which are commonly associated with the disease. Thus, the episode remained a mystery.

Then, one day, many months into the group's illness, Constance suddenly rose from her bed, to inform the others – and anyone else who would listen – that she had just received a vision (*okworekwa*) in which she had been told that the women's affliction was a direct result of her husband's actions, and would now be 'cured'. Following this vision, Juliet recalls, all four women, including Juliet herself, made a sudden, and miraculous, recovery from their existing state, and soon afterwards all three daughters returned to their jobs. Deeply moved by her own experience, some months later Constance made contact with an MRTC delegation which was visiting her sister-in-law's house, and a short time after this she left her marital home to join the MRTC.

Case 8: Byaruhanga Edith

A similar set of circumstances can be identified in the story of Byaruhanga Edith's decision to join the Movement, in 1995. As described to me by her daughter Doreen, in this instance both Edith and her husband (Doreen's father) had been born in Rwanda, and had migrated to South-western Uganda, with a number of their children, in the early 1980s. At the time of their arrival in the country the family had been quite poor, and it had taken them over three years to buy their first plot of land. However, during the following years their fortunes had slowly improved, and by the early 1990s the household had become reasonably well-off.

It was around this time, then, that Edith's husband – rather unexpectedly, Doreen thinks – decided to marry three additional wives, in quick succession. According to Doreen, at the time of these unions, the family already suspected that at least one of the young women must be an AIDS widow, given that she already had two small children from a previous marriage, but she steadfastly refused to reveal the identity of her former spouse. Within a short period of time, two of the new wives died of AIDS. However, following these deaths, Edith's husband again decided to take on still more wives, and began the arrangements for marrying two other young widows – two sisters – from a neighbouring village. According to Doreen, all five of these additional unions had created great tensions within her mother and father's marriage, in that all involved the latter paying at least some brideprice out of Edith's 'own' herds. Moreover, on three separate occasions, Edith's husband had also sold some of these animals in order to buy land for one of his new wives.

It is noteworthy that, by this time, Edith and her husband had 8 children – 5 girls and 3 boys – and three of the girls were already married (and had thus brought in a sizeable amount of livestock as brideprice). Moreover, that Edith had generally regarded all of these animals as hers alone to dispose of as she wished (she had intended to use some for the weddings of her two youngest sons, for example). Thus, according to Doreen, she had been greatly alarmed to discover that her husband had used them for such different ends. In these sorts of circumstances, a senior wife's best hope of 'defending' her herds from this sort of 'plundering' would lie with her adult sons, who might be able to literally 'defend' her stock – physically – from the father's advances. However, it is also noteworthy that Edith's position had been further worsened by the recent death of her eldest son, to AIDS, and by the subsequent sickness of her second boy (also, it was thought at the time, the victim of AIDS). Such, then, was Edith's situation when she first made contact with an MRTC delegation which was then staying at a neighbour's house. This was also the context in which, shortly afterwards, she left for the MRTC's main compound, at Kanungu.

Case 3: Jolly Habusa (Part 3)

Finally, let us return once more to the slightly later case of Jolly Habusa – details of which have already been discussed (in Case 3, Parts 1 and 2) – and to the mode of her entry into the MRTC. As I have already outlined, and as described to me in detail by her daughter Linda, Jolly's primary motivation in joining the Movement had stemmed from tensions created by her husband's decision to take on a second wife. In particular, strains resulted from Jolly's objections to her husband giving half of 'her' productive land to his new wife, and to his sharing some of her daughter's brideprice with the woman.

Let me just add a few further details of the story Linda told me. First, Linda felt sure that her father had always wanted to take on a second wife, but had never previously been able to 'afford' it. This apparently related to the fact that his two brothers, both of whom lived nearby him, had had more than one wife for many years. However, not least because of his being a 'very good drunkard' (Linda's words), her father had always mismanaged his wealth, and had thus never been able to save enough for a second brideprice of his own. Secondly, Linda added that her father had only been able to 'afford' a second wife on this occasion – in early 1999 – because the woman he took on then had been an AIDS widow, for whom he was required to pay no brideprice at all. Linda claimed that this woman, who was many years her father's junior, and who hailed from a village about five miles away from their place, had previously been married to a man who was widely rumoured to have died of AIDS. That she herself must therefore also have been HIV positive at the time of her second marriage was widely rumoured at the time. Moreover, this was subsequently proved beyond doubt when, in early 2001, she died of the disease (and indeed, on this point, my own interview with Linda was initially postponed in order that she could attend this young woman's funeral).[28]

Finally, there was at least one other way in which the emergent AIDS epidemic shaped people's motivations for joining the MRTC. Specifically, just as Kiconco turned to the MRTC in an attempt to gain redress for the malignant actions of *emandwa* (Case 1), so too many people afflicted by the ghosts of dead AIDS victims also turned to the Movement. Throughout the early to mid-1990s, as more and more people died from AIDS, so their surviving kin became ever more troubled by the growing number of 'ghosts' (*emandwa*) this generated. Indeed, as one respondent in Bugamba (Steven Ariko) put it to me, because of the growing epidemic at that time, the early 1990s are today still remembered as a period when afflictions from *emandwa* became particularly common or, in his exact words, as a time when 'the ghosts went crazy'. Thus, as one of my respondents on the Movement (Mr Sebataka), recalls, at the particular initiation course he had attended, the 'most common problem' from which people had been suffering was possession by *emandwa* (or some other form of affliction created by them). As a result of this, the whole group gathered there spent almost the entire week engaged in prayer aimed at 'freeing' one or other tortured soul. (Interestingly, Sebataka goes on to cite the failure of the course leadership in such 'curing' practices as the primary reason why he had first come to doubt the veracity of the Movement's claims.) Here once again, such spirits of the dead can – and still do – affect both men and women. However, given the latter's association with all aspects of household fertility, it follows that, throughout this period, it was women in particular who suffered the worst effects of these *emandwa*.

Case 9: Mary Namara

My final case concerns Mary Namara, who joined the Movement some time in 1996. As described to me by her son, Twinomugisha Gerald, Mary was

[28] Another example here concerns the former owners of the Buhunga compound (at which 155 bodies were later discovered). In that case, and as described to me by one of the compound's neighbours (Winifred Aheebwa), the original owners of the compound were a family of eight: a husband and wife, and their six children (three boys, and three girls, all of whom were in their later teens or early adulthood). Sometime in 1993, the husband had decided to take on a second wife – a young widow from Burambara – initially with the intention of installing her at Buhunga as well. However, when the first wife found out about this plan, she and her three grown-up sons vehemently protested against the move, objecting that a part of 'their' (sizeable) productive land would have to be given up as a result. After several months of serious tensions, the husband finally relented to the pressure, and moved out – with his new wife – to a new piece of land he had just bought (near to the second wife's home area). However, it later transpired that he had in large part funded this purchase through a secret sale of all of the Buhunga household's livestock (a move which left the first wife and all of her children, with very little wealth at all). This was the context, then, in which an MRTC delegation was first received at Buhunga, shortly afterwards. Introduced by the family's second daughter, the sect initially recruited all of the household's members (i.e. the first wife and her six children), and the compound itself was subsequently converted into an MRTC centre. However, it is not clear how many of the family – apart from the first wife and her second daughter – were still in the Movement at the time of the Kanungu fire. Incidentally, it is also noteworthy here that certain elements of the second daughter's story suggest that she may also have been an 'AIDS widow' at the time when she first introduced the MRTC delegation to her natal home.

born in Mbarara District, but at some time in the mid-1970s, had married a man in Kasese District and moved there. As far as Gerald knows, Mary's marital home had never been – and has still never been – affected by AIDS. However, her natal home was badly hit, and between the late 1980s and mid-1990s, she lost her father, mother, two brothers, two of their wives, and several other relatives, all to the disease. It was shortly after this, Gerald recalls, that his mother became quite sickly. At first complaining of (episodes of) 'pins-and-needles', sore ankles, and a painful chest, her condition gradually deteriorated, and she soon began to suffer from mysterious bouts of coughing, and 'fits' (Gerald's word). At first, her husband took her to the local hospital, but when this yielded no results, the couple instead visited a diviner (*omufumu*). The man identified the operation of (one or more) *emandwa* of her recently deceased kin, and gave her a herbal remedy to help 'banish' them. However, when this did not work, Mary instead sought out the MRTC, who had recently set up a study centre in a nearby village, and she later joined the Movement.

On those who 'used to give out so many things'[29]

Omuriro gw'ente nigwo mutuuro. Cows treasure their fireplace [because it keeps all the flies away]. People like to gather where food and beer are plentiful (because that is where the feast will be)[30]

I have argued that, throughout the early to mid-1990s at least, the Movement's main strategy for recruitment involved their projecting an image of the Virgin Mary as a divine female capable of helping women to gain redress for the same range of misfortunes as had previously been dealt with by Nyabingi – in particular, the misfortunes of infertility, problems of polygamy, and malignant *emandwa*. In and of itself, this image seems to have proved particularly compelling, especially to women, and especially in the context of the emergent AIDS epidemic. Yet, in addition, the MRTC also attempted to embed this image in practice, in ways which further reveal their intention to draw an analogy between their new Movement and the old Nyabingi. In particular here, shortly after the Movement's expulsion from the mainstream church, Ceredonia's visions began to place the Virgin Mary at the centre of an ever more elaborate network of exchange, one extensive enough to provide material assistance to all of the group's members for help with their misfortunes.[31] In this way, the Virgin Mary of the MRTC's projection became a 'giver of riches', and a material benefactor, one who *was* actually capable of offsetting the worst effects of the various hardships her followers faced. Just like the old Nyabingi.

First of all, it is important to note that all the independent attempts of the MRTC to recruit were always embedded in locally meaningful exchange

---

[29] Mr Sebataka.
[30] Cisternino, 1987: 447.
[31] It is particularly noteworthy that from the time of her very first visit to Nyabugoto, in 1988, Ceredonia herself had begun to receive a range of offerings in return for her communications with the Virgin.

practices, or relations of substance. Thus, the kind of formal visits to people's homes which the MRTC delegations made correspond to a practice which is known locally as *okuzinduka*. *Okuzinduka* is contrasted with more casual, everyday modes of visiting, which are instead referred to as *okutaayaayira*. Specifically, *okuzinduka* – a type of visiting I have engaged in on several occasions – requires the visitor to send ahead a formal request to be received, often several weeks or months in advance, and then to muster a delegation to accompany him or her on the trip (this group is known as the *abazinduki*). Most importantly, the visitor (and his/her delegation) must also prepare a range of goods – food, drink, vegetables, small livestock, and so on – to take with them on the day the visit begins (*okuzinduka* usually lasts for a few days, and sometimes longer). The bearing of these gifts is of crucial importance for the delegation, because the whole practice of *okuzinduka* revolves around a series of mutual material exchanges (which are often accompanied by much speech-making, eating, drinking and frivolity). Where the main visitor and receiver are male household heads, the event might culminate in an exchange of cattle – or a pledge thereof – to create a bond of *obukago* between the two (or else to reconfirm their existing *bakago* ties). As already noted, *obukago* is a reciprocal form of bond-partnership, and an extremely important social tie which, under normal circumstances, is enduring. Where the main visitor and receiver are female kin – as is more often the case with *okuzinduka* visits – the event might end instead with an exchange of agricultural produce, in order to reaffirm the women's natal bond. In both – indeed, all – cases, *okuzinduka* essentially revolves around various exchanges of substances, which serve to create, or to confirm, important social ties.

All the visits which were made by MRTC delegations to people's houses, whether these were headed by Kibweteere, by other of the Movement's leaders, or by its ordinary members, were always referred to as *okuzinduka* by all of my respondents. Moreover, a number of these same respondents recall that some of the delegations arrived with cylindrical food parcels (*omushenga*) on their heads, the distinctive feature of a *bazinduki* delegation (the *omushenga* parcel is made of banana, or some other, leaves, tied together in a particular pattern). In addition, almost all my respondents remember the MRTC delegations engaging in between their prayer sessions, in 'feasts' (*obugyenyi*, pl. *ebigyenyi*), and in other types of food exchange (although not in the exchange of alcohol). Moreover, one of my respondents (Mr Sebataka) describes being given several goats and a number of other animals – by Fr. Kasapuraari – during at least two of the courses which took place in his home (as a means, presumably, of thanking him for hosting the event). In addition, he remembers a number of other animals being slaughtered at these same courses, and their meat later being consumed by all those present. Another respondent (Francis D.) recalls a cow being given to the household head at the initiation course she attended, whilst another remembers a bull being killed and consumed at the one he participated in (at Kurambano's house). In these various ways, then, from the very outset, the Movement's leadership attempted to engage in locally meaningful exchange practices, and thereby to enter into relations of substance with potential new members, presumably with the aim of creating lasting social bonds with them (i.e. that they would subsequently become full members of the church).

Even more significantly, from the time the sect was expelled from the mainstream church, it began to intervene in property disputes. All of which is significant because practically every case outlined above, in addition to its other features, involved at least some element of contested property. For example, as Hilary Birungi pointed out to me, by expelling his recently widowed daughter-in-law from his home, Mbabazi Eunice's father-in-law had stood to gain all of the animals and goods which she had received as dowry, and would also be in a position to demand back any brideprice the family had paid for her (Case 6). Indeed, as noted there, the potential for such claims acted as the main deterrent against any natal families receiving back an AIDS widow in Mbabazi's position.

Just how costly such repayments could be is demonstrated in another of the above cases, that of Mrs Sebataka (Case 2). As described to me by Mr Sebataka, in this instance, the entry of Mrs Sebataka and her two sisters-in-law into the Movement resulted in attempts both by Mr Sebataka himself, and by his two brothers, to recover the brideprices they had paid for the women. For one of the brothers, this resulted in a protracted court battle with his former wife's family, which he went on to win. According to Mr Sebataka, the settlement in this case 'almost bankrupted' the other party involved. In these circumstances, then, all AIDS widows, and especially the younger ones, were placed in a particularly vulnerable position, caught as they effectively were between the competing property claims of their marital and natal homes.

Moreover, similar problems were faced by many senior wives living in new polygamous households. In these cases, disputes tended to relate less to properties which had been exchanged during their own marriages, as to animals which had been received in their daughters' marriages, to livestock which they had earned by other means, or to their productive lands. Thus, for example, Jolly Habusa's grievances related to her husband's 'inappropriate' use of her daughter's brideprice and 'her' productive land, Byaruhanga Edith's problems related to her husband's 'misuse' of her daughters' brideprice, Constance Tumuheki's issues stemmed from her husband's 'misuse' of cattle which had been purchased from her daughters' wages, and so on. However, such disputes were just as serious as those faced by AIDS widows, and had the potential to leave a senior wife in just as vulnerable a position in her marital home (especially where no sons – or any other actors – were available to 'defend' her position).

From the time of its expulsion from the mainstream church, the MRTC began to intervene in both kinds of property dispute. Thus, from about 1993 onwards – certainly, at some point after the group had left the Kibweteeres' home at Kabumba – the Movement's leadership began to claim that the Virgin would intervene in all sorts of property disputes, but only in return for some sort of offering (which they called *okutoija*). Thus, young widows were told that they would be protected from the competing property claims of their marital and natal kin, but only after they had, in effect, handed over all of their dowries to the Movement. Similarly, senior wives would be informed that they too would to be 'saved' from their husbands' misuse of their property, but only after they had also, in effect, sold all of their remaining property, and given the proceeds to the sect. Much was made in media accounts of Kanungu of the fact that MRTC members had to 'sell all of their property' in order to join the Movement.

However, it is more correct to say that only *some* members had to sell all of their property before joining. The key practices here revolved around the initiation courses that all new members were required to attend. As described to me in great detail by Mr Sebataka, in particular – although also mentioned by a number of other former members as well – at a given point during these courses, all initiands were given an exercise book in which they were required to write a list of all of the sins they had ever committed, since birth (for those who could not write, a leader was assigned to do this for them). Later, this book would form the basis of a private interview with a panel of leaders, at which each sin listed would be assigned a monetary value; from this, a total value for all of that individual's sins would be ascertained. At the end of the interview, the initiand would be told that Ceredonia would now request the Virgin to forgive all the sins listed, and in other ways to help the initiand with his or her troubles, but only after this total sum had been handed over to the Movement, as *okutoija*.

In practice, however, the amount assigned by the leaders to each individual sin varied from person to person, and thus, the total amount that any one initiand was required to pay at the end of their interview depended on who they were, and how they were placed in the various property disputes. Thus, for example, during these interviews, the sins of young women who were unmarried, or women who were newly married but barren, were assigned very low values, and as a result, these women had to pay almost nothing to enter the Movement. Such was the case with Deidre Masimbi (Case 4), who, at her interview with the leaders, was asked to pay only a nominal sum to join (a few thousand shillings). However, unable to afford even that amount, Ceredonia decided that Deidre could instead work for one month for a neighbour of the Rushojwa compound – as a house girl – in order to raise what was required of her. This Deidre did, and thus, one month later, became a full member of the sect. Moreover, the person she worked for at Rushojwa, my respondent Winifred, received at least half a dozen other young women in a similar position to Deidre's during the 1990s. In another example, Ceredonia told another woman who was unable to pay her (nominal) sum that she could 'pay off' the amount by selling some of the handicrafts she would be making as part of her daily economic round in the Movement's compounds (Patience N.).

For other categories of women, however, the amounts set at the interviews were much higher. Thus it was that younger AIDS widows were often required to pay the monetary equivalent of their entire dowry to join. For example, this was the case with Mbabazi Eunice (Case 6). Similarly, that senior wives in polygamous households were required to pay an amount roughly equal to all of their lands and animals. Thus, for example, following her own interview, Jolly Habusa returned home to sell all of her possessions, including the few animals remaining from her daughter's marriage, and a small piece of productive land she had bought independently of her husband, through a mutual support group she belonged to (*ekigombe*).[32]

We might also note here that men too, and sometimes even the heads of polygamous households, also attended MRTC initiation courses, and therefore also took part in these interviews. It is perhaps not surprising to discover here that although it was not entirely unheard of for some men also to be set nominal fees for joining (which could be 'paid off' over time),[33] it was more usual for the amounts required of men to be much higher than those required of women. This might simply be explained, of course, with reference to the fact that most men in South-western Uganda own more wealth – land and livestock – than women. However, it is also of particular interest, to my mind that, in the context of these interviews, the amounts required of men engaged in polygamy were often exceptionally high, and sometimes even absurdly so. Indeed, over the course of my research I recorded two cases in which the amounts asked for were between four and five times the value of the man's entire holdings. In this way, then, it seems that, if the sect's leadership used the initiation interviews as a primary mechanism through which to intervene in married couples' property disputes, they did so in a way which was designed to penalize the male parties within those disputes. Moreover, the interviews may even have been a device through which the leadership discouraged certain categories of men – such as the heads of polygamous households – from joining. This might well explain why, time and time again during my research on Kanungu, I came across households in which the only person not to have joined the Movement – and the only person therefore to have survived Kanungu – was the male head of the household (*nyin'eka*).[34]

Thus, many of the women who joined the MRTC were required to make sizeable payments of *okutoija* in order to do so. Presumably, most felt that this was simply 'the better option' in a context in which their properties were being – or were likely to be – 'stolen', or 'misused', anyway. It is also important to note here that the Movement's leadership was always careful to redistribute at least some of the wealth so gathered. Thus, the sect always provided ongoing, everyday material assistance to all its permanent residents, simply by housing and feeding them (including, on occasions, with meat slaughtered specifically for their benefit).

Then, from the time of their expulsion from the mainstream church – and again while they were still based at the Kibweteeres' home in Kabumba

[32] It is important to note here that the Movement's leaders had a good idea of the total wealth of all initiands at the time of these interviews. Thus, at the beginning of each course, the body of initiands was divided into groups of ten to fifteen people, for each of which a leader (or 'chairman') would be selected. Over the week-long enterprise, one of the jobs of the leader was to make a list of all of the property of the people in his or her group, in a separate exercise book. These lists were then handed over to the main course leaders, prior to their beginning their personal interviews with the initiands.

[33] For example, I did record one case in which an older man who was unable to pay his requisite joining fee was allowed to work for the sect as a carpenter, until his debt had been 'paid off' (Kazooba's sons).

[34] Although, in many instances, these men had gone on to subsequently start new families.

– the sect also started to provide its members with other sorts of material assistance as well. For example, as Mrs Kibweteere herself recalls, already by early 1992, one of the main attractions of coming to live at Kabumba on a full-time basis was the further promise, which had already by that time been made publicly by Joseph Kibweteere, that the sect would pay the full primary school fees for all its members' children. (In the period before Universal Primary Education was introduced in Uganda, in 1996, such fees were one of the major drains on a household's finances.) In practice, this meant that the sect educated the children themselves, first in a makeshift 'schoolhouse' in the Kibweteeres' compound, later at a large (6-classroom) dedicated school building at Kanungu.[35] However, under the direction of as senior an educator as Joseph Kibweteere, and staffed by a number of his former senior contacts in the education sector, the standard of education this provided was (initially at least) reasonably good. For example, this was one of the main reasons why the aunt of Tulinawe George – who was already, at the time, a member of the Movement, and a mother of five children – decided to take up permanent residence at Kabumba, in August 1992.

Furthermore, and of perhaps greater relevance, given my previous discussions, from at least this time onwards, the Movement also began to offer at least some of its members help with medical expenses. Thus, in addition to herbal remedies, at least some of the AIDS sufferers who entered the Movement also obtained fully-paid hospital treatment and other forms of medical care. For example, such was the case with the brother and sister-in-law of Kyarisiima Sarah, both of whom were in the final stages of the disease at the time of their entry into the Movement, also in 1992. Thus, for at least some of the women who joined the MRTC, the perception that the Movement represented 'the better option' must have been shaped by these actual material benefits, which full membership conferred.

Not only did the MRTC's particular brand of Marianism revive the old symbolism of Nyabingi, it also revived its old practices. Thus, in their projection, if the Virgin Mary was also a divine figure capable of helping people to gain redress during times of misfortune, she now also required sizeable *okutoija* payment in return for her intercessions. However, in return for this, she could provide people with actual, material assistance with their misfortunes. Thus, it was increasingly to the MRTC's Virgin that people now turned with their difficulties. Moreover, just as women with (what they perceived to be) permanent, or ongoing, difficulties had previously become Nyabingi 'handmaidens', so too these women now became full-time members of the Movement.

Areas of recruitment

Finally, here, it is necessary to say something about the areas from which all of these MRTC members were being recruited. I base my discussion here

---

[35] This school operated for several years before being registered, and officially 'opened', in 1997. At that time it was named as *Ishayuuriro rya Maria* (lit: 'the School of Mary').

on the various death lists which were drawn up after the Kanungu fire (working on the not unreasonable assumption that the people who died in Kanungu – and its associated events – would have been a representative sample of the MRTC's membership as a whole). Following the fire, at least two lists of the dead were drawn up, one by the Uganda Police, the other by the Kabale Catholic Diocese. In addition, in late March 2000, *The New Vision* published a 'register' of MRTC members which one of its reporters had found at the Movement's compound in Rutoma (this was reprinted in the 2 April edition of its Runyankore/Rukiga weekly, *Orumuri*). However, I can confirm that this latter list is not a register of members at all, but a list of all those who attended initiation courses at Rutoma during 1998 and 1999. Such lists were made at each course, for the reasons just described. However, as I have explained, many of those who attended initiation courses did not go on to join the Movement, and it is thus unsurprising that I have been able to track down a number of the people listed on the Rutoma register who were very much alive and well on the occasion of my visit. For these reasons, then, I do not take the Rutoma list as a reliable guide to Movement membership.

A much better indicator is, again unsurprisingly, the list compiled by the Uganda police. However, even this list must be regarded with a degree of caution. Specifically, it lists all of the Kanungu victims by district of origin, and thus includes separate registers of all those who died from Bushenyi District, all those who died from Kabale District, and so on. Significantly, each of these district lists was compiled by the Resident District Commissioner (RDC), or the Chief of Police – or sometimes by both men – in the days and weeks following the fire. However, it is clear that the task of drawing up these lists was carried out somewhat differently, and with varying degrees of diligence, by the different RDCs and Chiefs.

Thus, the resulting lists vary quite markedly from one district to another. For example, the RDC for Rukungiri seems to have interpreted his task as being to produce a list of *all* the people who died at Kanungu (and not just those from Rukungiri *per se*). So, the list for Rukungiri District includes a large number of people who were from other districts including, crucially, a number of individuals whose names appear on the lists for other districts as well. At the other end of the spectrum, the RDC for Mbarara seems to have produced only a partial list, and so only 33 of the dead are listed as having come from Mbarara (even though, over the course of my fieldwork, I collected evidence related to more than 100 people who had died from that district). In addition, in some cases, the district lists include such information as the gender and age of victims, whilst others they do not, and so on.[36] For these reasons, then, even the police list must be treated with caution, and several key adjustments – not least that of discounting names which appear on two different district registers – must be made before drawing any conclusions from it. However, it is still probably the best guide we have to the overall composition of the MRTC. For example, I would note that practically all of the names which appear on the Kabale Diocese list

[36] The list for Ntungamo District is anomalous as being the only one which also discriminates against some victims in terms of their having been 'juniors'.

are already accounted for on the police list, and that this register does not, therefore, add much to it – other than the age and gender of some victims (where these are missing from the police lists).

Having taken these various factors into account, and made the necessary adjustments to the lists, I have concluded that the police register records the deaths of – or at least, the names of – 650 people. Interestingly, the composition of this group – in terms of both age and gender – seems to correlate quite closely with the various cases I recorded during my own research on Kanungu. Thus, around half of all MRTC members were minors – included on these lists as people under 18 years of age, who would have joined the Movement, presumably, with their parents. Of the remainder, some 72 per cent were women. Moreover, of the adult female membership of the sect, the largest single age grade is that of women (listed as) between 20 and 29 years of age. This would presumably have been the cohort of young AIDS widows. In addition, the second largest grade is that of women listed as 50–59 years of age, which is the age range of many of the senior co-wives of my case studies. Thus, the details of the police list would appear to confirm my own case studies as indicative of the MRTC's membership as a whole.

Furthermore, I would note here that, over the course of my entire research, I interviewed respondents who were related to, or in some other way knew, 146 of the people named on this police register (as well as respondents connected with numerous other Kanungu victims, who are not mentioned on any of the above lists). However, the point here is that it is not surprising that the police list correlates with my own findings, given that my interviews in some way touched on the stories of almost one-quarter of the people on that list.

The police list also serves as a guide to the origin of the sect's members. It shows that the MRTC membership was drawn from every district in the southern and western parts of Uganda. In addition, that the sect had a small number of members from the central and eastern regions (from Mubende and Jinja, in particular). However, my comments about the varying quality of the individual district lists notwithstanding, it is clear that the majority of names on the list – representing as much as 62 per cent of the followers – came from just three districts: Bushenyi, Kabarole, and Rukungiri. It is also clear that, within each of these districts, the areas which provided the most recruits were those in and around the sites of the former assisted relocation scheme of the mid-1940s onwards. Thus, for example, most of the recruits from Bushenyi hailed from places in and around the former resettlement site of Kati and the 'unassisted settlement' locale of Bunyaruguru (in which Rugazi parish is also located). Those from Rukungiri were drawn particularly from areas around Kambuga (where Kanungu itself is located), and the Bugangari Valley. Meanwhile, a majority of the Kabarole recruits came from areas around the former resettlement site of Bigodi. To put this in other words, it is quite clear from all of these police lists that the MRTC membership was drawn primarily from among the Kiga Diaspora. Moreover, I might also note here that a large number of the people included on the police list for Mbarara District came from

Bisheshe, whilst a majority of the additional cases I recorded for this district
– who are missing from the police register – were associated with the
former resettlement site of Mwizi (the area adjacent to Bugamba).

My research has suggested a number of reasons why a large part of the
MRTC membership should have been drawn from the Kiga Diaspora. Firstly,
because many of the Movement's leadership were themselves members of
that Diaspora, and thus, their own personal networks – upon which the
Movement relied so heavily in the years immediately following its expulsion
(in particular) – would have been more extensive amongst this population
than within any other group. Secondly, because Ceredonia's various
references to the sites, language, and symbols of the old Nyabingi – in other
words, her attempts to represent the MRTC as a revival of the old religious
complex – would probably have resonated better with members of the
Diaspora than with, for example, those whose families had never left Kigezi.
This stems from the fact that a 'social memory' of the old fertility goddess
has been more actively maintained by, and cultivated within, the Diaspora,
than among the wider Kiga population. Thus, as my discussion in Chapter
2 demonstrated, most members of the Diaspora – at least, if those living in
and around the Bugamba area can be taken as representative – can recall
a range of stories concerning either their own experiences with, or else their
parents' or grandparents' engagements with, the Nyabingi spirit.

Thirdly, because from the time of the assisted relocation scheme onwards, changes in the structure of the polygamous household had resulted
in women in the Diaspora being more reliant on Marian intercession than
ever before (as discussed in Chapter 3). Thus, by the late 1980s, the
Diaspora was simply better represented within the Legion groups from
which the MRTC emerged at that time. Indeed, I can attest to this from my
own observations in Bugamba Village, where the local Legion of Mary
group – whose meetings I have attended on several occasions – is made up
of a high proportion of Kiga women, even though ethnic Kiga make up only
a small percentage of the overall population of the village. Moreover, if the
Diaspora was well represented within the Legion, this would then have
become further amplified within the Movement, especially following
Ceredonia's later pronouncement for the sect to recruit primarily through
its existing members' networks. As my case studies demonstrate, this
usually resulted in delegations being sent out to existing members' female
natal kin – to their sisters, to their mothers, and so on – or, in other words,
to other members of the Kiga Diaspora (and indeed, it was through this very
method that the MRTC network eventually spread out across all of the
former resettlement areas, thereby encompassing such a wide geographical
area overall).

However, there may also be more to it than this. Specifically, it is worth
making explicit that, given the overall timings here, it is simply not possible
that the women who joined the MRTC could possibly have been the very
same women who had formerly participated in Nyabingi practices (in the
first half of the twentieth century) or who had experienced the difficulties
which followed the assisted relocation scheme (in mid-century). Simply put,
none of the Movement's members, neither the 'senior co-wives' nor the

younger AIDS widows, could possibly have been old enough to have remembered those earlier happenings. Instead, then, the women who joined the MRTC must have been the daughters (in the case of the senior co-wives), or else the grand-daughters, or great-granddaughters (in the case of the AIDS widows), of the women who had formerly engaged in the old Nyabingi practice, or of those who had moved into the Diaspora.

Yet this fact may in itself be illuminating, given their apparently enthusiastic response to Ceredonia's revival of Nyabingi (in terms of their enthusiasm for attending former Nyabingi shrines, their engagement with the language of the old spirit, and their general embrace of secrecy). This is interesting, given one conclusion which can be drawn from the comparative ethnographic literature on revivalist movements, namely, that such a return to 'tradition' is often more appealing to those two or three generations removed from the original form than it is to to those who have experienced the earlier version first-hand. This stems from the fact that those further removed will usually have greater scope to imagine – or re-imagine – the original elements in different sorts of ways (and thus to reinterpret them in ways more appropriate to their own lives).[37]

Yet in addition, there would also be good grounds, to my mind, for supposing that the types of misfortunes which many women faced in the context of the emerging AIDS epidemic – as have been outlined at length here – would have been felt more acutely by the daughters, and grand-daughters, of those who had relocated in the mid-1940s, than they would have been by other women living in South-western Uganda at that time. For example, it is important to point out that the particular problems that were faced by that first generation of émigrés – and which had resulted in their becoming more reliant on Marian intercession than ever before – had all stemmed from a general dispersal of the polygamous household within the Diaspora (which frequently resulted in the *enju* of different co-wives being located some distance from each other). In other words, their greater devotion to the Virgin Mary had stemmed from their general isolation within their new social situation (as discussed in Chapter 3). Yet so too their daughters and grand-daughters were just as isolated at the time the AIDS epidemic struck in the mid-1990s. Indeed, these later generations may have been even more removed from mechanisms of support and assistance than that first generation ever had been.

After all, looking at the marriage patterns of these subsequent genera-tions, it is clear that most of these women seem to have married within the Diaspora. On the one hand, this meant that they were, in effect, marrying into the very same households in which that first generation of émigré women had spent their married lives. As a result, their own household arrangements were often just as dispersed as their mothers' or grand-mothers' situations had been (and in which the very same pressures on land, and other property, would therefore have held sway). On the other hand – given the dispersed nature of the Diaspora itself – it also meant that these

---

[37] The 'classic' anthropological work on revival movements is that done by Wallace in the mid-twentieth century (a good entry point is Wallace, 2003). See also the more recent collection of Harkin (2004).

women's marital homes were frequently located a considerable distance away from their natal villages (and thus, from their kin networks of assistance and support). For example, if we look again at my case studies of MRTC membership, it becomes clear that in only one instance – that of Deirdre Masimbi – had the woman involved married into a household within her natal village. In all the other cases, the woman had travelled a vast distance for marriage, from Rukungiri to Toro (in Kiconco's case), from Toro to Mbarara (Mrs Sebataka), and so on.[38] From this, it follows that when the kinds of misfortunes which accompanied the AIDS epidemic first struck in the mid-1990s, it was these women – as either senior co-wives or younger AIDS widows – who would have found themselves to be particularly vulnerable. As a result, these women may well have become even more committed to Marian devotion than even the first-generation émigrés had been. Thus it was then – for all of these reasons – that when the MRTC first began projecting its image of a Nyabingi revival (and reinstating all of the logics and practices which accompanied this), and when they first began preaching their particular message of Marian intercession, they found in these women of the Kiga Diaspora a particularly captive audience.

[38] Compare this with Bugamba Village, in which more than 80 per cent of women – my own census data would suggest – are married within 10 miles or less of their natal homesteads.

6
Chronicles
The History of an African-Initiated Church

The key purpose of the previous two chapters has been to show the various ways in which the MRTC attempted to reinforce a symbolic connection between Holy Mary of their projection and the figure of the old Nyabingi. In this way, they represented the Virgin as a divine figure capable of helping people with the same range of misfortunes – especially barrenness (*engumba*), 'problems' with polygamy, and afflictions by *emandwa* – as had previously been dealt with by the old goddess. Moreover, they further tried to embed this image in practice, by grounding it in the same kinds of local property relations and exchange networks, as had previously been so characteristic of Nyabingi practice. All of which seems to have made the Movement particularly compelling, especially for women, and especially for women in various positions within a (shifting) 'social structure' in the context of an emerging AIDS epidemic in the early to mid-1990s. As a result of this, the Movement grew rapidly throughout this period, recruiting especially from among second- and third-generation members of the Kiga Diaspora. Thus, the general thrust of my argument is that, in these ways, the MRTC represented a reconstruction, or a 'reversioning', of the kinds of empirical networks which had formerly attached to Nyabingi practice. Or, to put it in other words, for purposes of understanding the early part of the MRTC story, in particular, it is crucial to recognize the ways in which the sect grew out of, and was firmly located within, a specific – historically and geographically located – set of logics and practices.

However, in putting forward this argument about the importance of these local logics and practices, I do not wish to imply that the group's Christianity was therefore somehow unimportant, either to their thinking or to their activities, as these developed over time. As Joel Robbins has recently cautioned (2007), the anthropologist of indigenous Christianities must always guard against any tendency to in some sense 'prioritize' pre-existing, and 'local', ideas and practices over those of the wider, Christian religion which serves to shape these (and which is itself, in turn, shaped by them). In other words, one must be careful not to analyse local cultural logics and practices in such a way as to relegate Christianity itself to the level of façade, surface, superstructure, or whatever. Thus, it is important to stress that, if the Movement was indeed the latest in an historical sequence of transformations of the key symbol of Nyabingi, and its associated practices, then what made this particular transformation, at this particular point in time, distinctive was its framing by, and its location within, the various forms of 'new' Christianity which have become so prevalent on the African continent, and elsewhere, over the last 25 years or so.

Thus, the purpose of the present chapter is to provide a detailed examination of the various ways in which the Movement's doctrine and practice were also shaped by the leadership's exposure to, and engagement with, various forms of new Christianity (both Catholic and Protestant). I begin my discussion here with an examination of what later became one of the MRTC's key defining characteristics: its belief in an imminent end of the world.

The MRTC and millenarianism

Although both media reports, and early academic accounts, of the Kanungu fire made much of the MRTC's millenarian outlook, it is somewhat curious that few articles discussed the evolution of this perspective among the sect. In other words, few commentators seem to have explored how, when and why such eschatological concerns became one of the primary issues – if not *the* primary focus – for the Movement. This is strange, given that almost all of the journalists who covered Kanungu seem to have had access to the MRTC's publication *A Timely Message from Heaven: The End of the Present Times* (1996 [1991]), which in fact emerges as one of the best sources for tracing the evolution of the sect's millenarian thinking over time. A number of textual features of the book lend themselves to such an exercise, not least the fact that the book is set out in largely chronological order. Thus, all of the 10 chapters concerning individual leaders' 'initial visions' (*okworekwa*) are placed in chronological order, based on the timing of that particular leader's entry into the Movement. Thus, the book opens with the chapters concerning the visions of Ceredonia, Kibweteere and Ursula. These are followed by chapters which recount the visions of Byarugaba and Kamagara, followed by ones which relate the visions of Frs. Ikazire and Kataribaabo, and so on. Moreover, in most cases, specific dates are attached to these visions, and in a majority of instances, these dates correspond exactly to the timing of that particular individual's entry into the sect. For example, this is the case with the chapters referring to the visions of Kibweteere, Ursula, Byarugaba, Kataribaabo, Kasapuraari and others.[1]

Significantly, because all of the visionary chapters are recounted in chronological order, taken together, they constitute a reasonably accurate guide to the development of the sect's millenarian thinking over time. The first point to make here is that the end of the world is not a primary, or even a predominant, issue in *any* of the visions. As has already been

---

[1] Indeed, the only exception here is the chapter concerning the vision of Ceredonia, which dates that apparition as having occurred one month before she had first met Kibweteere, and moved to Kabumba (in July 1989). However, curiously, the body of the chapter also gives the date of 10 March 1981 (1996 [1991]: 1), which was a full 7 years before she received her first vision in Mazima's home. It could be that she has pushed the date back here in order to emphasize that she is the 'original' visionary of the Movement.

described in the previous chapter, all implore the faithful to return to a life based on the biblical ten commandments, to observe the rosary, to devote themselves to the Virgin, and so on. From here, each addresses a specific theme, and elaborates the ways in which a particular set of sinful behaviours contravenes a specific Commandment or Commandments while a number of the visions, including those of Ceredonia, Kibweteere, and Fr. Kasapuraari describe how people's current actions break all of the Ten Commandments. Within this context, then, the end of the world does not emerge as a key theme in any of the visionary chapters. Instead, references to the final judgement – which are nevertheless numerous – are only ever made in passing, in relation to some other issue or theme.

Nevertheless, these chapters concerning the visions offer a degree of insight into the development of the sect's millenarianism. In particular, taken together, they suggest a shift in the Movement's thinking, from Judgement Day as an inchoate future possibility, to the end of the world as an imminent event. Thus, in the earliest visions, such as that of Joseph Kibweteere, the rhetoric of a final judgement is used in much the same way as it would be in any mainstream Catholic pedagogy. The 'final day' is a vague, even hypothetical, future event for which all people should nevertheless prepare. People should repent of their sins and return to the true path – i.e. to the Ten Commandments – 'before it is too late'. For example: 'The Ten Commandments are steps or ladders which God gave to each person, to preserve very well and care for each one of them. They are the criteria on which God bases His Judgement' (*ibid.*, 21). It is nowhere stated exactly when this final hour will come. Similarly, in the vision of Ursula Komuhangi:

> I have already been saved...I am not prepared to put out this light, but rather to walk in that light to the end [*omuheru* – *lit*: 'the end' – a term which is commonly used in Catholic parlance to refer to the final day of judgement]...I have renounced these evil behaviours, you should also come out so that we all belong to the light. (*ibid.*: 42)

Again, no concept of timing is conveyed. Similarly in the vision of Henry Sempa (Chapter 5), it is forewarned that all those failing to mend their ways will face God's wrath on the judgement day (*ibid.*: 62–6). In all of these cases, then, reference to the end of the world seems to serve a purely rhetorical function. Nowhere is this clearer than in the vision of Byarugaba, which goes so far as to make fun of the idea (*ibid.*: 67–8). On the final day of judgement, this vision tells us, drunkards will have no chance of hiding their sinful behaviour. This is because the smell of stale alcohol and tobacco on their clothes will certainly give them away!

In only one of the early visions is there a marked difference from this general pattern: that of Ceredonia. In this instance, the chapter opens with a most extraordinary divine drama. As described to Ceredonia by one of the actors in this drama – the Virgin Mary – the scene opens with an angry God. He has 'looked at the world and He has seen that the people have abandoned the Ten Commandments...This grieved Him and He said: "The people of this generation are not worthy of me. I am going to destroy them by taking them one by one"' (*ibid.*: 2). Upon hearing these angry words, Mary kneels before God, begging him not to destroy humanity. She suggests that people might be persuaded to reform, if only she be allowed to go down among them. 'The Blessed Virgin Mary went on to say [i.e. in Ceredonia's vision]: "I, the Virgin Mary, knelt in front of God and begged Him saying, My Lord and God, before you destroy them allow me as a Mother, since you allowed me to give birth to the Messiah, to first go there and show myself to them".' God is unmoved. Mary weeps uncontrollably, begging to be given at least one chance. 'I prostrated myself before Him weeping', she said, 'and I said, "simply allow me, at least out of 1000 I could get two or one"' (ibid.).

Upon seeing the tears of his mother, Jesus is also moved to intervene on her behalf. He joins his mother in petitioning God to let her be sent down, and suggests that he could further assist her by also appearing to people in visions. God finally relents: 'I am merciful, you may go, talk to them and save them...[but] I will only take away that punishment from them when they all repent, when they cry out to me and restore my Commandments. If only a few repent, it is those only that I will forgive; if they are many, so many will be saved' (ibid.: 2–3). Thus, in this case, the biblical end of the world is not a hypothetical future, but a postponed event. Yet, even here it is an event which can remain postponed indefinitely, as long as people do actually repent of their sins and turn back to the true path.

However, by the time of the visions of Frs. Kataribaabo, Ikazire, and Kasapuraari, a shift had occurred. Here, the biblical end of the world is no longer referred to in terms of its being a hypothetical or postponed future, but an imminent event. This much is clearly stated in the vision of Kataribaabo, when it says, 'You learn from the holy writings and from your prayers that Christ would come again to judge the living and the dead. What is happening in the world today should indicate to you that this is the time for your salvation, what is written in the holy scriptures is actually being fulfilled' (ibid.: 84). In the vision of Ikazire, a number of references are made to the world having already entered the 'period of punishments' which precedes the final judgement (ibid.: 77–8).

The vision of Kasapuraari similarly opens with an ominous warning that 'She [the Virgin] started saying: "The time is getting near and the Almighty God is displeased with the world, crimes have become too many; unless there is a change of heart the world is not going to escape punishment"' (ibid., 86). It later explains that those who have sinned will now face 'the wrath of the Almighty God, and His chastisements'. Thus, 'you people in the world should pray for yourselves. God the Almighty is justified when He is condemning a person, when He is judging you He is right...However, you should keep in mind that He is displeased, my God and also your God is displeased. My children, please repent wholeheartedly from the bottom of your hearts' (ibid., 97-98).

Thus, the evidence of these ten visionary chapters would seem to suggest a certain progression in the nature of the MRTC's millenarian thinking over time. Moreover, additional evidence, taken from elsewhere in the same publication, suggests that the group's apocalyptic outlook developed even further in the period after the last of the leaders' visions (8 June 1991).

Specifically here, it is extremely important to note that Chapter 4, entitled 'The Chastisements and the Three Days of Darkness', appears to be a late addition to the book. Placed alongside all of the other chapters, it is anomalous in several ways, and is much longer than any of the others. In particular, whilst all of the other visionary chapters concern only one vision, received by one of the sect's leaders, Chapter 4 recounts a single vision experienced by all of the MRTC leadership.[2] A declaration to this effect, signed by all the sect's leaders, is included towards the beginning of the chapter. For each leader, the declaration includes the individual's full name, his/her date and place of birth, and a formal statement that they have been a witness to this particular vision (which the chapter is about to recount). In this way, the declaration is made to resemble the witness statements on a legal document.

But one crucial point here is that, if all the leaders had indeed put their names to this vision, then it is highly significant that none of the details of it appear in any of the chapters concerning the individual visions. The most likely explanation of this would be that this group vision of Chapter 4 was constructed only after the other – individual – visions had been written down. Furthermore, given that the last of the individual visions (Kasapuraari) is dated 8 June 1991, we might reasonably conclude that the group vision must, therefore, have been first recorded only after that date. Further evidence to support this inference is the fact that the name of Joseph Kibweteere's wife, Teresa, is absent from the list of leaders bearing witness in the declaration. This might well indicate that this group vision was first written down only after the Movement had left Kabumba, in late 1992.[3] Moreover, if this timing is correct, then one further inference might be that Chapter 4 was not included in the original edition of the book, which was published in 1991, but instead represents a later addition to the subsequent editions of the book. However, not having seen either the 1991 or 1994 editions, I am unable to offer any firm conclusions on this point.[4]

All of this timing is nevertheless relevant here, because what certainly *is* clear is that, by the time this group vision was written down, the imminent apocalypse had become an all-encompassing obsession for the MRTC leadership (and therefore, presumably, for the sect as a whole). Thus, whilst the visions of Frs. Kataribaabo, Ikazire and Kasapuraari had talked of the

[2] As already noted, the various visionary chapters take up most of the book. In addition, it includes a number of chapters at the end which are concerned with various practical matters, with reports of questions and answers sessions at the group's training courses, and so on.
[3] Although Mrs Kibweteere's name is attached to one chapter in the book – that concerned with the importance of rosary prayers (Chapter 12) – she is crucially *not* regarded as a visionary (in the book, at least). In other words, whilst the content of all the other leaders' chapters is credited to divine inspiration, the details of Mrs Kibweteere's section are cast as her words alone. This, despite the fact that Mrs Kibweteere had previously experienced visions from the Virgin (the details of which she described to me at length).
[4] One hypothesis for the fact that Mrs Kibweteere's chapter is not credited to divine inspiration might be that it was regarded as a vision in the first edition, but was then 'downgraded' following her withdrawal. The leadership may even have wanted to erase it completely, but perhaps could not, given that it is the only chapter to deal specifically with the rosary. Once again, all of this would be impossible to verify without seeing the earlier editions of the book.

end of the world as an imminent event, they were still primarily concerned with other issues (indeed, to such a degree that none of those chapters, in their overall content, differ markedly from any of the other chapters in the book). However, by contrast, Chapter 4 is *much* darker in tone than any of the book's other sections, and is concerned exclusively with the impending doom. It is subtitled 'The Fulfilment of God's Predictions for His People and the World', and it begins:

> [these messages are] to inform you all about the impending chastisements to the world for its disobedience, and about the termination of the present generation and the three days of darkness; some of what is being said below has already taken place, and some is surely going to come about (*ibid.*, 43).

The reader is left in little doubt as to the exact nature of these imminent events. 'There will be great tribulation [*obusaasi, lit:* 'pain'] upon all the people such that has never before been experienced by any person since the creation of the world' (*ibid.*, 46). There will be a famine. People will be forced to eat their children. 'Those without children will endeavour to steal children from other parents. Even people who are stronger than others will attempt to kill the weaker ones and eat them. This is the type of cannibalism that will come as a result of the famine that has never before been experienced by any person' (*ibid.*: 47). Even people's domestic herds will not be able to save them here, because some 'would be struck by thunder or destroyed by the storm or by hailstone', and others 'would be attacked by diseases of various types and they would not be cured by any veterinary doctor at all', whilst even those animals which survived all this 'would develop poison that would kill their masters...some other [animals] would kill their masters with horns and some with hoofs by kicking them' (*ibid.*).[5] Then, an animal 'as big as a mountain...[will be] ordered to eat the people...as many people as can be found in one whole county [*Ishaza ryoona*]', and the Earth will be covered with snakes, 'ten times the size of the tyre of a lorry' which will devour humans (*ibid.*, 48). There will be

> heavy hailstone to fall and also heavy storm at sea. We are as well expecting heavy earthquakes that will destroy what is on the earth such as buildings, trees, mountains... A strong whirlwind that has never before been seen since the creation of the world, it will destroy many things. There will be a certain disturbance of the soil that will cause the soil to break into several pieces. Inanimate objects such as mountains, lakes, rivers, stones...will move from one place and go to another place...the valleys will run to the mountains amidst a great roar and the trembling of the earth, the flashing of the lightning and the rumbling of thunder. The people will be trying to run away, and the mountains will collide with one other in fear of the wrath of God. Stones will then be rolling down and hurting the people as they move. The chastisements about the disturbance of the earth are painful but the victims do not die soon. (*ibid.*: 49)

---

[5] This passage on animals is particularly significant, because most people in the Southwest (and beyond) would typically expect to consume their own domestic beasts as a 'last resort' to survival, during any period of extreme famine. Thus, the story which is being conveyed here is of an 'ultimate' famine (one which is worse than anything previously known in history).

Finally, Satan, and his force of 'devils' (*emandwa*),[6] will come into the world.

> The devils from the under-world will come out to harass people; those devils that belong to men who died will rape women and those devils that belong to women will force me to fornicate with them...all those who are intent on and are observing the Commandments of God will be severely persecuted and some others will be killed. (*ibid.*: 50–1)

The world will be plunged into an age of darkness, during which people will be transformed into animals.

> Some women will give birth to animals and some animals will produce human beings. Women will give birth to children whose parts of the body will be in abnormal positions, namely the eyes will be on the neck, the lips on the chest, and so on...Some children will be born without arms or legs or nose. (*ibid.*: 53)

This age of darkness is a prelude to the final battle of good and evil. At that time, Jesus himself will come down into the world to do battle with Satan. Only a quarter of the people currently in the world will survive, as all those who have failed to repent are wiped out. For the survivors, however, a final, golden age of heaven on earth will prevail.

> I saw a new earth coming down from heaven. This new earth contained every good thing of every type that pertains to the spiritual and the material well-being of the human person. The new earth is very beautiful and it has plenty of light... This is the new earth that was promised to those who would repent. Death and the underworld are vanquished, Satan has been put in fetters as well as those who accepted to serve it. Satan will never attempt the redeemed ones. The new earth will be connected with Heaven. (*ibid.*: 59–60)

Thus, it would seem that, in the minds of the MRTC leaders, at least, the end of the world was indeed now nigh.

In summary, then, this reading of the MRTC's central text allows certain conclusions to be drawn about the evolution of the group's millenarianism. From the time the Movement was first formed, in 1984, until Frs. Kataribaabo, Ikazire and Kasapuraari joined the sect in 1991, the MRTC seems to have held no particular commitment to the idea of a millennial 'end of the world'. Its various leaders did talk about a future 'Judgement Day', but this served a largely rhetorical function in their teaching. Indeed, by simply speaking of repentance 'before it is too late', these early writings seem hardly distinguishable from any form of mainstream Catholic pedagogy. However, by 1991, the MRTC's thinking had changed, and the group had begun to consider the biblical apocalypse as a real, and imminent, future. Then, sometime between Mrs Kibweteere's departure from the sect in late 1992, and the publication of the last edition of the book, some time in 1996 (the edition upon which my discussion here is based), things changed again. During this period, the MRTC leadership became quite obsessed with eschatology, and all other ideas were pushed aside as the group began to focus exclusively on the concept of the biblical end of the world, an event they perceived to have already started. It is only during this period, then, that the MRTC emerged as a truly millenarian movement.

---

[6] The book uses the term '*emizimu*' here, although I have changed this to '*emandwa*' (for the reasons discussed in Chapter 4).

The MRTC and the global Marian movement

So how, then, might we begin to account for these shifting perspectives over time? Well, first of all, it is interesting that the MRTC should have first begun to demonstrate a commitment to the idea of apocalypse as an imminent event in the period immediately following Fr. Kataribaabo's entry into the sect. After all, prior to his entry into the group, Kataribaabo had already had exposure to the millenarian doctrines of a number of international Marian organizations (in particular, during his trip to California, in the mid-1980s; see Chapter 4). Thus, it it is quite likely that it was this senior priest who first emphasized eschatological thinking within the MRTC.

Moreover, it might also appear obvious why the Movement's worldview should have then become more markedly pessimistic around 1994. Firstly, this was the year during which the Movement's membership was expanding rapidly, as a direct result of the emerging AIDS epidemic (see Chapter 5). Given that the MRTC was a revival of Nyabingi – and given the propensity of historical Nyabingi networks to become more millennarian during times of 'general misfortune' – it follows that this context would probably have also shaped the group's shift towards a more apocalyptic perspective. Secondly, this was also the period during which the international coffee price spiked unexpectedly, an event which, in the context of Uganda's newly liberalized economy, had a sudden, and profound, impact on household incomes, and which resulted in some households unexpectedly having large amounts of cash.[7] As the Comaroffs have famously pointed out, such episodes of (what actors experience as) 'millennial capitalism' frequently result in a proliferation of apocalyptic imagery (2000). Indeed, these perceptions may have become especially marked in this particular case, given the peculiarly negative impact this new wealth had on the social situations of many younger wives in the Southwest (who subsequently formed a significant proportion of the MRTC's total membership, see Chapter 5). Finally, 1994 was also the year in which the Rwanda genocide occurred, an event which, although it had no direct connection with the MRTC's activities, must nevertheless have had at least some impact in shaping a general mood of uncertainty within the sect (as indeed it did for so many other people in the Great Lakes region during this period).[8]

[7] For example, one oft-told story in Bugamba recalls a coffee dealer who visited the village during this period, and from the back of his pick-up handed out fistfuls of money. The event is well remembered, because the party which followed, in the village's main bar, lasted for more than three days.

[8] It is certainly true that a number of MRTC leaders, including the Kibweteeres, had had contact with the Marian seers of Kibeho during the late 1980s. This is potentially significant, given that the Kibeho group had been receiving visions which were markedly apocalyptic from the early '80s onwards (and which had become ever more so in the period immediately preceding the genocide). Moreover, it is also interesting to note that much of the Kibeho seers' own version of millenarianism was also cast in terms of an imminent, and general, 'crisis of fertility' in Rwanda. However, against all this, there is simply no evidence that any of the MRTC's leaders had any further contact with the Kibeho group – or any other Rwandan visionaries, for that matter – after the group's move to Kabumba (in July 1989). In addition,

Thus, all of these factors may have played some part in shaping the MRTC's development of a more pessimistic outlook at this time. However, evidence from the group's own publication suggests that there may also have been another, even more important, influence as well. Specifically, a close reading of the sect's central text strongly suggests that this evolution in the sect's millenarianism was also significantly – perhaps even primarily – shaped by the particular form of 'global' Christianity with which they were engaged. Here, Fr. Kataribaabo's previous interactions with the MMP do not, in fact, emerge as the most significant part of the story. Instead, it is more important to note that during Joseph Kibweteere's brief spell in politics in the 1970s, both he and his wife Theresa also travelled abroad, and in 1979 visited the Vatican City, in Rome (a certificate commemorating the visit still hangs on the wall of their family home). The visit is important to our story here, because it was during this trip that Mrs Kibweteere – who was already, by that time, a Marian devotee of sorts – had first made contact with a number of Marian groups in Italy. Furthermore, over the following few years, Theresa had then used these contacts to trace other Marian groups, elsewhere in the world. As a result of these efforts, by the mid-1980s – at the same time as both she and her husband were starting to make contact with, and to attend the meetings of, Marian visionaries throughout South-western Uganda (and beyond) – Mrs Kibweteere was receiving literature from a wide array of, mostly Catholic, Marian groups around the world. By the mid-1990s, her post office box in Mbarara Town was regularly filled with Marian publications from organizations based as far apart as England, Spain, Ghana, Japan and Australia. Indeed, as a direct result of her industriousness, by the time the MRTC took up residence at the Kibweteeres' home, in July 1989, the sect was receiving literature from a quite startling array of worldwide Marian organizations. However, perhaps unsurprisingly, the vast majority of the organizations were based in the United States, in Vermont, New York, Massachusetts, Louisiana and Texas.[9]

The particular imaginary these texts helped to foster, of a global network within which the MRTC was located, must surely have been another factor in the group's early expansion. After all, this was a time before print media, commercial radio, or mobile phones had become widely available in South-

---

[8] (cont.) it is also clear that the MRTC had very few, if any, Rwandan members at all, either before, or after, 1994. This point was stressed by all of my respondents, on numerous occasions – often in response to my own speculations along these lines – that 'there were very few Rwandans in the MRTC', that 'almost none of the sect's members could speak Kinyarwanda', and so on. Moreover, this point is also borne out by my own examinations of the membership's composition (in Chapter 5). Thus, for these – and other – reasons, the early media speculation that the MRTC's membership may have been primarily made up of Rwandans who had escaped the genocide of 1994, can be largely dismissed. Nevertheless, it is still fair to say that the violence in Rwanda in 1994, occurring as it did such a short distance from the MRTC's field of operations, *must* have made at least some impression on the sect's outlook at this time. Therefore, it may well have been one of the factors which shaped the overall context in which the MRTC developed a more strongly millenarian perspective at this time (I would like to thank Wendy James for her clarifications on this point, pers. comm.).

[9] I am extremely grateful to Mrs Kibweteere for allowing me to photocopy all of this literature. I thank her also for granting me a number of interviews on the subject of the MRTC.

western Uganda, and when most people – in the rural areas, in particular – would have generally received very little information about the outside world. In this context, the information contained in these Marian texts, emanating as it did from the four corners of the earth, must have seemed extraordinary to the majority of the sect's membership. Moreover, a number of my respondents recall that the MRTC's leaders would sometimes claim that their own sect occupied a privileged position within this global network of Marian groups. For example, the end of Chapter 4 of the MRTC's publication contains a section entitled 'Uganda, A Chosen Nation, A New Israel', in which it is stated that 'Uganda is the Nation that the Lord has chosen to become the New Israel, second Israel. It is the Nation that is loved by God most. If Uganda accepts to comply with the messages coming from heaven...then it is Uganda that will convert other nations' (*ibid.*, 60).[10] Whether or not this claim to Uganda's pre-eminence was key to the MRTC's appeal, it is certainly clear that many people initially began to attend the group's meetings for the purpose of hearing readings from the Marian literature. Thus, as Mrs Kibweteere now recalls, throughout the period of the group's meetings at her home, readings from, and interpretations of, these texts formed the very basis of the MRTC's daily routine. Moreover, at least one former member also remembers that, even after the sect left the Kibweteeres' home, copies of the material continued to be widely drawn upon by MRTC delegations during their proselytizing missions. This apparently continued up until the publication of the MRTC's 1994 edition (after which time the text formed the basis of their worship). However, by that time, many of the key insights of the global Marian literature appear to have been already incorporated into the MRTC's own worldview.

Indeed, further close reading of the MRTC's own publication reveals a growing influence of the Marian literature on the sect's thinking over time. Thus, as one would expect, in the very earliest vision of Mwerinde (10 March 1981), one finds no reference at all to the Marian literature, since this vision was received before Mwerinde ever met Mrs Kibweteere. In the visions of 1989 (Kibweteere and Komuhangi), no reference is made to this source, either. However, by 1991, the leaders' visions were borrowing directly from the Marian texts. Although none of these visions explicitly reference the pamphlets, various ideas seem to have been lifted directly from them. Among these are Fr. Kasapuraari's notions of cosmetic surgery, as well as his ideas about IVF treatments, whereby 'there are some who satisfy their sexual desires through injections and one gets a baby in that way with the one she loves'; people have sex by way of injections for the purpose of conceiving children' (*ibid.*: 94). The latter, in particular, is a recurring theme in many of the pamphlets, which are often concerned with issues of abortion and new reproductive technologies.

However, the clearest example of borrowing is found in the vision of Fr Ikazire, which is primarily concerned with the sacrament of the Eucharist, and in particular with a return to an older practice in which the host was

---

[10] This perception of a privileged position for Uganda may have been further strengthened by visits to the MRTC's compounds, by members of other, international churches (see below).

FRANZ JOSEPH KEILER 409 RICHMOND AVE., BUFFALO, N. Y. 14222 AVE MARIA! +

Thursday, the 15th of August 1985- While walking in the grove early this morning, I came upon a most beautiful sight, Our Blessed Mother, dressed in white, wearing a blue mantle and a large gold crown. She said:

"My child, today is the Feast of My Assumption, yet it is not revered by many as a Feast. In a world of modernism and progressiveness, feast-days do not have any place. Awake, My children, from your slumber before it is too late. My Divine Son's cup is running over and I must appease Him constantly. Why do My children re-crucify their Saviour daily? Why do My children constantly only 'play' lip-service rather than practice their Faith? Too many are lazy and only follow the pleasures of life; this must change! Many of My children are guilty of leading lives that are far from Holy, yet, in the eyes of the world they are 'deeply religious'. Beware, My children! You can NOT fool your Saviour."

"My children, pray for the children of the dark continent; they suffer a great deal at the hands of a few. Pray for them, for they suffer greatly for their Faith. Many are strong Pillars of faith in the world of materialism. Look UP to these martyrs, My children. Do not be fooled by the idols of today; many are worldly - and their lives are just full of emptiness. Pray, My children, PRAY, for in prayers many will find the solace they need."

"Pray, My children, for the Holy Father, for he is really a man of peace, much maligned by the Media because he cannot be manipulated. Pray for his safety during his travels. Beware of C U R I A, My children, for they try to change much but are restrained. Through prayer much can be changed. Pray."

"My child, tell My children in your travels the importance of attending Mass daily and receiving Communion. I also wish My children to say FIFTEEN decades of the Rosary daily and to meditate. Is it too much to ask? Far too many only complain when their lives are difficult - they do not pray for the Mercy of the Eternal Father. Through prayer much is received; have more Faith, and criticise less! I wish My children to continue their novenas, for many more months. There will be many blessings for those that persevere. Prayer is the Key to Heaven and the solace of the oppressed. Pray for the poor and the oppressed, for many are overlooked by the world, but are beloved by their Saviour. Pray for (the) elderly, for their lives are saddened by the lack-of-Love many of their children show them. Remember the Commandment: Honor Thy Father and Mother. Far too many children are too concerned with their own lives that they forget the past. Are YOU guilty of this, My children; are you interested in helping others?"

"My children, what more can be said; abortion is, pure and simply, MURDER; yet many try o justify this! It deeply grieves My heart to see the slaughter of the Innocents. Beware, My daughters! Beware! Abortion is a grave sin, not to be taken lightly. Pray for your legislatures - that they may change these laws that allow these murders. Pray! Pray! Pray! This does more than just talk."

"My child, I wish My children to teach their innocents the beauty of life, for many get a distorted view outside the homes. Prayer is the important part of every life but, to many innocents, it is nothing. Teach them, My children, for it is your responsibility to reach them."

"Good-bye for now and God bless you, continue as you are sending out My Messages. Tell My children to pray and make sacrifices. Remember, My children, I come to many Voice-Boxes and send My blessings to ALL. Guard your health and especially your door."

DEAR FRIENDS: Be assured of my prayers for everyone during the Novena to Our Blessed Mother. Please, dear friends, do NOT send 'LIST' of names for the messages. I send ONLY to those that have personally written. Please help us - we still need a great deal more to send the Messages to Africa and the East.   FRANZ

6.1 Many of the leaflets used by the MRTC were text-only, and detailed Marian visions received elsewhere in the world. This one, produced by Franz Joseph Keiler (Buffalo, USA), describes an apparition Keiler had received in which he was asked to pray for 'the children of the dark continent'.

placed directly on the tongue of the receiver, rather than being laid in the communicant's palm (*ibid.*, 76–7). All of Ikazire's ideas on this issue are taken directly from a pamphlet entitled 'Communion in the Hand is a Sacrilege' written by the organization Our Lady of the Roses of New York City. Moreover, the growing influence of the Marian literature on the individual visions coincides directly with the sect's adoption of a 'final' millenarian outlook (i.e. one in which the end of the world is regarded as an imminent event).

This correlation is more than coincidental, as evidenced by the fact that, aside from talk about cosmetic surgery, abortion and the sacraments, a coming apocalypse emerges as perhaps *the* key theme across all of the Marian texts which the MRTC was receiving during this period. Moreover, this primary preoccupation with the imminent end of the world is particularly marked in the literature of the US-based Marian organizations. Thus, a number of these groups' publications quote predictions by the Virgin Mary that the apocalypse is either imminent or has already begun. For example, as one pamphlet, from an organization based in Buffalo, NY, begins, 'Our Blessed Mother...[has] said: "...Many of my children must change their lives drastically, and soon! For time is SHORT; much shorter than people think".' A booklet from the St Paul's Guild of Vermont, quotes from a vision received at Fatima, Spain. 'Our Lady has repeatedly told me: "Many nations are going to disappear from the face of the earth, Godless nations will be picked up by God as His scourge to punish the human race...tell them, Father, that the Devil is waging his decisive battle against Our Lady".' Another leaflet from the Marian Workers of Atonement, of New South Wales, Australia, quotes a seer in Poland. 'At 12.30 pm...Holy Mary entered...[she said] "Turn back, for time is short. You are living in the days where the signs are given in the sky and on the earth...If the people do not turn to God, then will come down terrible continuous thunder and lightning and the earth will start to crack".'

It is beyond my scope here to explore fully the reasons why the publications of these – mostly US-based – Marian organizations should themselves have been so millenarian in tone during this period. However, I would note in passing that the texts often relate the predicted biblical end of the world to the then ongoing Cold War struggle (most of the texts in the MRTC's possession had been produced before the fall of the Soviet Union). Rather, my aim here is to demonstrate the influence of this international literature on the development of the sect's own millenarian thinking. I have already noted that the leaders' visions of 1991, the first to borrow directly from the international Marian literature, were also the first to suggest the end of the world to be an imminent event.

Even more significantly, the entire group vision of Chapter 4 of the MRTC publication, by far the most millenarian in tone in the whole book, appears to be almost entirely derived from the international Marian publications. Thus, at the very outset of the chapter, before even the declarations of the MRTC's own leaders, the text explicitly lists other people, around the world, who have received the same vision which is to follow. Significantly, this list includes the names of *all* of the Marian seers who are mentioned in the various international Marian texts (*ibid.*: 44). Furthermore, many of the details of the group vision (outlined above) appear to have been lifted directly from the pamphlets. Finally, at the end of the chapter – following the details of the vision itself – a list is included of a number of countries worldwide, and details given of the specific fate which awaits them on judgement day (*ibid.*, 55–8). Again, this list bears a striking resemblance to the places named in the international Marian publications. Most significantly here, the country which tops this list, whose people are destined for the greatest suffering during the forthcoming apocalypse, is none other than Russia![11]

Moreover, a close examination of the Marian literature itself suggests a further reason why any serious reader of this material should have taken its apocalyptic message increasingly seriously over time, because at several points in the various books and pamphlets, the predicted end of the world is given a specific timing. For example, one crucial section in a booklet from the St. Paul's Guild reads: 'a great chastisement will come over all of mankind; not today or tomorrow but in the second half of the twentieth century...the great, great war will come in the second half of the twentieth century.'

This section is crucial, because its timing is explicitly referenced in the group vision of Chapter 4, which states – in capital letters, and bold type – that although 'some of the following messages give the dates on which they were delivered and some others do not' (Chap. 4: 46), the fact that a prediction has been made of 'the second half of the twentieth century' suggests that the end of the world will probably occur at the millennium, in the year 2000. Thus, 'All of you who are living on the planet, listen to what I am going to say: When the year 2000 is completed, the year that will follow will not be year two thousand-and-one. The year that will follow shall be called Year One in a generation that will follow the present generation' (*ibid.*, 53–4). Again, 'the person who will not repent, his or her end is between now and the year 2000. Each person from the time he or she has heard this message to the year 2000, should carefully decide about the destiny of his or her soul and then plan how he or she will use the remaining time profitably' (*ibid.*, 54). Finally, to close the whole apocalyptic vision of Chapter 4: 'The Blessed Virgin Mary...is warning us so often that if the people persist in disobeying and displeasing God, He will shorten the period stated and will close this generation before reaching to the year 2000. She says that that day will come like a thief' (*ibid.*: 61). Thus, on the evidence of this Chapter 4, at least, it would seem that the increasing

[11] As further evidence of the influence that this (primarily) American literature was having on the sect during this period, it is also noteworthy that, by 1996, whenever MRTC leaders spoke about the end of the world – in the context of their initiation courses, or during daily prayer sessions at the sect's various compounds – they invariably did so with reference to apocalyptic visions which had been received in the US. Thus, as one respondent put it to me (in his broken English): 'It was America mostly. America mainly. That [in] America there are some religious people who came from there and gave them some messages telling them that one day a star will collide with the sun, and the echo that would come would doom the whole world, and only about one quarter of the whole world would survive. So [they were] fighting to be that quarter' (Mr Sebataka).

FURTHER WARNINGS FROM OUR LADY OF FATIMA

MESSAGE OF SISTER LUCY – MAY 22nd 1958

Why was the third message of Our Lady of Fatima not to be opened before 1960? Cardinal Ottaviani at the opening meeting for the celebration of the Golden Jubilee of Fatima, held in Rome on February 11, 1967, said that he had submitted that very question to Lucy, who answered that the message will be clearer in 1960. "This made me think." said the Cardinal, "that the message might be a prophecy." The message was published by the magazine "La Immaculada," of January-February 1959.

The message was transmitted to Rev. Father Agosto Fuertes, Postular General for the beautification of Francisco and Jacinta at Fatima. On receiving the message, Father Fuertes disclosed: "the Holy Father gave me permission to pay a visit to Lucy now in Coimbra as a Discalceate Carmelite, who received me with great sorrow; she had grown thin, and was very sad when said:

"Father, Our Lady is very displeased because no one had heeded Her message of 1917. Neither the good nor the bad paid any attention to it. The good ones go their way unconcerned and heeding not the Celestial directives; the bad, pursuing the broad way of perdition, completely ignoring the threatened punishment. Father, please tell everyone what Our Lady had repeatedly told me: 'Many nations are going to disappear from the face of the earth, Godless nations will be picked up by God as His scourge to punish the human race, if we through prayers and the Sacraments, will not bring about their conversion.' Tell them, Father, that the Devil is waging his decisive battle against Our Lady, in that, <u>the fall of religious and priestly souls is the thing that most</u> saddens the Immaculate Heart of Mary and Jesus. The Devil knows too well that when <u>religious and priests betray their high calling, they drag behind them many souls to Hell</u>. We have hardly any time left to stave off the punishment of God. There are at our disposal two very effective means, <u>PRAYER and SACRIFICE</u>, but the Devil is doing his utmost to divert our minds from, and <u>take away the taste for prayer.</u> The outcome will be that either we shall be saved or doomed. One thing, Father, <u>you must make clear to the people though; not to wait or hope for any call to Prayer and Penance either from the Supreme Pontiff, the Bishops, the Pastors, or the Superior Generals.</u> It is time that <u>each one, on his own initiative</u>, undertake to do works of sanctity, <u>and to reform his life</u>, according to the admonitions of our Blessed Lady. The Devil is striving to get hold of consecrated souls, working by little, to induce them to a state of complete atheism; it is using all the artful tricks even to the extent of suggesting 'updating of Religious life.' (The word used by Lucy is the one subsequently employed by Pope John XXIII, that is, "aggiornare," "Aggiornamento." That was in 1958. – Note of the translator.)

"What comes out of this is sterility of the interior life, <u>and in lay people, unconcern in regard to abstaining from sensual pleasures and total immolation.</u> Remember, Father, that two facts contributed to the sanctification of Jacinta and Francisco: <u>The sadness of Our Lady and the vision of Hell.</u> Our Lady is placed between two fires; on the one hand the stubborn humanity, indifferent to threatened chastisements and on the other, we, whom She sees setting at naught the Sacraments and disregarding the approaching punishment, while remaining unbelieving, sensual and materialistic. The Holy Mother has expressly said, 'We are approaching the last days.' She expressed three times; the first time, She stated that the Devil is waging decisive (that is to say a 'final') battle from which we will come out either a winner or a loser.

"The second time, more than once, She told us that the final remedies given to the world are 'The Holy Rosary and devotion to the Immaculate Heart of Mary.' The third time, she said to me that having exhausted all other means which men have ignored, She is now offering with apprehension, as the last resource of salvation Herself in Person, Her numerous apparations, Her tears and messages given through seers scattered in various parts of the world. Our Lady added that if we do not heed Her pleas and will keep going on with our offenses, then there will be no more pardons. It is urgent, Father, that we face reality, terrible as it may be. The purpose is not that of scaring the souls, but of recalling the seriousness of the situation; since in fact, Our Lady gave such powers to the Holy Rosary, there is no problem whether material or moral, national or international, that cannot be solved effectively through the Holy Rosary and our sacrifices. Received with love and devotion, the Rosary will please Mary and compensate for the disappointments of Her Immaculate Heart."

(Pro Manuscripto)

6.2 Another of the Marian leaflets used by the MRTC, entitled: 'Further warnings from Our Lady of Fatima', and produced by St Paul's Guild (Vermont, USA)

Saint Michael
Guardian
of the Faith

ROSES

Redemption
Grace
Peace

The Message of Our Lady and Our Lord to Veronica Lueken

Our Lady of the Roses Shrine • P.O. Box 52 • Bayside, New York 11361

October 1, 1988 • Eve of the Guardian Angels & in honor of St. Theresa

New York City targeted for destruction

Bombs to be placed in strategic places

Veronica—There are blue lights now coming down from the sky, high overhead. Oh, the lights are so beautiful! Oh, I've seen lights before, but there is something different about these lights. They're magnificent. They're blue. And, also, now beyond the blue, on the right side of each rivulet of blue, there are pink cascading lights coming down now. They're actually lights because they flow out from the blue. I never saw anything like it before.

And—oh, there they are: all about the lights now are coming out—I know they're angels. They're all different ages and different sizes, but I do believe it registers their age. These are all, I know, guardian angels. They are dressed in the most beautiful pastel shades of blue and pink and white. And I feel that the blue stands for the masculine angel, if there is such a thing; and the pink also for the feminine angels; and the whites are for babies. They are—there are hundreds of them all about the trees. Oh, I'm sure you must see them. They are so clear, they're almost human-like in appearance, except for the translucency of their faces. They are so beautiful.

Now high up into the sky—oh, about maybe 20 feet beyond the statue up into the sky, there is now a very white light. The light is opening up; it's as though it's piercing the sky, and there coming through the light is Jesus. Oh, He's just beautiful! He has on the most magnificent robe. It's cut quite differently than He wore the last apparition time. But it is a beautiful robe, all of a classic type of weave. It's—it almost looks like it comes from a foreign country, the robe. But it is so beautiful.

Now—oh, right behind Him now, as the light is opening up, I can see Our Lady coming with someone else. Oh! It's Saint Theresa! I'd know her anywhere, since she's been practically living with me in 1968 and '69. She has on a habit now. It's white and black. However she has a cape; the cape is a cream color.

Now they're all together, side by side. Jesus is on our right side; Our Lady is right next to Him on His right side, and Saint Theresa is also standing on Our Lady's right side.

Now Jesus is touching His lips, which means He's going to talk. Oh no, He's pointing over to Saint Theresa; she's going to talk. But I can't speak French!

Jesus—"You will understand, My child."

Veronica—Oh, Jesus said that I will understand.

St. Theresa—"My sister, my dear sister Veronica, how happy I am to see you again after all these years. I have been around, but not permitted by the Eternal Father to appear before you as I did in the early years. But I have been guiding you. I wish at

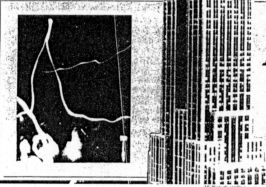

EMPIRE STATE BLDG. ONE TARGET

Miraculous photo (with an SX-70 Polaroid camera), taken within inner circle, of Veronica holding three votive lights (far left). Incredibly, the whole outline of the Empire State Bldg. comes out, even with the needle and airport light at the summit. The beads of prayer cutting through the upper part of structure indicate what floor these terrorists plan to install the bomb, but also that prayers can still avert this disaster. A sword, complete with handle, with its blade cutting through the skyscraper, appears in the lower forefront of photo. Also, a missile-like object facing downwards (lower right) is clearly visible.

6.3 Leaflet, 'New York City targeted for destruction', produced by Our Lady of the Roses Shrine (New York, USA)

urgency with which the MRTC had come to regard the predicted apocalypse – as was predicted, above all, by the Marian literature – stemmed, at least in part, from the sect's own interpretation of the specific timings which were attached to that prediction.

However, it later became clear that, at the time the group vision of Chapter 4 was written down, not everyone in the MRTC was entirely convinced of the validity of this timing. Indeed, jumping ahead to the year 2000, it appears that still by that time, some members of the sect remained sceptical on this point. For example, four days after the Kanungu fire, James Mujuni reported a letter, written in Runyankore, which had earlier been received by the *The New Vision*'s sister paper, the vernacular *Orumuri*, from Joseph Kibweteere. Written sometime in January 2000, the letter explicitly addressed a then ongoing argument within the MRTC as to the exact date for the end of the world. Apparently seeking to clarify internal discussions on this point, Kibweteere stated in the letter that, 'I Joseph Kibweteere, my boss Jesus Christ has appeared to me and given me a message to all of you that there are some people arguing over the message that this generation ends on 1 January 2000. On the contrary, the generation ends at the end of the year 2000 and no other year will follow' (*New Vision*, 21 March 2000; the letter was translated from the Runyankore by Mujuni).[12]

This new vision of Kibweteere seems finally to have been accepted by all. Thus, when the MRTC handed in a report on their activities to the Ugandan Ministry of Internal Affairs three days before the fire, it stated that 'their mission was coming to an end, and there would be no 2001. Instead, next year would be year number 1, starting with a new generation' (*ibid.*). As it turned out, of course, for the majority of the MRTC membership, the world was due to end several months before that date.

An African-Initiated Church

Thus, if the MRTC's leadership became increasingly concerned with questions of eschatology in the years between 1992 and 1996, it would seem that this cannot be explained only by reference to such factors as the sect's membership expanding rapidly during this period, as a result of an emergent AIDS epidemic. In addition, based on the evidence of the Movement's own publication, at least, it is evident that this shift was also profoundly shaped by the group's engagement with a worldwide network of Marian organizations, and by the MRTC leadership's particular interpretation of these other groups' own concerns.

Yet, in fact, this was not the only way in which the Movement's doctrine and practice were shaped by their engagement with various forms of 'new'

---

[12] This vision is itself remarkable, not least because it is claimed for Kibweteere himself. As described to me by *all* of my respondents on Kanungu, following their 'initial visions', no leaders of the sect, other than Ceredonia, had any further apparitions. As I have detailed at length, within the Movement such visitations quickly became the sole preserve of Ceredonia herself. Thus, we might speculate that Kibweteere's claim of a vision at this particular point in time – and one from Jesus, not Mary – might perhaps have been indicative of tension between himself and Ceredonia on the above point.

Christianity. In addition, it is clear that much of the leadership's earliest innovation – i.e. that which occurred in the period immediately following the sect's expulsion from the mainstream church – was primarily driven by a desire to return to a more 'authentic', or 'pure', form of Catholicism. Thus, during this time – and no doubt partly as a response to the fact that the sect had just been expelled from the Roman church – a number of my respondents recall Movement leaders, or other recruiters, telling would-be members that the sect represented an 'improvement' on an erstwhile Roman church, which had become 'corrupted', or 'flawed' (for example, Lucy Kamuli). In addition, many of the sect's Sunday masses came to be conducted entirely in Latin (in which both Fr. Kataribaabo and Fr. Ikazire, as senior clergymen, were fluent).[13] Within these services, the liturgy was also purged of anything which the leadership considered to be 'recent innovation'; the Eucharist was placed on the tongue of communicants, rather than in their hands, and so on.[14] However, it is also clear that, as time went on, the various innovations that were introduced by the sect's leaders – and increasingly, by Ceredonia alone – came to have a quite different emphasis, one which betrays the growing influence that various new forms of Christianity were also starting to have over the group.

It is not clear with exactly which forms of 'new' Christianity, or which specific churches, or other Christian organizations – either Uganda-based, or international – individual MRTC leaders ever had contact (either in the years immediately before, or after, the sect's expulsion from the mainstream church). Certainly, from the mid-1980s onwards, the nascent Movement was receiving materials from the worldwide Marian organizations. In addition, it has also been established that, as part of their engagement with local Marian networks during the late 1980s, Joseph and Theresa Kibweteere also attended meetings held in Uganda by a number of other international Christian organizations. For example, in October 1989, the pair attended at least one session which was held in Kampala by the charismatic Australian visionary, William Kamm (aka the 'Little Pebble', Borzello, 19 April 2000). In addition, as already discussed, Fr. Kataribaabo would also almost certainly have had contact with a range of other charismatic Catholic organizations, including the International Catholic Charismatic Renewal (ICCR), during his time at Loyola Marymount University (the ICCR was at that time well represented on most Catholic campuses in the US). By the early 1990s, the group would certainly also have been aware of the activities of the local branch of the ICCR, in South-western

---

[13] In addition to Sunday services, the MRTC also held masses on any day carrying Marian significance. Thus, for example, the Feast of the Immaculate Conception was observed as the most holy day of the entire year.

[14] In a further example here, the argument between Ceredonia and Fr. Ikazire which eventually led to the latter's withdrawal from the group involved an argument over whose interpretation of the Liturgy of Santo Dadao represented the more 'correct' version. In this instance, Ceredonia had insisted on the group praying first to the Virgin, with Ikazire arguing that this was not the correct sequence (see Chapter 4). In this example, it would appear that the Movement's general commitment to Marianism, and their attempt to return to a more 'authentic' version of Catholicism, existed in a state of tension (although we might also note here that in this same example, it was *Ceredonia's* argument – i.e. the Marian imperative – that finally won the day).

Uganda. (Although still very small at this time, throughout Uganda, the ICCR did nevertheless have a presence in the Southwest by this time. Moreover, its leader, Fr. John Baptist Bashobora, was a former close associate of Fr. Kataribaabo).[15]

However, beyond this, the picture is far from certain. Nevertheless, it is highly likely that, throughout the early 1990s, the Movement's leadership, at least, did have some interaction with other religious organizations as well. Following its accession to power in 1986, the government of President Yoweri Museveni's National Resistance Movement passed a series of laws aimed at increasing religious freedom in Uganda, with the result that by the early 1990s, the number of new Christian churches – both Ugandan and international – which were operating in the country had increased dramatically.[16] In this context, it is simply inconceivable that any sect such as the MRTC – especially in the years following its expulsion from the church – would not, therefore, have had at least some interaction with other such groups. Moreover, several of my respondents recall delegations being received from other independent churches – including several delegations which were made up entirely of 'bazungu' (white people) – at a number of the Movement's compounds, including Kanungu, in the period after the group left Kabumba (in late 1992). However, I have never been able to substantiate these claims, especially on the question of from which churches these delegations might have come.[17]

To my mind, it is reasonable to surmise, however, that at least some of this contact – in whatever form it might have taken – may have been with groups other than purely Catholic ones, and might even have included some of the new Pentecostal-charismatic Churches (PCCs) which were burgeoning in Uganda at that time. Such can be ascertained from the nature of several innovations the MRTC introduced to its doctrine, and to its general ritual practice, from (roughly) the mid-1990s onwards. For example, if, sometime between 1992 and 1996, the MRTC leadership became primarily concerned with an imminent end of the world, so during the following period, into the late 1990s, this millenarianism came to be

---

[15] I have never been able to construct a reliable history of the introduction of the ICCR to the dioceses of the Southwest. Nevertheless, it is clear that the organization did have some sort of presence by this time, and may well have influenced the MRTC's own practice, in a number of ways (a point to which I shall return).

[16] The NRM's relaxing of the country's former restrictions on religious organization in the country culminated in their inclusion of religious rights in their new constitution, in 1995.

[17] However, it is clear from respondents accounts that these delegations probably did come from different churches (as opposed to their representing members of one church who visited on multiple occasions). On the issue of the 'bazungu' delegation, two reports published in The New Vision after the fire claimed that the Kanungu compound had been visited by 11 Spanish nationals in August 1999. This group was reportedly made up of Fr. Kasapuraari's brother's wife, and a number of her relatives. Fr. Kasapuraari's brother had met his wife while studying for a Masters degree in Australia, and was on this occasion visiting Uganda with her, and with some members of her family (see: 'Spanish Visited Kanungu', by Betty Kagoro, and 'Kanungu Spanish Visitors Were In-Laws', by Vision Reporter, in The New Vision, 5 and 6 April 2000, respectively). However, both in its timing and in the number of people involved, this cannot possibly have been the same 'bazungu' delegation that was described to me. Thus, it would seem that the Kanungu compound may in fact have received a number of foreign delegations. This would no doubt have further bolstered its claims to have had a 'global' reach.

tinged with a distinctly Pentecostal hue. In this way, from about 1995 onwards, Ceredonia's daily visitations from the Virgin began to be inflected by the Protestant doctrine of dispensational pre-millenarianism. Tracing, ultimately to the writings of John Nelson Darby, the nineteenth-century, Anglo-Irish evangelist, dispensational pre-millenarianism is similar to various other versions of Christian eschatology which posit that the Final Judgement is imminent (as evidenced by a series of biblical 'clues').[18] However, it also differs from other forms, in further postulating that all of the 'true believers' will be protected from the impending Armageddon, by being taken up on an arc to heaven for the duration of the 'final battle'. Thus, all the believers will be delivered to the Millennium unharmed.

From the time of the genesis of the Pentecostal-charismatic (PC) Movement – at the Asuza Street Revival, in Los Angeles, in 1906 – this doctrine of dispensational pre-millenarianism has been frequently adopted by a large number of PC churches, including a number of the new PC churches which have burgeoned in Africa over the last two and a half decades or so (Douglas, cited in Robbins, 2004: 121, note 1). Now, interestingly, before the mid-1990s, the MRTC made no allusion to the doctrine of dispensational pre-millenarianism at all. Thus, for example, the sect's own publication – up to and including the apocalyptic group vision of Chapter 4 – made no reference whatsoever to the concept of 'an arc' for the saved. However, from about 1995 onwards, the idea became an increasing concern both of Ceredonia's visions and, as a result, of the sect's wider preaching as well. A number of my respondents recall the delegations which visited their home areas speaking openly of an arc which, on the day of the final battle, would be sent by Mary to save all her true followers (for example, Mr Sebataka, Linda). Moreover, and perhaps more importantly, in the week leading up to the Kanungu fire, a number of members were heard speaking openly about the imminent arrival of 'the arc' (Kahuru Richard).

Further clues here relate to the Movement's later adoption of another distinctly Protestant doctrine: that of sanctification. Sometimes referred to as 'Christian perfectionism', sanctification is a concept that became particularly emphasized within US Methodism in the nineteenth century. In essence transformational, sanctification posits that all those who receive a 'second birth in the Spirit' may also experience a 'second blessing', or a 'second grace', during which 'the inbred sin people carry, owing to Adam's fall, is removed' (Robbins, 2004: 120). The notion is historically anathema to the Roman Church, because it reifies the basic Protestant notion of salvation as individual experience. For Catholics, of course, salvation can only be achieved through the mediation of the Church. However, the idea is central to the theology of practically all PCCs (indeed, it might well be described as the key element of the Pentecostal creed). Thus, it is again

---

[18] Writing in the mid-nineteenth century, Darby put forward the idea that, within the text of the Bible, a series of chronologically successive dispensations could be identified, each based on a specific covenant (each of which, in turn, implied a particular form of communion between the believer and God). The notion was later made popular by the US evangelist Cyrus Scofield (1843–1921) who further elaborated that the Bible referenced seven distinct dispensations, the last of which represented an impending Christian millennium, during which Christ would return to earth to rule for a thousand years.

interesting that whilst the MRTC appears to have made no reference to the concept during the early years of its existence, from about the mid-1990s onwards, members' achievement of sanctification became of increasing concern for the Movement's leadership.

Thus, as the sect's membership grew dramatically, from late 1993 onwards, the mode of entry into the group became ever more complex. Specifically, in order to achieve full membership of the Movement, new recruits were now required to take not one initiation 'course' – as before – but three. In this way, the three key functions of the initiation process – teaching in the Movement's mode of Marian devotion, confession of sins (in the context of formal confessional meetings), and full entry into the group – were now spread over three separate week-long courses, which initiands were often required to take at different Movement centres (by about the mid-1990s, the sect's network of 'study centres' had increased, through the processes described, to include at least 13 separate sites – and possibly many more as well).

The very fact that the MRTC had relied, from the very beginning, on the 'course' structure as a primary means of entry into the sect, might once again be read in terms of the sect's attempts to revitalize Nyabingi. After all, in an earlier period, it had been the White Fathers' catechism courses which had previously most closely resembled former Nyabingi practice, and had drawn most heavily on Nyabingi language (as a result of which they had become central to the initial transformation of Nyabingi into a Catholic idiom). Certainly, the MRTC's own courses, in many of their aspects – in their emphasis on residence, fasting, quiet prayer and inward reflection – closely resembled these earlier catechist training courses. In addition, the sect's reliance upon the course structure might also be interpreted as part of the group's more general attempt to realize a more 'authentic' form of Catholicism. After all, in all of their features, these MRTC courses also resembled 'traditional' Catholic retreats. Moreover, there is a long history of Catholic organizations in Africa using the retreat structure as a means for marking entry into their ranks, and for defining their own distinctive vision of – a markedly 'African' – Catholicism (cf. Simpson's work in Zambia, 2004). Yet in addition here, we might also infer the influence of the then newly established local branch of the ICCR, given that that organization, as a whole, also emphasises a course structure, as a means of communicating with the Holy Spirit (Fr. Thaddeus). More generally, the decision of the MRTC leadership around 1994 to develop a more elaborate course structure in 1993 could also have been influenced by the wider practices of non-governmental 'development' organizations (NGOs), a majority of which continue to use training courses as a primary means for training new staff, educating target populations, and so on. By 1994, the number of NGOs – both international and national organizations – was burgeoning massively in Uganda. It was around this time that the MRTC first attempted to register itself as an NGO with the Ministry of Internal Affairs.[19]

---

[19] The Uganda Human Rights Commission report on Kanungu reproduces a letter, dated 7 November 1994, concerning the sect's application to register as an NGO. Written by

The MRTC's emphasis upon the course structure may well therefore have been influenced by a range of different factors. However, the aspect of the story which is of particular interest here is the fact that the MRTC's overall course/retreat structure also came to be marked, unusually for any sort of Catholic organization, by a particular emphasis upon sanctification. For example, from about 1994 onwards, the first course, now called *okuramaara* (lit: 'to live a long time', from the root *okurama*, 'to keep a fire alight'), involved mostly study of the MRTC's book, rosary prayers, and so on. Following the successful completion of *okuramaara*, the initiand would then move to another of the Movement's compounds to take a second course, termed *okwaturebibi* (lit: 'to confess one's sins'), at which she would confess her past sins (in the manner described).[20] Following this, the initiand would return home to organize her payment of entry into the Movement, following which she would become eligible to take her third and final course, after which she could become a full member. Significantly, this final course was formally called *okwezibwa* (lit: 'to be sanctified'), although it seems to have been more usually referred to simply by the English term 'sanctification' (for example, the third course was constantly referred to as 'sanctification' by *all* of my respondents, including by all of those who otherwise spoke little or no English).[21]

Moreover, as part of this final course, all initiands were expected to demonstrate their 'second birth', by being publicly 'struck down' by the

---

[19] (cont.) Yorokamu Kamacerere, then Resident District Commissioner (RDC) of Rukungiri District, to the Secretary to the Board of Trustees for NGOs at the Ministry of Internal Affairs in Kampala, it states the RDC's opinion that the application be refused, on the grounds that 'the services of this religious cult are not required in this district'. 'However', he goes on, 'the NGO could be duly licenced to operate anywhere else in the country [*sic*] where their services may be required' (UHRC, 2002: 74). In the end, it was not until 1997 that the registration was finally accepted (at which time it was supported by the Reverend Richard Mutazindwa, then Assistant RDC for Rukungiri). The following year, the MRTC also lodged articles of association, and was duly issued with a certificate of incorporation (thereby also making it an 'Unlimited Company Without a Share Capital', see *ibid.*: 55 and 75–84).

[20] At least one of my respondents (Winifred Aheebwa) also referred to this second course as *okwozya* (lit: to wash, or to cleanse [as in: 'to wash away one's sins']).

[21] A number of my respondents stressed that the MRTC used the English word 'sanctification' here, rather than the Runyankore/Rukiga *okujunwa* (lit: 'to be saved'). This is further evidence that the sect was significantly influenced by 'new' PC forms. Specifically, it is significant here that the term *okujunwa* has been used to describe the Christian 'rebirth in the Spirit' at least since the arrival of the Protestant Buchmanite Movement – the so-called Oxford Group – in the region (in 1928, Stenning, n.d.). From that time onwards, followers of the Buchmanite Movement – who are known locally as the Balokole, and whose numbers are still significant in Protestant parshes throughout Uganda – have stressed a concept of 'being saved' (*okujunwa*) as a means of being 'reborn' in the faith (and into their Movement). However, unlike many of the 'new' PC churches, Balokole versions of rebirth have rarely stressed such concepts as perfectionism, or the removal of 'original sin', but have focused instead on the ideas of 'surrender' (to God's will), and – betraying the Buchmanite Movement's Lutheran roots – of 'labour' (in His cause). In these ways, then, the 'saved' person of the Balokole's projection is one who accepts being controlled by God's power, and who becomes devoted to the assistance of others, especially other members of the Movement. Against this, many of the new PC churches which emerged in Uganda in the early 1990s sought ways in which to mark their own version of rebirth as different from that of the Balokole Movement. One of the primary ways in which many did this in the Southwest (at least) was through a general adoption of the Methodist word 'sanctification' as an alternative to the older *okujunwa*.

Holy Spirit. This was stressed to me by one of my respondents, Patience N., who witnessed the conclusion of a number of these courses at the Rushojwa compound. According to Patience N., each sanctification course ended with a particular night ritual, during which a number of paraffin lanterns were lit, and placed in a semi-circle around the compound. All those present would then gather in the compound, and kneeling down – again, in a semi-circle – would begin their usual session of night rosary prayers. However, unlike the sect's typical evening prayer sessions, on these occasions the 'leader' who had been running that particular course – usually Ceredonia, although sometimes also Fr. Kataribaabo, or someone else besides – would move amongst the group, and would touch each initiand on the forehead, in turn. Following this contact, the individual involved would begin to scream and 'bark like a dog' (as evidence that they had indeed been 'struck down' by the Spirit). Later, the same leader would move among the group for a second time, and again touching each initiand on the head, would gradually bring the whole collective back to its senses. Interestingly, these displays of religiosity, although they seem to have usually taken place during sessions of rosary prayers, were apparently always ascribed to the actions of not Mary, but the Holy Spirit (Patience N., also Mr Sebataka, Vincent Bwenungi, and others). This is interesting because it is practically the only time that the figure of the Holy Spirit appears in any of my respondents' narratives about the MRTC, a sect which was in all other respects predominantly Marian in nature. (Another point here is that such displays seem to have taken place only during the sanctification courses. None of my respondents recall having seen any member being 'struck down' on any other occasion.)

Thus, over time, sanctification seems to have become not only a key part of the initiation process, but indeed a necessary requirement for full entry into the Movement. One result of this was that at least some of the long-standing membership of the Movement – i.e. those who had joined the sect when only one course was required – began also to attend the new *okwezibwa* courses (presumably with a view to demonstrating that they, too, had now also become sanctified). Later, the central significance of sanctification became marked in other ways, too. For example, sometime during this period, Ceredonia received a further message from the Virgin commanding all those who had become sanctified to wear only black robes, and to sit as a group, away from the other members, during the sect's daily prayer sessions (Mr Sebataka). This served to distinguish the sanctified from all categories of initiands – in a further elaboration, those who had attended only the first initiation course were made to wear red robes, those who had attended the second, green ones (John Kihama) – although this probably did not, in practice, introduce any social distinctions within the permanent membership itself (given that by this time, practically all the members would have become sanctified, anyway).

Later, an additional pronouncement from the Virgin ordered all those who had received the second birth (i.e. practically all the sect's membership) also to shave off all of their bodily hair, and never let it regrow (Vincent Bwenungi, Kahuru Richard). By some accounts, the hair removed in this way – which included the hair on people's heads, the hair in their armpits, even their pubic hair – was then prayed over and ritually burnt (Mr Sebataka, Winifred Aheebwa).[22] However, the pronouncement to remove hair is of particular significance, and demonstrates just how important the concept of sanctification had by then become within the MRTC leadership. Throughout South-western Uganda, such hair-cutting rituals have for long been deeply symbolic of the severance of pre-existing social ties, and the regeneration of new ones. Under normal circumstances, this hair-cutting would usually take place only following the death of a household head (*nyin'eka*). Specifically, the burial of a household head is far more elaborate than any other funeral, and includes all surviving members of the household cutting off all of their hair for the duration of the rites. Yet such rites used to occur during other periods of heightened social significance as well, for example during the ritual purification of murderers (Edel, 1957: 139.)

Thus, just as almost all African PCCs promote some concept of spiritual transformation through a radical rupture with, or separation from, both one's past life and one's surrounding social world, as a necessary precursor to the achievement of sanctification (Gill, 1990; Martin, 1990; Meyer, 1998), so too it would seem that the MRTC developed an ever more elaborate set of 'rituals of rupture' as part of its own version of sanctification. Finally, in another apparent borrowing from PC doctrine, another of Ceredonia's visitations from the Virgin claimed that all those who had achieved sanctification would also be bestowed with the 'enduement of power'. In this way, all those who had experienced the second birth – i.e. practically all of the sect's membership – would be granted divine powers to spread the Word, and to proselytize amongst non-believers. These powers would, of course, assist all those Movement members who were already, by this time, taking part in delegations to villages all over South-western Uganda and beyond, in the search for new members.

Thus, the overall picture which emerges here is of a sect with a complex vision of Christianity, one which was shaped by a number of different strands. In addition to the various historical trends I have identified, one of the most significant influences was a series of pamphlets that some sect leaders were receiving from a range of Marian organizations worldwide. This is perhaps not surprising, given the social and historical context from which the Movement emerged, and in the light of the powerful 'global' imaginaries which this literature helped to inculcate. Yet it is certainly the most important development in terms of the overall MRTC story, in that it significantly shaped the sect's subsequent adoption of a millenarian outlook, which was in turn to play an increasingly consequential role in the run-up to the year 2000, and to the Kanungu fire itself (the events to which I shall turn in the next chapter).

[22] Ceredonia's visions had first spoken of hair-cutting after her earliest visits to the Nyabugoto caves (Chapter 4). However, it was only with this elaboration of the course structure that members began to carry out the practice in a systematic way. Later on, it also became the norm for the initiands' old clothes to be burned as part of this ritual as well, following which they would wear only the robes provided by the sect (Winifred Aheebwa).

Nevertheless, this Marian literature is still only part of the story here. In addition, a number of the sect's other innovations owed more to its Catholic heritage, and reflected their ambition to return to a more authentic version of the 'mother' religion. It is somewhat ironic here – given its wider revival of the symbols and practices of Nyabingi – that its efforts to realize a more 'pure' form of Catholicism should have involved its rejecting all of the innovations that had been introduced by the Second Vatican Council (many of which had been designed, of course, to institutionalize the very concept of inculturation). On the other hand, perhaps these two strands should be seen as less a contradiction than a source of tension, within the sect. After all, the argument which had led to Fr. Ikazire's departure from the group had involved a dispute between precisely these two themes: over whether the sect should emphasize Marian devotion as primary or 'authentic' liturgy (see Chapter 4). Yet if these two elements *did* constitute a tension, then there is no doubt which strand eventually won out, given that so much of the group's subsequent activity came to be focused upon Ceredonia's visions alone. Even with these visions, still further sources of influence can be discerned, however, given that so many of these visions – and the practices which stemmed from them – later came to be tinged with a distinctly PC hue (not least, in their emphases upon dispensational pre-millenarianism and individual sanctification).

Thus, once again here – this time in relation to the sect's version of Christianity – it would seem that a series of temporally and geographically diffuse networks had acted to produce something which was essentially complex, and deeply hybrid, in nature. Yet in this regard, at least, there may be little which is particularly remarkable in the MRTC story. After all, much of the recent anthropological and historical literature on African Christianities has argued that such hybridity may indeed be the very defining characteristic of all the new African-Initiated Churches which have emerged on the continent over the last twenty years (and therefore, of all the new forms of Christianity themselves). However, if this is indeed the case – that all AICs are, in effect, assemblages or hybridities – then it nevertheless remains crucial for us to keep in view the specific elements which were involved here, or, in other words, to understand the exact form this assemblage took, in this particular case. Certainly, it is only by so doing, by paying close attention to the specificities of this particular AIC, that we can possibly hope to understand what finally became of the MRTC.

7
Revelation
The Last Days of the MRTC

'It is an old maxim of mine that when you have excluded the impossible, whatever remains, however improbable, must be the truth'[1]

Amaisho gareeba, omutima gubeiha. The eyes see, but the soul lies. Stick to the facts[2]

So what did finally become of the MRTC? What took place in the final months of the sect's existence? How did those who were buried in the pit graves die? And why did so many of their members burn to death on Friday 17 March 2000?

I think this is where we came in:

The primary interpreters of events, in the days immediately following the fire, were the Uganda police. Thus, already by Saturday 18 March, the police had ascertained that the MRTC had for long been millenarian in outlook, had recently been preparing for some sort of 'big event', had a few days earlier purchased two drums of sulphuric acid, and so on. In addition, their initial analysis report of the fire site had observed that some of the building's windows had been nailed shut at the time of the fire. The report also stated that the bodies inside the building were piled in one spot (a later report by Dr. Kalyemanya described them as having formed a 'heap'), suggesting that they had all died quite quickly. Finally, the description added that the 'surging in of the roof and walls of the building indicat[ed] a big blast ... probably [caused by] an inflammable accelerant' (an interpretation which the report apparently goes on to confirm, in its results of chemical residue tests at the site, all of which indicated the presence of petrol amongst the human remains). Taken together, then, all of these facts seemed to provide a relatively straightforward narrative, of a sect which, having decided that the end was nigh, had locked themselves in their main church building and (presumably in a state of high ritual excitement) had ignited an explosion in which all present had perished. In short, a 'simple' case of mass suicide. In addition, on Tuesday 21 March, James Mujuni reported a letter, written in Runyankore/ Rukiga, which had earlier been received by The New Vision's *sister paper,* Orumuri, *from Joseph Kibweteere. The letter, written sometime in January 2000, spoke openly about the end of the world.*

However, within a few days of the fire, the police had changed tack, and were instead treating the demise of the MRTC as a case of mass murder. This interpretation was then seemingly confirmed by the Buhunga excavations (on Friday 24 March), from which it was concluded that, of the 153 bodies exhumed at that site, 21 showed signs of strangulation, 3 had fractured skulls, and 1 had been stabbed. A

[1] Conan Doyle, 1892, *The Adventure of the Beryl Coronet.*
[2] Cisternino, 1987: 209.

*few days later, the Chief Pathologist, Dr. Birungi, further concluded that of the 74
bodies found in the two pit graves in the garden of the Rugazi compound, 20 had died
of strangulation (as evidenced primarily by their having a broken hyoid bone in their
neck, with some also showing signs of cyanosis of the tongue – which might be
caused by a lack of oxygen to the tongue prior to death), 1 of stabbing, and 1 of a
fractured skull. In addition, he concluded that 3 of the bodies found in the grave in the
former wine cellar at Rugazi had died of strangulation. He also reported the presence
of numerous small green and white bottles, like medicine vials, strewn around the
house, which could have contained poison, possibly as an instrument of murder.
These vials he immediately sent away for toxological analysis (although at the time I
read the police file on Kanungu, in May 2004, no record of any toxological findings
was contained therein). However, all of this seemed to provide ample evidence of mass
murder, as did Birungi's later findings at Rushojwa as well (where he concluded that,
of the 81 bodies recovered, 3 showed signs of strangulation).*

*Thus, over the following days and weeks, media representations of the episode
became much darker, and journalists now sought to develop an explanation as to why
this sect should have suddenly committed mass murder on quite the scale that it
appeared to have done. Only one plausible explanation ever really emerged here, based
on the fact – quickly established by the foreign journalists who visited Kanungu – that
most of the MRTC's members had been required to sell all of their property, and to
hand over the proceeds to the sect's leadership, upon entry into the group. The theory
ran that, if such payments had been made in expectation of a coming end of the
world, and if this was expected to arrive at the turn of the year 2000, but then had
not, some members might have become disgruntled, and have started to demand their
money back. In reaction to this, the leadership had presumably decided to quash the
dissent by killing the worst complainants (such killings as could be hidden by them
among the frequent transfers that were made between the sect's various compounds).
Hence, then, the bodies in the pits. However, as dissent continued to grow – so the
story went – an even grander scheme was hatched, to kill off all of the sect's
members, in a staged suicide, in a move that would allow the leaders to make off with
whatever remained of the members' property.*[3]

On the academic detective

What, then, can the anthropologist possibly contribute to an overall
interpretation of events here? I begin with the observation that, in recent
decades, a growing number of scholars, across a range of different
disciplines, have sought to draw an analogy between their own disciplinary
research practices and those of the police detective (albeit usually those of
the purely fictional detective). For example, Richard Cobb has argued that
the historian's methods are similar to those of the detective, reliant as they
often are on the observation of 'habit, routine, assumptions, banality, every-
dayness...[with a view to disclosing] the nature of the everyday in local
settings' (cited in Austrin & Farnsworth, 2005: 152). Philip Howell,
following Schmid, has similarly suggested that urban geographical inquiry

---

[3] For a fuller description of these various developments, see the Prologue.

is like detective work, in that both require connections to be made, and followed, across economically, politically and spatially disparate parts of the city (1998: 357–8). David Glover draws an equivalent connection between the sociologist and the detective, arguing that both are most likely to succeed in their investigations when those enquiries are informed by an 'inner knowledge of the people and processes' involved (1979: 21). However, in perhaps no other discipline has this analogy between the practitioner and the detective been pursued so consistently as it has been in (certain branches of) anthropology (for a good overview of this literature, see Gross, 2005; see also MacFarlane, n.d.).

However, usefully for my purposes here, these discussions on the anthropological detective have seldom focused on what is elsewhere generally taken to be the primary advantage of participant-observation: its placement of the researcher as a direct observer of the events he or she is studying (which is itself central, of course, to a subsequent narrative of the anthropologist as having 'been there'). I say 'usefully' here because, as is by now obvious from my account, when it comes to events in Kanungu, I most certainly was 'not there' (neither at the events themselves nor, indeed, during the subsequent investigations). Instead, my own account of the whole affair is based on 26 months of research begun long after the fire had occurred, and which instead involved my interviewing surviving protagonists of the MRTC drama, the friends and relatives of those who died, local clergymen, and various others who could be identified through a method of 'snowball sampling' (it also involved some archival study). In other words, from the very beginning, my own research was always framed as a process *not* of observation, but of reconstruction (although I hope that it was a relatively thorough one at that). Yet I would argue that this lack of direct observation was not, in and of itself, a hindrance to the final analysis which emerged here (not least because, as I shall discuss below, one of the primary findings of my reconstruction of the fire itself is that practically every eyewitness statement of the event turns out to have been, in some aspect, wrong).

However, as I have said, this element of direct observation is anyway not central to the analogy anthropologists have drawn between their own research practices and those of the detective (not least given that the detective is also generally absent, of course, when the crime itself takes place). Those trying to explore this parallel have focused instead on other features of the anthropological method and, in particular, on the peculiar position in which it places the researcher, as one who – like the (successful) detective – is located both within and outside the situation he or she is studying. In other words, as one who has established what Gross calls a 'network of useful relationships' (2005: 162) – and who has developed enough contextual knowledge to make at least some sense of what these respondents, or 'contacts', might be telling him or her – yet who remains distant enough to also gain some critical reflection on the character of those relationships, and on the nature of the information derived from them.

As James Weiner (1996) points out in his discussion of the anthropologist and the fictional detective Sherlock Holmes, such skills are

7.1 An aerial view of the Kanungu compound, taken from the police video of the scene. The burned-out building can be seen on the upper left-hand side. (Note that the whole compound stands on a ridge line, with steep drops on both sides.)

7.2 A sketch map of the Kanungu compound

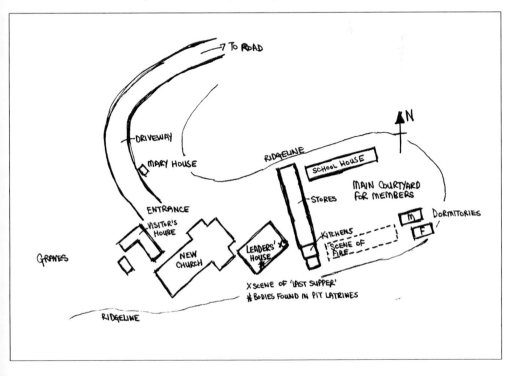

7.3 A view of the compound from the nearest road. Standing on a ridge line, and only accessible via the 1/2-mile-long, and very steep, driveway visible on the right, the site is almost entirely secluded from surrounding properties. **7.4** The main entrance to the compound. The structure on the right is the visitors' house, beyond which non-members were not permitted to pass. Straight ahead is the new church, and behind that the leader's house.

7.5 The main compound (now overgrown). This photograph looks out from the dormitory buildings towards the schoolhouse (on the right) and the main storeroom and kitchen complex (straight ahead). The building in which the fire took place stood behind the tree on the left.

central both to ethnographic research and to (good) detective work (Nick Thomas has made a similar point in his examination of anthropological epistemologies, 1997). Moreover, for both the participant-observer, and the detective, this ability to reflect, and to make sense of the information he or she gathers, generally increases over time. Thus, just as the ethnographer may not fully appreciate the significance of particular utterances, practices or events, until some time after he or she has first recorded them, so too the detective will probably be unaware of the relevance of specific clues until well into his or her investigations (cf. Strathern, 1994 and Jameson, cited in Gross, 2005: 4). In both instances, it is the extended period of time taken over the enquiries which is important here, because it is this – beyond all else – that enables the crucial process of informed analysis to develop. I would note here that, from this perspective, my own research on Kanungu was perhaps not so different, after all, from that which is conducted by any ethnographer. Although I did not witness the events I was researching, my enquiries into them were nevertheless still illuminated by just this sort of informed reflection, itself based on understandings developed over a (lengthy) period of fieldwork.

In addition to these ideas, it seems to me that the detective analogy could be pushed even further still. For example, it is also noteworthy, to my mind, that for both the ethnographer and the detective, amidst the masses of (different sorts of) data each collects during his or her investigations, the testimony, or insights, of one or two key people often emerge as crucial. Thus, anthropologists have recognized the significance of (what used to be called) the 'key informant' from at least the publication of Casagrande's *In The Company of Man* (1960) onwards; (and in recent years, this figure has come to define the burgeoning genre of ethnographic life-history). Meanwhile, few detectives would deny that criminal investigations frequently hinge on the testimony of one or two key witnesses. Moreover, this fact once again emerges as important in the present case, given that, over the course of the hundreds of hours of interviews I conducted on Kanungu, one particular respondent's recollections did indeed emerge as crucial.

From these perspectives, then, *all* ethnographers who engage in long-term fieldwork may be understood to, in some senses, 'play the detective'. Yet even so, I should note that, at the outset of my own research on the MRTC, it was not my intention to explore this group's ultimate demise. After all, what could I possibly contribute to this investigation, given that I was 'not there'? Instead, then, I always framed my own research around such questions as how and why had the MRTC emerged in the first place? Why had so many, mostly women, left the mainstream Catholic church to join the sect? And how had it come to have such a profound impact on their lives, during the middle years of the 1990s, in particular? However, curiosity is a strange master, and over the course of the research, my intrigue in the question of how the group had died simply grew and grew. Moreover, it later occurred to me that, were I to not broach this question, I would also be presented with a number of practical problems. Not least, it is difficult to imagine how this book could possibly have been ended, without some sort of explanation as to what had happened in the fire itself?

Yet if aspects of my research did therefore highlight the analogy between the ethnographer and the detective, they also demonstrated the limitations of that connection. In particular, my research showed that, whilst an ethnographer could gain some insight into the circumstances leading up to the final event, it turns out that I was simply not qualified to interpret certain key pieces of evidence from that incident, including the bodies in the pits, the fire itself, and so on. Of course I could not, having had no training in pathology, fire investigation, or whatever. Thus, it later occurred to me that the detective part of this story would also require a move beyond my own disciplinary boundaries *per se*, to mobilize alternative frames of understanding (a move which is also encouraged, incidentally, by Austrin & Farnsworth, in their discussion of the sociological detective, 2005). However, in order to do *this*, it was also necessary for me to mobilize an alternative set of evidence and artefacts (given that my own disciplinary data set – i.e. my fieldnotes – proved to be of only limited interpretative value within any of these other frameworks). Thus, in the final analysis, I would have to argue that what makes my own account of Kanungu so compelling – over and above those of eye-witnesses, journalists, even the Ugandan Police themselves – is probably less any one or other field method I myself employed, so much as the opportunities I have had over the course of such a long research project (eight years or so) to mobilize an ever wider assemblage of disciplinary experts, and of (different sorts of) material evidence, in pursuit of the story of what did, then, happen at Kanungu.

On the origins of violence

So what did happen here? As I have argued at length in this book, the MRTC's major period of growth occurred around 1994, largely in response to the then emerging AIDS epidemic. Some of those joining the group were themselves AIDS victims (or else those who suspected themselves to be carriers of the disease). More significantly, a greater proportion of the membership was made up of certain categories of women who had been made particularly vulnerable by the epidemic: especially young brides (*bagole*), and senior co-wives in polygamous households. For both of these categories of women, the primary problems they faced related to the mis-appropriation of their property. It was in this context, then, that many seem to have reasoned that the 'better option' was for them to sell everything they had left, and to hand over the proceeds to the MRTC, a move which – according to the redistributive logic of Nyabingi – would then take care of their future material needs (as indeed, the Movement was able to provide – during the early years at least – out of the payments it was receiving).

Interestingly, the logic of these processes already poses a number of challenges to the 'mass murder' hypothesis. The main claim of that narra-tive was that the members had handed over their property in expectation of the coming end of the world, but when this had not arrived, they had demanded these possessions back (following which a decision was taken to kill them all). Yet, in the light of what I have just said, much of this cannot possibly be correct. First of all, women were *not* handing over their property in expectation of the end of the world, but instead, in response to the serious misfortunes they were experiencing in the here and now. Moreover, at least some of these women would have joined the Movement sometime *before* it had developed a millenarian outlook (given that this shift was a later development). It is therefore unlikely that millenarianism could have been part of these women's initial decision to join. One further challenge to the murder thesis is that it is difficult to imagine how any of these women could possibly have ever wanted to demand their properties *back*. In other words, given that most of these women had only turned to the MRTC in the first place out of desperation, with the sect representing some sort of 'option of last resort', it is difficult to imagine that any would have then later concluded that they probably were better-off on their own, after all.

However, a process of informed reflection, based on understandings developed over a lengthy enquiry into the history and sociology of the MRTC, anyway offers a potentially entirely different perspective as to the origins of violence amongst this sect. Indeed, it might even be argued that, as in any good detective story, the key clues have in fact been 'under our noses' all the time. After all, whether or not it has always been made explicit, violence has been a significant component of much of what I have so far described. Thus, for example, the kinds of misfortunes that first led people into the MRTC – especially during its period of rapid expansion, around 1994 – were often violent in nature. On the one hand, the kind of sicknesses for which people turned to the sect for assistance often had a violent impact upon the body. This was especially true of AIDS which, in the period before Anti-Retroviral Drugs (ARVs) or any other forms of treatment, were widely available in Uganda, invariably caused its victims to develop extreme skin problems, to suffer chronic diarrhoea, and to experience rapid weight loss (to name just a few of the more common symptoms).

On the other hand, the kinds of wider social problems that the AIDS epidemic created – those which had a particularly detrimental impact upon both young AIDS widows and senior co-wives – often engendered an additional degree of violence of their own. Not only was the theft of these women's property itself a form of symbolic violence against their means of reproduction (and by extension, against their personhood in general). In addition, as I look back now over all of my respondents' accounts of Kanungu, I realize that, in practically every case I recorded of a young AIDS widow being 'expelled' from her marital home, this expulsion also involved at least some degree of actual physical force. To cite just the case of Mbabazi Eunice, it is noteworthy that the episode during which 'her father-in-law...tried to run Mbabazi off his family's land' (Chapter 5, Case 6), involved the old man making repeated visits to Mbabazi's *enju*, usually in the dead of night, and frequently in a drunken state, in order to punch her, kick her, and beat her with a stick. According to my respondent (Hilary Birungi), these attacks went on for several months in early 1994, and left Mbabazi with a fractured arm, a broken tooth, severe scarring across her back, and various other injuries besides.

So too, in most instances I recorded of senior co-wives' having had their properties 'stolen' by their husbands (in their pursuit of additional wives), some degree of violence was involved. Thus, for example, on the occasion of Constance Tumuheki's husband's theft of her daughters' two cows (Chapter 5, Case 7), Constance later confronted the man over his actions and was 'severely beaten' for her efforts (Juliet). Similarly, when Jolly Habusa's husband reassigned her fields to his new wife (Chapter 5, Case 3), a number of loud arguments, and physical fights, resulted (Linda). More-over, when Jolly's husband later got wind that, as a result of his actions, Jolly had begun planning to leave with their children for an MRTC compound, he assigned two adult men in his family to watch her 'night and day', and to (physically) prevent her from going. It appears that the two men took this duty seriously; according to Linda, they beat her on at least two occasions before she finally managed to get away.

However, the example I most vividly recall here concerns the senior co-wife of a man called Julian Kansanga, a woman from Kabale District who had joined the sect in 1995. In this instance, my own interviews on Mrs Kansanga's case, and the circumstances surrounding her entry into the MRTC, had been conducted with Julian himself. Thus, over the course of several visits, Julian had explained to me his decision, sometime in 1993, to take on a second wife, he had described the arguments that had resulted from this, and had told me about the MRTC delegation which arrived at their home shortly afterwards. However, the part of Julian's testimony that made the most lasting impression on me was divulged shortly after I had completed my final interview with him. I had packed up my equipment and was strolling up through the banana plantation with Julian, when he suddenly turned to me and said: 'You know, she did come back once, after she had joined that group. But she had become *so* stubborn. When I raised my hand [as if to hit her] she said that if I tried to hit her, then my hand would become crippled...So I gave her a *thorough* whipping, and then I asked her 'do you think it [i.e. the hand] is crippled then?'...She had become *so* stubborn.'[4]

Thus, the context from which the MRTC emerged was a markedly violent one. Or, to put it in other words, violence was deeply embedded in the very rationale of the networks through which this sect recruited its membership. Moreover, all of this might go some way towards explaining why the sect itself should have later demonstrated a propensity for violence of its own. Thus, from the earliest accounts onwards, testimonies of life inside the MRTC are punctuated by moments of violent outburst. For example, one of the key features of Ceredonia's daily visitations – which were themselves the central element in the group's entire ritual practice – was their inherently violent nature. Thus, as Mrs Kibweteere recalls, whenever Ceredonia entered one of her trance-like states – as happened every afternoon whilst the group was still at Kabumba, at least – this was invariably accompanied by her going into some sort of fit, during which she would either drop to the floor, or else scream and flail around (often crashing into people, or smashing furniture, as she did so). Other respondents described the manner in which Ceredonia entered the night prayer sessions – to deliver details of a vision she had just received in her room – in similar terms. On these occasions, Ceredonia's physical arrival was frequently preceded by her screaming, or making some other noise, in another part of the compound. Following this, she would suddenly appear in the place of public gathering, again in a highly agitated, and markedly violent, state, and would remain in this condition for at least the first few minutes or so (until such time as she had 'returned' from her visitation).

In other ways, too, daily life within the MRTC, from the beginning, involved incidents of violence. For example, a number of respondents recall the violent punishment that would sometimes be meted out to those members who transgressed the sect's strict behavioural codes. As Mrs. Kibweteere describes, Ceredonia would occasionally receive a vision in which the Virgin named a specific member of the group as having been particularly lazy, as having told lies, or as having committed some other type of sin. Following a message of this type, the person so named would

---

[4] My interviews with Julian were conducted in Runyankore/Rukiga. However, he did speak some English, and so a number of conversations with him, including this one, were conducted in English. Although these comments of Julian were not captured on tape, I wrote them down as soon as possible after he had spoken them (perhaps 10 minutes or so later), in order to capture what he had said as accurately as possible. The quote which is reproduced here is taken directly from these fieldnotes.

be beaten by other members. However, more typically (although it should be stressed that such incidents were not in themselves common), the collective group would reach their own decision to simply 'turn in' on someone who was deemed to have broken the rules.

Thus, on one occasion, a young woman who had 'refused to take orders' was given 'a terrible beating'. Indeed, so bad were this woman's injuries, that she later required treatment for them in a Kampala hospital (Mrs. Kibweteere). Fr. Ikazire describes a similar incident in which members 'beat one [woman] who broke the rule of talking. They beat her severely and blood came out of her' (interview with MBC). The *Monitor* newspaper also described one incident in which a member who inadvertently became pregnant was beaten until she aborted (cited in Behrend, 2000: 88). One of Ceredonia's own nieces – her brother's daughter, who was forced into the sect following the death of her father (Ceredonia's brother), sometime in the early 1990s – describes another incident in which she was involved. According to this young woman, shortly after Ikazire's departure from the Movement, in 1994, she too was accused of having 'broken the rules'. Following this, she was locked up in a small store cupboard (in her compound of residence, at Rugazi). There she remained for a period of what she estimates to have been a month, during which time she was starved and on one occasion attacked by a column of safari ants (*empazi*).

Yet, if the MRTC did emerge from a setting of violence against new wives (*bagole*), and senior co-wives, it is also true to say that its main intention, and purpose, within that context was to assuage the suffering of these women. After all, the main message that sect delegations took to the villages was that the Movement could assist women in *ending* their troubles. In addition, the reason why some women later took up residence with the sect – selling almost everything they owned in order to do so – was precisely in order to escape the violent treatment they were experiencing in their marital homes. Thus, from this perspective, the MRTC also represented a mechanism for dissipating violence, for 'controlling anger'. Indeed, in one very important sense, this was its *raison d'être*. Moreover, a comparative perspective offers few clues as to why it should not ultimately have been successful in this endeavour. After all, the historical literature on African Christianities is replete with examples of AICs which emerged from violent settings, yet which later managed to regulate, and dissipate, the emotions and responses that these contexts inevitably engendered (see Fernandez, 1978; Ranger & Weller, 1975; Spear, 1999). So too the wider ethnographic record on Africa is full of examples of networks, and 'cults', of affliction which similarly draw on violence, and in some cases also engender violence of their own, yet which continue to operate for extended periods of time without ever breaking down in the way that the MRTC did (see Janzen, 2005). How, then, can we possibly account for the dramatic breakdown which occurred in this particular case?

I would argue that a process of informed reflection on the history and sociology of the MRTC also reveals a series of clues as to how we might go about addressing this question. In particular here, my earlier analysis of the group's development of a more millenarian outlook, sometime around the mid-1990s, emerges as crucial. On the one hand, that development is itself a key part of the story, given the inherently violent nature of that world-view. Yet, on the other hand, and perhaps more importantly, my examina-tion of that development also revealed the central role played by various non-human agents in bringing about the group's shift in perspective. In other words, my analysis highlighted the fact that the MRTC's development of a more eschatological worldview could not be explained with reference to only images and ideas generated by Movement participants themselves. Just as important here, if not more so, were the operations of various material objects – in particular a series of leaflets that the group had been receiving from worldwide Marian groups – which, once introduced by the leadership, acted to shape developments in a way that no one within the sect could possibly have predicted. Yet another way of putting this is to say that it was necessary for me to shift my entire frame of analysis, and to understand that particular event as an 'actor-network' – as an assemblage of both semiotic and material elements, in which both types of elements exerted a degree of agency in shaping the final outcome (see also Latour, 2005). All of which is relevant because this same move turns out also to be crucial for making sense of the events which led to the final breakdown of the MRTC, from 1998 onwards. Specifically, what emerges from an examination of these events is that they were also equally shaped *both* by the participants' own intentions *and* by various forms of non-human agency (which once again acted to alter the course of events in ways that no one among the Movement's participants could possibly have foreseen, or intended). In other words, what did finally happen to the MRTC – the sequence of events which led to the Movement's final breakdown – is also best understood as an actor-network, as itself the outcome of an assemblage of both human, and non-human, forms of agency.

The 'last revelation'

This insight first occurred to me during my first interview with one John Kihama, in November 2001. Although I could not have known it when I first arrived at his home, Kihama was subsequently to become one of my key respondents on the events leading up to the Kanungu fire. Kihama turned out to have been a member of the MRTC from about 1992 until a few weeks before the fire itself, during which he had climbed the ranks to become 'Chief Messenger' for the whole sect. As such, it was his job to coordinate all movement between the group's various compounds – as was decided by more senior leaders within the organization – to inform people when, and to where, they were to be moved, and to pass on messages to those who had recently changed sites. Thus, not only did he spend the whole time moving around the various compounds, which were spread all over the South of Uganda, and beyond, but it was his job to know where each individual member was, at any given point in time. In his discussion of this role, Kihama's testimony provides a further challenge to the 'mass murder' thesis when he states that he knows of *no* case of an individual member disappearing whilst in transit. Indeed, he was very explicit on this point (remember that the murder thesis posited that the 'killing' of members had been concealed by the transfer system between compounds). Yet what Kihama *does* recall is an episode which in any case puts an entirely different spin on the whole Kanungu story.

I was about three hours into my first interview with Kihama when he suddenly turned to me and asked, 'But you do know about the bodies in the pits, don't you?' to which I, of course, replied in the negative. He then went on to describe a major malaria epidemic (*omushwija*) that had struck the Kanungu camp in early 1998, and which – in the cramped dormitory conditions in which most of the members were living – had killed several hundred people. As he put it, 'no sooner had we dug one big pit, than it would be full, and we would have to start digging the next one'. Indeed, according to Kihama, so many people had died in this outbreak, that the group had soon run out of space to bury more people in Kanungu itself. Thus, from that time onwards, additional bodies were driven, in the back of the Movement's pick-up – always at night – to the sect's compound at Rushojwa. Indeed, the main driver for these deliveries was one of Kihama's good friends in the group.

So what weight should we give to this apparently crucial testimony? First of all, it is certainly interesting to note that the timing of Kihama's story coincides precisely with that of a major outbreak of highland malaria in South-western Uganda in February-May 1998, and which is well documented in the scientific literature on the region.[5] According to this literature, the outbreak was caused by abnormally high rainfall during the previous rainy season (late 1997), which was in turn created by the *El Nino* weather cycle of that year (Kilian *et al.*, 1999; Lindblade *et al.*, 1999, 2000a, 2000b; Lindsay & Martens, 1998; Lindsay *et al.*, 2000; Snow *et al.*, 1999).[6] Moreover, for various reasons, including the fact that malaria is not well established in these parts of highland East Africa, outbreaks such as this are marked by abnormally high rates of endemicity and mortality (on the evolution of malaria in these highlands, see Lindsay & Martens, 1998 and Mouchet *et al.*, 1998). As Lindblade *et al.* describe, 'because malaria

---

[5] As Lindblade *et al.* describe, this 'epidemic began in February 1998...and peaked in March with a malaria incidence almost 3 times greater than the mean of the previous 5 years. Incidence remained elevated through May and then returned to the historical monthly average. From January to June 1998, the proportion of clinical malaria patients positive for malaria parasites remained fairly constant (between 61.5% and 77.9%), indicating that increased incidence was not due to a change in diagnostic criteria or another febrile illness' (1999: 482).

[6] One of the key papers on this outbreak is Lindblade *et al.* 1999, which concludes thus: 'our data suggest that this epidemic was precipitated by excessive rainfall from mid-October 1997 through January 1998 which has been attributed to a strong El Nino event' (1999: 483). In addition, the authors suggest that temperature fluctuations may have also played a part here as well, given that 'it is well established that temperature modifies mosquito development rates, biting rates and the extrinsic incubation period of malaria parasites within their mosquito host', and given that throughout highland South-western Uganda 'minimum bimonthly temperatures from mid-October 1997 through mid-May 1998 ranged from 1.0 to 2.5 degrees C above normal' (again as a result of the El Nino event, *ibid.*; see also Kilian *et al.*, 1999).

transmission is unstable at these highland altitudes and the human population has little or no immunity, the highlands are prone to *explosive* outbreaks when the density of *Anopheles* increases and weather conditions favour transmission' (2000b: 664, emphasis mine). Thus, during the 1998 outbreak in South-western Uganda, 'up to 40 per cent of the population was diagnosed with clinical malaria' (*ibid.*).[7] And whilst the published data on this Ugandan epidemic do not relate how many people died as a result of it, it is quite likely that mortality rates would have been in excess of 10 per cent. This figure can be deduced from a comparison with a contemporaneous outbreak in Kenya (which was caused by the same *El Nino* event which had precipitated the Ugandan epidemic). That epidemic centred around lowland areas of Northeast Kenya – areas in which malaria immunity is much higher than it is in highland regions – yet still produced mortality rates of 8.2 per cent and above (Snow *et al.*, 1999: 79).[8]

In addition, it is important to note here that several of the MRTC's largest and most important centres – including that of Kanungu itself – were located close to the centre of the 1998 outbreak.[9] Thus, it is almost certain that all of those centres would have been badly affected by this epidemic. At the time, Kihama estimates, the number of people living in the Kanungu compound alone was about 5000. This is almost certainly an overestimate, but even if there were, say, 2000 people in the sect as a whole,[10] the kind of endemicity and mortality rates described above (of 40 per cent, and between 10 and 15 per cent, respectively) would still have killed at least 80–120 people.

Moreover, it must also be borne in mind that a range of factors would have resulted in endemicity and mortality rates being much higher in the MRTC membership than amongst the surrounding populations. Specifically, from July 1989 onwards, all the group's members had slept in communal dormitories, in which malaria would easily have spread. In addition, we may assume that, during this outbreak, few members would have received direct medical treatment. There is little evidence that the MRTC leadership were sceptical of 'modern' medicine. Indeed, their earlier provision of HIV treatments for some new members would suggest quite the opposite. Nevertheless, it is also highly unlikely that, during such an epidemic, the leadership would have permitted all those affected to visit a hospital *en*

---

[7] Elsewhere, Lindblade et al. give the exact figure as 41.1%. Moreover, they also state that 'of blood slides taken from 694 (1.9%) of these patients to confirm diagnosis, 61.5% were parasitaemic' (1999: 482).

[8] Moreover, this figure of 8.2% is likely to be a conservative estimate of total mortality rates during the Kenyan outbreak as a whole, given that it was recorded at the 'special malaria unit' of Wajir District Hospital (which is particularly well-equipped as compared with other health units in the region, Snow *et al.*, 1999: 79).

[9] Indeed, Lindblade *et al.*'s description of the epidemic is based on a study area which extended to within 10 miles of the Kanungu site. In addition, I have seen monthly 'outpatient diagnoses' data for Nyakibaale and Kisiizi Hospitals which confirm that the epidemic was also experienced – in a pattern similar to that of Lindblade *et al.*'s description – at both those locations (both of which are located within a 15-mile radius of Kanungu). The authorities at both these hospitals allowed me to view their historical outpatient data, but not to reproduce them in print.

[10] A figure which is based on the size of the membership from about 1994 onwards (see Chapter 5).

7.6 An image of the male dormitory at Kanungu. The female dormitory – which is identical to this structure – stands just behind this building. By 1998, each of these buildings was sleeping as many as 1,000 people (in shifts)

masse, given the extremely negative scrutiny that this would certainly have invited from the local authorities.[11] Finally here, rates of HIV/AIDS would have been much higher amongst the sect's membership than amongst surrounding populations (with AIDS-related illnesses often acting as a significant catalyst to malaria mortality). Thus, if all of these additional factors are taken into account, then it is in fact quite possible that the malaria outbreak of 1998 could account for a number of mass graves at Kanungu (as described by Kihama),[12] and for the 81 bodies that were later recovered from the Rushojwa site.

Moreover, we might also note that there is nothing in the various pathologists' reports on any of these sites to really dispute this hypothesis. After all, as I have described, no report was ever received on the bodies at Kanungu or Buhunga – indeed, no detailed autopsies were carried out at either site – and few signs of violence were recorded on any of the bodies at Rushojwa. Moreover, having now seen a range of video and photo-

[11] This being around the same time that the sect's school had been closed down, due to its poor standards of hygiene.
[12] It is also noteworthy that the Kanungu compound contains a large burial site – marked by wooden crosses and cairns of stones – that was never excavated by the police during their investigations at the site. It is possible that this burial site contains the additional mass graves to which Kihama refers.

graphic footage of the grave excavations at the Rugazi, Rushojwa, and Kampala compounds – and having discussed all this footage with a leading forensic anthropologist, and with three forensic pathologists – I now think it quite likely that the people buried at Rushojwa had indeed died some time before those who were placed in the other pits. This much is indicated by the apparently more advanced state of decomposition of the bodies at Rushojwa, at the time of their exhumation.[13]

[13] Following his investigations at Rugazi and Rushojwa, Dr Birungi concluded that all the bodies, at both sites, must have been buried shortly after death. This conclusion is based on his observation that all the bodies were tightly packed in all of the graves, which he took to indicate that they must have been buried before *rigor mortis* had set in. Moreover, he also concluded that if all the bodies had been buried before *rigor mortis* had set in, then this also indicated that they had died close to the place of burial (given that the bodies could not have been transported over any great distance in the period between death and the onset of rigor mortis). In addition, Birungi concluded that all the bodies, at both sites, had died at around the same time, around 2 to 3 weeks prior to exhumation – and 'certainly less than 1 month' beforehand – as evidenced by the 'lack of saponification of body fats' on them. However, he also noted that the bodies in the wine cellar were more decomposed than those of the other pits, something which he put down to a small opening in the wine cellar grave, which would have allowed air to enter the pit (thereby speeding up decomposition). All these conclusions were contained in the 'Final pathology report on Kanungu' (above).

However, according to the various specialists with whom I have discussed the footage of the scenes, Dr Birungi's various conclusions here are either invalid or equivocal. For example, Dr Nicholas Hunt, one of the UK Home Office's leading forensic pathologists, has said that the fact that the bodies were tightly packed in the graves cannot be taken as evidence that they were buried before *rigor mortis* had set in. On the contrary, it might also indicate that they were buried *after rigor mortis* had passed off – as happens immediately a body starts to decompose – following which a number of corpses placed in a mass grave 'would collapse into one another, and compact' in exactly the manner observed. Moreover, Hunt went on that, in an environment as rich as this one, in tropical Africa, he 'would imagine that [dead bodies] would start decomposing rapidly'. Thus, there is no evidence here that these people must have died close to their place of burial. On this point, Hunt indicated that the most reliable guide as to the length of time between death and interment is entomological analysis – given that dead bodies are exposed to a much wider range of insect predators before they are buried, than afterwards (especially in a tropical environment such as this) – none of which was carried out in this particular case.

In terms of establishing the overall post-mortem interval for these bodies, Hunt indicated that changes in fatty acid composition would be one indicator here. However, he went on that it would be impossible to make any more accurate prediction of timing without comparing these bodies to average rates of taphonomization – the rate at which a buried body becomes fossilized – in this particular environment (given environmental variables, such rates vary greatly from context to context). Given that such comparisons were not made in this case, Birungi's conclusion that the bodies had been buried 'certainly less than 1 month' before exhumation, seems equivocal.

Moreover, the two forensic pathologists to whom I showed this footage in New Zealand threw further doubt on Birungi's conclusion that all the bodies, at all three sites, had experienced a similar post-mortem interval (i.e. that they had all died at around the same time). Specifically, they argued that although the video footage of the various sites could not be used to ascertain an accurate timing of death at any of the sites, it could nevertheless be used to draw certain relational conclusions. Specifically, they argued that one could conclude from this footage – indeed, with '99% certainty' – the bodies at Rushojwa were relatively much more decomposed than were those at either Rugazi or Kampala. Moreover, that although one could not draw any 'definite conclusions' from this – given potential differences in the period between death and internment, and in differing rates of taphonomization at the three sites – in most instances, based on their experience, this would indicate that these bodies had experienced a longer post-partum interval. In other words, although it is difficult to draw any hard and fast conclusions on this point, it seems highly likely that the bodies at Rushojwa had indeed been dead for a significantly longer period than the corpses at either of the other two sites, prior to exhumation.

Thus, Kihama's claim that the bodies in the Rushojwa pits were the victims of a major outbreak of highland malaria is supported by a range of circumstantial data, and is not challenged by any of the police evidence from the various burial sites. Yet Kihama's description of this outbreak was only the first part of his testimony on what happened to the MRTC. In addition, he went on that, whilst the outbreak did turn at least some people away from the sect, for many others, the epidemic instead seemed to *increase* their zeal for the group. Thus, still by mid-1999, all of the sect's compounds – and especially that of Kanungu itself – remained significantly overcrowded. Therefore, when a major drought, and subsequent famine, struck the area later that year, there was simply not enough food to go around. Indeed, according to Kihama, by late 1999, it became a frequent occurrence for members at Kanungu to have to go all day without any food, and to survive on only a meagre supper (which often consisted of as little as 'a few maize seeds soaked in water', or 'a few small pieces of [raw] sugar cane'). As a result, many members soon became emaciated, and eventually, quite sickly as well (as a result of which, a few people even died). Once again here, some members, including Kihama himself, began to drift away from the sect, for want of food. However, before departing the group, Kihama once again noted that the famine – as with the earlier malaria outbreak – seemed to also result in remaining members engaging in their daily prayer sessions with ever greater enthusiasm (prayer sessions which, perhaps because of the lack of food, became longer than ever, often lasting for 12 hours or more at a time).

Once again, it is interesting to note that much of this description tallies with the available evidence. Thus, in addition to Kihama, a number of my other respondents also spoke of just how crowded the MRTC compounds – and especially that of Kanungu – were in 1999 (for example, Kahuru Richard).[14] Moreover, climatological data indicate that there was indeed a marked failure of rainfall in 1999 throughout East Africa, as an outcome of the *La Nina* weather system (the 'down-cycle' of the same *El Nino* that had caused the malaria epidemic of the previous year). In South-western Uganda, the 1999 system was experienced as a marked failure in that year of both the short rains of April–May (*katumba*) and the long rains of October–December (*eitumba*) (for a good introduction to the vast body of

---

[13] (cont.) Moreover, it makes sense that in the event of a malaria outbreak, the sect would have taken the bodies to Rushojwa – rather than to any of their other compounds – given that this centre was in some ways the most secluded of their compounds (after Kanungu).

[14] MRTC numbers may have been further bolstered, in early 1999, by a series of broadcasts the group made on a local radio station, Radio Voice of Toro FM. In an important break from their earlier practice of recruiting primarily through personal networks, the sect's leaders broadcast programmes on the station three times a week over a three-month period (at 8pm on a Monday and a Thursday, and 8.45am on a Saturday). These programmes – each of which lasted for between 10 and 15 minutes, and each of which cost the group UgSh 70,000 – consisted mainly of sermons on 'spiritual' matters (see: 'Cult boss used Toro FM radio', by Moses Sserwanga, *The New Vision*, 31 March 2000). In the context of Uganda's new radio broadcasting environment, which had been inaugurated by the 'structural-adjustment' programmes of the early 1990s, these broadcasts would have proved particularly compelling, and may well have resulted in at least some listeners seeking to join the group (for a much fuller discussion, see Vokes, 2007).

climatological data on the impact of La Nina systems on rainfall in East Africa, see Nicholson & Selato, 2000). The fact that all of this did indeed cause a major drought is the one part of the story that I can also confirm from my own observations, given that this impacted on other villages throughout the wider region, including that of Bugamba (see also Anyamba *et al.*, 2002). Not only were people in Bugamba still talking about the drought at the time I first arrived in the village (on Thursday 30 March 2000). In addition, as I look back at the photographs I took during that initial visit, I realize just how abnormally dry the whole place still was (even though, by then, the rains had long since returned). Moreover, this event did indeed cause a major food crisis, not only across South-western Uganda, but also across large parts of the Eastern continent. In fact, so bad was the crisis, that it resulted in the United Nations, and the US government's Famine Early Warning System, and other agencies as well, launching a region-wide emergency response plan.[15]

Moreover, Kihama's descriptions of the impact that this drought, and subsequent famine, had specifically on the MRTC, are also corroborated by other respondents' testimonies. Thus, for example, Winifred Aheebwa similarly recalls that, during this period, the members at Buhunga also appeared to be 'starving'. As a result, not only did they become increasingly reliant on 'handouts' – from the centre's various neighbours – but they also began to engage in itinerant labour on nearby estates, in return for payments of food. Thus it was, for example, that a small party of MRTC members once came to work in Winifred Aheebwa's own banana plantation (*orutookye*), for which she paid them 5 bunches of bananas. In addition, it is also noteworthy that all of the Buhunga centre's cattle were slaughtered for food at this time.[16] Moreover, this general situation seems to have been repeated at other of the MRTC's compounds as well. For example, a neighbour of the Movement's centre at Rushojwa (Patience N.) recalls that many of the members who visited that compound during this period were similarly 'suffering' from 'hunger' (*enjara*), and occasionally had to buy in food (either from local stores, or from town). In addition, they too began to engage in work parties in neighbouring estates. Even at Kanungu itself, a former neighbour told me, there was similarly 'no food' by this time. Thus, many people were also 'going hungry' (*enjara*), often surviving on as little as one cup of maize porridge (*posho*) and one piece of yam (*barugu*) per day (Kahuru Richard).

These same respondents also attest to how much more intense the

---

[15] See: 'La Nina brings food crisis to Horn of Africa', by Kieran Murray, *Reuters News Service*, 9 November 1999.

[16] It should be stressed that killing cows for food is regarded as an 'option of absolutely last resort' throughout South-western Uganda and beyond, because it effectively entails destroying a large part of one's household wealth. However, so bad was the famine of 1999 that it became quite common for households throughout the Southwest to have to eat their cattle. Indeed, such was the case in Bugamba (which is one reason why the event was still being frequently discussed at the time I first arrived in the village in March 2000, even though the rains had long since returned by then). Thus, even today, people in Bugamba still describe the 1999 famine, which was the worst in most people's living memory, as the famine 'in which we ate our cows'.

Movement's ritual practice became as a result of all this. In particular, Winifred Aheebwa, who occasionally attended the group's various prayer sessions, recalls that, during this period, it became permitted for individual members to start attending Ceredonia *during* one of her Marian visitations. In this way, it became possible, for the first time, for members to have private, and direct, consultations with the Virgin herself (as She spoke through Ceredonia). As Winifred describes it, 'she [Ceredonia] would become possessed ... with the Virgin Mary speaking through her', following which 'people consult[ed] her one on one on spiritual issues' (order of quotes reversed).[17] Moreover, following this development, the prayer sessions themselves became ever longer still. Eventually, they appeared to be 'full time praying [*sic*], during the day, and during the night'. Both Patience N. and Kahuru Richard also commented on a generally increased 'excitement' amongst MRTC members at this time.

Thus, the overall picture that seems to emerge is of a group which initially grew in response to the trauma of the AIDS epidemic, but which subsequently became millenarian in nature. This shift was initially shaped by various external influences and, in particular, by the group's exposure to a global Marian literature which was itself becoming increasingly apocalyptic in expectation of the coming year 2000. However, once the sect *had* become millenarian, this outlook was later confirmed, and deepened, by a series of more proximal events – a famine and a drought – which were themselves an outcome of the unpredictable operations of various other sorts of non-human agents (including rainfall patterns, malaria vectors, crop yields, and so on). However, the overall effect of these various assemblages was that by the time the Year 2000 did finally arrive, expectations of the end were particularly sharply drawn within the MRTC. The letter from Joseph Kibweteere to the *Orumuri* newspaper, sent in January 2000, confirms this point (see the Prologue, and also the letter of Elly Baryaruha, note 20 below).

Moreover, in this context, it is perhaps not surprising to discover that the Kanungu fire itself turns out to have been an event that probably *is* best described as having been a 'mass suicide', after all. It was during a fieldwork trip in 2005 that I finally secured a copy of the police video of the fire scene. However, it was showing this video to an expert in fire investigation – Dr. Mark Chubb of the New Zealand Fire Service – a few months later, that produced the crucial insights. Specifically, Chubb's analysis revealed that the smoke marks on the walls above the windows of the burnt-out building were in fact quite shallow, indicating that the fire itself had been slow burning, with relatively little fuel. Indeed, a calculation

---

[17] If, from 1989 onwards, the MRTC's ritual practice had revolved entirely around Ceredonia's Marian apparitions, then the usual format here had involved Ceredonia going into a trance-like state while she received her visitation (either in public, or in a private 'back-room'). Upon her return from trance, Ceredonia would then pass on details of her apparition, and answer questions about it (see Chapter 4). Thus, the only way in which members could have any direct access to the Virgin themselves was by listening to one of the tape recordings of the Virgin speaking through her, which Ceredonia occasionally made (always in private). Against all this, then, the new practice of individual members being invited to 'converse with the Virgin directly' – through Ceredonia – represented a significant innovation.

7.7 The shallow smoke marks above the windows of the burned-out building indicate a slow-burning fire, with relatively little fuel. The image shows the window on the north side of the building. (Source: police video)
7.8 The same pattern of smoke marks can be seen on the south side of the building as well. (Source: police video)

7.9 The even buckling of the roof suggests a steady blaze, one which produced an even amount of heat. This indicates that there was no explosion here. (Source: police video)

based on the size of the building, the number of people killed in the blaze, and so on, reveals that, in all likelihood, the only fuel present had been the people's bodies themselves. In other words, no accelerant had been used. Thus, there was simply no explosion of the sort the eyewitness described, a fact which is confirmed by (what turns out to be) the very even buckling of the roofing materials.[18] Moreover, the fire investigator's analysis further challenges other aspects of the scene, as this was described by journalists and others. For example, much was made, in early accounts, of the fact that some of the windows may have been nailed shut from the outside at the time of the fire. Yet, whether or not this is true, it turns out to be in any case irrelevant, given that at the time the fire began, most of the people inside the building were probably already dead.

Most early reports on the fire – including several of those prepared by the police themselves – recorded that the bodies in the burned-out building were 'piled in a heap' (which was presumed to indicate that these people had been trying desperately to escape the blaze when they met their end). However, from the fire investigator's point of view, this is simply not true.

---

[18] According to Chubb, an explosion would have caused a significant depression in that part of the roof which lay above the centre of the blast. However, this is not present in this case. Instead, the roof here has been subject to an even degree of buckling along its entire length.

Indeed, upon his initial viewing of the video, the *very first* comment Chubb made – without any input from myself – was that these bodies were '*remarkably* evenly spread', and showed no signs at all of the kind of clustering around the doorways that one would generally expect to see – that, on many occasions, Chubb has seen – following a fire in a crowded and confined space. Indeed, so evenly spread are these bodies that, in Chubb's view, the only possible interpretation is that all of these people must have been already dead, or else completely incapacitated, when the fire began. However, in addition to the general mass of bodies in the centre of the room, there are also some individual bodies, perhaps 5 or 6, located at intervals around the outside. From the contorted shapes of these bodies – known, technically, as their 'pugilistic stance' – it would seem that these individuals, at least, had been alive when the fire started. Yet even here, there is something unusual, in that all these bodies are in some way turned away from the various doors and windows to which they are adjacent (with the instinctive reaction of a person in a burning building being to head towards the nearest source of air). Indeed, so unusual is this feature that it may well be indicative of people who had made a conscious effort *not* to survive the inferno.

Thus, the most likely interpretation of events here is that all the members were gathered together in this building, then poisoned by a small group of (presumably particularly committed) members, who then went on to set fire to all the other bodies, killing themselves in the process. Whether or not the ordinary members were aware that they were going to die at the time they ingested the poison remains unclear, of course, from this analysis. On the one hand here, members certainly had been talking openly of a coming 'big event' in the days and weeks leading up to the fire, and at least some had also been 'tying up' their affairs in preparation for it. Thus, for example, one member with whom Winfried Aheebwa had become quite friendly brought her a pile of children's clothes, claiming that she would no longer need these on the journey she was about to undertake, and so had decided to donate them to Winifred's children instead.[19] At Rushojwa, another member told Patience N. a similar story, while handing over some pots and pans, a large pile of unused firewood, and various other items. At least one member – a former soldier, Lt. Elly Baryaruha – wrote to his family telling them that he was about to join an 'Ark', and wishing them farewell.[20]

[19] Although members were prohibited from speaking to each other, and were instead permitted to communicate only through sign-language (see Chapter 4), it seems that they did sometimes communicate with people outside the sect (and especially with those neighbours – such as Winifred Aheebwa – for whom they occasionally worked).
[20] This handwritten letter, which was reproduced in the report of the Uganda Human Rights Commission on Kanungu (2002: 71–3) was dated 4 March 2000, and states the following [in English, *verbatim*]:

I have felt in ungodly and on the other hand unhuman to go away forever without a word of farewell! Now, this is to say farewell to the whole family and if you do not see me once again, then do not ask! Throughout my 38 years existence, I might have sinned [?] or gravely (mortally) against some members or all of the family, and as per now, I request kindly to be pardoned.
I have hardly remained with over 10 days here before I join all the other members of the Restoration of the 10 Commandments of God before the closure of the 'ARK'. That will

In addition, on 14 March, 60 members talked of an upcoming journey whilst paying off their graduated tax arrears in Kanungu trading centre (UHRC, 2002; 62).[21] Also in that last week before the fire, the sect hired a local photographer to take all the members' photographs which, they told him, were to be used in 'passports' for the journey ahead.[22] In addition, a series of large bonfires were lit in the Kanungu compound, in which members burned all of their remaining property (which by this stage amounted, in most cases, to little more than their copies of the MRTC's book, their mattresses and blankets, a few clothes, and so on).[23] Finally, many members also spoke openly about an imminent event, and a 'coming journey', at the huge party which was held at the Kanungu compound on the evening of 16 March.[24] Indeed, one local person who attended that

[20] (cont.) mean therefore that we shall never meet once again. To me, it sounds sad, but that is what it must be. As we follow directives from Heaven, we are supposed to gather in the selected area before the wrath of the Almighty God the creator is let down on non-repentants.

Keep my words on your hearts; there will never be these year 2001.

Catastrophes will befall human kind and the indicators of such will be war, crime increased such as murders, rape, robbery etc. These will be a lot of fear for among the human races!

Appearance of strange animals and people will be noticed. I would [?] you that if you come across such, simply run and look for me I will not fail to seek refugee for you. Who [?] ever wanted his brother's family to perish?

Do not stick to people simply leave it to be and run for your dear lives.

I will always pray for you as I have nothing else to do! May God guide you. Your ever loving brother, and in-law. Elly.

I will always be there to welcome whoever comes for refugee'.

[21] Moreover, both the tone of Lt. Baryaruha's letter, and this practice of settling outstanding debts, convey a sense of a group of people who were trying to 'cleanse themselves of sin' in anticipation of this coming event.

[22] Moreover, all of this was taking place in a context in which the MRTC as a whole was winding up its – by now extensive – network of 'centres'. It was sometime in November 1999 when Ceredonia first decreed that all the Movement's centres were to be closed down, and the entire membership to be centralized at Kanungu. Following this edict, large fences were put up around a number of the compounds, and no further courses took place within them (although, in most instances, a small number of individuals did stay on as 'caretakers'). Thus, for example, in November 1999, a fence was erected around the compound at Buhunga (Winifried Aheebwa), whilst in December, a similar process took place at both Rugazi and Rushojwa (Galasiano and Patience N., respectively).

[23] The remains of at least five major bonfires can be clearly seen on the police video of the Kanungu site (prompting Assuman Mugyenyi to later remark to me, rather sardonically, that 'these people really liked fire!). The decision of the sect to burn all their remaining belongings in the days before the fire may have carried a symbolic meaning, given the sect's earlier use of ritual burnings as a means of marking spiritual transition (as in their earlier use of ritual hair, and clothes, burning as part of the rites of sanctification, see Chapter 6). However, it may just as well have served a purely pragmatic purpose, as a means of emphasizing the fact – both to the membership, and to outsiders – that the end had arrived.

[24] The function of 16 March was attended by a large number of local people, and by all members of the MRTC. In preparation for this, the group's pick-up had spent most of the previous week touring the sect's other compounds, to pick up any members who still remained at those other sites, and to bring them to Kanungu. In this way, this function became one of the biggest parties that the village had ever seen. In addition, the sect had also killed several cows, and various other animals, in preparation for it. At the party, the meat from these animals was then served up, along with various other special foods, and numerous crates of soda. A feast on this scale would normally only be served on the occasion of, for example, a major wedding celebration, or else during the visit of an important dignitary.

function even recalls one member telling him – in quite excited tones – that this party was in fact only the preliminary event, and that the 'real function' was to take place the following morning (Mugarura Nathan).

However, on the other hand, at least one piece of evidence *would* seem to indicate that the ordinary members may well have been deceived at the time they ingested the poison: the simple fact, apparently lost on all previous commentators on Kanungu, that the building in which these people had ingested this poison – and in which the fire then took place – was not the group's main church at all, but their *dining-room* (in which, presumably, it would have been much easier to surreptitiously administer a noxious substance, without raising immediate suspicion).[25] Yet whether or not the ordinary members did know that they were going to die at the time they ingested the poison, the main point here is that the profile of the deaths at Kanungu is exactly that of the 'classic' mass suicide. For example, the mass suicide undertaken by the People's Temple cult in 'Jonestown', in Guyana in 1978, similarly involved a group of 'hardcore' followers poisoning all of the other members, before turning on themselves.

Finally, let me turn to the remaining bodies in the pits. As I have already indicated, at least some of the bodies in the pits were probably those who had died in the earlier malaria outbreak. However, according to at least two of the forensic pathologists to whom I showed the police video, the bodies in at least two of the other pit graves – those of the wine cellar in Rugazi, and the one at the compound in Kampala – probably had been buried more recently. Yet in both these instances, all the pathologists also indicated that certain other of the conclusions drawn by the police investigators at the time were unreliable. Specifically, all of them also questioned Dr Birungi's original conclusion that some of these people must have been strangled,

[25] The Kanungu compound had two major centres of worship, the 'old chapel', which was located at the front of the main 'administration building', and the 'new church', a much larger structure sited some 100 yards or so down the hill from this main block. Whilst the old chapel had been the group's primary place of worship in the first few years of their stay at the compound, as the numbers grew – especially during the mid-1990s – a plan was developed to build a much larger, and grander, place of worship on the site (and certainly, the very finest building materials, including aluminium-and-glass window frames, were used in the project). The building project itself was overseen by Mzee Kurumbano, who was a trained carpenter. The choice of Kurumbano is itself illustrative, because at the time of his entry into the Movement, this senior – and wealthy – member of the local Catholic laity had refused to sell any of his property, or to pay any fee whatsoever, in order to enter the sect. Thus, the plan here was that Kurumbano would undertake all of this building work, free of charge, in lieu of these 'arrears' (all of which was described to me by members of Kurumbano's family). Indeed, the project was in fact close to completion in early March 2000. So it was that when Fr. Kataribaabo arrived at Kurumbano's home, just outside Mbarara Town, on 16 March, and requested that the man should accompany him back to Kanungu, to attend a function which was to be held the next day in order to mark the 'official opening' of the new church – i.e. the near-completion of Kurumbano's building work – nothing seemed particularly amiss. And so it was that later that day, on 16 March, Kurumbano hired a young taxi driver from Mbarara Town to drive him to Kanungu, and to his death. (Having arrived at the compound late at night on 16 March, the taxi driver stayed the night in the Movement's 'guest block' – which was located near to the entrance of the compound, and then left at dawn, before the fire.)

Against all this, then, the building in which the fire took place, which was located in the main 'residential area' of the Kanungu compound – between the kitchen and the two dormitory buildings, and adjacent to the former school buildings – was in fact the compound's main dining room.

7.10 An 'interesting technique' for exhumation (Dr Nick Hunt). The rope on which these prisoners are about to pull is tied around the neck of one of the bodies which was buried in the garden of the Rugazi compound. The police pathologist later concluded that signs of broken neck bones on some of these bodies indicated that strangulation was the cause of death.
(Source: police video)

given that they had broken hyoid bones, and showed signs of cyanosis of the tongue. In relation to the former, all three forensic pathologists pointed out that earlier in the police video, these bodies were shown being brought up out of their pit graves, by means of a pulley system. A rope was tied around the neck of each corpse in turn, upon which four or five of the prison labourers then heaved. In the experts' opinion, this method of exhumation was just as likely to have been the cause of the observed broken neck bones as anything that had happened to these people at the time of death. Moreover, Dr Hunt simply dismissed out of hand the notion that the observed cyanosis of the tongue could be taken as evidence of cause of death here. According to Hunt, the observed cyanosis in some of the bodies was much more likely to be an outcome of post-mortem decomposition.[26] Yet if all of the supposed evidence of strangulation can be

[26] Given that all these bodies had clearly experienced at least some degree of decomposition. As Hunt put it, in relation to this question of the observed cyanosis of the tongue: 'that is decomposition. I certainly would not make any assumption about the colour of the tongue after that degree of post-mortem change and the fact that it [the tongue, on one particular corpse in the video] is protruding is almost certainly due to gas formation in the soft tissue [as would occur after death]'.

dismissed, then we are left with only one possible sign of foul play at Rugazi – that of the aforementioned medicine vials, which were described at the time as having being like many small bottles of poison. This alone may make perfect sense, in the light of what I have just said about the fire. In other words, if (at least some) members of the group had been intending to kill the rest of the members by poisoning, then would it not have made perfect sense for them to have wanted to test their method here, on some smaller group, ahead of time? Thus, it is my surmise that the bodies in the wine cellar at Rugazi – and presumably also those in the pits in Buhunga and Kampala – had indeed also been killed by poisoning, most likely administered by the same small group of 'hardcore' followers who later went on to do the killings at Kanungu, by way of a series of 'experiments' for that larger event to come.[27]

Of course, as with even the best detective story, I realize that the narrative I have put forward here is both partial, and contingent. Thus, were some new piece of evidence to come to light, or better still were one of the surviving leaders – best of all Ceredonia herself – to be found, then all of this would no doubt require at least some further revisions.[28] However, until

[27] Moreover, this interpretation would tally with the one piece of corroborating evidence that we do have here. Specifically, it would make sense of Assuman Mugyenyi's later comments to the *New York Times* that 'the bodies which were buried in the pits had been poisoned, police pathologists have told us'. However, the reason why this apparently crucial insight – the basis of which is not known – was never confirmed is contained in the second part of what Mugyenyi had to tell the newspaper. Specifically, he went on: 'but we have not got the detailed report from forensic experts of the type of poisoning because we have not yet paid to get the results' (See: 'Cult in Uganda Poisoned Many, Police Say', in *The New York Times*, 28 July 2000). Thus, it would seem that we have the reason as to why this potentially key conclusion was never confirmed: because the requisite monies were never paid. Certainly, still by the time I read the police file on Kanungu, in 2005, no such report was contained therein.

Furthermore, Behrend cites an unnamed police source as claiming that the poison was administered here by two Rwandan *Inteerahamwe* (i.e. former *génocidaires*) whom the MRTC leadership had hired for the task (as evidence for this claim, Behrend's source further observed that none of the bodies in the pits showed any sign of a fight; 2000: 79 & 92 fn. 4). However, I have never come across any evidence to support this claim of a Rwandan connection. Instead, I think it is much more likely that the 'hardcore' element to which I refer here would have been drawn from the sect's own class of 'leaders', especially from that group of leaders who had only been promoted to the rank following a specific order in one of Ceredonia's visions. According to at least one of my respondents, individuals who had been promoted in this way tended to display a particularly loyal attitude towards Ceredonia (Winifred Aheebwa).
[28] It is simply impossible to know whether Ceredonia, and the other leaders, did also die in the fire, or whether she, and they, simply motivated others to engage in the mass suicide, before escaping themselves. Certainly, eye-witnesses of the scene of the fire (including James Mujuni) recall that at least one of the charred bodies was dressed in priestly robes, which would indicate that at least one of the leaders – presumably either Joseph Kibweteere, or Fr. Kataribaabo, or Fr. Kasapuraari – did indeed die there. However, it is also the case that both Ceredonia and Fr. Kataribaabo had instigated the sale of much of the sect's property in the weeks leading up to the fire. Thus, for example, Ceredonia oversaw the sale of the Movement's two shops in Kanungu, and of its remaining herd of cattle (which by then amounted to some 60 beasts; see also UHRC, 2002: 6). In addition, in late February, Fr. Kataribaabo began the sale of the sect's Rugazi property – i.e. his former home (although, because of complications related to various family interests, and for other reasons besides, the sale was not completed until 11 March, at which time it was sold to one of Fr. Kataribaabo's nephews, Bart Bainomukama). Certainly, the amounts raised through these various sales – in total, around UgSh 11 million – would have been more than enough for at least two or three of the sect's leadership to undertake almost any conceivable form of escape plan from the scene of the fire.

such a time, the story I have presented here may well remain the best account we have of just what did, then, happen at Kanungu.

---

[28] (cont.) On this point, one local man also told a documentary film team from the MBC production company that he had seen Ceredonia, and a number of the other leaders, drive away from the village, in a pick-up truck, about one hour or so before the fire. However, having interviewed this witness myself, I have concluded that his evidence is entirely unreliable, and for that reason, I do not give any credence to this testimony.

Epilogue

It is now more than eight years since the Kanungu Fire. But, in that time, no one has yet been brought to account for the events which took place in early 2000, in this small corner of the African Great Lakes. In the weeks and months following the fire – and especially in the period following the widespread adoption of the 'mass murder' hypothesis – both the national and international media reported a number of apparent 'sightings' of the sect's leaders (especially Ceredonia and Kibweteere) in locations as far apart as Eastern Congo, Rwanda, Sudan, Tanzania and elsewhere. However, although at least some of these leads were followed up – for example, in early 2001 a police team was sent to Rwanda to investigate one particularly credible sighting of Joseph Kibweteere – on no occasion did they amount to anything concrete. In addition, a number of rumours soon began to circulate in the urban centres of Rukungiri, Mbarara and Kampala, in particular, as to what might have become of the sect's leadership, and as to the reasons why nothing more had been heard publicly about them.

For example, one particularly good rumour I was told – by a very high ranking official in Kampala – was that Ceredonia had in fact survived the inferno, and had flown to Belgium, on Sabena Airlines, just a couple of weeks after the fire. Moreover, that the reason why this information was never made public was that, rather embarrassingly for the authorities – given that Ceredonia was, at that time, the most wanted person in Uganda (if not in the whole of Africa) – she had made the flight on her own passport, travelling under her own name. In addition, this same official also told me that Fr. Kataribaabo had also survived, and had been tracked by the intelligence services as far as a Nairobi slum, before that trail also went cold. However, as with all rumours of this type, it is simply impossible to judge their veracity. Thus, in the absence of any corroborating evidence, or any further disclosures, such rumours – however interesting they might appear to be on the surface – must continue to be regarded as exactly that, as nothing more than speculative hearsay.[1] So although international arrest warrants continue to be placed against all of the MRTC leaders, and

---

[1] Although we can say that the suggestion that Fr. Kataribaabo had survived the fire is slightly more plausible than some of the 'sightings' of MRTC leaders, given that there is at least one piece of corroborating evidence here: that his mobile phone had continued to be used for some days *after* the fire. Press reports at the time suggested that the relevant network provider (MTN Uganda) was preparing transcripts of the calls made on the handset for the Uganda police (see 'Kataribaabo Phoned After the Kanungu Fire', *The New Vision*, 21 April 2000). However, by the time I read the police file (in 2005), no such transcripts were included therein.

although a number of international law enforcement agencies – including Interpol, and the US Federal Bureau of Investigation (FBI) – have continued to keep their files on the Kanungu case open, to date no significant arrests have ever been made.[2]

However, this is not to say that no activity at all has stemmed from the Kanungu fire. On the contrary, in fact, the event has led directly to a number of significant shifts in the political landscape of Uganda, both at the local and national levels. In terms of the former, the local authorities in (what was then) Rukungiri District were initially highly embarrassed by the whole affair. This stemmed from the fact, later disclosures in both regional and national newspapers were to reveal, that a number of local officials had themselves been engaged in exchange relations with the MRTC. It would seem that, in the period following the closure of its school in Kanungu, in particular, the Movement had begun a campaign of distributing cattle among various officials within the local 'LC' (Local Council) system, all of which appear to have been gratefully received.[3] In addition, one report in *The New Vision* alleged that members of the sect had even worked in the household of the Assistant Resident District Commissioner (RDC) for the area, the Reverend Richard Mutazindwa (who was at the time based near the Kanungu trading centre, and would thus have been ultimately in charge of security for the whole area).[4] Certainly, in its annual report to the

[1] (cont.) It may be that these transcripts were produced, but were then removed from the file – for example, by the intelligence services, in their pursuit of Fr. Kataribaabo towards Kenya (as in the above rumour) – or else that they were produced but then lost, or that they were simply never produced at all. However, until such time as these articles do eventually appear, we shall never know exactly what happened here. And, in the continuing absence of these transcripts, we will also never know whether the calls made on Fr. Kataribaabo's phone after 17 March 2000 were made by him or by, for example, someone to whom he had previously sold the phone.

[2] In fact, the police investigation did lead to a number of minor arrests, mostly of individuals who had formerly converted their homes into 'study centres' for the Movement, but who had not – for one reason or another – gone on to die in Kanungu themselves. (For example, see: 'Rakai Arrests Another Suspected Cult Leader', by Eddie Ssejjoba and Dismus Buregyeya, *The New Vision*, March 2000.) The police strategy here seems to have been to try to use these individuals to 'flush out' some of the more senior leaders. However, if this was indeed the aim, then it resulted in disappointment, because none of these arrests ever led to the netting of a senior sect leader.

[3] The closure of the MRTC's school house at the Kanungu compound was the only occasion on which the local authorities made any significant intervention in the sect's affairs. The move was instigated by the then RDC of Rukungiri District, Yorokamu Kamacerere – the same individual who had earlier refused to support the sect's application to be registered as an NGO (see Chapter 6) – following a report from government inspectors that conditions in the school were unhygienic. Interestingly, the visit upon which this report was based had taken place in mid-1998, which would have been either during the malaria outbreak, or else shortly after its conclusion (in other words, at a time when conditions in the compound as a whole would have reached a particularly low point). It was following the school's closure that the MRTC leadership began to expand their exchange relations with local government officials. Moreover, this might explain why the LC chairmen in the Kanungu area did not make more of an effort to monitor the Movement's activities in the period leading up to the Kanungu fire. Certainly, it is my experience that LC1 (village-level) and LC3 (sub-county-level) chairmen, in particular, tend to make it their business to get to know everything which is going on in their areas, and to alert higher authorities when anything out of the ordinary comes to their attention.

[4] See: 'Cult Nuns Used to Cook for RDC', by John Kakande, *The New Vision*, March 2000. Mutazindwa had previously supported the sect's application to be registered as an NGO (see Chapter 6).

Ministry of Internal Affairs of January 2000, the MRTC had reserved special praise for Mutazindwa, hoping that 'the Lord [may] be his guide throughout all his life' (for further discussion of this report from the MRTC, see *The New Vision* report of 26 March 2000, cited in the Prologue).

At the same time, in the months following the Kanungu fire, a number of other local political actors also saw in the event an opportunity for political gain, if it could be established that the primary cause of the incident had been a general lack of 'development' in the area. Thus, throughout the second half of 2000, in particular, various individuals – and in particular the local Member of Parliament, Dr Stanley Kinyata – pushed for the fire to be primarily understood as an outcome of 'poverty', 'lack of investment', and so on. In one sense, such factors *had*, of course, contributed to the whole affair. However, local politicians' real reasons for interpreting it in this way became clear in early 2001, when, in the context of an ongoing government review of district boundaries in Uganda – which, admittedly, had begun before the fire took place – they deployed the argument as part of their attempts to gain full District status for Kanungu (at that time, Kanungu was only a County within the wider Rukungiri District). Such is the nature of the national political discourse in contemporary Uganda – with its key emphasis upon the notion of the 'developmental state' – that the argument appears to have been particularly compelling. Thus, in their final judgement on the review, in July 2001, the government panel cited the fire as one of the main reasons why they had finally decided to grant Kanungu full District status (and thus to confer all the various benefits, including a massively increased budget, a guarantee to build a hospital in the area, and so on, which that entailed). It is therefore quite symbolic, to my mind, that the headquarters of the new Kanungu District should now be located less than half a mile or so from the site of the fire (it is in fact the very same building in which Rutembo Didas had first made contact with Corporal Stephen Mujuni on that fateful morning, in the incident with which this book opened). It is for these reasons, then, that, on at least two separate occasions, I have heard people in Kanungu express a sentiment to the effect that the fire itself was 'probably the best thing that ever happened around here'.

If the local authorities were initially embarrassed by the Kanungu fire, so too were their national counterparts. Not only was the fire incredibly damaging for the international image of the country as a whole (which was at the time still recovering from the 'Bwindi Massacre' of the previous March – when Rwandan rebels had killed eight Western tourists in the nearby Bwindi National Park, in what had become front-page news around the world). In addition, it soon transpired that the national government had in fact received a number of warnings about the MRTC's activities, but had failed to act on them. In an interview with the BBC in London, on 29 March 2000, President Museveni himself expressed incredulity that a series of intelligence reports outlining 'the potential dangers of the Movement for the Restoration of the Ten Commandments' had been 'sat on',[5] and not brought

---

[5] See: 'Death Cult Activities Ignored', *BBC News Online*, 30 March 2000.

to his attention (with the result that 'until the recent incident' he had 'never heard of the cult' before).[6] The President's comments were almost certainly made with reference to two reports on the MRTC that had been prepared earlier by Godfrey Karabenda, an officer in the Internal Security Organization (the ISO, Uganda's domestic intelligence agency), but apparently had never been passed on to higher authorities.

However, by the time of these interviews, the President would doubtless have also become aware that a number of the senior members of his government had received even more direct warnings on the MRTC, from relatives of Movement members. For example, I have seen copies of a series of letters that were sent to one senior member of Museveni's cabinet in 1996, by the husband of a Movement member who hailed from that Minister's home area. The letters – which are written in the strongest possible terms (using words and phrases such as 'evil', 'brainwashing' and 'causing misery')[7] – describe the husband's concerns with the MRTC's practices of seeking donations from its members, of requiring its followers to take up residence at Movement centres, of separating husbands and wives once they had done so, and so on. Yet in this instance, at least, it would seem that, whether or not these missives were ever taken seriously, they were certainly never acted upon. Indeed, the old man who wrote the letters now claims that he never even received a reply. In addition, in 1998, one Goretti Mitima had contacted the Inspector General of Government, the Administrator General, and finally the Uganda Human Rights Commission, to complain about the Movement. In particular, Mitima had requested that the authorities investigate the circumstances in which her mother had died at one of the sect's compounds some months previously, and to look into the well-being of her sister-in-law's six children (following the death of Mitima's brother, his widow had joined the Movement along with her six children, taking up residence at the Kanungu compound; UHRC, 2002: 60-62). Once again, it would seem that very little action was taken here.[8] All of which might go some of the way towards explaining why a government commission of enquiry into Kanungu, something which was promised in the weeks following the fire, was in fact never set up.[9]

In addition to these issues, in the weeks and months following the Kanungu fire, the government also came in for more general sorts of criticism as well. For example, the editor of the opposition newspaper *The Monitor*, Charles Onyango-Obbo, claimed that the very emergence of a group such as the MRTC could be understood as an outcome of government policy. Onyango-Obbo expressed a sentiment which was then widely held among opposition groups, when he argued that Museveni's dictatorial presidential style, and his move towards a 'one-party state', had effectively closed the political space in Uganda. Moreover, he went on, it was

[6] See: 'Kibweteere Gave Leaders Gifts', by Alfred Wasike, *The New Vision*, 26 March 2000 (order of quotes reversed).
[7] All these letters were written in English.
[8] Of the three agencies to whom Mitima wrote, only the Human Rights Commission replied. However, they asked her to provide a series of documents that she could not provide, and so her enquiry effectively came to nothing (UHRC, 2002: 61).
[9] See: 'Who Cares About Kanungu?', by Bernard Atuhaire, *The New Vision*, 17 March 2005.

inevitable, in this context, that people would seek expression elsewhere (given that it 'creates a vacuum, and something will fill it'). According to Onyango-Obbo, it was primarily this, then, that had led to a proliferation of small religious groups such as the MRTC, during the 1990s.[10]

Thus, the national government, too, was both embarrassed by, and criticized for, the whole Kanungu episode. It is no doubt because of these factors that its subsequent actions were so decisive. Specifically, in the period after the fire, the government introduced a series of measures to ensure that such an incident could not happen again. Interestingly – given the central arguments of this book – their efforts in the Southwest initially focused on either closing, or else monitoring activities at, many 'traditional' shrines. Thus, for example, the former shrine at Nyabugoto – in which many of Ceredonia's earliest visions had taken place – was completely shut, with a ban imposed on any form of public gathering at the site. Indeed, this ban was still in place by the time I made my last visit to the caves, in November 2001, and a policeman was still on permanent guard at the location. Yet Nyabugoto was not the only 'traditional' shrine to come under such scrutiny at this time. In the months following Kanungu, various other sites – throughout the Southwest, and beyond – were also visited by the police, or by senior government officials, and in at least two cases were monitored for an extended period of time.

Even more significantly, in the aftermath of Kanungu, the government also introduced a series of countrywide measures aimed at overseeing, and in some aspects curtailing, the activities of all independent religious groups. Thus, for example, following the fire, the national NGO registration laws – under which most religious sects in the country are registered (and under which the MRTC were themselves registered) – was amended, and more stringent conditions introduced. Following these changes, it has become a requirement not only for all sects to register their existence, and to provide some description of their beliefs and activities (both to the local LC officials *and* to their local RDC), but also for all of them to have one senior member of the LC system, or the RDC, actually sitting on their official 'Board of Governance'. In addition, today no sect is allowed to hold 'night vigils' – i.e. all-night prayer sessions – more than once a month (and even then, only with the express permission either of a senior LC Chairman, or of the RDC himself). In addition, no sect is allowed to create a centre of 'permanent residence'. And so on.

Moreover, these measures have been invoked on a number of occasions – indeed, regularly – as a means of controlling the activities of independent religious groups throughout Uganda. Thus, although the authorities had in fact disbanded a number of sects in the period before the Kanungu fire – for example, they had broken up the World Message Last Warning Church, in Luwero District, in late 1999[11] – such actions have increased dramatically in the time since the inferno. For example, during the period of my most recent fieldwork in Uganda alone – in early 2005 – the government used

[10] See: 'Uganda: Religion That Kills', by Logan Nakyanzi, *ABC News Online*, 14 February 2001.
[11] Although the leader of this sect, the 'prophet' Wilson Bushara, was not apprehended until July 2000, when he was arrested in Iganga Town.

their new powers to break up two sects, those of Pastor Toya's Church, in Gulu Municipality, and Ssali Kilima Mwaka's Holy Rock Movement, in Kikandwa, Mubende District. In the first case, the sect was disbanded on the grounds that it had been holding unauthorized night prayers. In the second example, the Movement's alleged infringement related to some of its members having taken up residence at their 'prophet' Mwaka's own house.[12] In both instances, memories of Kanungu were explicitly invoked by the officials involved in the actions, as a means for justifying their interventions. Thus, in these ways, the government has certainly used the Kanungu fire as a means through which to cut back some of the former freedoms of religious worship which had been introduced in Uganda following the 'structural adjustment' programmes of the 1980s and early 90s. Although there is no suggestion that the closure of any one or other cult has ever been undertaken for overtly political reasons, there is also no doubt that, in these various ways, the fire has proved a useful instrument for extending state control over (at least some aspects of) civil society in Uganda.

Finally here, there was the reaction of the local Catholic hierarchy, which it is fair to say extended beyond embarrassment. Indeed, on the number of occasions when I have met the now retired Bishop Kakubi – including on the occasion he granted me a full interview about Kanungu (also during my 2005 field trip) – he has expressed his deep remorse at the way things turned out with the MRTC, especially concerning the group's final demise. Apart from his former wrangles with Fr. Kataribaabo and the other Movement priests – which had led, of course, to his initial decision to interdict the group – the Bishop, who is a deeply sincere man, is today greatly troubled that he may not have acted decisively enough earlier on in the affair, or may not have fully appreciated exactly what the MRTC had later come to represent. Although, as he put it to me in 2005, at the time it was simply impossible for him to imagine that someone as 'wise', and as 'moral', as Fr. Kataribaabo could ever have become involved in events of this nature.

For his part, Bishop Kakubi's successor in the See of Mbarara, the now Archbishop Paul Bakyenga,[13] was primarily concerned, of course – like the government – with making sure that nothing like Kanungu ever happened again. The Archbishop's efforts here primarily focused on understanding what had led people into the MRTC – and therefore away from the main-stream Catholic church – in the first place. Thus, in the weeks following the fire, the Archbishop asked parish priests throughout the Southwest to consult widely on the MRTC, to draw up a list of all those who had joined the Movement (an activity which was coordinated by the diocese of Kabale, see Chapter 5) and to make contact with the families of those who had died.

[12] See: 'Gulu Church Closed Over Night Prayers', by Cornes Lubanakene, *The New Vision*, 7 February 2005, and 'Police Arrest Suspected Cult Leader in Mubende District', by Herbert Ssempogo, *The New Vision*, 5 May 2005 (respectively).
[13] On the occasion of John Kakubi's retirement, in November 1991, Paul Bakyenga had taken over as Bishop of Mbarara. However, in January 1999, the former diocese of Mbarara was elevated to become an archdiocese – the greater entity also incorporating the dioceses of Fort Portal, Hoima, Kabale and Kasese – at which time Bakyenga became an Archbishop.

Following this, the Archbishop announced plans for a major 'Pastoral Conference' on the history and future of 'evangelization' in the region, to be held at the Archdiocese headquarters at Nyamitanga – just outside Mbarara Town – in January 2001.

Few of the ten or so 'position papers' that were prepared for the conference – all of which were put together by some committee or other of senior church members[14] – mentioned the MRTC directly. Nevertheless, it is quite clear from their subject matter that most of these discussion pieces were specifically designed to address the Kanungu case. Thus, for example, the opening Position Paper 1 was aptly entitled: 'Inculturation as a New Means of Evangelization in the New Millennium', and examined under what conditions 'traditional' religious practices could be accepted into mainstream church practice, and in which contexts they must be rejected. The paper included one section on 'new religious movements' which identified the emphasis of these movements on residency – and the concomitant break-up of the family which this entails – as a specific flaw in these groups' version of inculturation (n.d.: 7). In another example, Position Paper 2 explored the history of 'Church Use of Mass Media to Promote Evangelization', and asked why the Archdiocese had not been as successful in its use of new media – especially newspapers and radio – for evangelization as had other religious groups in the region. (It will be recalled that the MRTC's 'global literature' had proved to be a particularly powerful draw in the early days of the Movement, and that the sect had later gone on to use radio advertising as a means of attracting new members). In one of the few papers which does explicitly reference the MRTC, Position Paper 6A looked at 'The Proliferation of New Religions and Churches in Mbarara Archdiocese'. Perhaps rather tellingly, it suggests that 'the main reason for the spread of these [new] movements and groups is the breakdown of the traditional social structures, cultural patterns, and traditional sets of value. This has been caused by migration, rapid development of communication systems and other modern technologies' (n.d.: 2). Based on the arguments put forward in this book, I would argue that this statement is partially correct. Yet, in an even more interesting reference, the paper also observes that one of the primary reasons why people had been leaving the mainstream Church to join these new groups related to their having 'received visions and dreams compelling them to change' (n.d.: 3). In yet other examples, Position Paper 7 explored the subject of 'The Family as an Agent of Evangelization'. Another looked at why so few people had been taking Church-run courses – especially catechism courses – in recent years. And so on.

In these various ways, then, although many of the papers did not explicitly refer to the MRTC case directly, most of them spoke directly to one

---

[14] Some of these committees were set up especially for the conference, whilst others were made up of pre-existing councils within the church. In addition, some were made up entirely of clergymen, whilst others included a mixture of both clergy (male and female), and senior members of the laity. So, for example, Position Paper 6A was prepared by a specially convened Commission of Priests' Council, whilst Position Paper 7 was written by a mixed group of priests, nuns, and lay members of the long-standing Laity Council.

or other element of the Kanungu story, and to the various issues it had raised (especially as these related to the Catholic Church's own practice). Moreover, given that the fire had occurred only a few months previously, and given that many of the clergymen present had spent the intervening period making enquiries into the former membership of the MRTC, it follows that Kanungu was at the time still fresh in most delegates' minds. So it was, then, that, as one delegate described it to me – I was not able to attend the conference in person – the topic of Kanungu dominated most of the discussions at the meeting.

In addition to instigating this process of reflection, the local Catholic hierarchy also took some more practical steps to guard against any such incident ever happening again. For example, in June 2000, copies of a pastoral letter signed by all the Catholic Bishops of Uganda were distributed in parishes throughout the Southwest, as a leaflet called *Testing the Spirits: [A] Pastoral Letter...to the Faithful on Cults, Sects and 'Religious' Groups*. To give some idea of the emphasis which was placed on the publication, it is notable that several hundred copies of the leaflet were handed out to Catholic parishioners in Bugamba alone. The purpose of the letter, which had been produced at a Bishops' Plenary Conference in Kampala earlier that month, was to remind all Catholics of canonical law in regard to 'private associations': that they are only acceptable where they are subject to the appropriate ecclesiastical authority, that they can only acquire 'status of juridic personality' through a formal decree from the appropriate authority, and so on. It then went on to identify a number of Catholic organizations that had failed to meet these standards in recent times. Although the document lists five such organizations here – drawn from all over the country – it is little surprise which organization topped this particular list.

Finally, in the months following the Kanungu fire, the local Church hierarchy appear to have also taken steps to promote the ICCR more actively, presumably as an officially sanctioned 'alternative' to sects such as the MRTC. The fact that the Archbishop wanted to advance the ICCR in this way is already indicated by the fact that the local leader of that Movement, Fr. Bashobora, was one of the authors of Position Paper 1 at the Mbarara Conference. Yet more significantly, in the period following the Kanungu fire, the ICCR's activities – under the leadership of Fr. Bashobora, and latterly four other priests as well – increased dramatically. In particular, the group's various public ceremonies became much more frequent, much larger in scale, and were conducted over a much wider geographical area (indeed, for this reason, I was able to attend a large number of these ceremonies over the course of my original doctoral fieldwork). If all this did much to increase the ICCR's popularity, an even bigger factor in this regard was its later intro-duction of a system of competitive secondary school scholarships for the group's members and their children. Today, the organization gives out several hundreds, if not thousands, of these scholarships every year to local families. On more than one occasion, respondents have expressed the opinion that this scholarship scheme may have contributed to the fact that the ICCR today attracts a regular membership of many thousands, if not tens of thousands, of people, throughout South-western Uganda.

Much has changed in Uganda, and in the wider Great Lakes region, in the period since the Kanungu fire. In particular, important questions over the reliability of all forms of HIV/AIDS data notwithstanding (Allen, 2006), it is clear that mortality rates from the disease have dropped from their peak in the early to mid-1990s. Wider knowledge about the disease, shifting patterns of behaviour (however one might try to define these), and latterly the wider availability of Anti-Retroviral Drugs[15] have all meant that, today, AIDS no longer kills on quite the scale it once did. As a result, the types of complications over property ownership which formerly led to so many women joining the MRTC are also no longer as acute as they once were. In addition, and perhaps more importantly, after nearly two decades of having lived with the epidemic, the people of South-western Uganda and beyond have developed much better personal, and social, 'coping' mechanisms for living with the ongoing effects of the disease. Thus, the virus no longer generates the kind of social panic that it did formerly, which had formed part of the general ferment in which the MRTC made its initial shift towards a millenarian outlook. Moreover, it is also true to say that the 'global' Marian literature upon which the MRTC drew – and which was the other major influence on its subsequent adoption of an eschatological worldview – would today no longer have the same power that it did at the time. Simply put, were this same literature to circulate today, it would be in competition with all of the other networks of transnational communication which have become so well established in Uganda over the last five years or so. Thus, the steady growth over this period in the number of radio and television stations broadcasting in, and to, the country, the explosion in mobile phone ownership (and more importantly, the spread of mobile network coverage), and the increasing numbers of Ugandans travelling out of the country for either work or study – many of whom now stay 'in touch' with home via mobile phones and the internet – have all combined to alter radically the ways in which Ugandans engage with, and (more importantly) perceive, the rest of the world. At least one outcome of this – there are many others besides – is that it is no longer possible for any individual, or group, to monopolize an imaginary of *buraeya* for their own ends (as the MRTC formerly did, through the international literature, for the purposes of amplifying the power of its own image of the Virgin Mary).

However, while I am on the subject of imaginaries, let me finish here with some imaginaries about what became of the Kanungu dead. Thus, on more than one occasion over the course of my fieldwork, one or other respondent told me that they had experienced the haunting presence of a Kanungu ghost. In several instances, friends and relatives of those who died

[15] To take Bugamba Village as one example, by the end of my doctoral fieldwork in 2001, only one person in the area, to my knowledge, was on ARV treatment. In this case, the man involved was paying for the drugs privately. However, by the time of my fieldwork in 2005, I recorded a total of 15 cases of people on the treatments. Of these, 9 were receiving the drugs free of charge (through the local health centre), whilst the remainder were buying them privately (which had become much more affordable by this time, the cost of the drugs having reduced dramatically in the intervening period).

[16] See: 'Strange, Ghostly Voices Terrorize Kanungu', by Mugisha Matthias, *The New Vision*, 29 September 2001.

described their ongoing sorrow as the outcome of an unsettled spirit (or spirits). More specifically, one young woman who had introduced a delegation to her home area, but who herself subsequently withdrew from the Movement, spoke of the ongoing troubles that the Kanungu dead had been causing her. In another instance, a respondent described a death in her family, in 2001, as the outcome of her dead co-wife's malevolence. In more general terms, throughout 2001 several neighbours of the Kanungu compound reported that the ghosts of the dead could be heard crying and wailing at night.[16] This may have reflected a widely held perception at the time that because none of the Kanungu dead had been (in one respondent's words) 'properly buried' – i.e. interred in a culturally appropriate way – all of their ghosts would probably remain forever unsettled.[17] However, against this, Bishop Kakubi finished our interview on the Movement (in 2005) by saying that, in his darker moments, he instead chose to imagine that all of those who had died at Kanungu were now in heaven. After all, he reasoned, they were all 'martyrs', in that they had all – one way or the other – died for their religious beliefs. Therefore, they all deserved to rest in peace.[18]

However, over the last eight years of studying the MRTC – of seeking to understand why this group emerged in the first place, how and why it grew so rapidly during the early 1990s, and how it came to have such a profound influence over so many people's lives – I have also developed at least one imaginary of my own. Over the course of this long project I have begun to imagine that the ghosts of Kanungu have at least acknowledged my own humble endeavours, to record the details of their lives, and to make some little sense of how and why they met their final, tragic ends.

Christchurch, New Zealand, July 2008

[17] Throughout South-western Uganda and beyond a great emphasis is usually placed on bodies being buried at home. For example, over the course of my research in the region, I have recorded instances too numerous to recount of families going to sometimes quite extraordinary lengths in order to bring home the body of a relative who had died elsewhere – in another rural area, in a distant town, even in another country – for a 'proper' burial. Thus, in the days and weeks following the Kanungu fire, a number of families did travel to the various sites with the intention of collecting their relatives' bodies, and taking them home. However, quite early on the authorities decided that no bodies were to be removed from the sites. There is little doubt that this decision was taken, in large part, in response to the fact that, in most cases, identification would have anyway been impossible (given that most of the bodies in the fire were charred, many of the corpses in the pits decomposed beyond recognition).
[18] Mayer also reports a Marian group based in Masaka Town, the Daughters of Mary, who have similarly come to regard the MRTC dead as 'martyrs' (cited in Behrend, 2000: 95).

Appendix
Marian Literature Used by the MRTC

The following is a sample list of some of the Marian literature used by the MRTC:

1988 Vigil Calendar. Produced by: Our Lady of the Roses Shrine (New York, USA).

1991 Vigil Calendar. Produced by: Our Lady of the Roses Shrine (New York, USA).

Ash Wednesday March 7ᵗʰ 1984. Produced by: Mary's House, Little Nazareth (Canvey Island, UK).

Dedicated decades (Several editions). Produced by: The Universal Living Rosary Association (Texas, USA).

Five articles on the dignity of man. Produced by: The Kingdom of Our Lady (Japan).

Further warnings from Our Lady of Fatima. Produced by: St. Paul's Guild (Vermont, USA).

Litany of the Sacred Heart of Jesus. Produced by: The Marian Workers of Uganda.

Mary our mother, help us Christians. Produced by: Little Pebble (Australia).

Mary, queen and mother of the children of the world (Several editions). Produced by: Mary's House, Little Nazareth (Canvey Island, UK).

No title (Various documents). Produced by Franz Joseph Keiler (New York, USA).

Our Lady comes to Australia (Several editions). Produced by: Little Pebble (Australia).

Our Lady speaks to the world under the title of Our Lady of Unity... Produced by: The Knotted Cord of Love Rosary Mission (Louisiana, USA).

Progress on the prevention of abortion in Japan. Produced by: The Kingdom of Our Lady (Japan).

Roses: New York City targeted for destruction. Produced by: Our Lady of the Roses Shrine (New York, USA).

San Damiano. Produced by: J. M. J. San Damiano Centre Inc. (Massachusetts, USA).

The Little Pebble of Australia: fact-sheet (No. 1). Produced by: Little Pebble (Australia).

True messages and seers. Produced by: The Marian Workers of Atonement (Australia).

Bibliography

Archival Sources

Kabale District Archive

Given the poor quality of the Kabale District Archive, it is difficult to give accurate file references for all of the documents referred to in the text. The following files are still intact:

C. Adm. 27: District history and historical notes
Dev. 4/1 II: Kigezi Resettlement Scheme: policy reports and general.
Dev. 4/3 VI: Resettlement in Toro
Dev. 4/3 VII: Resettlement in Toro
Dev. 4/10 I: Resettlement in Toro – Kibale etc.
Kigezi District Annual Report, 1928.
Kigezi District Annual Report, 1949.
Kigezi Police Quarterly Report for the third quarter of 1935.
Uganda Monthly Intelligence Report No. 13, June 1922.
However, for the following documents, it is impossible to give accurate file references:
DC to PC Western Province, 21 September 1917.
DC to PC Western Province, 30 September 1917.
DC to PC Western Province, 3 March 1928.
DC Toro to ADC (Land Settlement) Kigezi, 16 September 1957.
J. R. Mcd. Elliott, Acting DC, 20 March 1925.
Philipps to PC Western Province, 1 January 1929.
S. C. Dwankey to DC Kigezi District, 23 September 1949.
Summary of Lukiko Case: Kinyoni son of Nyabuhende vs. T. Tebanyururwa, 15 October 1937.

Uganda National Archive, Entebbe Secretariat

In the Entebbe Archive, the vast majority of files on Nyabingi, which have been referred to in previous texts, are now missing. However, I did find the following useful:

ES A43/92 – Murders at Kagaru, Ankole (March 1907–March 1908).
ES A43/118 – Ankole: Saza Chief Hezikiah Kabututu.
ES A44/242 – Western Province: Major Treffrey's tour along the Anglo-German boundary of Ankole District.
ES A44/291 – Ankole District: Kabilimi to be confirmed as Saza Chief of Bunyaruguru.
ES A46/829 – Ankole District: Fighting in Rwampara. Rule of Ankole through chiefs.

Published books and articles

Allen, T. 1991. Understanding Alice: Uganda's Holy Spirit Movement in context. In *Africa* 61 (3): 370–99.

—— 2006. AIDS and evidence: interrogating some Ugandan myths. In *Journal of Biosocial Science* 38: 7–28.

Anderson, A. H. 2001. Types and butterflies: African initiated churches and European typologies. In *The International Bulletin of Missionary Research* 25: 107–13.

Anderson, D. & D. H. Johnson. 1995. Revealing prophets. In *Revealing Prophets* (eds) D. Anderson & D. H. Johnson. London: James Currey.

Anyamba, A., C. J. Tucker & R. Mahoney. 2002. From El Nino to La Nina: vegetation response patterns over East and Southern Africa during the 1997-2000 period. In *Journal of Climate* 15 (21): 3096–3103.

Ardener, E. 1970. Witchcraft, economics and the continuity of belief. In *Witchcraft confessions and accusations* [ASA Monograph Series, Volume 9] (ed.) Mary Douglas. London: Tavistock.

Austrin, T. & J. Farnsworth. 2005. Hybrid genres: fieldwork, detection and the method of Bruno Latour. In *Qualitative Research* 5 (2): 147–65.

Banura, G., S. Kabazzi-Kisirinya & R. K. D. Nkurunziza. 2000. *The Kanungu cult saga: suicide, murder or salvation?* Kampala: The Department of Religious Studies. Makerere University.

Becker, F. & P. W. Geissler. 2007. Searching for pathways in a landscape of death: religion and AIDS in East Africa. In *Journal of Religion in Africa* 37: 1–15.

Behrend, H. 1999. *Alice Lakwena and the Holy Spirits: war in Northern Uganda 1986-97.* Oxford: James Currey.

—— 2000. Salvation and terror in Western Uganda: the Movement for the Restoration of the Ten Commandments of God. In *Millenarian Movements in Africa and the Diaspora* (Royal Academy of Overseas Sciences: Bulletin des Seances). (ed.) Jan-Lodewijk Grootaers. Brussels: Belgian Association of Africanists.

Bellman, B. L. 1984. *The language of secrecy: symbols and metaphors in Poro ritual.* New Brunswick, NJ: Rutgers University Press.

Berger, I. 1981. *Religion and resistance: East African kingdoms in the pre-colonial period.* Tervuren: Koninklijk Museum voor Midden-Africa.

—— 1995. Fertility as power: spirit mediums, priestesses & the pre-colonial state in Inter-lacustrine East Africa. In *Revealing Prophets* (eds) D. Anderson & D. H. Johnson. London: James Currey.

Bessell, M. J. 1938. Nyabingi. In *Uganda Journal* 2 (2): 73–86.

Boissevain, J. & J. Clyde Mitchell (eds). 1973. *Network analysis: studies in human interactions.* The Hague: Mouton and Co.

Brazier, F. S. 1968. The incident at Nyakishenyi, 1917. In *Uganda Journal* 32 (1): 17–27.

Buckser. A. & S. D. Glazier (eds). 2003. *The anthropology of religious conversion.* Lanham, MD: Rowman and Littlefield.

Bugingo, G., A. Ntilivamunda, D. Nzaramba, P. Van de Perre, A. Ndikuyeze, S. Munyantore, A. Mutwewingabo and C. Bizimungu, 1988. Etude sur la séropositivité liée à l'infection du Virus de l'Immuno-déficience Humaine au Rwanda. In *Revue Médicale Rwandaise* 20 (54): 37–42.

Callon, M. 1986. Some elements of a sociology of translation: domestication of the scallops and the fishermen of St. Brieuc Bay. In *Power, action and belief: a new sociology of knowledge* (ed.). John Law. London: Routledge & Kegan Paul.

Carswell, J. W., G. Lloyd & J. Howells. 1989. Prevalence of HIV-1 in East-African lorry drivers. In *AIDS* 3, 759–61.

Casagrande, J. (ed.). 1960. *In the company of man: twenty portraits by anthropologists.* New York: Harper & Bros.

Cisternino, M. 1987. *The proverbs of Kigezi and Ankole.* Rome: Museum Combonianum.

Clifford, J. & G. E. Marcus. (eds). 1986. *Writing culture: the poetics and politics of ethnography.* Berkeley, CA and London: University of California Press.

Clyde Mitchell, J. 1969. *Social networks in urban situations: analysis of personal relationships in Central African towns.* Manchester: Manchester University Press.

Comaroff, J. & J. Comaroff. 2000. Millennial capitalism: first thoughts on a second coming. In *Public Culture* 12 (2): 291–343.

—— 2003. Ethnography at an awkward scale. In *Ethnography* 4 (2): 147–79.

Comoro, C. & J. Sivalon. 1999. The Marian Faith Healing Ministry: an expression of popular Catholicicsm in Tanzania. In *East African expressions of Christianity* (eds) T. Spear and I. N. Kimambo. Oxford: James Currey.

Conan Doyle, A. 1892. *The adventures of Sherlock Holmes.* London: George Newnes Ltd.

Deleuze, G. & F. Guattari. 1972. *Anti-oedipus.* New York: Viking Press.

—— 1980. *Capitalisme et schizophrenie.* Paris: Les Editions de minuit.

Des Forges, A. 1999. *Leave none to tell the story: genocide in Rwanda.* New York: Human Rights.

Droz, Y. 1997. Si Dieu veut...ou suppots de Satan: incertitudes, millenarisme et sorcellerie parmi des migrants Kikuyus. In *Cahiers d'Etudes Africaines* 145: 85- 114.

Edel, M. M. 1957. *The Chiga of Western Uganda.* London: Dawsons of Pall Mall.

Ellis, S. & G. Ter Haar. 2004. *Worlds of power: religious thought and political practice in Africa.* Oxford: Oxford University Press.

Englund, H. 2003. Christian independency and global membership: Pentecostal extraversions in Malawi. In *Journal of Religion in Africa* 33 (1): 83-111.

Evans-Pritchard, E. E. 1937. *Witchcraft, oracles and magic among the Azande.* Oxford: Clarendon Press.

—— 1940. *The Nuer: a description of the modes of the livelihood and political institutions of a Nilotic people.* Oxford: Clarendon Press.

Favret-Saada, J. 1980. *Deadly words: witchcraft in the Bocage.* Cambridge: Cambridge University Press.

Ferme, M.C. 2001. *The underneath of things: violence, history, and the everyday in Sierra Leone.* Berkeley, CA and London: University of California Press.

Fernandez, J. W. 1978. African religious movements. In *Annual Review of Anthropology* 7: 195–234.

Freedman, J. 1984. *Nyabingi: the social history of an African divinity.* Tervuren: Koninklijk Museum voor Midden-Africa.

Gifford, P. 2003. *Ghana's new Christianity: Pentecostalism in a globalising African economy.* London: Hurst.

Gill, L. 1990. 'Like a veil to cover them': women and the Pentecostal movement in La Paz. In *American Ethnologist* 17: 708-21.

Glover, D. 1979. Sociology and the thriller. In *Sociological Review* 27 (1):21–40.

Gluckman, M. 1950. Kinship and marriage among the Lozi of Northern Rhodesia and the Zulu of Natal. In *African systems of kinship and marriage* (eds) A. R. Radcliffe-Brown & D. Forde. London: Routledge & Kegan Paul.

Gross, C. 2005. What difference can culture make? A social anthropologist looks at detective fiction. In *A polymath anthropologist: essays in honour of Ann Chowning* [Research in Anthropology and Linguistics Monograph No. 6] (eds) C. Gross, H.D. Lyons & D. A. Counts. Auckland: Department of Anthropology, University of Auckland.

Hage, H. 2005. A not so multi-sited ethnography of a not so imagined community. In *Anthropological Theory* 5 (4): 463–75.

Hansen, H. B. 1984. *Mission, church and state in a colonial setting: Uganda 1890–1925.*

London: Heinemann.

—— 1995. The colonial control of spirit cults in Uganda. In *Revealing Prophets* (eds) D. M. Anderson & D. H. Johnson. Oxford: James Currey.

Harkin, M. E. (ed.). 2004. *Reassessing revitalization movements: perspectives from North America and the Pacific Islands*. Lincoln, NE: University of Nebraska Press.

Hastings, A. 1979. *A history of African Christianity, 1950-1975*. Cambridge: Cambridge University Press.

Hegel, G. W. F. 2004 [1807]. *The phenomenology of mind* [translated by J. B. Baillie]. Mineola: Dover.

Hendry, J. & C. W. Watson. 2001. *An anthropology of indirect communication* (ASA Monograph No. 37). London: Routledge.

Hooper, E. 1999. *The river: a journey back to the source of HIV and AIDS*. London: Allen Lane.

Hopkins, E. 1970. The Nyabingi cult of South-western Uganda. In *Protest and power in Black Africa* (eds) R. L. Rotberg & A. Mazrui. New York: Oxford University Press.

Howell, P. 1998. Crime and the city solution: crime fiction, urban knowledge, and radical geography. In *Antipode* 30 (4): 357-78.

Infield, M. 2003. *The names of Ankole cows*. Kampala: Fountain.

Isichei, E. 1995. *A history of Christianity in Africa: from antiquity to the present*. Grand Rapids, MI: William B. Eerdmans.

James, W. & D. H. Johnson (eds). 1988. *Vernacular Christianity: essays in the social anthropology of religion* (JASO Occasional Paper No.7). Oxford: JASO.

Janzen, J. M. 2005. Affliction: African cults of affliction. In *Encyclopedia of Religion* [2nd Edition]. (ed.) Lindsay Jones. London: Macmillan Reference Books.

Johnson, D. H. 1991. Criminal Secrecy – the Case of the Zande Secret Societies. In *Past & Present*: 170-200.

Kassimir, R. 1999. The politics of Popular Catholicism in Uganda. In *East African expressions of Christianity* (eds) T. Spear & I. N. Kimambo. Oxford: James Currey.

Kilian, A. H. D., P. Langi, A. Talisuna & G. Kbagambe. 1999. Rainfall pattern, El Nino and malaria in Uganda. In *Transactions of the Royal Society of Tropical Medicine and Hygiene* 93: 22–3.

Lanternari, V. 1963. *The religions of the oppressed: a study of modern messianic cults*. London: MacGibbon and Kee.

Latour, B. 1988. *The pasteurization of France*. Cambridge, MA and London: Harvard University Press.

—— 1996. *Aramis, or the love of technology*. Cambridge, MA and London: Harvard University Press.

—— 1999. *Pandora's hope: an essay on the reality of science studies*. Cambridge, MA and London: Harvard University Press.

—— 2005. *Reassembling the social: an introduction to actor-network theory*. Oxford: Oxford University Press.

Latour, B. & S. Woolgar. 1979. *Laboratory life*. Princeton, NJ: Princeton University Press.

Likoudis, P. 2000. Cult suicide exposes deep troubles of church in Uganda. In *The Wanderer* (Ohio).

Lindblade, K. A., E. D. Walker, A. W. Onapa, J. Katungu & M. L. Wilson. 1999. Highland malaria in Uganda: prospective analysis of an epidemic associated with El Nino. In *Transactions of the Royal Society of Tropical Medicine and Hygiene* 93 (5), 480–7.

—— 2000a. Land use change alters malaria transmission parameters by modifying temperature in a highland area of Uganda. In *Tropical Medicine and International Health* 5 (4): 263–74.

Lindblade, K. A., E. D.Walker, & M. L. Wilson. 2000b. Early warning of malaria epidemics in African highlands using anopheles (diptera: culicidae) indoor resting density. In *Journal of Medical Entomology* 37 (5): 664–74.

Linden, I. & J. Linden. 1977. *Church and revolution in Rwanda.* Manchester: Manchester University Press.

Lindsay, S. W. & W. J. M. Martens. 1998. Malaria in the African highlands: past, present and future. In *Bulletin of the World Health Organization* 76 (1): 33–45.

Lindsay, S. W., R. Bodker, R. Malima, H. A. Msangeni & W. Kisinza. 2000. Effect of 1997–98 El Nino on highland malaria in Tanzania. *Lancet* 355: 989–90.

Lindstrom, L. 1996. Millennial movements, millennialism. In Alan Barnard & Jonathan Spencer (eds) *Encyclopedia of social and cultural anthropology.* London: Routledge.

Lukyn-Willliams, F. 1934. Blood-brotherhood in Ankole (omukago). In *Uganda Journal* 2(10): 33–41.

Lyman, S. M. 1964, Chinese Secret Societies in the Occident: notes and suggestions for research in the sociology of secrecy, In *Canadian Review of Sociology and Anthropology* 1 (2): 79–102.

Lyons, M. 1998. AIDS and development in Uganda. In *Developing Uganda* (eds) H. Hansen & M. Twaddle. Oxford: James Currey.

MacGaffey, J. 1991. *The real economy of Zaire: the contribution of smuggling and other unofficial activities to national wealth.* Oxford: James Currey.

MacGaffey, W. 1983. *Modern Kongo prophets: religion in a plural society.* Bloomington, IN: Indiana University Press.

Mair, L. P. 1959. Independent religious movements in three continents. In *Comparative Studies in Society and History* 1: 113–36.

Mamdani, M. 1977. *Politics and class formation in Uganda.* New York: Monthly Review Press.

—— 2001. *When victims become killers: colonialism, nativism and the genocide in Rwanda.* Oxford: James Currey.

Martin, D. 1990. *Tongues of fire: the explosion of Protestantism in Latin America.* Oxford: Blackwell.

Mauder, C. J. 1991. Marian apparitions. In *Modern Catholicism: Vatican II and after.* (ed.) Adrian Hastings. New York: Oxford University Press.

Maxwell, D. 1999a. *Christians and chiefs in Zimbabwe: a social history of the Hwesa people c. 1870s–1990s.* Edinburgh: Edinburgh University Press.

—— 1999b. Historicizing Christian independency: the Southern African Pentecostal Movement ca 1908–1960. In *Journal of African History* 39 (2): 243–64.

—— 2006a. *African gifts of the spirit.* Oxford: James Currey.

—— 2006b. Writing the history of African Christianity: reflections of an editor. In *Journal of Religion in Africa* 36 (3-4): 379–99.

Meyer, B. 1998. 'Make a complete break with the past': memory and post-colonial modernity in Ghanaian Pentecostalist discourse. In *Journal of Religion in Africa* 27 (3): 316-49.

—— 2004. Christianity in Africa: from African Independent Churches to Pentecostal-charismatic Churches. In *Annual Review of Anthropology* 33: 447-74.

Meyer, B. & P. Geschiere (eds). 1999. *Globalization and identity: dialectics of flow and closure.* Oxford: Blackwell.

Mouchet, J. S. Manguin, J. Sircoulon, S. Laventure, O. Faye, A. W. Onapa, P. Carnevale, J. Julvez & D. Fontenille. 1998. Evolution of malaria in Africa for the past 40 years: impact of climatic and human factors. In *Journal of the American Mosquito Control Association* 14 (2): 121–30.

Mushanga, M. T. 1970. The clan system among the Banyankole. In *Uganda Journal* 34: 29–34.

Namaara, W., F. Plummer *et al.* 1987. *Cross sectional study of HIV infection in South Western Uganda.* Naples: Second International Symposium on AIDS and Associated Cancers in Africa.

Ngologoza, P. 1998 [1968]. *Kigezi and its people.* Dar es Salaam: East African Literature Bureau.

Nicholson, S. E. & J. C. Selato. 2000. The influence of La Nina on African rainfall. In *International Journal of Climatology* 20: 1761–76.

Oberg, K. 1938. Kinship organization of the Banyankole. In *Africa* 11 (2): 129–59.

——— 1940. The kingdom of Ankole in Uganda. In *African political systems* (eds) M. Fortes and E. E. Evans-Pritchard. London: Oxford University Press.

——— 1949. Analysis of the Bahima marriage ceremony. In *Africa* 19: 107–20.

Oboler, R. S. 1994. The house-property complex and African social organization. In *Africa* 64 (3): 342–58.

Oliver, R. 1952. *The missionary factor in East Africa.* London: Longmans, Green & Co.

Otunnu, O. 1999. Rwandese refugees and immigrants in Uganda. In *The Rwanda crisis from Uganda to Zaire* (eds) H. Adelman & A. Suhrke. New Brunswick, NJ: Transaction Publishers.

Pauwels, M. 1949. La magie au Rwanda. In *Grands Lacs* 65 (1): 17–48.

——— 1951. Le culte de Nyabingi. In *Anthropos*. 46: 3–4.

——— 1954. La divination au Rwanda. In *Kongo-Overzee*. 20: 4–5.

Peel, J. D. T. 2003. *Religious encounter and the making of the Yoruba.* Bloomington: Indiana University Press.

Phillips, J. 1928. The Nyabingi. In *Congo* 1 (3): 310–21.

Piot, C. D. 1993. Secrecy, ambiguity, and the everyday in Kabre culture. In *American Anthropologist* 95 (2): 353–70.

Prunier, G. 1995. *The Rwanda crisis: history of a genocide.* New York: Columbia University Press.

Ranger, T. O. & J. C. Weller. 1975. *Themes in the Christian history of Central Africa.* Berkeley, CA: University of California Press.

Richards, A. I. 1952. *Economic development and tribal change: a study of imigrant labour in Buganda.* Cambridge: W. Heffer.

Robbins, J. 2004. The globalization of Pentecostal and charismatic Christianity. In *Annual Review of Anthropology* 33: 117–43.

——— 2007. Continuity thinking and the problem of Christian culture. In *Annual Review of Anthropology* 48 (1): 5–38.

Roberts, J. M. 1972. *The mythology of the secret societies.* London: Secker & Warburg.

Robertshaw, P. & D. Taylor. 2000. Climate change and the rise of political complexity in western Uganda. In *Journal of African History* 41: 1–28.

Rutanga, M. 1991. *Nyabingi movement: people's anti-colonial struggles in Kigezi 1910–1930.* Kampala: Centre for Basic Research.

Schoenbrun, D. L. 1998. *A green place, a good place: agrarian change, gender, and social identity in the Great Lakes region to the 15th century.* Oxford: James Currey.

Schwartz, N. 2005. Dreaming in color: anti-essentialism in Legio Maria dream narratives. In *Journal of Religion in Africa* 35 (2): 159–96.

Simmel, G. 1950 [1900]. The secret and the secret society. In *The sociology of Georg Simmel* (ed.) K. H. Wolff. New York: Free Press.

Simpson, A. 2004. *'Half London' in Zambia: contested identities in a Catholic mission school.* Edinburgh: International African Institute.

Snow, R. W., A. Ikoku, J. Omumbo & J. Ouma. 1999. *The epidemiology, politics and control of malaria epidemics in Kenya: 1900–1998.* Geneva: The Resource Network on Epidemics, World Health Organization.

Spear, T. 1999. Toward the history of African Christianity. In *East African expressions of Christianity* (eds) T. Spear & I. N. Kimambo. Oxford: James Currey.

Strathern, M. 1994. *After nature: English kinship in the late twentieth century.* Cambridge: Cambridge University Press.

———1996. Cutting the network. In *Journal of the Royal Anthropological Institute (N.S.)* 2 (3): 517–35.

Taussig, M. T. 1999. *Defacement: public secrecy and the labor of the negative.* Stanford, CA: Stanford University Press.

Taylor, C. 1959. *A simplified Runyankore-Rukiga-English and English-Runyankore- Rukiga dictionary.* Kampala: Fountain.

Taylor, C. C. 1988. The concept of flow in Rwandan popular medicine. In *Social Science and Medicine* 27 (12): 1343–48.

———— 1990. Condoms and cosmology: the 'fractal' person and sexual risk in Rwanda, In *Social Science and Medicine* 31 (9): 1023–38.

———— 1992. *Milk, honey, and money: changing concepts in Rwandan healing.* Washington, D.C.: Smithsonian Institution Press.

Ter Haar, G. 2003. A wondrous God: miracles in contemporary Africa. In *African Affairs* 102: 409–28.

The Bible Society of Uganda. 1989. *Ekitabo ekirikwera: n'ebitabo eby'omubonano Apokurufa/Dyutrokanoniko.* Kampala: The United Bible Society.

The Catholic Bishops of Uganda. June 2000. *Test the spirits: pastoral letter of Catholic Bishops of Uganda to the faithful on cults, sects, and 'religious' groups.* Entebbe: Marianum Press.

The Movement for the Restoration of the Ten Commandments of God. 1996 [1991]. *Obutumwa bwaruga omu eiguru: okuhwaho kw'obusingye obu* (English Version: *A timely message from heaven: the end of the present times*). Kampala: The Movement for the Restoration of the Ten Commandments of God.

The Uganda Human Rights Commission (UHRC). 2002. *The Kanungu massacre: the Movement for the Restoration of the Ten Commandments of God indicted.* Kampala: The Uganda Human Rights Commission.

Thomas, N. 1997. Anthropological epistemologies. In *International Social Science Journal* 49 (3): 333-43.

Thrupp, S. (ed.) 1962. *Millennial dreams in action: essays in comparative sociology.* The Hague: Mouton.

Trouwborst, A. 1973. Two types of partial networks in Burundi. In *Network analysis: studies in human interaction* (eds) J. Boissevain & J. Clyde-Mitchell. The Hague: Mouton.

Vokes, R. 2005. The Kanungu fire: millenarianism and the millennium in South-western Uganda. In *The qualities of time: anthropological approaches* [ASA Monograph Series, Vol. 41] (eds) D. Mills & W. James. Oxford: Berg.

———— 2007. Charisma, creativity and cosmopolitanism: a perspective on the power of the new radio broadcasting in Uganda and Rwanda. In *Journal of the Royal Anthropological Institute* (N.S.) 13 (4): 805–24.

Waliggo, J. M. 1995. The Catholic Church and the root cause of instability in Uganda. In *Religion and politics in East Africa* (eds) H. B. Hansen & M. Twaddle. Oxford: James Currey.

Wallace, A. F. C. 2003. *Revitalization and mazeways: essays on culture change, Volume 1 (Robert C. Grumet, ed.).* Lincoln, NE: University of Nebraska Press.

Waller, R. D. 1995. Kidongoi's kin: prophecy and power in Maasailand. In *Revealing Prophets* (eds) D. Anderson & D. H. Johnson. London: James Currey.

Weiner, J. F. 1996. Sherlock Holmes and Martin Heidegger: a discussion of Julian Thomas' 'Time, culture and identity'. In *Archaeological Dialogues* 3 (1): 35–9.

West, H. G. 2005. *Kupilikula: governance and the invisible realm in Mozambique.* Chicago: Chicago University Press.

Wilson, B. R, 1963. Millennialism in comparative perspective. In *Comparative studies in society and history* 6: 93–114.

Wood, W. B. 1988. AIDS north and south: diffusion patterns of a global epidemic and a research agenda for geographers. In *Professional Geographer* 40: 266–79.

Unpublished works

Heck, S. 1998. In the presence of neighbours: land, property and community in Ankole, Uganda. (PhD thesis, Boston University).

Job, S. Pioneers of Uganda: The White Fathers of Uganda and especially His Excellency Bishop Francis Xavier Lacoursiere OBE. (Radio talk given on Uganda Broadcasting Service).

MacFarlane, A. On creative and analytical methods.

Neema, S. B. 1994. Mothers and midwives: maternity care options in Ankole, South-western Uganda. (PhD thesis, University of Copenhagen).

Stenning, D. J. Preliminary observations on the Balokole Movement particularly among Bahima in Ankole District. (East African Institute of Social Research, Kampala).

Yeld, E. R. 1969. The family in social change: a study among the Kiga of Kigezi District, South-west Uganda. (PhD thesis, University of East Africa).

Wright, M. Varieties of Catholic action in a time of nationalist mobilization in East-Central Africa, 1953–1958.

Index